Hidden Financial Risk

Understanding Off–Balance Sheet Accounting

Hidden Financial Risk

Understanding Off–Balance Sheet Accounting

J. Edward Ketz

WILEY

JOHN WILEY & SONS, INC.

Copyright © 2003 by J. Edward Ketz. All rights reserved.

Published by John Wiley & Sons, Inc., Hoboken, New Jersey
Published simultaneously in Canada

Copyright 2002 SmartPros Ltd. www.smartpros.com. Reprinted with permission.

For general information on our other products and services, or technical support, please contact our Customer Care Department within the United States at 800-762-2974, outside the United States at 317-572-3993 or fax 317-572-4002.

Wiley also publishes its books in a variety of electronic formats. Some content that appears in print may not be available in electronic books.

For more information about Wiley products, visit our web site at www.wiley.com.

Library of Congress Cataloging-in-Publication Data

Ketz, J. Edward.
   Hidden financial risk : understanding off-balance sheet accounting / J. Edward Ketz.
      p.   cm.
Includes bibliographical references and index.
   ISBN 0-471-43376-4 (CLOTH)
   1. Accounting—Case studies.   2. Accounting firms—Corrupt
practices—Case studies.   3. Business ethics—Case studies.   I. Title.
   HF5635 .K43 2003
      658.15′5—dc21

                                                           2003003952

Printed in the United States of America

10 9 8 7 6 5 4 3 2 1

For Charity and Benjamin

About the Author

J. Edward Ketz is MBA Faculty Director and Associate Professor of Accounting at the Penn State Smeal College of Business. He has been a member of the Penn State faculty since 1981. He holds a bachelor's degree in political science, a master's degree in accountancy, and a Ph.D. in business administration, all from Virginia Tech.

The teaching and research interests of Dr. Ketz focus on financial accounting, accounting information systems, and accounting ethics. He has published numerous academic and professional articles, and he has written seven books. Also, he is coeditor of *Advances in Accounting Education*.

Dr. Ketz writes two columns about financial reporting issues. *Accounting Today* publishes "Accounting Annotations," while "Accounting Cycle: Wash, Rinse, and Spin" appears on SmartPros.com. He has been cited in the popular and business press, including *The Wall Street Journal*, *The New York Times*, *The Washington Post*, *Business Week*, and *USA Today*, and he has served as an accounting commentator on CNNfn.

Contents

Contents

Preface

When I graduated with a doctorate in 1977, I researched and published articles on mainstream topics, particularly current value accounting and the interaction between earnings and cash flows. After a while, it occurred to me that these are not the crucial issues of financial accounting and reporting. Ethics and honesty and fairness to financial statement users comprise the foundational issues of the profession. If a business enterprise adopted the best methods for accounting but did so with treachery and duplicity, it would not help any capital market agent. If I have to choose between the best accounting methods and managerial integrity, I always prefer the latter.

I started writing articles on such topics in the 1980s and published them in obscure academic journals. Then in January 1996 I began writing the "Spirit of Accounting" column for *Accounting Today* with my friend Paul Miller. I needed a break in 2000, so I quit the column; Paul Bahnson joined Paul Miller on it. After a year's respite, I found myself writing "Accounting Annotations" for *Accounting Today* and "The Accounting Cycle: Wash, Rinse, and Spin" for SmartPros.com.

Then Enron disclosed problems in its third-quarter report of 2001 and soon declared bankruptcy. All of a sudden people were interested in accounting at levels I had never experienced previously. During the first half of 2002 I had at least 500 interviews with the media, and I discussed at length issues about Enron, Global Crossing, WorldCom, Tyco, Adelphia, and Arthur Andersen. My main message was simple: The culture of financial reporting that began around 1990 brought about this mess. When managers engage in "earnings management," what they really mean is that when they cannot make profits legitimately, they will exaggerate and abuse accounting numbers until the reported numbers make them look good. Aiding and abetting this process of "earnings management" have been board directors who never asked serious questions, corporate lawyers who were eager to push the limits, stock brokers and investment bankers who did not care how they made a buck, financial analysts who worried little that they served as used-car salesmen for their investment banking firms, auditors who looked the other way, an impotent Financial Accounting Standards Board, an overextended Securities and Exchange Commission, and members of Congress who would tolerate almost anything for sufficiently large campaign contributions.

Writing short essays or talking a few minutes with a reporter necessarily involves a partial examination of some identifiable, circumscribed issue of financial accounting. This book allows me to address these concerns in a broader and more coherent fashion. I see three purposes of this book: (1) to lay out in some detail several specific problems in the financial reporting arena, (2) to describe how the system failed to correct any of these problems during 2001 and 2002, and (3) to suggest a course of action for improving things. The latter is critical if the stock market crash of 2001/2002 is not to be replicated. Ironically, the thrust of my suggestions rests on the work of former partners in Arthur Andersen.

When one says and writes the things I do, it is not surprising that some people object. During the spring of 2002 I received a number of e-mails from Arthur Andersen personnel. I wish to share two of them here, both sent to me on March 21, 2002. The first e-mail came from a lawyer/certified public accountant at Arthur Andersen.

> I am deeply disturbed at some of the public comments you are making to the media with respect to Arthur Andersen and the Enron matter.
>
> To quote you as quoted in the Houston Chronicle: "Rightly or wrongly they are looking at Andersen in part for that justice because Andersen obviously had an audit failure here in approving things that shouldn't have been done." What did we approve that shouldn't have been approved [sic]. How much do you know about what went on at Enron? Where is your information coming from?
>
> Because you are a professor of accounting, I would expect more rationale, reasoned, and knowledgeable statements from you. I would refer you to AU 316, Consideration of Fraud in a Financial Statement Audit. The statement clearly indicates that an auditor cannot obtain absolute assurance that a material misstatement will be detected. Because of the concealment aspects of fraudulent activity (i.e. collusion and falsification of documents), even a properly planned and executed audit may not detect material misstatements resulting from fraud. Whether Arthur Andersen did or did not perform at the requisite level of professional competency is yet to be determined. We have admitted to making mistakes, but those mistakes are not the cause of the downfall of Enron and should not be the cause of the downfall of my firm.
>
> You are doing my firm, the accounting profession, and the public a great disservice by disseminating inaccurate information. Audits are not designed to detect fraud. Never have been. Auditors to [sic] not go into client offices and put a gun to the client's head and demand that they tell them about all of their fraudulent activities while searching through the secret drawer in the client's desk for the second set of books. Auditors perform a professional service that can be subverted by management fraud. This is the point you should be making.
>
> I would ask that you utilize your bully pulpit to strengthen the profession, not aid in its demise.

The second e-mail also criticizes my comments. It comes from an accounting alumnus.

> I am an Arthur Andersen audit partner and Penn State alumni. I have read your name and related quotes throughout articles over the past several months and I have a few questions for you. In an article I read today you are quoted as saying "I think the story of Enron has resonated basically to the bone for so many Americans that they want justice done. Rightly or wrongly they are looking at Andersen in part for that justice because Andersen obviously had an audit failure here in approving things that shouldn't have been done." I was wondering if I could get a copy of research/study or whatever you have to support your statement. Please provide me with a list of these things that Andersen approved that created an audit failure. This could really save everyone a lot of time and money. Have you

ever worked outside of academia? Ever audited a public company? Ever worked in public accounting? Do you really know anything about Arthur Andersen? I guess I would not be as troubled with your quote if it was the first one. However, I have read these idiotic, unsupported opinions from you over the last several months. I find it curious that you seem to be the only accounting professor in the United States with any opinion what so ever. Could it be that other accounting professors feel that they just don't have enough facts to reach these conclusions that are obvious to you? Or maybe other accounting professors don't thirst for the limelight like you do. What ever the answer is, I really don't care. I just wanted to let you know that I will not support Penn State financially in the future and I will implore all my fellow Penn State partners and other alumni to do the same while you are employed there. I don't believe a University should employ someone who would make such careless, unsupportable remarks. Whatever happens to Andersen, my partners and I will survive and thrive and I will go out of my way to share my views like you seem to go out of you way to share yours.

These accusations inspired me to write this book. While this text responds to the questions and allegations just listed in depth, I wish to provide a summary response at this stage. If Arthur Andersen is so innocent in the Enron case, how do you explain Boston Chicken, Waste Management, Sunbeam, Arizona Baptist Foundation, Global Crossing, and WorldCom? It expands one's credulity past the breaking point to think that Arthur Andersen could be the victim with respect to all of these failures.

With respect to the first e-mail written by the Arthur Andersen lawyer/CPA, I have three additional points. First, to the best of my knowledge, I have not disseminated inaccurate information. I have responded with the facts that I had at the time, coupled with my analysis. If I have disseminated inaccurate information, show me my specific mistakes instead of merely asserting that I have made errors. It seems to me, given what we now know, that I was right in what I said and wrote. Second, you are correct in alleging that auditors often claim that audits are not designed to detect fraud. What you are forgetting is that the investment community thinks differently. To their collective mind, if you are not checking on the accuracy and completeness of the disclosures and verifying that managers are not lying to us, what is the point? If you do not check these things, we are wasting our money on your audits. Third, it was not my intent to aid in the demise of Arthur Andersen. My goal was and remains to talk about the culture of financial reporting and seek for improvements. It appears to me that Arthur Andersen undid itself. Your firm screwed up the audits at Boston Chicken, Waste Management, Sunbeam, Arizona Baptist Foundation, Global Crossing, as well as at Enron and WorldCom. Your firm committed these audit failures, not I.

To the gentleman who wrote the second e-mail, I have four further points. First, I have been writing about accounting ethics for 20 years. While you may be unaware of my work, it is out there in the public domain and you can read and critique it as you choose. But please do not accuse me of doing no research just because you are too lazy to determine what my previous work has been. Second, I admit that I have never audited a company, although I have studied and researched the nexus between financial reporting and stock investments for 30 years. My expertise in financial accounting and reporting is foundation enough to enable me to make comments about shoddy audits. Third, I do not understand why other accounting professors have not responded to the events of the past two years. Perhaps they are timid and shy; perhaps they are too busy doing their research in financial economics; perhaps they do not wish to work with the media; or perhaps they or their departments have received money from your firm, which caused them to be afraid to speak out. Last, I think it unfortunate that you will not support Penn State because of what I have said. Your commentary shows that you do not understand the university system, nor do you approve of my First Amendment right to free speech. My statements are my own; I do not speak for the university. Fortunately, the tenure system allows me to make unpopular testimonials even when university officials do not agree with my remarks. Business contributions to universities benefit society because they foster research and teaching efforts and because the money can support the education of students who otherwise would not get the chance to attend. Lack of donations will hurt poor and needy potential students, not me.

From this tête-à-tête between two (former) partners at Arthur Andersen and me, the reader should see what is at stake. Do we preserve the status quo, claiming that there are only a few rotten apples, and hope things improve? Or do we acknowledge that an infectious problem exists when managers lust to "manage earnings" while directors, lawyers, auditors, stock brokers, and members of Congress do not have the fortitude to stop them?

In my judgment, a serious problem exists in the world of financial reporting; indeed, the problem is so deep-seated that only a fundamental change in the system will restore credibility to financial reports. In this book I shall explore how managers hide corporate liabilities and why the economic system has not responded appropriately to repair the underlying causes of the problems. I conclude with a chapter on how to improve the system and exhort readers to work toward this goal.

I wish to thank John DeRemegis at John Wiley & Sons for encouraging me to write this book and for sufficient prodding to finish it. I appreciate the help of Penn State MBA students Hsiuwen ("Wendy") Lin and Puntawat Sirisuksakulchai, CMA and CFM, who conducted some of the financial analyses and assisted with library and other research activities. I also thank Judy Howarth, who edited the book.

Part I

My Investments
Went Ouch!

CHAPTER ONE

What? Another Accounting Scandal?

Financial events in the last two years raise questions about the role of modern-day managers. Do they really work as the stewards of their shareholders, as business orators say, or is it all a sham in which the managers work for themselves, stealing whatever they can and covering up their tracks with accounting tricks?

The American public views professional advisers no better. From a former view of sweet innocence and presumed utility, society now perceives accountants as conniving and manipulative; worse, it considers them willing pawns in the hands of corrupt managers who employ their positions to steal the assets of investors and creditors. Even the standards and principles of the accounting profession are challenged for lacking substance and foundation and for merely providing rhetoric to reach any conclusion that managers desire.

In this book I explore the substantive issues surrounding the plethora of accounting and corporate scandals in recent years. I examine the nature of the accounting scandals, why they have occurred, and how to overcome them. I also inspect the failure of corporate governance, the failure of regulation, and the failure of the accounting profession in preventing these scandals from taking place.

Unfortunately, there have been so many accounting and corporate scandals that to do the topic justice would require a multivolume work; after this chapter I shall restrict most of the analysis to those accounting scandals dealing with the underreporting of corporate liabilities. These scandals include Enron, Global Crossing, Adelphia, and WorldCom, so I certainly take account of the important scandals of this time period.

While I start with an overview of the many accounting and auditing failures in corporate America, I focus on financial risk. As clarified later in this chapter and in the next, financial risk concerns the bad stuff that can happen to a company when it takes on too much debt. Investors and creditors recognize this concept, so they monitor how much debt exists in the financial structure of a corporation. But managers realize that investors and creditors are monitoring their firms, so sometimes they attempt to mask the quantity of debt they possess, sometimes even by lying about it. In this book I attempt to raise the awareness of the business community about this issue because such deception is hurtful to all.

The predicament about corporate liabilities worsens as we understand how generally accepted accounting principles (GAAP) have aided and abetted corporate managers.

This situation is most poignantly seen in the case of Enron, in which some of the company's swindles actually followed the profession's rules. I also discuss how auditors could better understand their purpose and assist capital markets by requiring better and more accurate and more complete disclosures—even if GAAP does not require such disclosures. Later I expand these points by looking at the equity method, lease accounting, and pension accounting. From that base, I then look more carefully at special-purpose entities, their use and their abuse, and examine more carefully the amount of debts involved and how firms have deceitfully hidden these debts from their balance sheets.

The rest of this chapter provides a thumbnail sketch about accounting and auditing abuses, including how the investment community aches because we did not listen to the warning voices of Abraham Briloff and Eli Mason. After this, I review the concept of financial risk and then take a more in-depth look at Adelphia, Enron, Global Crossing, and WorldCom, since these malfunctions specifically entail lies about each firm's true amount of debt. I conclude with some thoughts on accounting ethics and why I think these accounting frauds form a serious threat to American society.

ACCOUNTING PROPHETS: "THEY HAVE NO PROFITS"[1]

Some writers have criticized corporate accounting, but until recently they have been few in number. Perhaps the best-known accounting critic is Abraham Briloff, who wrote *Unaccountable Accounting* (1972), *More Debits Than Credits* (1976), and *The Truth About Corporate Accounting* (1981).[2] These books have two themes. First, accounting distortions, improprieties, and even frauds are more widespread than commonly believed. Briloff documented his assertions with scores of examples, principally from the 1960s and 1970s. Second, he goes on to ask why the independent, external auditor did not do enough to stop these distortions and peccadilloes. If the auditor cannot stop them—and often he or she cannot—at least the audit firm ought to unearth the problem on a timely basis and minimize the damages. Even this goal is not always achieved.

The large accounting firms have attempted to silence Briloff's voice through litigation. Each and every one of the previous Big Eight firms sued him, but the fact that Briloff has never lost one of these suits speaks volumes. Firms continue to persecute him, however, as can be seen in trumped-up ethics charges brought by the American Institute of Certified Public Accountants (AICPA). Happily, Briloff continues to write about accounting scandals, but unhappily the stock market decline due to accounting lies has proven his allegations correct. We all would have been better off if the accounting profession had listened to Briloff's wisdom instead of throwing stones at him.

Eli Mason has also performed diligently the role of accounting critic. He has served the profession in a variety of roles, including a stint as president of the New York Society of Certified Public Accountants (CPAs). He has written many articles that have appeared in a variety of professional journals, and the most important have been collected in his book *Random Thoughts*.[3] Mason continues to write, with occasional essays in *Accounting Today*. He has focused his attention on the profession itself and has clamored for better ethics and more professionalism and fewer conflicts of interest. Regrettably, the AICPA and the large accounting firms have not listened to his sage advice either.

Instead of ignoring Briloff and Mason, the business world should have listened to them because the business world of the 1990s and 2000s contains many similarities to the 1960s and the 1970s about which Briloff and Mason began their critiques. Improper accounting still occurs, and audit firms still do not stop it, nor do they always detect the fraud until great losses arise. In fact, it appears that these illicit practices have increased greatly.

Even today we ignore their prophecies only at our peril. While these issues are not life-and-death issues, they are matters of wealth and poverty. America's economic system remains mostly one of finance capitalism. As accounting serves as the lubricant to make this engine run, it also can act as the sand that grinds the machinery to a halt. Which it will be depends on whether we listen and make substantive and long-lasting changes to the system. In particular, government and business leaders must change today's culture that encourages managers to exaggerate or outright lie to investors and creditors. Before we can talk about reform, we must carefully examine where we are and how we got into this mess.

A RASH OF BAD ACCOUNTING[4]

In this section I review some of these accounting scandals. My attempt is not to provide an encyclopedic reading of them but merely a sampling. The reading, however, will provide enough examples that readers can make some inferences about what is wrong in the business world and what needs to be done to improve the system of corporate reporting. Exhibit 1.1 provides a detailed list of 50 companies that have experienced accounting scandals of one type or another; many were frauds carried out by the management team. Fifty firms with accounting scandals is 50 too many.

Exhibit 1.1 Corporations with Recent Accounting Scandals

Adelphia	Delta Financial Corp.
Amazon	Duke Energy
AOL Time Warner	Dynegy
Arizona Baptist Foundation	El Paso
Aurora Foods	Enron
Boston Chicken	Global Crossing
Bristol-Myers Squibb	Homestore
Cendant	Informix
Cerner	JDS Uniphase
CMS Energy	Kmart
Commercial Financial Services	Lernout & Hauspie
Conseco	Livenet
Creditrust	Lucent

Exhibit 1.1 *(Continued)*

Medaphis	Phar Mor
Merck	Qualcomm
Mercury Finance	Qwest
MicroStrategy	Reliant Energy
MiniScribe	Rite Aid
Mirant	Sapient
Nicor Energy	Sunbeam
Omnicom	Tyco
Orbital Sciences	W. R. Grace
Oxford Health Plan	Waste Management
Pediatrix	WorldCom
Peregrine Systems	Xerox

Boston Chicken

In 1993, Boston Chicken's initial public offering (IPO) was very warmly received by Wall Street, and its stock price went up, up, and up. Boston Chicken also successfully raised millions of dollars through the bond market. Analysts, brokers, and investors felt that this firm could deliver the right goods to the consumer food market. Earnings reports bolstered these forecasts, as the net income numbers met or exceeded all expectations. But something was fowl. Subsidiaries of Boston Chicken lost money, and none of these losses hit the parent's income statement.

Managers played this game by creating what Boston Chicken called financed area developers (FADs). The mother hen loaned money to these large franchisees/FADs, often up to 75 percent of the necessary capital, and it had a right to convert the debt into an equity interest. During the start-up phase, the FAD typically lost money. Boston Chicken reported its franchise fees and interest revenue from the FADs but indicated no losses. When the FAD started to generate profits, Boston Chicken would exercise its right to enjoy an equity interest in the FAD. In this manner, Boston Chicken would start allowing the franchisee's profits into its income statement via the equity method.

The problem with this arrangement is that the accounting did not reflect the economic substance of what was going on. Clearly, the FADs operated as subsidiaries from the very beginning in terms of their operating, financing, and investing decisions. Boston Chicken controlled these FADs in reality, and the FADs were not independent entities. Since the FADs owed their lives entirely to Boston Chicken, the economic truth is that Boston Chicken was the parent company while the FADs were subsidiaries, regardless of the legal form under which the FADs were constructed. This truth implies that Boston Chicken ought to have employed the equity method throughout, and not just when the debt was converted into equity.

6

The accuracy of the setup dawned on the market participants in 1997. In just a few months, the stock lost over half its value, just desserts for giving the market financial indigestion. Interestingly, a number of major analysts and brokers knew what was going on at Boston Chicken but continued to believe in the stock. This observation indicates that even professionals can allow their feelings to overpower the facts.

While Boston Chicken did disclose these facts deep in the footnotes, the company should not be exonerated. Disclosure does not redeem bad accounting. And echoing in the background is that oft-asked question, "Where were the auditors?" More specifically, where was Arthur Andersen?

Waste Management

Founded by Wayne Huizenga and Dean Buntrock, Waste Management hauls trash in the United States. Unfortunately, its financial statements were part of the garbage that it should have transported to the landfill. The SEC accused the firm and its executives of perpetrating accounting fraud from at least 1992 through 1997.

The creative accounting employed by Waste Management was quite simple, for much of it dealt with depreciation and amortization charges. Elementary accounting students learn that straight-line depreciation equals cost minus salvage, all divided by the life of the asset. To minimize the impact on the income statement, the bookkeeper can increase the estimate of salvage value or increase the estimate of the asset life. Waste Management did both, for example, by adding two to four years to the life of its trucks and claiming up to $25,000 as salvage. Depreciation on other plant and equipment was similarly contorted. In addition, Waste Management started booking ordinary losses as "one-time" special charges. It also lied about the useful life of landfills by alleging that the landfills would be expanded. A number of them were never expanded.

Waste Management cleaned up its act in 1999 by replacing the old management team with a new one, by restructuring the board of directors and the audit committee, and by supplanting Arthur Andersen with Ernst & Young. The after-tax effect of all the shenanigans was a mere $2.9 billion!

Given the uncomplicated nature of these accounting games, did the auditors know what was going on? If so, why did they not stop this fraud? If not, how diligently were they conducting their audits of Waste Management? After all, $2.9 billion is a material sum of money in anyone's books.

While we are at, we should also wonder about the Securities and Exchange Commission (SEC) and the Department of Justice. It took them several years before they put together a case against these wrongdoers. Why did it take so long to bring justice to the managers and Arthur Andersen?

Sunbeam

"Chainsaw" Al Dunlop was everyone's favorite chief executive officer (CEO) and chairman of the board—everyone except for those who worked for him. Dunlop fired many employees to cut costs and restructured much of Sunbeam's businesses during the mid 1990s. He apparently also managed the books to give the firm a healthy set of financial figures in 1996, 1997, and 1998.

The legerdemain here was that old chestnut of recognizing revenues whether the firm did anything to earn them or not. Specifically, Sunbeam designed a new policy called a "bill and hold" program in which Sunbeam's customers (i.e., retailers) would "buy" goods but have Sunbeam hold them until the customers wanted shipment. The problem is that customers did not pay cash and they had a right of cancellation. Under these circumstances, such transactions exist only in the mind of the manager and should not be booked under GAAP. Only when cash is tendered or when the right of cancellation expires can the firm recognize any revenues.

Sunbeam has since chopped the chainsaw man himself. On September 4, 2002, the SEC settled with Chainsaw Al. He has to pay a ticket of $500,000, and he agrees not to serve ever again as an officer or director for an SEC registrant.

Arthur Andersen apparently was asleep on this one as well, with Deloitte & Touche called in in 1998 to provide light on the situation. This deception is such an old hoax and it was so easy to detect that I return to the refrain, "Where were the auditors?"

Cendant

Another example is Cendant, a corporation that emerged as a marriage between Household Financial Services (HFS) and CUC. After the wedding ceremony, the HFS half of the team discovered accounting irregularities by the CUC team. It is as if HFS was too love-struck to see the blemishes of its intended.

One problem centered on the coding of services provided to customers as short term instead of long term. This coding allowed the company to recognize all the revenue in the current period instead of apportioning it between the current and future periods. In fact, many of these services were long term in nature; thus only a part of the revenues should have been booked currently.

A second aspect dealt with the amortization of various charges related to various clubs sponsored by CUC, including marketing costs. The firm capitalized these costs as an asset and amortized them over a relatively long period. Wall Street caught CUC playing this game in the late 1980s and hammered the firm by cutting its value in half. Evidently CUC's management did not learn the lesson.

Another gimmick was the delay in recognizing any cancellations, thereby overstating current earnings.

Michael Monaco, chief financial officer (CFO) at Cendant, announced on April 15, 1998 that CUC's earnings over the past few years were filled with fictitious revenues: "These accounting [fictions] were widespread and systemic." He also said that the errors were made "with an intent to deceive." Walter Forbes, the former chairman, dismisses these statements, but recently he has been dismissed from Cendant. The SEC is examining this matter also.

This time Ernst & Young is in the hot seat. Deloitte & Touche is now the external auditor at Cendant, but Arthur Andersen was called in to assist the investigation. From our vantage point in time, we of course ask why.

Sensormatic Electronics Corporation

A variation on the theme can be found in the fraud by Sensormatic's managers. Ronald G. Assaf, CEO, Michael E. Pardue, chief operating officer (COO), and Lawrence J. Simmons, vice president of finance, became concerned when Sensormatic was not making enough profits during certain quarters. Whenever they projected quarterly earnings in the past, actual earnings were never off by more than one cent. The stock market was happy to have such a stable firm, and it rewarded Sensormatic with increased share prices. But there came a point when the top officers found themselves in the embarrassing situation that they could not deliver on the projections. Rather than admitting that business was slowing, they lied about the earnings.

Assaf, Pardue, and Simmons altered the dates in the computer clocks so that invoices and shipping documents and other source documents would record sales that actually occurred in (say) January as if the revenues had taken place in December. They continued this process until enough revenues were logged into the old quarter and the financial projections were achieved, always within one penny of the original forecast. Once they had enough revenues, they would adjust the clock so the documents were correctly date-stamped.

The controller of U.S. operations, Joy Green, stumbled onto this conspiracy around 1995. She apparently discussed the matter with these officers but no one else. This response was feeble. The SEC not only sanctioned Assaf, Pardue, and Simmons for their fraud, but it also censured Green for her failure to notify the firm's audit committee or the independent auditors.

What do you do when the boss cheats? Managers and accountants do not relish the responsibility; nonetheless, keeping quiet is itself a crime. The SEC demands disclosure of the fraud to those within the firm who have oversight responsibility. If the audit committee or the internal auditors do not follow up, the SEC believes that the discoverer of the fraud has a responsibility to report the fraud to the commission.

AOL Time Warner

AOL illustrates the maxim "If at first you don't succeed, try, try again." Of course, Momma was not talking about creative accounting.

Several years ago managers at AOL decided that they could up net income by reducing expenses. One of the easiest ways to reduce costs is by ignoring them, and that is what they did with their marketing and selling costs. Of course, to make the books balance, somebody has to debit something, so the accountants put these costs as assets. AOL justified this decision by saying that these marketing and selling costs, such as mailing computer disks to potential customers, have long benefits that extend several years. Thus, the managers at AOL capitalized the costs and then amortized them over a three- to five-year period.

The problem with this accounting is that it borders on silliness to believe that the benefits from marketing efforts last so long. Rarely does anyone in any industry capitalize these costs, so AOL stands alone on this one. If some business enterprise could prove that the benefits extended over several years, I would not object to this accounting. The burden of proof rests with corporate management and the auditors. So if, for example, some investors decide to sue them, corporate managers and auditors ought to have demonstrable evidence to show that their stand is proper. I submit that AOL has no such evidence.

When the SEC took the company to task, AOL agreed to pay a fine of $3.5 million and to cease and desist from such accounting. That was in 2000.

In 2002 the Justice Department began probing whether these managers were at it again. AOL managers seem to have exaggerated sales by recording barter deals as revenues and by grossing up commissions earned on creating advertising deals to pretend that AOL earned the entire advertising revenue. If these allegations prove true, Momma may not want AOL's managers ever to try again.

Qwest

Managers at Qwest and darn near every other telecommunications company played the capacity-swap game. Apparently, Arthur Andersen dreamed up this scheme as a way for everyone to show a profit. Unhappily for them, Accounting Principles Board (APB) Opinion No. 29 is reasonably clear about these transactions.

APB Opinion No. 29 covers the accounting for barter transactions, which the APB referred to as nonmonetary transactions. The APB divided these transactions into two types, those comprising similar assets and those embracing dissimilar assets. We can illustrate the first category with the trade of one refrigerator for another. An example of the second group is the trade of a refrigerator for artwork. The APB concluded that the trading of similar assets should not entail the recognition of any profit or loss because the earnings process is not complete, but the trading of dissimilar assets does require the recognition of a gain or loss on the exchange. (Giving or receiving cash makes the situation more complex, for the APB says we need to treat the transaction as part monetary and part nonmonetary. This treatment, however, does not change the basic scheme.)

Managers at Qwest and at other telecommunication firms tried to hide the fact that they were not making any money by inventing revenue streams. They engaged in swaps of bandwidth; a typical contract had one company selling some of its bandwidth in return for obtaining access to some of the bandwidth of another corporation. How should the telecoms account for these transactions? APB Opinion 29 clearly says that no income should be recognized because one bandwidth is quite similar to another bandwidth. If only they had put all of their hard work into making honest profits!

Tyco

The big news about Tyco, of course, is charges of its looting by its own CEO, Dennis Kozlowski. He apparently covered up his tracks with improper business combination accounting along with insufficient disclosures about transactions with related parties. Given that the list of miscreants has achieved a considerable length, let me just say Kozlowski has given a new name to greed, for he has become the Gordon Gecko of the 21st century.[5]

On the other hand, the new managers at Tyco may not be doing much better. While there is plenty of evidence that Tyco has managed earnings, there is no evidence that a change in culture has taken place.[6] Alex Berenson reports that in its latest quarterly report, Tyco's new managers have devised a new definition of "free cash flow." It should come as no surprise that this new definition biases the figures and makes management look better than it is really doing. Coupled with the failure to acknowledge the impairment of the firm's goodwill, this path seems a desperate attempt to arrange debt refinancing on favorable terms in early 2003.

The Boies report may help to perpetuate this debauched culture.[7] After examining only two-thirds of the questionable entries and not scratching too deeply on the ones they did investigate, the report claims that "there was no significant or systemic fraud." Purposeful errors are mentioned on virtually every page of the report. If they were not purposeful, why do they all benefit management? Additionally, the authors of the report grumble about poor controls and the lack of documentation that helped Tyco managers enter erroneous data in the accounting records. The report also states that "aggressive accounting is not necessarily improper accounting." While it is true as written, this assertion is a bit misleading. The point is that financial statements should communicate information to shareholders. A little aggressive accounting may not impede this process too much, but there comes a point when a lot of aggressive accounting virtually destroys the communication process. In my judgment, the Boies report gives the reader enough facts to realize that Tyco managers may have passed that threshold with its many errors and a culture that fostered "aggressive accounting."

DEBT? WHAT DEBT?

Financial Leverage

The theory of finance posits that expected returns are a function of risk. Risk itself is comprised of many different aspects, including business risk, inflation risk, political risk, and financial risk. Here I am concerned primarily with *financial risk*, which deals with the negative aspects of having too much debt. The problem with too much debt is that the interest costs become high, and the corporation must pay the interest regardless of its revenues or cash inflows.[8]

To make this concept more concrete, financial economists talk about *financial leverage*, which attempts to measure either the amount of debt in the financial structure or the amount of fixed interest charges in relation to the overall cost structure. Since the latter is difficult for analysts to glean from public financial statements, here I shall operationalize financial leverage as some ratio of debt that occurs in the financial structure. Commonly used ratios that quantify financial leverage are total debts to total assets, long-term debts to total assets, and debt to equity.

The other accounting scandals I wish to discuss involve managers' hiding liabilities under some carpet. When the liabilities got too big, the carpet split and the dirt went everywhere.

Adelphia

Adelphia is another cable company that is in trouble because of its accounting. In this case, the accounting improprieties at Adelphia center on its $2.3 billion in loans to the Rigas family, the founders of Adelphia. As is becoming increasingly popular, the firm issued the loan via an SPE (special-purpose entity). The worthless notes receivable are also lodged with the SPE.

The major reporting deficiency arises because the parent corporation should consolidate the SPE's financial results with its own. Even though the Financial Accounting Standards Board (FASB) and the SEC have both been incredibly slow to acknowledge this reality, this conclusion requires only some common sense. Adelphia must service the debts, so properly they belong on Adelphia's balance sheet. Financial statement readers can have a clue as to what is going on only if these debts are reported as debts of Adelphia.

Enron[9]

Enron was an energy enterprise, dealing in natural gas and electricity both with wholesalers and with retail consumers, providing broadband services, and developing a market for energy-related financial commodities. The most intriguing aspect of Enron, however, was its evolution from an energy company to a hedge fund characterized by high-risk investments and a mass of debt. For a while it seemed to perform adequately, but then those high-risk investments yielded poor results. In particular, in 1999 Enron's managers and its board of directors decided to create financing vehicles and specialized partnerships that seemingly permitted in some cases off-balance sheet financing. However, the management team at Enron then engaged in hanky-panky, for they did not disclose what the firm was really doing, especially with respect to its liabilities.

The case against Enron focuses on at least five aspects, the first of which deals with its energy contracts. At the risk of oversimplifying the accounting, the rules require entities to report such contracts on the balance sheet at fair market value. When the firm holds a long position in an energy contract and energy prices rise (fall), then the balance sheet reports these contracts at higher (lower) amounts and the unrealized gain (loss) is placed in the income statement. The opposite is true when the company maintains a short position in the energy contract. What investors have to remember is that these portions of income are paper gains, and what goes up can and often does come down; accordingly, they need to investigate the firm's quality of earnings. Investors need to assess the degree to which earnings have been or soon will be associated with cash inflows. They also need to examine the degree to which management is cooking the books. Having said this, I find Enron's $1 billion write-down in the third quarter of 2001, most of it relating to losses due to its energy contracts, interesting. This huge loss suggests a lack of proper accounting in earlier periods.

The second charge against Enron concerns its use of SPEs. Generically, SPEs work as an entity that goes between the corporation (in this case Enron) and a group of investors, usually in the form of creditors. The creditor lends money to the SPE and the SPE in turn transfers the cash to Enron; simultaneously, Enron transfers assets to the SPE. As these assets generate cash, the SPE pays off its debts to the creditors. All SPEs serve two purposes, one legitimate and one illegitimate. The legitimate purpose of the SPE occurs when the corporation dedicates assets in sufficient quantity and quality to entice creditors to give the corporation a loan at a favorable interest rate. The creditors willingly do this because of the credit enhancements given to the assets contained in the SPE. The illegitimate purpose comes when business enterprises employ SPEs to hide debt, because GAAP by and large allow firms not to reveal the liability. The FASB and the SEC should have closed this loophole a long time ago. These regulatory bodies do require some disclosures with respect to the SPEs, but Enron did not meet these disclosure rules.

I turn next to the issue of related parties. Related party transactions occur when the firm participates in a transaction with another entity or person that is not at "arm's length." In other words, the business enterprise transacts with another party that is somehow related to it, such as between a parent company and its subsidiaries, a corporation and its pension plan, or a firm and its managers. Because the firm might not engage in transactions with related parties that are competitive (e.g., giving a manager a loan with an unusually low interest rate), the FASB requires in Statement of Financial Accounting Standards (SFAS) No. 57 that the entity disclose the related party transactions, including the dollar amounts involved. Apparently beginning in 1999, Enron created several limited partnerships, such as the LJM Cayman LP and LJM2 Co-Investment LP, which were run by and partially owned by top managers within Enron. Clearly, the creation of these limited partnerships and the subsequent transactions between them and Enron constituted related party transactions. Enron's disclosures about these related party transactions were cryptic and obscure, and made it very hard for a reader of the financial statements to discern their true nature. Of course, this was done on purpose.

The fourth charge against Enron focuses on the lack of consolidation of the limited partnerships. When one company owns more than 50 percent of another entity, the investor company must consolidate the financial statements of the investee with its own financial statements. Briefly, this means that the assets and liabilities of the subsidiary or investee are added to the assets and liabilities of the parent or investor company. It also requires the elimination of intercompany transactions, including the elimination of the parent's investment account and the subsidiary's stockholders' equity. In like manner, the accountant also would consolidate the income statements and the cash flow statements. However, if the company owned less than a controlling interest in the investee, then it would apply the equity method instead of consolidation. Under the equity method, the investor company places the proportional net assets (assets less liabilities) of the investee it owns on its own balance sheet. Notice that the liabilities of the investee are unreported, thus demonstrating that the equity method is itself a tool for off-balance sheet reporting. Trouble arises when the parent firm has virtual control of what the subsidiary can do even though the parent has less than 50 percent ownership interests in the subsidiary. This deficiency shows that FASB ought to change the rules about consolidation so as to require controlled entities to be included in the financial reports of the controlling entity.

Enron did not consolidate some of the limited partnerships it owned, but it should have. Apparently, Enron had a controlling interest in some of these partnerships but somehow talked Arthur Andersen into allowing the firm to apply the equity method instead. Given the related parties involved, I would argue that even those limited partnerships in which Enron did not possess a controlling interest should have been consolidated. The reason is that senior managers of Enron owned and managed these limited partnerships, so in effect Enron had substantive control over them. The substance of the transactions should dictate the accounting, not the letter of some FASB pronouncement.

The last aspect of Enron's faulty accounting deals with improperly recorded notes receivable on its balance sheet at $1.2 billion. These notes arose from Enron's equity partners in the various limited partnerships. Certain partners apparently promised to ante up some assets in the future for an equity claim in the limited partnership today. Displaying these notes receivable as assets on the balance sheet, however, is clearly a violation of GAAP. Whenever there is subscribed stock for corporations or subscribed equity interests in partnerships, the SEC requires the subscription receivable to be reported as a contra stockholders' equity account, that is, it must be deducted from the enterprise's stockholders' equity. The rationale for this regulation is that state laws generally do not require subscribed stockholders or subscribed partners to pay off the notes. If these stockholders or partners do not pay off the notes, state laws generally stipulate that they have no claims to the equity of the business. Given these rules, Enron should not have reported the receivable on the asset side of the balance sheet. Enron corrected this irregularity in a public statement on October 16, 2001. This shrinkage of the assets by $1.2 billion not only reflects decreased asset values but also implies that the debt-to-equity ratio was systematically underreported. In other words, this manipulation deceived investors about the true financial risk of the enterprise.

The net effect of these five schemes is that Enron greatly underreported its debts and provided opaque disclosures about its business. When the investments of Enron and its subsidiaries and its limited partnerships went south, the underreported assets had evaporated, leaving only the underreported liabilities. As everyone gained this knowledge, Enron's stock value eroded and Enron declared bankruptcy on December 2, 2002.

Global Crossing

Some pundits refer to Global Crossing as the other Enron because of the incredible similarity between the two frauds. Both involve lies about financial leverage, accounting cover-ups, feeble and spineless boards of directors, a lack of corporate governance, and Arthur Andersen as its public auditors. It therefore comes as no surprise that the firm declared bankruptcy only a month after Enron—and that the government has been slow to prosecute the criminals who perpetrated the frauds.

WorldCom

Not to be outdone by others, Bernard Ebbers, the former CEO, decided to combine the worst of AOL and Enron. WorldCom had experienced operating expenses of around $7 billion but, like AOL Time Warner, WorldCom reported them as capital expenditures and depreciated them over a long period of time. In addition, WorldCom created its own SPEs so that it could hide at least hundreds of millions of dollars in debts. Recently we also have learned that various officers received huge loans from the company, possibly in an attempt to buy some influence over them to keep things quiet. It worked for a while.

SUMMARY AND CONCLUSION

Accounting improprieties have always occurred, because every period has had some CEOs who feel that they can fool people with accounting lies. The current period has its problems, as seen in Boston Chicken, Waste Management, Sunbeam, Cendant, Sensormatic Electronics, AOL Time Warner, Qwest, Tyco, Adelphia, Enron, Global Crossing, and WorldCom. Others not discussed in this chapter include Amazon, Informix, KMart, and Peregrine Systems. Despite what CEOs, CFOs, and auditors are currently espousing, this quantity of problems seems excessive. There exist more than a few bad apples.

Corroborating evidence is found in the GAO's 2002 report *Financial Statement Restatements*.[10] The GAO found that from 1997 until June 2002, there were 919 accounting restatements. The GAO's list is presented in Exhibit 1.2. Firms certainly make mistakes from time to time, but 919 changes is a ridiculously high number, and it makes me wonder whether any manager tells the truth. At the least, I believe that 919 restatements of the accounting numbers provide a prima facie case that the American system is facing a major cultural problem because it appears that the norm for managers is to deceive investors and creditors.

Representative John Dingell (D-Michigan) recently said in House debate that the occurrence of securities fraud is rising. (Dingell blames passage of litigation reform, which is discussed in Chapter 9.) While it remains difficult to measure just how much accounting fraud is occurring, the same might be said about it.

Managers and their lawyers and accountants face every day the ethical dilemma of whether to disclose or not disclose the truth. As documented in the cases presented in this chapter, managers and their representatives have erred too often. If this country is to clear up this accounting mess and the doldrums in the stock market and the economy at large, much has to be changed. These reforms must affect the culture of how managers manage their business, or the country will see these accounting scandals played over in the future. The names and the companies and the schemes may change, but the scheming itself goes on. Effecting real change will require the business community to stop this conspiracy.

Exhibit 1.2   Recent Accounting Restatements with the SEC

1997

1. Acacia Research Corporation
2. Alabama National BanCorp
3. America Online, Incorporated
4. American Business Information, Incorporated
5. American Standard Companies Incorporated
6. AMNEX, Incorporated
7. Ancor Communications, Incorporated
8. Arrhythmia Research Technology, Incorporated
9. Arzan International (1991) Limited
10. Ascent Entertainment Group, Incorporated
11. Astrocom Corporation
12. Caribbean Cigar Company
13. Carrington Laboratories, Incorporated
14. Centennial Technologies Incorporated
15. Computron Software, Incorporated
16. Concorde Career Colleges, Incorporated
17. Craig Consumer Electronics Incorporated
18. Discount Auto Parts Incorporated
19. Donnkenny, Incorporated
20. Dyna Group International Incorporated
21. Electrosource, Incorporated
22. Eltek Limited
23. Federal-Mogul Corporation
24. Fidelity Bancorp, Incorporated
25. Fine Host Corporation
26. First Colorado Bancorp, Incorporated
27. First Merchants Acceptance Corporation
28. First USA Paymentech, Incorporated
29. First USA, Incorporated
30. FOCUS Enhancements, Incorporated
31. Fonix Corporation
32. Foxmoor Industries Limited
33. Genesco Incorporated
34. Geographics, Incorporated
35. GranCare, Incorporated
36. Health Management, Incorporated
37. HealthPlan Services Corporation
38. Healthplex, Incorporated
39. HMI Industries Incorporated
40. Hudson Technologies Incorporated
41. In Home Health, Incorporated
42. Informix Corporation
43. InPhyNet Medical Management, Incorporated
44. International Nursing Services, Incorporated
45. Israel Land Development Company
46. Macerich Company
47. Management Technologies Incorporated
48. Material Sciences Corporation
49. Medaphis Corporation
50. Medaphis Corporation
51. Mercury Finance Company
52. Meridian National Corporation
53. Micro-Integration Corporation
54. Molten Metal Technology, Incorporated
55. MRV Communications, Incorporated
56. National Health Enhancement Systems, Incorporated
57. National Steel Corporation
58. National TechTeam, Incorporated
59. Oak Industries Incorporated

Exhibit 1.2 *(Continued)*

60. Paging Network, Incorporated
61. Paracelsus Healthcare Corporation
62. Pegasystems Incorporated
63. PennCorp Financial Group, Incorporated
64. Perceptron, Incorporated
65. Perceptronics, Incorporated
66. Photran Corporation
67. Physicians Laser Services, Incorporated
68. PictureTel Corporation
69. Room Plus, Incorporated
70. S3 Incorporated
71. Safe Alternatives Corporation of America, Incorporated
72. Santa Anita Companies
73. Silicon Valley Research, Incorporated
74. Simula, Incorporated
75. Soligen Technologies, Incorporated
76. St. Francis Capital Corporation
77. Summit Medical Systems, Incorporated
78. System Software Associates, Incorporated
79. Thousand Trails, Incorporated
80. Today's Man, Incorporated
81. Unison HealthCare Corporation
82. United Dental Care, Incorporated
83. Universal Seismic Associates, Incorporated
84. Unocal Corporation
85. UROHEALTH Systems, Incorporated
86. USA Detergents Incorporated
87. UStel Incorporated
88. Video Display Corporation
89. Waste Management Incorporated
90. WebSecure Incorporated
91. Wilshire Financial Services Group Incorporated
92. Wiz Technology, Incorporated

1998

93. 3Com Corporation
94. 4Health, Incorporated
95. ADAC Laboratories
96. Altris Software, Incorporated
97. American Skiing Company
98. Aspec Technology, Incorporated
99. AutoBond Acceptance Corporation
100. Boca Research, Incorporated
101. Boston Scientific Corporation
102. Breed Technologies, Incorporated
103. Cabletron Systems, Incorporated
104. Canmax Incorporated
105. Castelle Incorporated
106. Cendant Corporation
107. COHR Incorporated
108. Corel Corporation
109. Cotton Valley Resources Corporation
110. CPS Systems, Incorporated
111. Creative Gaming Incorporated
112. Cross Medical Products, Incorporated
113. CyberGuard Corporation
114. CyberMedia Incorporated
115. Cylink Corporation
116. Data I/O Corporation
117. Data Systems Network Corporation
118. Detection Systems, Incorporated
119. Digital Lightwave, Incorporated
120. Egobilt Incorporated
121. Envoy Corporation
122. EquiMed Incorporated
123. Female Health Company
124. Florafax International Incorporated
125. Food Lion, Incorporated

Exhibit 1.2 *(Continued)*

126. Forecross Corporation
127. Foster Wheeler Corporation
128. Galileo Corporation
129. General Automation, Incorporated
130. Glenayre Technologies, Incorporated
131. Golden Bear Golf, Incorporated
132. Green Tree Financial Corporation
133. Guilford Mills, Incorporated
134. Gunther International, Limited
135. H.T.E., Incorporated
136. Harnischfeger Industries
137. Hybrid Networks, Incorporated
138. Hybrid Networks, Incorporated
139. IKON Office Solutions Incorporated
140. Informix Corporation
141. Integrated Sensor Solutions, Incorporated
142. Interactive Limited
143. International Home Foods, Incorporated
144. International Total Services, Incorporated
145. Kyzen Corporation
146. Lernout & Hauspie Speech Products N.V.
147. Livent, Incorporated
148. McDonald's Corporation
149. MCI Communications Corporation
150. Media Logic, Incorporated
151. Mego Mortgage Corporation
152. Metal Management, Incorporated
153. Microelectronic Packaging Incorporated
154. Morrow Snowboards Incorporated
155. MSB Financial Corporation
156. National HealthCare Corporation
157. Neoware Systems, Incorporated
158. Newriders Incorporated
159. Norland Medical Systems, Incorporated
160. Outboard Marine Corporation
161. Pegasystems Incorporated
162. Peritus Software Services, Incorporated
163. Peritus Software Services, Incorporated
164. Philip Services Corporation
165. Physician Computer Network, Incorporated
166. Premier Laser Systems Incorporated
167. Prosoft I-Net Solutions, Incorporated
168. Raster Graphics, Incorporated
169. Room Plus, Incorporated
170. Rushmore Financial Group Incorporated
171. Saf T Lok Incorporated
172. Schlotzsky's Incorporated
173. ShoLodge, Incorporated
174. Signal Technology Corporation
175. SmarTalk Teleservices, Incorporated
176. Sobieski Bancorp Incorporated
177. Starbase Corporation
178. Starmet Corporation
179. Sterling Vision Incorporated
180. SunTrust Banks, Incorporated
181. Sunbeam Corporation
182. Sybase Incorporated
183. Telxon Corporation
184. Total Renal Care Holdings, Incorporated
185. Transcrypt International, Incorporated
186. Trex Medical Corporation
187. TriTeal Corporation
188. Unitel Video, Incorporated
189. Universal Seismic Associates, Incorporated

Exhibit 1.2 *(Continued)*

190. USWeb Corporation
191. Versar, Incorporated
192. Versatility Incorporated
193. Vesta Insurance Group Incorporated
194. Wheelabrator Technologies Incorporated

1999

195. Acorn Products, Incorporated
196. Advanced Polymer Systems, Incorporated
197. Aegis Communications Group, Incorporated
198. Allied Products Corporation
199. Alydaar Software Corporation
200. America Service Group Incorporated
201. American Bank Note Holographics
202. American Banknote Corporation
203. AmeriCredit Corporation
204. Annapolis National Bancorp
205. Armor Holdings, Incorporated
206. Assisted Living Concepts, Incorporated
207. Assisted Living Concepts, Incorporated
208. At Home Corporation
209. Autodesk, Incorporated
210. Avid Technology, Incorporated
211. AvTel Communications Incorporated
212. Aztec Technology Partners, Incorporated
213. Baker Hughes Incorporated
214. Bausch & Lomb, Incorporated
215. BellSouth Corporation
216. Belmont Bancorp
217. Best Buy Incorporated
218. Blimpie International, Incorporated

219. Blue Rhino Corporation
220. BMC Software, Incorporated
221. Boston Chicken Incorporated
222. Cabletron Systems, Incorporated
223. Candence Design Systems, Incorporated
224. Candie's Incorporated
225. Carleton Corporation
226. Carnegie International Corporation
227. CellStar Corporation
228. CenterPoint Properties Trust
229. Central Illinois Bancorp, Incorporated
230. CHS Electronics, Incorporated
231. CMGI Incorporated
232. Colorado Casino Resorts, Incorporated
233. Community West Bancshares
234. CompUSA Incorporated
235. CoreCare Systems, Incorporated
236. Crown Group, Incorporated
237. Cumetrix Data Systems Corporation
238. CVS Corporation
239. Cyberguard Corporation
240. Dassault Systemes S.A.
241. Day Runner, Incorporated
242. DCI Telecommunications, Incorporated
243. Digi International Incorporated
244. Discreet Logic, Incorporated
245. Diversinet Corporation
246. DSI Toys, Incorporated
247. Dynamex Incorporated
248. Engineering Animation, Incorporated
249. Engineering Animation, Incorporated
250. Evans Systems, Incorporated
251. Fair Grounds Corporation

Exhibit 1.2 *(Continued)*

252. FCNB Corporation
253. Fidelity National Corporation
254. Financial Security Assurance Holdings Limited
255. Finova Group, Incorporated
256. First Union Real Estate Equity and Mortgage Investments
257. First Union Real Estate Equity and Mortgage Investments
258. FlexiInternational Software, Incorporated
259. Flowers Industries Incorporated
260. Forest City Enterprises, Incorporated
261. Friedman's Incorporated
262. GameTech International, Incorporated
263. Gencor Industries, Incorporated
264. GenRad, Incorporated
265. Graham-Field Health Products, Incorporated
266. GTS Duratek, Incorporated
267. Gunther International, Limited
268. Halifax Corporation
269. Harken Energy Corporation
270. High Plains Corporation
271. Hitsgalore.com, Incorporated
272. Hungarian Broadcasting Corporation
273. Image Guided Technologies, Incorporated
274. IMRglobal Corporation
275. IMSI, Incorporated
276. Infinium Software, Incorporated
277. InfoUSA
278. INSO Corporation
279. Intasys Corporation
280. INTERLINQ Software Corporation
281. International Total Services, Incorporated

282. ION Networks, Incorporated
283. Kimberly-Clark Corporation
284. Lab Holdings, Incorporated
285. LabOne, Incorporated
286. Leisureplanet Holdings, Limited
287. Level 8 Systems
288. Lightbridge, Incorporated
289. LSI Logic Corporation
290. Lycos, Incorporated
291. Made2Manage Systems, Incorporated
292. Maxim Group, Incorporated
293. McKesson HBOC, Incorporated
294. MCN Energy Group, Incorporated
295. Medical Graphics Corporation
296. Medical Manager Corporation
297. Medical Waste Management
298. MEMC Electronic Materials, Incorporated
299. Metrowerks Incorporated
300. Miller Industries, Incorporated
301. Motorcar Parts & Accessories, Incorporated
302. National Auto Credit, Incorporated
303. National City Bancorp
304. Network Associates, Incorporated
305. Nichols Research Corporation
306. North Face, Incorporated
307. Northrop Grumman Corporation
308. Novametrix Medical Systems Incorporated
309. Nutramax Products, Incorporated
310. ObjectShare, Incorporated
311. ODS Networks, Incorporated
312. Olsten Corporation
313. Open Market, Incorporated
314. Open Text Corporation
315. Orbital Sciences Corporation
316. Orbital Sciences Corporation

Exhibit 1.2 (Continued)

317. Pacific Aerospace & Electronics, Incorporated
318. Pacific Research & Engineering Corporation
319. P-Com, Incorporated
320. PDG Environmental Incorporated
321. Pegasystems Incorporated
322. Peregrine Systems, Incorporated
323. Pharamaceutical Formulations, Incorporated
324. Protection One, Incorporated
325. PSS World Medical, Incorporated
326. Rite Aid Corporation
327. SafeGuard Health Enterprises, Incorporated
328. Safeskin Corporation
329. Safety Components International, Incorporated
330. SatCon Technology Corporation
331. Saucony, Incorporated
332. Schick Technologies, Incorporated
333. Schick Technologies, Incorporated
334. Segue Software, Incorporated
335. Signal Apparel Company, Incorporated
336. The Sirena Apparel Group, Incorporated
337. SITEK Incorporated
338. Smart Choice Automotive Group
339. SmarTalk TeleServices, Incorporated
340. Spectrum Signal Processing Incorporated
341. SS&C Technologies, Incorporated
342. Styling Technology Corporation
343. Sun Healthcare Group, Incorporated
344. Telxon Corporation
345. Texas Instruments Incorporated
346. The Timber Company
347. Thomas & Betts Corporation

348. Total Renal Care Holdings, Incorporated
349. TRW Incorporated
350. Twinlab Corporation
351. Unisys Corporation
352. Vesta Insurance Group Incorporated
353. Voxware, Incorporated
354. VTEL Corporation
355. Wabash National Corporation
356. Wall Data Incorporated
357. Wang Global
358. Warrantech Corporation
359. Waste Management Incorporated
360. WellCare Management Group Incorporated
361. Western Resources, Incorporated
362. Wickes Incorporated
363. Williams Companies
364. Xilinx, Incorporated
365. Yahoo! Incorporated
366. Zenith National Insurance Corporation
367. Ziegler Companies, Incorporated
368. Zions Bancorp

2000

369. 1st Source Corporation
370. 3D Systems Corporation
371. Able Telcom Holding Corporation
372. Acrodyne Communications, Incorporated
373. Activision, Incorporated
374. Advanced Technical Products, Incorporated
375. Aetna Incorporated
376. Allscripts Incorporated
377. Alpharma Incorporated
378. American Physicians Service Group, Incorporated

Exhibit 1.2 *(Continued)*

379. American Xtal Technology
380. Analytical Surveys, Incorporated
381. Anicom Incorporated
382. Asche Transportation Services, Incorporated
383. Aspeon, Incorporated
384. Atchison Casting Corporation
385. Auburn National Bancorp
386. Aurora Foods Incorporated
387. Avon Products, Incorporated
388. Aztec Technology Partners, Incorporated
389. Baan Company
390. BarPoint.com, Incorporated
391. Bindley Western Industries, Incorporated
392. Biomet, Incorporated
393. Bion Environmental Technologies, Incorporated
394. Boise Cascade Corporation
395. BPI Packaging Technologies, Incorporated
396. California Software Corporation
397. CareMatrix Corporation
398. Carnegie International Corporation
399. Carver Bancorp, Incorporated
400. Castle Dental Centers, Incorporated
401. Cato Corporation
402. Chesapeake Corporation
403. Children's Comprehensive Services, Incorporated
404. CIMA LABS Incorporated
405. CINAR Corporation
406. Clearnet Communications Incorporated
407. ClearWorks.net, Incorporated
408. CMI Corporation
409. CMI Corporation
410. Computer Learning Centers, Incorporated
411. Covad Communications Group
412. Cover-All Technologies Incorporated
413. Cumulus Media Incorporated
414. Del Global Technologies Corporation
415. Delphi Financial Group, Incorporated
416. Detour Magazine, Incorporated
417. Dicom Imaging Systems, Incorporated
418. Digital Lava Incorporated
419. Discovery Laboratories, Incorporated
420. DocuCorp International
421. DT Industries, Incorporated
422. e.spire Communications, Incorporated
423. EA Engineering, Science, and Technology, Incorporated
424. ebix.com, Incorporated
425. ebix.com, Incorporated
426. EDAP TMS S.A.
427. eMagin Corporation
428. Environmental Power Corporation
429. Epicor Software Corporation
430. eSAT Incorporated
431. Exide Corporation
432. FFW Corporation
433. FinancialWeb.com, Incorporated
434. First American Financial Corporation
435. First American Health Concepts, Incorporated
436. First American Health Concepts, Incorporated
437. First Tennessee National Corporation
438. FLIR Systems, Incorporated
439. Flooring America, Incorporated

Exhibit 1.2   *(Continued)*

440. FOCUS Enhancements, Incorporated
441. Gadzoox Networks, Incorporated
442. Geographics, Incorporated
443. Geron Corporation
444. Global Med Technologies, Incorporated
445. Good Guys, Incorporated
446. Goody's Family Clothing, Incorporated
447. Goody's Family Clothing, Incorporated
448. Guess ?, Incorporated
449. Hamilton Bancorp
450. Harmonic Incorporated
451. Hastings Entertainment, Incorporated
452. Heartland Technology, Incorporated
453. Hirsch International Corporation
454. Host Marriott Corporation
455. IBP, Incorporated
456. Image Sensing Systems, Incorporated
457. Imperial Credit Industries
458. Inacom Corporation
459. Indus International, Incorporated
460. Industrial Holdings, Incorporated
461. Information Management Associates, Incorporated
462. Innovative Gaming Corporation
463. Interiors, Incorporated
464. International Total Services, Incorporated
465. Internet America, Incorporated
466. Interplay Entertainment Corporation
467. Interspeed, Incorporated
468. Intimate Brands, Incorporated
469. Intranet, Incorporated
470. J. C. Penney Company, Incorporated

471. JDN Realty Corporation
472. Jenna Lane, Incorporated
473. Kitty Hawk Incorporated
474. Kmart Corporation
475. Laidlaw Incorporated
476. LanguageWare.net Limited
477. Legato Systems, Incorporated
478. Lernout & Hauspie Speech Products N.V.
479. Lodgian, Incorporated
480. Louis Dreyfus Natural Gas Corporation
481. Lucent Technologies, Incorporated
482. Magellan Health Services, Incorporated
483. Magna International Incorporated
484. Master Graphics, Incorporated
485. MAX Internet Communications Incorporated
486. Mediconsult.com, Incorporated
487. Mercator Software, Incorporated
488. MerchantOnline.com, Incorporated
489. MetaCreations Corporation
490. MicroStrategy Incorporated
491. Mikohn Gaming Corporation
492. Mitek Systems, Incorporated
493. MITY Enterprises Incorporated
494. Monarch Investment Properties, Incorporated
495. National Fuel Gas Company
496. Network Systems International, Incorporated
497. Northeast Indiana Bancorp
498. Northpoint Communications Group
499. Nx Networks, Incorporated
500. Oil-Dri Corporation of America
501. Omega Worldwide Incorporated
502. Omni Nutraceuticals, Incorporated
503. OnHealth Network Company

Exhibit 1.2   (Continued)

504. On-Point Technology Systems Incorporated
505. Orbital Sciences Corporation
506. Oriental Financial Group Incorporated
507. Pacific Bank
508. Pacific Gateway Exchange, Incorporated
509. Parexel International Corporation
510. Paulson Capital Corporation
511. Phoenix International, Incorporated
512. Plains All American Pipeline, L.P.
513. Plains Resources Incorporated
514. Planet411.com Incorporated
515. Potlatch Corporation
516. Precept Business Service, Incorporated
517. Profit Recovery Group International, Incorporated
518. 18 Pulaski Financial Corporation
519. Quintus Corporation
520. Ramp Networks, Incorporated
521. RAVISENT Technologies Incorporated
522. Raytheon Corporation
523. Rentrak Corporation
524. Rent-Way, Incorporated
525. RFS Hotel Investors, Incorporated
526. Roanoke Electric Steel Corporation
527. Safety Kleen Corporation
528. SatCon Technology Corporation
529. Scan-Optics, Incorporated
530. SCB Computer Technology, Incorporated
531. Seaboard Corporation
532. Segue Software, Incorporated
533. Serologicals Corporation
534. Shuffle Master, Incorporated
535. Source Media, Incorporated
536. Southwall Technologies, Incorporated
537. Sport-Haley, Incorporated
538. Sterling Financial Corporation
539. Stryker Corporation
540. SunStar Healthcare, Incorporated
541. Superconductive Components, Incorporated
542. Sykes Enterprises, Incorporated
543. Sykes Enterprises, Incorporated
544. Taubman Centers, Incorporated
545. TeleHubLink Corporation
546. Telemonde, Incorporated
547. Telescan, Incorporated
548. Telxon Corporation
549. Limited, Incorporated
550. Thomas & Betts Corporation
551. TJX Companies, Incorporated
552. Today's Man, Incorporated
553. Too, Incorporated
554. Transport Corporation of America, Incorporated
555. Travel Dynamics Incorporated
556. TREEV, Incorporated
557. Tyco International Limited
558. UICI
559. Ultimate Electronics, Incorporated
560. Unify Corporation
561. Vari-L Company, Incorporated
562. Vari-L Company, Incorporated
563. Vertex Industries, Incorporated
564. W.R. Grace & Company
565. Westmark Group Holdings, Incorporated
566. Whitney Information Network, Incorporated
567. Winnebago Industries, Incorporated
568. WorldWide Web NetworX Corporation

Exhibit 1.2 *(Continued)*

569. Wyant Corporation

2001

570. Accelerated Networks, Incorporated
571. The Ackerley Group, Incorporated
572. Actuant Corporation
573. Adaptive Broadband Corporation
574. Advanced Remote Communication Solutions Incorporated
575. Air Canada Incorporated
576. Alcoa Incorporated
577. ALZA Corporation
578. AMC Entertainment, Incorporated
579. American HomePatient, Incorporated
580. American Physicians Service Group, Incorporated
581. Anchor Gaming
582. Andrew Corporation
583. Angiotech Pharmaceuticals, Incorporated
584. Anika Therapeutics Incorporated
585. Applied Materials, Incorporated
586. Argosy Education Group, Incorporated
587. ARI Network Services, Incorporated
588. Aronex Pharmaceuticals, Incorporated
589. Atchison Casting Corporation
590. Aviron
591. Avnet, Incorporated
592. Avon Products, Incorporated
593. BakBone Software Incorporated
594. Baldor Electric Company
595. Banner Corporation
596. Beyond.com Corporation
597. Brightpoint, Incorporated
598. BroadVision, Incorporated
599. Bull Run Corporation

600. California Amplifier, Incorporated
601. Cambior Incorporated
602. Campbell Soup Company
603. Cantel Medical Corporation
604. Cardiac Pathways Corporation
605. Cardiac Pathways Corporation
606. CellStar Corporation
607. CellStar Corporation
608. Centennial Communications Corporation
609. Centex Construction Products, Incorporated
610. Centex Corporation
611. Century Business Services, Incorporated
612. Charming Shoppes, Incorporated
613. Cheap Tickets, Incorporated
614. Checkpoint Systems, Incorporated
615. Chromaline Corporation
616. Chronimed, Incorporated
617. Cincinnati Financial Corporation
618. Clorox Company
619. Cohesion Technologies, Incorporated
620. Cohu, Incorporated
621. Commtouch Software Limited
622. ConAgra Foods, Incorporated
623. Concord Camera Corporation
624. Corel Corporation
625. Corixa Corporation
626. Credence Systems Corporation
627. Critical Path, Incorporated
628. Cyber Merchants Exchange, Incorporated
629. Daw Technologies, Incorporated
630. Dean Foods Company
631. Derma Sciences, Incorporated
632. Dial-Thru International Corporation
633. Digital Insight Corporation

Exhibit 1.2 *(Continued)*

634. Dillard's, Incorporated
635. Dollar General Corporation
636. Donnelly Corporation
637. ECI Telecom Limited
638. ECI Telecom Limited
639. EGames, Incorporated
640. Embrex Incorporated
641. Encad Incorporated
642. Energy West, Incorporated
643. Enron Corporation
644. ESPS, Incorporated
645. FindWhat.com
646. First Data Corporation
647. Fleming Companies, Incorporated
648. FLIR Systems, Incorporated
649. Fortune Brands, Incorporated
650. FreeMarkets, Incorporated
651. Gateway, Incorporated
652. GATX Corporation
653. Genentech, Incorporated
654. Greka Energy Corporation
655. Guardian International, Incorporated
656. Guess ?, Incorporated
657. HALO Industries Incorporated
658. Hamilton Bancorp
659. Hanover Compressor Company
660. Harrah's Entertainment Incorporated
661. Harrah's Entertainment Incorporated
662. Hayes Lemmerz International, Incorporated
663. Health Care Property Investors, Incorporated
664. Health Grades, Incorporated
665. Health Risk Management, Incorporated
666. Hemispherx Biopharma, Incorporated
667. Herman Miller, Incorporated
668. Hewlett-Packard Company
669. High Speed Net Solutions, Incorporated
670. Hollywood Casino Corporation
671. Homestake Mining Company
672. Homestore.com, Incorporated
673. IBP, Incorporated
674. ICNB Financial Corporation
675. IDEC Pharmaceuticals Corporation
676. IMAX Corporation
677. Immune Response Corporation
678. Industrial Distribution Group, Incorporated
679. Integrated Measurement Systems, Incorporated
680. Israel Land Development Company
681. J Jill Group, Incorporated
682. JDS Uniphase Corporation
683. Jones Lang LaSalle Incorporated
684. Kaneb Services, Incorporated
685. KCS Energy, Incorporated
686. Kennametal Incorporated
687. Kindred Healthcare, Incorporated
688. Krispy Kreme Doughnuts, Incorporated
689. Kroger Company
690. Lafarge North America Incorporated
691. Laidlaw Incorporated
692. Lancaster Colony Corporation
693. Lance Incorporated
694. Landec Corporation
695. Lands' End, Incorporated
696. Lason Incorporated
697. Learn2, Incorporated
698. LeCroy Corporation
699. Ledger Capital Corporation
700. Lions Gate Entertainment Corporation
701. LoJack Corporation
702. Lucent Technologies Incorporated

Exhibit 1.2   *(Continued)*

703. Lufkin Industries, Incorporated
704. Magna International Incorporated
705. Manitowoc Company, Incorporated
706. Marlton Technologies, Incorporated
707. MasTec Incorporated
708. MCK Communications, Incorporated
709. MERANT PLC
710. META Group Incorporated
711. Method Products Corporation
712. Midland Company
713. Minuteman International, Incorporated
714. Monsanto Company
715. Motor Club of America
716. National Commerce Financial Corporation
717. National Steel Corporation
718. NCI Building Systems, Incorporated
719. NESCO, Incorporated
720. Net4Music Incorporated
721. NetEase.com, Incorporated
722. New England Business Service, Incorporated
723. NexPub, Incorporated
724. NextPath Technologies, Incorporated
725. Nice Systems Limited
726. Northrop Grumman Corporation
727. NPS Pharmaceuticals, Incorporated
728. Online Resources Corporation
729. Onyx Software Corporation
730. Opal Technologies, Incorporated
731. Orthodontic Centers of America, Incorporated
732. Parallel Petroleum Corporation
733. Paulson Capital Corporation
734. Pennzoil-Quaker State Company
735. Pinnacle Holdings, Incorporated

736. Placer Dome Incorporated
737. PlanetCAD, Incorporated
738. Pre-Paid Legal Services, Incorporated
739. Pre-Paid Legal Services, Incorporated
740. Private Media Group, Incorporated
741. Provident Bankshares
742. Proxim, Incorporated
743. PurchasePro.com, Incorporated
744. PXRE Group Limited
745. Rare Medium Group, Incorporated
746. Rayovac Corporation
747. Reader's Digest Association, Incorporated
748. Reynolds and Reynolds Company
749. Riviana Foods Incorporated
750. Roadhouse Grill, Incorporated
751. Robotic Vision Systems, Incorporated
752. Rock-Tenn Company
753. SCB Computer Technology, Incorporated
754. SeaView Video Technology, Incorporated
755. Semitool, Incorporated
756. Service Corporation International
757. Shurgard Storage Centers, Incorporated
758. Sonus Corporation
759. Sony Corporation
760. Southern Union Company
761. Southwest Securities Group, Incorporated
762. SRI/Surgical Express, Incorporated
763. StarMedia Network, Incorporated
764. Stolt-Nielsen S.A.
765. Sykes Enterprises, Incorporated
766. Take-Two Interactive Incorporated

Exhibit 1.2 *(Continued)*

767. Team Communications Group, Incorporated
768. TeleCorp PCS, Incorporated
769. Toro Company
770. Trikon Technologies, Incorporated
771. True North Communications Incorporated
772. Tyco International Limited
773. U.S. Aggregates, Incorporated
774. U.S. Wireless Corporation
775. Unify Corporation
776. Urban Outfitters, Incorporated
777. UTStarcom, Incorporated
778. Vans, Incorporated
779. Varian, Incorporated
780. VIA NET.WORKS, Incorporated
781. Vical Incorporated
782. Vicon Fiber Optics Corporation
783. Wackenhut Corporation
784. Wackenhut Corporation
785. Wallace Computer Services, Incorporated
786. Warnaco Group, Incorporated
787. Warnaco Group, Incorporated
788. Webb Interactive Services, Incorporated
789. Western Digital Corporation
790. Westfield America, Incorporated
791. Westvaco Corporation
792. Williams Controls, Incorporated
793. Woodhead Industries, Incorporated
794. Xerox Corporation

2002

795. ACTV, Incorporated
796. Adelphia Communications Corporation
797. Advanced Magnetics, Incorporated
798. Advanced Remote Communication Solutions Incorporated
799. Akorn Incorporated
800. Alliant Energy Corporation
801. Allied Irish Banks PLC
802. Almost Family, Incorporated
803. American Physicians Service Group, Incorporated
804. Anadarko Petroleum Corporation
805. Avanex Corporation
806. AvantGo, Incorporated
807. Avista Corporation
808. Baltimore Technologies PLC
809. Barrett Business Services, Incorporated
810. BroadVision, Incorporated
811. Calpine Corporation
812. CIT Group Incorporated
813. CMS Energy Corporation
814. Cognos, Incorporated
815. Collins & Aikman Corporation
816. Computer Associates International, Incorporated
817. Cornell Companies
818. Corrpro Companies, Incorporated
819. Cost-U-Less, Incorporated
820. Creo Incorporated
821. Del Global Technologies Corporation
822. Del Monte Foods Company
823. Dillard's, Incorporated
824. DOV Pharmaceutical, Incorporated
825. Dover Corporation
826. Drexler Technology Corporation
827. DuPont Company
828. Eagle Building Technologies, Incorporated
829. eDiets.com, Incorporated
830. Edison Schools Incorporated

Exhibit 1.2 *(Continued)*

831. eFunds Corporation
832. Eidos PLC
833. Enterasys Network, Incorporated
834. EOTT Energy Partners, L.P.
835. Escalon Medical Corporation
836. Exelon Corporation
837. FFP Marketing Company, Incorporated
838. FiberNet Telecom Group, Incorporated
839. Fields Technologies, Incorporated
840. Flagstar Bancorp, Incorporated
841. FloridaFirst Bancorp, Incorporated
842. Flow International Corporation
843. Foamex International
844. Foster Wheeler Limited
845. Gemstar-TV Guide International, Incorporated
846. GenCorp Incorporated
847. Gerber Scientific, Incorporated
848. Great Pee Dee Bancorp, Incorporated
849. Haemonetics Corporation
850. Hanover Compressor Company
851. Hanover Compressor Company
852. Hometown Auto Retailers Incorporated
853. HPSC, Incorporated
854. Hub Group, Incorporated
855. I/Omagic Corporation
856. iGo Corporation
857. ImmunoGen, Incorporated
858. Imperial Tobacco Group PLC
859. Input/Output, Incorporated
860. JNI Corporation
861. Key Production Company, Incorporated
862. Kmart Corporation
863. Kraft Foods Incorporated

864. L90, Incorporated
865. Lantronix, Incorporated
866. Measurement Specialties, Incorporated
867. Medis Technologies, Limited
868. Metromedia Fiber Network, Incorporated
869. Minuteman International, Incorporated
870. Monsanto Company
871. Network Associates, Incorporated
872. Northwest Bancorp, Incorporated
873. NuWay Energy Incorporated
874. NVIDIA Corporation
875. Omega Protein Corporation
876. OneSource Technologies, Incorporated
877. PAB Bankshares Incorporated
878. Pennzoil-Quaker State Company
879. Peregrine Systems, Incorporated
880. Peregrine Systems, Incorporated
881. Performance Food Group Company
882. Petroleum Geo-Services ASA
883. PG&E Corporation
884. Pharmaceutical Resources, Incorporated
885. Phar-Mor, Incorporated
886. Phillips Petroleum Company
887. Photon Dynamics, Incorporated
888. The PNC Financial Services Group, Incorporated
889. The PNC Financial Services Group, Incorporated
890. Pyramid Breweries Incorporated
891. Qiao Xing Universal Telephone, Incorporated
892. Raining Data Corporation
893. Reliant Energy, Incorporated
894. Reliant Resources, Incorporated

Exhibit 1.2 *(Continued)*

---

895. Reliant Resources, Incorporated
896. Restoration Hardware, Incorporated
897. Rotonics Manufacturing Incorporated
898. SeaView Video Technology, Incorporated
899. Seitel, Incorporated
900. Smart & Final Incorporated
901. Standard Commercial Corporation
902. Star Buffet, Incorporated
903. Stratus Properties Incorporated
904. Superior Financial Corporation
905. Supervalu Incorporated
906. Sybron Dental Specialties, Incorporated
907. The Hain Celestial Group, Incorporated

908. Transmation, Incorporated
909. United Pan-Europe Communications N.V.
910. United States Lime & Minerals, Incorporated
911. Univision Communications Incorporated
912. USABancShares.com, Incorporated
913. Vail Resorts, Incorporated
914. Viad Corporation
915. Williams-Sonoma Incorporated
916. WorldCom, Incorporated
917. Xerox Corporation
918. Xplore Technologies Corporation
919. Zapata Corporation

Source: General Accounting Office, *Financial Statement Restatements: Trends, Market Impacts, Regulatory Responses, and Remaining Challenges.* Report to the Chairman, Committee on Banking, Housing, and Urban Affairs, U.S. Senate. Washington, DC: GAO, October 2002, Appendix III.

NOTES

1. Parts of this section first appeared in my 1998 article "Is There an Epidemic of Underauditing?" *Journal of Corporate Accounting and Finance* (Fall 1998): 25–35.

2. Abraham J. Briloff, *Unaccountable Accounting* (New York: Harper & Row, 1972); *More Debits than Credits* (New York: Harper & Row, 1976); and *The Truth about Corporate Accounting* (New York: Harper & Row, 1981).

3. Eli Mason, *Random Thoughts: The Writings of Eli Mason* (New York: Eli Mason, 1998).

4. *Forbes* provides details about these accounting problems in its "The Corporate Scandal Sheet," at *www.forbes.com/2002/07/25/accountingtracker.html.* Schilit provides great documentation of these accounting scandals, and he categorizes them into seven "financial shenanigans": H. Schilit, *Financial Shenanigans: How to Detect Accounting Gimmicks and Fraud in Financial Reports* (New York: McGraw-Hill, 2002). The General Accounting Office describes many of these as well in appendixes V through XX of *Financial Statement Restatements: Trends, Market Impacts, Regulatory Responses, and Remaining Challenges.* Report to the Chairman, Committee on Banking, Housing, and Urban Affairs, U.S. Senate (Washington, DC: GAO, October 2002).

5. Gordon Gecko is a character in the movie *Wall Street,* who says "Greed Is Good."

6. M. Maremont and L. P. Cohen, "Tyco's Internal Report Finds Extensive Accounting Tricks," *Wall Street Journal,* December 31, 2002; A. R. Sorkin and A. Berenson, "Tyco Admits Using Accounting Tricks to Inflate Earnings," *New York Times,* December 31, 2002.

7. See Tyco 8-K filed on December 30, 2002.

8. For more details, see G. I. White et al. (1998), pp. 983–1026.

9. Parts of this section first appeared in my 2002 article "Can We Prevent Future Enrons?" *Journal of Corporate Accounting and Finance* (May-June 2002): 3–11. For greater details about Enron, see: A. L. Berkowitz, *Enron: A Professional's Guide to the Events, Ethical Issues, and Proposed Reforms* (Chicago: Commerce Clearing House, 2002); R. Bryce, *Pipe Dreams: Greed, Ego, and the Death of Enron* (Perseus Book Group, 2002); L. Fox, *Enron: The Rise and* Fall (Hoboken, NJ: John Wiley & Sons, 2003); D. Q. Mills, *Buy, Lie, and Sell High: How Investors Lost Out on Enron and the Internet Bubble* (Upper Saddle River, NJ: Prentice-Hall, 2002); W. Powers, R. S. Troubh, and H. S. Winokur Jr., *Report of Investigation by the Special Investigative Committee of the Board of Directors of Enron Corp,* February 1, 2002; and the series of columns by *Washington Post* staff writers Peter Behr and April Witt: "Visionary's Dream Led to Risky Business," July 28, 2002, p. A01; "Dream Job Turns into a Nightmare," July 29, 2002, p. A01; "Concerns Grow Amid Conflicts," July 20, 2002, p. A01; "Losses, Conflicts Threaten Survival," July 31, 2002, p. A01; "Hidden Debts, Deals Scuttle Last Chance," August 1, p. A01.

10. GAO's 2002 report *Financial Statement Restatements.* The 919 restatements do not imply 919 firms because some companies issued two or more restatements. As depicted in Exhibit 1.2, this set of multiple restaters includes Cardiac Pathways, CMI Corporation, ECI Telecom, Goody's Family Clothing, Orbital Sciences, Peregrine Systems, PNC, Pre-Paid Legal Services, Reliant Resources, Schick Technologies, Sykes Enterprises, Var-L Company, Wachkenhut, and Warnaco.

CHAPTER TWO

Balance Sheet Woes

During the 2002 congressional hearings on the Enron bankruptcy, some senators asked Jeff Skilling, former chief executive officer (CEO) of Enron, about the firm's liabilities. In a huff Skilling retorted, "I think your question suggests that there's some issue of hiding debt!" Well, Jeff, there is an issue.

Corporate managers have an array of tools and techniques in their toolbox by which they can hide their liabilities. Some of the older methods include such things as the equity method, lease accounting, pension accounting, take-or-pay contracts, and throughput arrangements. Newer schemes create special-purpose entities (SPEs) and hide their debts from loan securitizations, synthetic leases, and other borrowings. We are aware that managers have fashioned accounting practices for the sole purpose of lying about the corporate liabilities, methods that the accounting profession and the Securities and Exchange Commission (SEC) have implicitly or explicitly endorsed within the body of generally accepted accounting principles (GAAP).

Besides these legal ways of hiding corporate debts, managers of some business enterprises have misrepresented their firm's financial leverage. Among these companies are Enron, Global Crossing, Adelphia, and WorldCom. The CEOs and chief financial officers (CFOs) purposely and deliberately understated the financial risk of their firms. As I discuss in this chapter, one perceived benefit of such prevarication comes about because lower perceived liabilities might bring lower interest rates if creditors incorrectly believe that the firm has low financial risk. In addition, investors and creditors might perceive a lower probability of bankruptcy that large amounts of debt could cause, and so have higher stock prices as well as higher bond prices. Managers thus hoodwink investors and creditors into thinking that the firm is doing better than it actually is.

In this chapter I explore the woes brought on by balance sheet deceptions. I begin with a definition of financial risk, a look at some simple metrics of financial risk, and examine why managers finance the firm with debt. I then explore the relationship of corporate liabilities with stock prices, probability of bankruptcy, and bond ratings. With this foundation, I conclude with a closer examination of the motivations for managerial lying about corporate liabilities and how the market fights back by lowering stock and bond prices.

INVESTMENT RISKS

Financial economists have argued that expected returns depend on the investment's risk. *Risk* generally refers to the uncertainty of returns on whatever investment vehicle is relevant to the user. While no one worries about the upside potential—that is, when the investment returns more than one thought—most people do fret over the possibility of an investment's losing money. Assessing the riskiness of an investment is a crucial aspect of any portfolio analysis, however large or small. While there are different types of risk, including business risk, inflation risk, political risk, and exchange rate risk, I shall focus on financial risk.

As I shall soon show, there are positive and negative benefits to a firm's taking on too much debt. *Financial risk* concentrates on those negative consequences of having too much debt. Too much debt can lead to at least three problems for the business enterprise, so investors and creditors need to recognize these issues. First, too much debt can magnify the shareholders' returns. It can do this both in a positive and a negative way, but the risk to the shareholder occurs, of course, when return on equity is lowered by the corporation's having too many liabilities. A second problem with too much debt is that the interest costs are fixed, so that the corporation must pay the interest regardless of its revenues or cash inflows. If the organization does not generate enough revenues to cover all of these fixed costs, then the firm might go bankrupt. The third issue is that well before the company gets to the point of corporate failure, banks and other creditors might recognize the increased financial risk and increase the interest rates they charge the corporation. Increases in financial risk compel these creditors to protect themselves by requiring higher rates of return.

A balance sheet depicts an entity's assets and its liabilities and its shareholders' equity. In other words, it shows the firm's resources and the claims to those resources. For the most part I am going to ignore the asset side of the balance sheet and study the claims to the entity's resources. *Financial structure* means that part of the balance sheet displaying those claims to the resources of the firm. The term *capital structure* sometimes is equivalent to financial structure, but more often it refers to the long-term components of financial structure. With the second meaning, capital structure is equal to financial structure minus short-term liabilities.

I define *financial leverage* as the ratio of total liabilities to total assets. This ratio then allows us a way to investigate what happens as a business enterprise assumes more debt in its financial structure. As the examples unfold, the reader should notice that adding debt to the financial structure, which is equivalent to increases in the corporations' financial leverage, does indeed lead to greater uncertainty about the investment's expected returns.

SOME RATIOS[1] THAT INDEX FINANCIAL RISK

Exhibit 2.1 lists the liabilities and stockholders' equities for Ford in 2001 and 2000. As typical in this country, Ford separates current debt from noncurrent debt, where current debt is that which typically comes due in one year. (If the length of the operating cycle is longer than one year—where the *length of the operating cycle* refers to the time it takes to convert cash into inventory, sell the inventory, and receive cash from the customer—then use the length of the operating cycle to determine which liabilities are current.) Current debts consist of accounts payable, the current portion of long-term debt, accrued expenses, income taxes payable, and other current liabilities. Noncurrent liabilities include deferred income taxes, long-term debt, other noncurrent liabilities, and minority interest (though some analysts consider minority interest a special form of shareholders' equity).[2]

Shareholders' equity comprises both preferred stock and common equity; however, Ford has no preferred stock. Common equity embraces common stock at par value, additional paid-in capital, retained earnings, other equity, and treasury stock.

Exhibit 2.1 Financial Structure of Ford (in Millions of Dollars)

Liabilities & Shareholders' Equity	2001	2000
Liabilities		
Accounts Payable	15,677	21,959
Current Portion Long-Term Debt	302	277
Accrued Expenses	23,990	23,515
Income Taxes Payable	0	449
Other Current Liabilities	5,515	4,011
Total Current Liabilities	45,484	50,211
Deferred Income Taxes	10,065	9,030
Long-Term Debt	167,035	165,279
Other Non-Current Liabilities	45,501	40,618
Minority Interest(Liabilities)	672	673
Total Liabilities	268,757	265,811
Shareholders' Equity		
Common Stock (Par)	19	19
Additional Paid-in Capital	6,001	6,174
Retained Earnings	10,502	17,884
Other Equity	(8,736)	(3,432)
Treasury Stock	0	(2,035)
Total Shareholders' Equity	7,786	18,610
Total Liabilities & Shareholders' Equity	276,543	284,421

Note: Parentheses denote negative numbers.

Financial leverage is total debts divided by total assets; since total assets equal total equities, we could say that financial leverage is total debts divided by total liabilities and shareholders' equity. Other measures of risk include the debt-to-equity ratio, which is total liabilities divided by shareholders' equity. Ford's financial leverage was 0.97 in 2001 and 0.93 in 2000. Its debt to equity was 34.5 in 2001 and 14.3 in 2000. These figures denote quite high levels of financial structure in the United States.

While I concentrate on the balance sheet in this book, one income statement ratio that bears mentioning is times interest earned. This ratio indexes the safety of the creditors by assessing how well operating earnings cover the fixed interest charges. Times interest earned equals the firm's earnings before interest and taxes divided by the firm's interest expense. Ford's times-interest-earned ratio (numbers are not in the exhibit) was 0.30 in 2001 and 1.62 in 2000. The 2000 ratio is marginal at best, while the 2001 ratio indicates weakness because of Ford's financial structure.

FINANCIAL LEVERAGE AND ITS EFFECTS

Let us now look at an extended example to see how these definitions and concepts play out. The idea is to comprehend the impact of financial leverage on some metric of shareholder interest; in particular, to notice, under certain circumstances, how the use of financial leverage can hurt the firm and its investors and creditors.

As stated earlier, financial structure means that part of the balance sheet displaying those claims to the resources of the firm. For example, Exhibit 2.2 contains several balance sheets in which total assets and total equities equal $100. I do not break down the total assets into constituent parts, such as current and long-term assets, to drive home the idea that this aspect is unimportant. How the assets are structured is irrelevant to this discussion about financial structure.

Exhibit 2.2   Different Financial Structures

Panel A: No debt; all common equity

		Liabilities	$ 0
		Common equity	100
Total assets	$100	Total equities	$100

Panel B: 25 percent debt; 75 percent common equity

		Liabilities	$ 25
		Common equity	75
Total assets	$100	Total equities	$100

Exhibit 2.2 *(Continued)*

Panel C: 50 percent debt; 50 percent common equity

		Liabilities	$ 50
		Common equity	50
Total assets	$100	Total equities	$100

Panel D: 75 percent debt; 25 percent common equity

		Liabilities	$ 75
		Common equity	25
Total assets	$100	Total equities	$100

The four balance sheets in panels A through D of Exhibit 2.2 show liabilities as 0, 25, 50, and 75 percent of total equities (and thus also of total assets). As defined, we have these four levels of financial leverage and now turn our attention to what difference financial leverage makes. These effects are captured in Exhibit 2.3.

Exhibit 2.3   Effects of Financial Leverage on ROE

Assume cost of debt is 8 percent and total assets = $100.

EBIT = earnings before interest and taxes

EBT = earnings before taxes = EBIT − interest expense

ROE = return on equity

Tax rate = 50 percent. Assume losses result in income tax credits.

Rates of return on assets	0%	4%	8%	12%	16%
EBIT	$0	$4	$8	$12	$16

Panel A: 0 percent leverage

EBIT	$0	$4	$8	$12	$16
Interest expense	0	0	0	0	0
EBT	$0	$4	$8	$12	$16
Taxes	0	2	4	6	8
Earnings available to common equity	$0	$2	$4	$ 6	$ 8
ROE	0%	2%	4%	6%	8%

Exhibit 2.3 *(Continued)*

Panel B: 25 percent leverage

EBIT	$ 0	$ 4	$8	$12	$16
Interest expense	2	2	2	2	2
EBT	$(2)	$ 2	$6	$10	$14
Taxes	(1)	1	3	5	7
Earnings available to common equity	$(1)	$ 1	$3	$ 5	$ 7
ROE	(1.3%)	1.3%	4%	6.7%	9.3%

Panel C: 50 percent leverage

EBIT	$ 0	$ 4	$8	$12	$16
Interest expense	4	4	4	4	4
EBT	$(4)	$ 0	$4	$ 8	$12
Taxes	(2)	0	2	4	6
Earnings available to common equity	$(2)	$ 0	$2	$ 4	$ 6
ROE	(4%)	0%	4%	8%	12%

Panel D: 75 percent leverage

EBIT	$ 0	$4	$8	$12	$16
Interest expense	6	6	6	6	6
EBT	$(6)	$(2)	$2	$ 6	$10
Taxes	(3)	(1)	1	3	5
Earnings available to common equity	$(3)	$(1)	$1	$ 3	$ 5
ROE	(12%)	(4%)	4%	12%	20%

Note: Parentheses denote negative numbers.

Exhibit 2.3 shows the return on equity (ROE) for a particular business enterprise under various scenarios. Assume that the pretax cost of debt (the interest rate) is 8 percent and that total assets and total equities equal $100. Also assume that the income tax rate is 50 percent. (While higher than the real world, this figure makes the computations easier and does not affect the conclusions.)

Note that I say nothing about the asset structure, only that the total assets are $100. We shall assume various rates of return on assets in the exercise to show how the rate of return on assets intersects with the cost of debt to affect the rate of return on equity.

Panels A through D portray four different levels of financial leverage: 0 percent debt, 25 percent debt, 50 percent debt, and 75 percent debt. Exhibit 2.3 shows the results for each of these levels of financial leverage under five different economic scenarios, differing by the presumed return on assets. These scenarios assume 0, 4, 8, 12, and 16 percent rates of return on assets. This table thus contains 20 different possibilities, four possible levels of financial leverage times five possible rates of return on assets.

In each of the 20 different situations, Exhibit 2.3 reveals the return on equity and its computation. The calculation begins with the earnings before interest and taxes (EBIT), which equals the total assets (remember that this remains $100 in every case) times the presumed rate of return on the total assets. For example, when the return is 8 percent, EBIT becomes $100 times 8 percent, so EBIT is $8.

From EBIT we subtract the interest expense, which equals the total liabilities multiplied by the cost of debt (remember that this is always 8 percent). When financial leverage happens to be 50 percent, total liabilities are $50, so interest expense is $50 times 8 percent interest times one year, resulting in an interest expense of $4.

Earnings before taxes (EBT) amounts to EBIT minus interest expense. Recalling that the presumed income tax rate is 50 percent, we recognize that taxes are 50 percent of EBT. When EBT is negative, we assume that the organization can ask for a refund from the federal government via a tax carryback, so the income taxes are actually negative amounts. Earnings available to common equity (i.e., shareholders) are then EBT minus the income taxes (we assume no preferred stock).

Return on equity (ROE) indicates how well the business enterprise satisfies the investors. It shows how much return an investor acquired from his or her investment during the year. We compute this metric by dividing the earnings available to common equity by the amount of common equity in the company. Common equity is composed of the common stock, additional paid-in capital, and retained earnings of the entity. In each of our cases, the common equity is the residual interest in the firm computed as the total assets or total equities ($100) minus the amount of debt in the financial structure. As an example, consider the case when financial leverage is 75 percent and the rate of return on assets is 16 percent. From the chart, we can observe that in this case the income available to common equity is $5. Common equity is $100 minus total liabilities of $75, for an amount of $25. Return on equity equals $5 divided by $25 for 20 percent.

Now that we understand the construction of Exhibit 2.3, let us turn to its implications. The first reflection is that the return on assets positively affects the return on equity. This commonsense deduction can be observed by going across the ROE rows in the exhibit. For whichever ROE row is chosen, the ROE increases as the rate of return on assets increases. The second conclusion is that financial leverage generally changes the return on equity, as can be detected by examining the columns in the exhibit. As more and more debt is added to the financial structure, the ROE varies in amount, except when the rate of return on assets equals the interest rate. The third point is just an extension of the second—this modification of the ROE can be either a good thing or a bad thing. It can increase or lower ROE.

Before stating the fourth and most important conclusion, let us look at the column when the rate of return on assets equals 8 percent. Notice that in each instance as we vary financial leverage, the ROE stays at 4 percent. Whenever the return on assets is the same as the cost of debt, there is no effect on ROE. Now examine the previous two columns in which the rate of return on assets is zero or 4 percent, amounts that are lower than the cost of debt. In each of these cases, the ROE deteriorates as financial leverage increases. Shareholders lose more value as the debt level increases. Now let us move to the last two columns in the exhibit and assess what takes place when the rate of return on assets is 12 or 16 percent, amounts that exceed the cost of debt. In each of these two instances, the ROE increases felicitously for the shareholders. As debt increases in the corporate financial structure, the shareholders gain value. Putting it all together, return on equity increases, stays constant, or decreases as the rate of return on assets is greater than, equal to, or less than the cost of debt.

I can sum up this discussion with a chart. Exhibit 2.4 displays the five scenarios in a graph in which the x-axis represents the different levels of financial leverage while the y-axis represents return on equity. The five different lines in the chart depict the effects of financial leverage on ROE for five specific returns on assets. When the return on assets equals the cost of debt, a straight line indicates that ROE stays constant. When the return on assets is greater than the cost of debt, the lines turn upward as financial leverage increases, thus showing the positive effects of magnifying ROE. When, however, the return on assets is lower than the cost of debt, the lines turn downward as financial leverage increases, which indicates the negative effects on ROE.

Exhibit 2.4   Relationship between Financial Leverage and Return on Equity

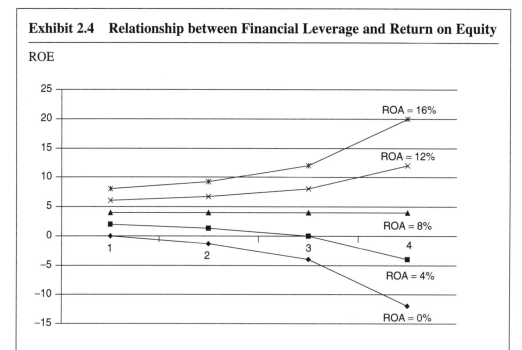

The four points along the x-axis track changes in the financial leverage. The four points represent 0 percent, 25 percent, 50 percent, and 75 percent financial leverage.

The y-axis shows the return on equity (ROE).

The five different lines in the chart depict the effects of financial leverage on return on equity (ROE) for a specific return on assets (ROA).

Corporate managers can try to add value to their shareholders by adding in enough debt to obtain positive magnification of the returns.[3] The trick is not to add in so much debt to run the risk of a negative magnification of those returns. Investors would like managers to find the right amount of debt to add the most value to them, and investors evaluate managers in part on that basis. This analysis, however, assumes that managers tell shareholders the whole truth in the financial statements.

STOCK PRICES AND FINANCIAL LEVERAGE

The theory of finance hypothesizes a relationship between stock returns and stock risk-iness.[4] The simplest such model speculates a linear relationship, as shown in Exhibit 2.5. Panel A of this display graphs the *capital market line*. The capital market line asserts that the expected return on a portfolio E (R_p) is a straight-line function of the portfolio's risk as measured by its standard deviation σ (R_p). The y-intercept of this line is the risk-free rate (R_f), for example, the return on U.S. treasury bonds, while the slope measures the price per unit of risk. This theory asserts that all assets lie on the straight line, so the price of any asset can be found once its risk is known. For example, given the market risk as σ (R_m), the expected market return is E (R_m).

Actually calculating the risk is sometimes difficult, so the process can be standardized by focusing instead on the asset's beta. Panel B of Exhibit 2.5 depicts the *security market line*, which is a graph of the capital asset pricing model, which posits a relationship between the asset's expected return and its risk as measured by beta. This model standardizes the measurement of risk by comparing the asset's standard deviation to the market's risk. The resulting risk metric is termed *beta*. The security market line asserts that the expected return on a portfolio E (R_p) is a straight-line function of the portfolio's risk as measured by its beta β_p. The y-intercept of this line is the risk-free rate (R_f), and the slope measures the price per unit of beta. As with the capital market line, this model also claims that all assets lie on the straight line, so the price of any asset can be found once its risk is known. The market has a beta equal to one, yielding the expected market return of E (R_m).

The key thing for purposes of this book is that financial leverage affects the risk of the business enterprise. Adding debt to the financial structure of a firm increases the standard deviation of the stock returns and increases the company's beta. In terms of the graphs in Exhibit 2.5, adding debt to the financial structure moves the firm up the line. For example, if a company is at point P on the capital market line in Panel A or point P on the security market line, then adding debt moves the company to (say) point Q. More debt in the financial structure therefore increases the corporation's financial risk.

Expected stock returns are a function of the corporate risk, where corporate risk includes not only the operating aspects of the firm but also the financial risk. Investors and creditors will price securities with higher amounts of financial risk so that the investors and creditors can expect higher returns. This process of pricing securities requires information about the capital asset, especially to allow the market to determine the asset's risk. If managers understate the liabilities of the firm, then the investment community might not correctly price the firm's securities. While overpricing securities

Exhibit 2.5 Capital Market Line and Security Market Line

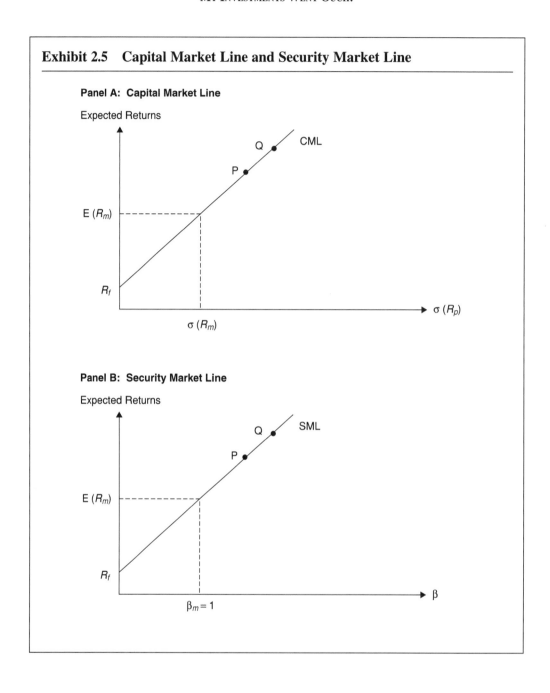

in the short run might be good for managers, sooner or later investors and creditors learn the truth and the prices plummet.

Before leaving this topic, I should also introduce the concept of *cost of capital*. The *pretax cost of debt* is the interest charges, often expressed in terms of the interest rate. The *after-tax cost of debt* is the interest rate minus the percentage of cash recouped by deducting interest expense on the income tax statement. The *cost of equity* may be thought of as the required rate of return that investors demand because of the stock's risk, as defined by either the capital market line or the security market line.[5] The firm's *weighted average cost of capital* combines these two elements in proportion to their weights in the financial structure. Thus, the weighted average cost of capital equals the after-tax cost of debt times the financial leverage plus the cost of equity times the ratio of common equities divided by the total equities.

This weighted average cost of capital is important to managers because it represents what the corporation has to pay whenever it taps the investment community for more funds. Initially, as debt is added to the financial structure, the weighted average cost of capital declines because the cost of debt is usually lower than the cost of equity. After a while, however, more debt becomes a concern to the marketplace and the cost of debt rises. As the cost of debt rises, the weighted average cost of capital rises as well. I shall make use of this notion of cost of capital later as I discuss the impact of management deceptions on the firm's cost of capital. In particular, truthfulness lowers the corporate cost of capital while management lies increase this cost of capital.

BANKRUPTCY PREDICTION MODELS

Investors and creditors and their analysts employ accounting numbers in a variety of ways, and one of the enduring practices is the prediction of corporate failure. Bankruptcy is an important event to predict because of the dire consequences when it occurs. Investors and creditors stand a chance to lose some or all of their investment as well as forfeit chances for profits if a business enterprise collapses.

A number of statistical models have been around for decades, and one of the most popular prediction schemes is the Altman model.[6] Edward Altman paired 33 failed and 33 nonfailed firms in an attempt to control for industry and size differences. He then employed a method called discriminant analysis to a list of 22 financial ratios. This method builds the best linear model possible so that it can explain the firms as failed or not failed with as little error as possible. The dependent variable in this model denotes the bankruptcy status, in which a value of 1 denotes a company that has not failed, while a value of 0 denotes that the entity has failed.

Altman started with a list of 22 financial ratios for the independent variables. From this list he chose five that embrace the best possible model:

1. Working capital/total assets
2. Retained earnings/total assets
3. Earnings before interest and taxes/total assets
4. Market value of equity/book value of total debt
5. Sales/total assets

The coefficients for the model are shown in Exhibit 2.6. These coefficients of the function were developed using the data from the first year prior to bankruptcy. The same function was then used to predict corporate failure (regardless of the time frame). Testing the model on the original data and on a fresh set of data, Altman found that the

---

Exhibit 2.6   Altman's Bankruptcy Prediction Model

Altman (1968 and 1971) applied a statistical method termed *discriminant analysis* to a set of bankrupt firms that were paired to similar nonbankrupt firms. The dependent variable Z denotes the firm's bankruptcy status. A value of $Z = 1$ indicated healthy firms, but a value of $Z = 0$ denoted unhealthy companies.

Altman examined several possible independent variables and derived the following model as his best prediction model.

$$Z = 1.2\,X_1 + 1.4\,X_2 + 3.3\,X_3 + 0.66\,X_4 + 1.0\,X_5$$

where: X_1 = working capital / total assets

X_2 = retained earnings / total assets

X_3 = earnings before interest and taxes / total assets

X_4 = market value of equity / book value of total debt

X_5 = sales / total assets

To use the model, determine the values of the five independent variables and substitute them into the model and determine the resulting Z-score. Then evaluate this Z-score as follows.

- If $Z > 2.99$ predict healthy.
- If $Z < 1.81$ predict failing.
- Otherwise, it is too close to call.

---

multiple discriminant analysis model seemed to be a reliable model up to two years prior to bankruptcy.

The model can be used by entering the data into the model given in Exhibit 2.6. Compute what is termed the Z-score by using the equation in the exhibit. Then interpret the Z-score, depending on the resulting value. When the Z-score exceeds 2.99, predict that the business enterprise will not fail. If the Z-score is less than 1.81, then predict bankruptcy. If the value of the Z-score is between 1.81 and 2.99, then the model is unable to categorize the firm as one that is likely to fail or not fail.

The key point to notice in yet another application is the importance of financial risk. One of the most important variables in the Altman model is market value of equity divided by book value of total debts. This measure is merely a variation of the more common debt-to-equity measure of financial risk. The coefficient of this variable is 0.66, which of course is positive. This means that as there is more equity in the financial structure, the less likely the business enterprise will collapse. Alternatively, as debt is added to the financial structure, the lower this variable will be, which in turn lowers the Z-score and indicates that there is greater risk of corporate failure.

BOND RATINGS PREDICTION MODELS

Another example of a model that investors and creditors employ in practice is a model to predict bond ratings. Obviously, such models help to explain how ratings agencies arrive at the particular assessments for particular corporate bonds. Since better bond ratings typically mean lower bond interest rates, these models help to explain bond premiums. They also are important for investors and creditors to assess the quality of new bond issuances and the quality of privately placed bonds that ratings agencies do not review. Finally, these models prove helpful in evaluating those bonds that the rating agencies have not reassessed recently, such as Enron's bonds in 2001.

James Horrigan was the first to investigate this issue.[7] He took a variety of firms whose bonds were relatively stable during a certain period of time and applied multiple linear regression. This method builds the best linear model it can so that it can explain the firm's bond ratings with as little error as possible. In this context the dependent variable Z represented the bond ratings at that time. Horrigan explored a number of possible variables for the independent variables. Unique to his study, Horrigan divided each variable by the industry average for that variable; this is one way by which the research can minimize the impact of industry on the financial ratios and make the model more generalizable. Horrigan's best model exploited these variables:

- Subordination status (whether the particular bond was subordinated to another debt issue)
- Total assets
- Common equities/total debts[8]
- Working capital/sales
- Operating profit/sales
- Sales/stockholders' equity

The coefficients for this model are tabulated in Exhibit 2.7. To apply the model, gather the values of the independent variables, multiply them by the coefficients as indicated in the exhibit, and sum up the products. The resulting number is called the Z-score. Then interpret the Z-score according to the table in the exhibit. For example, if a Z-score of 1.8 is obtained, since it lies between 1.602 and 2.094, we would predict that the corporate bond would have a rating of A.

The key point for us is similar to what I said for the Altman model, and that is to recognize another instance in which financial structure is crucial to investors and creditors. One of the most important variables in the Horrigan model is common equities divided by total debts, which is just the reciprocal of the more popular debt-to-equity ratio, so they are both measures of financial risk. The fact that the coefficient of this variable is 0.272, a positive number, implies that as there is more equity in the financial structure, the higher the bond rating will be. Conversely, as debt is added to the financial structure, the lower this independent variable will be, thereby decreasing the Z-score, which indicates that the bond rating will be lower.

Exhibit 2.7   Horrigan's Model to Predict Bond Ratings

In 1996 Horrigan ran multiple linear regressions on a sample of firms whose bond ratings were stable within a certain time period. In this case the dependent variable Z stands for bond rating, while the independent variables (the Xs) correspond to various financial dimensions considered important to the bond rating process. Horrigan obtained the following as his best model.

$$Z = 1.197 \, X_0 + .034 \, X_1 + .272 \, X_2 - .501 \, X_3 + 4.519 \, X_4 - .203 \, X_5$$

where X_0 = subordination status (1 if the bond is unsubordinated;
0 if the bond is subordinated)

X_1 = total assets

X_2 = common equities / total debt

X_3 = working capital / sales

X_4 = operating profit / sales

X_5 = sales / stockholders' equity

The financial ratios are divided by the industry averages to minimize the impact of industry on the financial ratios.

To apply the model, determine the values of the six independent variables, substitute them into the model, and determine the resulting Z-score. The Z-score predicts the bond rating as follows.

$2.855 < Z$	AAA
$2.094 < Z < 2.855$	AA
$1.602 < Z < 2.094$	A
$0.838 < Z < 1.602$	BBB
$0.360 < Z < 0.838$	BB
$Z < 0.360$	B or lower

COST OF LYING

Managers have some incentives to lie in the balance sheets issued to the investment community. They know that investors and creditors are evaluating them in part on how much debt is in the financial structure of the enterprise. The ability to raise capital depends on whether investors and creditors perceive the debt level to be too high. Even if they would choose to provide capital, investors and creditors impose a cost of capital that is partly a function of the firm's financial structure. Thus, to obtain capital at a lower cost, managers might choose to distort the accounting numbers in their balance sheets.

This story seems rather shortsighted, however, because it assumes that investors and creditors are fools who have no idea what is really going on. When they learn about the deceptions, investors and creditors will raise the cost of capital by adding what I term a *financial reporting risk premium* to this cost.[9] Consider the next scenario.

When banks approve loans and charge interest on their loans, they establish interest rates that depend on at least three factors: (1) the real interest rate, (2) the expected inflation rate, and (3) the risk that the loan applicant will not repay the loan in part or in whole. The real interest rate is the interest rate that would exist in a world without inflation and for a party who has no credit risk. Inflation, of course, implies that future dollars are weaker than current dollars because the currency cannot fetch as much as it once could. Bankers realize that inflation could potentially hurt them because the dollars repaid by borrowers have less value. Because the lenders comprehend the problem, they protect themselves by increasing interest rates to offset the problem of inflation. In addition, banks worry about the credit risk of the loan applicant. Will the party pay off the loan in full and on time? Banks shelter themselves from this credit risk by adding a premium to the interest rate, an amount that depends on the perceived credit risk of the borrower.

Just as creditors adjust the cost of debt—the interest rates—to compensate them for expected inflation and for credit risk, investors do the same. The cost of equity also depends on expected inflation and on financial leverage. Present and potential shareholders want to be remunerated for the risks that they bear.

In the same way that investors and creditors add risk premiums to their required costs to obtain payment for risk taking, they also require recompense for the additional risks they incur because managers might lie in the financial reports. This financial reporting risk premium covers the potential investment losses due to accounting chicanery. During periods when accounting frauds and misstatements are high, as documented in Exhibits 1.1 and 1.2, investors and creditors get scared about other possible cons and ruses and defend their investments by charging higher premiums for this financial reporting risk. Increases in these premiums increase the cost of capital and reduce stock prices and bond prices. When investors perceive a decline in accounting fraud, they will reduce these premiums, thus increasing stock and bond values.

Paul Miller and Paul Bahnson address this same issue, but label it *quality financial reporting*.[10] They advocate a culture change in which managers, directors, and auditors perceive the value of financial reporting and treat investors and creditors as customers of the business enterprise. By treating these customers better with more and more information, the customers would respond by rewarding the firm with higher stock and bond valuations. The clarion for managers to hear is that investors and creditors desire more and better information in financial reports, schedules, footnotes, and management's discussion and analysis. Heeding the clear and piercing call leads to greater wealth for everyone; damping that sound, however, carries a cost to the firm and its managers. I hope there are managers who have ears to hear this music.

SUMMARY AND CONCLUSION

Debt matters. As managers begin to add debt to the financial structure, felicitous benefits take place since the liabilities magnify the returns to shareholders. This result occurs whenever the assets are generating returns that exceed the cost of debt. This good fortune has its limits, however, and after that, as managers add more debt, the liabilities begin to magnify the decline in returns. Because of this double-edged sword, investors and creditors scrutinize the financial leverage of any institution.

Such a close inspection by the investment community might tempt some managers to lie about their liabilities. These managers could apply the equity method or operating leases or pension accounting in such a way as to hide the liabilities. The managers might also create special-purpose entities in which they could park the debt. Either way, the managers and their professional advisers are lying to the public. In some cases, as with WorldCom and Adelphia, the managers are downright fraudulent. But even in the more common case in which managers follow generally accepted accounting principles, the managers are still deceiving the investment community, and so they should reject use of these flawed rules.

Lying about debt matters. Whenever investors and creditors are afraid they will be stiffed, they just increase the financial reporting risk premium. The cost of capital goes up and stock prices and bond prices go down. Managers can add value to their firms by telling the truth.

NOTES

1. Some good discussions on financial ratios can be found in: R. A. Brealey and S. C. Myers, *Principles of Corporate Finance,* 7th ed. (New York: McGraw-Hill Irwin, 2002; E. F. Brigham and J. F. Houston, *Fundamentals of Financial Management,* 8th ed. (New York: Dryden, 1998); R. C. Higgins, *Analysis for Financial Management* (New York: Irwin, 2000); J. E. Ketz, R. Doogar, and D. E. Jensen, *Cross-Industry Analysis of Financial Ratios: Comparabilities and Corporate Performance* (New York: Quorum Books, 1990); F. K. Reilly and K. C. Brown, *Investment Analysis and Portfolio Management,* 6th ed. (New York: Dryden, 2000); L. Revsine, D. W. Collins, and W. B. Johnson, *Financial Reporting and Analysis,* 2nd ed. (Upper Saddle River, NJ: Prentice-Hall, 2002); and G. I. White, A. C. Sondhi, and D. Fried, *The Analysis and Use of Financial Statements*, 2nd ed. (New York: John Wiley & Sons, 1998) and 3rd ed. (New York: John Wiley & Sons, 2003).

2. A variety of issues present themselves when constructing financial ratios. Questions arise, for example, whether deferred income taxes are really debt and, even if they are, whether they are incorrectly measured because they are not discounted. I ignore those concerns, for I am more interested in whether managers report truthfully than in the utility of what they present. Texts such as those mentioned in note 1 address the latter issue.

3. For more information about the corporate financial structure, see Brigham and Houston, *Fundamentals of Financial Management,* and Reilly and Brown, *Investment Analysis and Portfolio Management.*

4. I simplify things by assuming that the capital asset pricing model is the correct model. For further discussion, see Brealey and Myers, *Principles of Corporate Finance*; Brigham and Houston, *Fundamentals of Financial Management*; and Reilly and Brown, *Investment Analysis and Portfolio Management.*

5. Here, too, I simplify things by not considering the so-called cost of retained earnings, nor by including flotation costs in the cost of obtaining funds from new equity.

6. See the Altman model, described in E. I. Altman: "Financial Ratios, Discriminant Analysis and the Prediction of Corporate Bankruptcy," *Journal of Finance* (September 1968:

589–609; *Corporate Bankruptcy in America* (New York: Heath, 1971); and *Corporate Financial Distress and Bankruptcy: A Complete Guide to Predicting and Avoiding Distress and Profiting from Bankruptcy* (New York: John Wiley & Sons, 1993). In the last three decades researchers have made many improvements to the original Altman model. Unfortunately, some of them are quite sophisticated statistically, and so here I rely on the original Altman model, which suffices for our purposes. Details about this line of research can be found in Altman, *Corporate Financial Distress and Bankruptcy* and in White, Sondhi, and Fried, *Analysis and Use of Financial Statements,* 3rd ed.

7. J. O. Horrigan, "The Determination of Long-term Credit Standing with Financial Ratios," *Journal of Accounting Research* (1966 supplement): 44–62.

8. Horrigan actually calls this ratio net worth divided by total debt, but his notion of net worth is what I have termed common equities (common stock plus additional paid-in capital plus retained earnings).

9. For greater discussion about adjusting the cost of capital for risk, see S. P. Pratt, *Cost of Capital: Estimation and Applications*, 2nd ed. (Hoboken, NJ: John Wiley & Sons, 2002), especially Chapters 5 and 8.

10. Miller and Bahnson document a variety of academic studies that support the notion that capital markets reward those corporations that show increases in the quantity and quality of disclosure with higher stock prices; see P. B. W. Miller and P. R. Bahnson, *Quality Financial Reporting* (New York: McGraw-Hill, 2002). Not a single academic study exists that arrives at the opposite conclusion.

Part II

Hiding Financial Risk

CHAPTER THREE

How to Hide Debt
with the Equity Method

A variety of accounting methods and techniques exist by which corporate managers can give the illusion that the business entity possesses less debt than it actually has. Chapters 3 through 5 explore three of these schemes: the equity method in this chapter, lease accounting in Chapter 4, and pension accounting in Chapter 5. Chapter 6 explores utilization of special-purpose entities (SPEs) to conceal a firm's true obligations using asset securitizations, borrowing with SPEs, and synthetic leases.

The good news of the first set of accounting techniques (equity method, lease accounting, and pension accounting) for sweeping liabilities under the corporate carpet is that readers of financial statements sometimes can adjust the accounting numbers by incorporating the footnote disclosures into their analysis. Whether readers actually can do this depends on the quality of the disclosures by the organization's chief executive officer (CEO) and chief financial officer (CFO). If these managers care at all about the needs of investors and creditors, they will make sure that such disclosures are forthcoming, that these disclosures quantify what is going on accurately, and that the disclosures are complete.

The process of taking the reported numbers and adjusting them for what is really taking place is called *making analytical adjustments*. The financial statement user would then proceed to analyze the business enterprise in terms of these adjusted numbers rather than the reported numbers that appear in the financial statements. For example, by computing financial ratios with the adjusted numbers, investors obtain a better picture of the corporate health than if they calculated these ratios with the reported numbers.

In the equity method, lease accounting, and pension accounting, when firms give sufficient detail in their footnotes, readers can make analytical adjustments and integrate the hidden debt with the reported liabilities. Combining these items aids investors and creditors in better understanding the company's financial risk.

The bad news of the second set of accounting methods (hiding debt with asset securitizations, SPE borrowings, and synthetic leases) is that no such disclosures currently exist. Too many of the footnotes employ double speak and gobbledy-gook so that no one has the foggiest idea of what is being conveyed. Even when managers are aboveboard and attempt to provide transparent and truthful disclosures, the footnotes involving SPEs rarely provide enough detail to make analytical adjustments. With the accounting problems at Enron, WorldCom, and similar corporations, the investment community did not have much of a chance because of the virtual impossibility to disentangle the web of footnotes and make any sense of what the firms were doing. Readers might perceive that there is a problem but be unable to rectify the numbers and understand the economic reality. I discuss this matter later in the book.

In this chapter I explore the equity method and discuss how managers can employ this accounting ploy to reduce reported debt. The first section of the chapter summarizes accounting for investments, and the second section compares and contrasts the equity method with the trading-security and available-for-sale methods. The third section indicates the superiority of the equity method over the cost method when the investor can influence significantly the operations of the investee, using Boston Chicken as an exemplar of what not to do. The fourth section explains and illustrates the equity method and consolidation in greater detail. The last section of the chapter discusses the examples of Elan and Coca-Cola and demonstrates how the equity method helped managers at these companies appear to have fewer liabilities than their respective firms actually did. It also gives one pause to consider why WorldCom recently deconsolidated its investment in Embratel. I adjust the statements of Coca-Cola and examine its debt-to-equity ratios, noting that these ratios deteriorate with the inclusion of the hidden debts.

BRIEF OVERVIEW OF ACCOUNTING FOR INVESTMENTS

Let me place the topic into context by giving an overview of accounting for investments. Among other things, this synopsis will help readers understand the panoply of techniques available to managers when accounting for investments.[1]

When an entity buys some investment, it purchases either debt securities or equity securities. Debt securities imply a creditor-debtor relationship, while equity securities represent some type of ownership interest.

Accounting rules require an investor in debt securities to classify them into one of three categories: (1) trading securities, (2) held-to-maturity securities, and (3) available-for-sale securities. Trading securities are those securities that managers plan to hold only a short while and sell in the short run in an attempt to gain trading profits. Held-to-maturity securities are those securities that managers plan to hold until the debt matures. Available-for-sale securities are anything else.

Investors account for trading securities by recording them at fair value in the balance sheet and recognizing changes in fair value in the income statement as gains and losses. Available-for-sale securities are recorded at fair value in the balance sheet and are reported as gains and losses on the income statement only when the investor sells them. Investors put held-to maturity securities on the balance sheet at amortized cost[2] and do not recognize any changes in fair value on the income statement. Of course, interest revenue would appear on the income statement under all three approaches.

Accounting for investments in equity securities proceeds in this way. If the investor does not have significant influence over the investee (often interpreted as having less than 20 percent of the total capital stock of the company), then it classifies the investment as either trading securities or available-for-sale securities. The criteria for classi-fication and the accounting for these two categories are essentially the same for equity securities as they were for debt securities. The only difference is that the investor would report dividend income instead of interest revenue.

If the firm has significant influence over the activities of the investee but owns no more than 50 percent of the capital stock, then it would apply the equity method. If it holds more than 50 percent of the common stock of the company, then the investing cor-poration would apply the consolidation method. Under the equity method, the invest-ment account is adjusted for the investor's proportionate share of the investee's income. Under consolidation, the investor eliminates the investments account and replaces it with the assets and the liabilities of the investee. A subtle but important relationship exists between the equity method and consolidation, namely that the investor company will have exactly the same net income whether it employs the equity method or whether it consolidates the statements.

There are two key points to be gleaned from this overview. The first concerns when it is appropriate for an investor to utilize the equity method or to account for the invest-ments as either trading securities or available-for-sale securities—it depends on whether the investor has significant control over the investee. We need to understand why it makes a difference and of what sin Boston Chicken was guilty. The second key point concerns when it is appropriate for an investor to account for an investment with the equity method versus when it should consolidate the investment. Here too we need to understand the difference and investigate Coke's motivation for not consolidating its bottling operations. It also might help us understand why Elan did not consolidate its joint ventures and why WorldCom recently deconsolidated one of its Mexican subsidiaries. Before I discuss these issues, I examine the equity method in greater detail.

EQUITY METHOD VERSUS TRADING-SECURITY AND AVAILABLE-FOR-SALE METHODS

Consider the following hypothetical example. On January 2, Buzzards, Inc., buys 1,000 shares of High Flying stock at $32 per share. This purchase represents a 20 percent interest in High Flying, Ltd. During the year, High Flying earns net income of $23,000 and declares and pays dividends of $1.50 per share. At year end the capital stock of High Flying circulates at $40 per share. How do we do the accounting?

Trading and Available-for-Sale Securities

If Buzzards, Inc., determines that it does not have significant influence over the operat-ing activities at High Flying, then it needs to classify the stock investment either as trading securities or as available for sale. Let us begin by looking at what happens if management at Buzzards, Inc., adopts the former approach. On the balance sheet, the firm should value the stock investment at fair value, which is 1,000 shares at $40 per share, for a total of $40,000. The income statement shows two types of earnings. Buzzards receives dividends from High Flying of 1,000 shares at $1.50 per share, or

$1,500. In addition, Buzzards displays its unrealized holding gain, which is the difference in the fair value of the investment at the end of the year as compared with its fair value at the beginning of the year. In this case, Buzzards has an unrealized holding gain of 1,000 shares times the difference between $40 and $32, or $8,000.

If Buzzards, Inc., considers the investment available for sale, then it also records its value on the balance sheet at the fair value of $40,000. Unlike the previous example, however, the company would show only the dividends income of $1,500. The business enterprise would not show the unrealized holding gain in the income statement.[3]

Whereas the trading-security approach each year breaks out trading gains (or losses) that take place during the year, the available-for-sale tactic does not record any gain or loss until the securities are sold. For example, if Buzzards, Inc., sells the High Flying securities in the second year for $44 per share, the first approach records the gain on the sale as the number of shares times the difference between the price per share and the fair value at which it is recorded. Here that amount is 1,000 shares times $44 minus $40, or 1,000 times $4 for a gain of $4,000 in the second year. The second approach records the gain on the sale as the number of shares sold times the difference between the price per share and the book value per share when the securities were first acquired. In this example, the amount is 1,000 shares times $44 minus $32, or 1,000 times $12 for a gain of $12,000 per share. The contrast is seen as:

	Trading Security	Available for Sale
First year	$ 8,000	$ 0
Second year	4,000	12,000
Total profit	$12,000	$12,000

The two methods give the same income over the time period that the investor owns the stock, but they differ in the year-to-year recognition of gains and losses.

In practice, firms record equity investments far more often as available-for-sale securities than as trading securities because they do not have much say about when to record the gains and losses when the investments are trading securities. Instead, company managers can arrange when to recognize the gains or losses on available-for-sale securities by selling them when they want. If the income statement could use a boost, managers might sell some of these available-for-sale securities to provide that lift. If the income statement looks good, managers might delay any recognition until that rainy day appears, and they achieve this delay by not selling any of the securities. Managers yearn for this type of flexibility so they can "manage" their earnings, but this type of management does not help the investment community.

Equity Method

The equity method differs from both of these methods because it does not adjust the investments account for fair value changes; instead, the equity method adjusts the investments account for the investor's proportional share in the investee's earnings, which also serves as the investment income. The equity method reduces the investments account for any dividends it receives. Let us use the Buzzards, Inc., investment in High Flying, Ltd., to illustrate this technique.

Under the equity method, Buzzards initially records the investment at 1,000 shares times $32, the price paid per share; the amount is $32,000, the same as with the previous two accounting methods. During the year, High Flying has income of $23,000 and issues dividends of $1.50 per share.

Buzzards recognizes investment income of 20 percent of $23,000, or $4,600. Its share of the dividends is 1,000 shares time $1.50 per share, or $1,500. The investments account is increased for the investment income and decreased for the dividends. At year end, the investment has a balance of $32,000 plus $4,600 minus $1,500, or $35,100.

There are other aspects of the equity method, but before examining them, let us stop to ask when a firm would not want to employ this method.

BOSTON CHICKEN

Boston Chicken[4] created what it called financed area developers (FADs), which, from an accounting point of view, were just investments of Boston Chicken. In some cases, the corporation had a small equity interest in the FADs, and in other cases it did not. In all cases, the corporation had a right to convert the debt into an equity interest, usually giving Boston Chicken over 50 percent ownership in the FADs.

How should Boston Chicken have accounted for its investments in these FADs? When this question arises, it usually helps to ask what motivates the managers in their choices. The FADs had operating losses during the early years of their existence. If Boston Chicken had accounted for its investments with the equity method, then it would be reporting investment losses. By using a different method, Boston Chicken did not have to report any investment losses.[5] Thus, managers at Boston Chicken had incentives not to employ the equity method until the operating losses disappeared. Once the FADs started earning money, Boston Chicken could exercise the options and start adding the FADs' share of these profits into investment income.

Not surprisingly, managers did just that. They argued that Boston Chicken had less than 20 percent ownership in these FADs, so it did not have to apply the equity method. This argument errs because Accounting Principles Board (APB) Opinion No. 18 says that the threshold is whether the investor has significant control over the investee. The board issued the 20 percent demarcation only as a rule of thumb to help accountants determine which accounting method to employ.

In this case, clearly the managers of Boston Chicken had control over the operations of the FADs and assisted Boston Chicken in expanding its relationships with its franchisees. More important, Boston Chicken held options to convert the FADs' debt or small equity positions into large and often majority ownership positions. The options are clearly the key to understanding what is going on. The Securities and Exchange Commission (SEC) later acted against these managers, principally because of the existence of these options.

DETAILS ABOUT THE EQUITY METHOD AND CONSOLIDATION

To learn more about the equity method and to introduce the consolidation method, let us take a close look at an academic illustration. Later I present some real-world cases. Suppose that Publius Corporation acquires 80 percent of the capital stock of Serpentino Inc. on January 1 for $100,000. Before the purchase, the two companies have the balance sheets depicted in Exhibit 3.1. To effect the transaction, Publius borrows $52,000 with a note payable. Publius gives this amount plus $48,000 cash to obtain the 80 percent interest in Serpentino. Under any of the accounting methods, the investment is initially recorded on the books of Publius for $100,000.

Exhibit 3.2 portrays the new balance sheet of Publius, reports the old balance sheet of Serpentino, and displays the consolidated balance sheet. Serpentino's balance sheet, of course, stays the same. The assets in Publius's balance sheet differ because of the $100,000 investment and the net decrease in cash of $48,000. The liabilities in its balance sheet show an increase in notes payable of $52,000. Shareholders' equity stays the same. (Whenever a company buys more than 50 percent equity of another firm, the acquirer is termed the *parent* and the investee the *subsidiary*.)

Exhibit 3.1   Balance Sheets of Investor and Investee Prior to Acquisition (in Dollars)

	Publius Corporation	Serpentino Inc.
Cash	50,000	2,000
Accounts Receivable	16,000	5,000
Inventory	40,000	10,000
Land	100,000	40,000
Buildings	200,000	50,000
Accumulated Depreciation	(50,000)	(7,000)
Total Assets	356,000	100,000
Accounts Payable	10,000	5,000
Wages Payable	10,000	5,000
Mortgage Payable	100,000	30,000
Minority Interest		
Common Stock	50,000	5,000
Additional Paid-in Capital	86,000	20,000
Retained Earnings	100,000	35,000
Liabilities and Stockholders' Equity	356,000	100,000

Note: Parentheses denote negative numbers.

Exhibit 3.2 Balance Sheets Immediately after Purchase (in Dollars)

	Publius Corporation	Serpentino Inc.	Consolidated
Cash	2,000	2,000	4,000
Accounts Receivable	16,000	5,000	21,000
Inventory	40,000	10,000	50,000
Land	100,000	40,000	140,000
Buildings	200,000	50,000	274,000
Accumulated Depreciation	(50,000)	(7,000)	(57,000)
Investment in Serpentino	100,000		
Goodwill			28,000
Total Assets	408,000	100,000	460,000
Accounts Payable	10,000	5,000	15,000
Wages Payable	10,000	5,000	15,000
Notes Payable	52,000		52,000
Mortgage Payable	100,000	30,000	130,000
Minority Interest			12,000
Common Stock	50,000	5,000	50,000
Additional Paid-in Capital	86,000	20,000	86,000
Retained Earnings	100,000	35,000	100,000
Liabilities and Stockholders' Equity	408,000	100,000	460,000

Note: Parentheses denote negative numbers.

Differences between Equity Method and Consolidation at Date of Acquisition

Think about what Publius receives in exchange for its $100,000 cash. The reported net assets (assets minus liabilities, which equals stockholders' equity) of the investee or subsidiary are $60,000. Assets of Serpentino equal $100,000, liabilities equal $40,000 (accounts payable of $5,000 plus wages payable of $5,000 plus mortgage payable of $30,000), and so shareholders' equity equals $60,000. The latter number is obtained either by subtracting liabilities from assets ($100,000 minus $40,000 equals $60,000) or by adding the components of shareholders' equity (common stock of $5,000 plus additional paid-in capital of $20,000 plus retained earnings of $35,000).

Now assume that all assets and liabilities of Serpentino have fair values equal to book values, except for buildings, which have a fair value of $73,000 but a book value of $43,000 (*book value* equals the cost of the asset less its accumulated depreciation, which equals $50,000 minus $7,000). This assumption implies that Publius is acquiring

80 percent of net assets with a fair value of $90,000 (reported book value of $100,000 plus the fair value increment of the buildings of $30,000 minus the fair value of the liabilities, $40,000). Publius is therefore buying net assets worth $72,000.

Accountants term the difference between what is paid for the investment and the fair value of the net assets acquired *goodwill*. In this case, goodwill equals $100,000 minus $72,000, or $28,000.

Minority interest reflects the equity interests in Serpentino by the other shareholders in the corporation, the minority shareholders. Given that Publius owns 80 percent of Serpentino, the minority shareholders have claim to 20 percent of the net assets of the entity. In this case, minority interest is 20 percent of $60,000, or $12,000.[6]

If Publius Corporation prepares a consolidated balance sheet at the date of acquisition, it removes the investments in Serpentino and the shareholders' equity of Serpentino. It adds the goodwill of $28,000 and the minority interest of $12,000. Then the company combines all of the other accounts. Consolidated cash is the parent's cash ($2,000) plus the subsidiary's cash ($2,000) for $4,000, and so forth.

The key point shows up when we compare some financial ratios computed on numbers of Publius's balance sheet versus what values these ratios take on when they are based on the consolidated balance sheet. In particular, differences appear for the financial leverage ratios. The results are:

Financial Ratio	Equity Method	Consolidated #1	Consolidated #2
Debt/total assets	.42	.46	.49
Debt/equity	.73	.85	.95
Long-term debt/equity	.42	.52	.55

There are two columns for the consolidated method, depending on one's viewpoint about the nature of minority interest. Some people perceive that minority interest is part of equity, and that is how it is treated in the first consolidated column. Others, however, claim that, from the parent's point of view, minority interest is like debt and should be analyzed as if it were debt. That is how the ratios were computed in the second consolidated column.

The thing to notice is that the equity method understates the financial leverage of the entity because it excludes the subsidiary's debts from the analysis. Whatever measure of financial leverage is considered, the equity method presents results that look better than the consolidated numbers. When minority interest is treated as a liability, this consequence becomes exacerbated. These results always occur because the equity method in essence nets the debts of the subsidiary with its assets in the parent's investment account.

Differences between Equity Method and Consolidation after Acquisition

To illustrate the income effects from applying these two methods, look at these two companies one year after acquisition. Income statements, statements of retained earnings, and balance sheets are presented in Exhibit 3.3. Before reviewing them, two things must be done. First, with respect to the subsidiary's buildings, the parent company has

Exhibit 3.3   Financial Statements One Year after Purchase (in Dollars)

	Publius Corporation	Serpentino Inc.	Consolidated
Income Statement			
Sales	100,000	40,000	140,000
Cost of Sales	(60,000)	(20,000)	(80,000)
Other Expenses	(20,000)	(10,000)	(35,400)
Investment Income	2,600		
Minority Interest Net Income			(2,000)
Net Income	22,600	10,000	22,600
Retained Earnings			
Beginning	100,000	35,000	100,000
Net Income	22,600	10,000	22,600
Dividends	(14,000)	(5,000)	(14,000)
Ending	108,600	40,000	108,600
Balance Sheet			
Cash	9,000	5,000	14,000
Accounts Receivable	20,000	6,000	26,000
Inventory	39,000	12,000	51,000
Land	100,000	40,000	140,000
Buildings	200,000	50,000	274,000
Accumulated Depreciation	(55,000)	(8,000)	(65,400)
Investment in Serpentino	98,600		
Goodwill			25,000
Total Assets	411,600	105,000	464,600
Accounts Payable	12,000	8,000	20,000
Wages Payable	8,000	3,000	11,000
Notes Payable	52,000		52,000
Mortgage Payable	95,000	29,000	124,000
Minority Interest			13,000
Common Stock	50,000	5,000	50,000
Additional Paid-in Capital	86,000	20,000	86,000
Retained Earnings	108,600	40,000	108,600
Liabilities and Stockholders' Equity	411,600	105,000	464,600

Note: Parentheses denote negative numbers.

to depreciate the full fair value of the building. The subsidiary already depreciates the book value of the building, so the parent only has to pick up the incremental amount. Assume the building has a 10-year life and no salvage value and Publius uses the straight-line formula. The fair value increment over the book value of the building is $30,000 by assumption; the parent's portion of this is 80 percent of $30,000, or $24,000. The depreciation of the excess therefore will be $2,400 per year, calculated as $24,000 minus the salvage value of $0, all divided by 10 years. Under the equity method, this extra depreciation is subtracted from the investment income; under consolidation, it is added to the depreciation expense.

In addition, we have to ask whether goodwill has at least its original fair value. If not, an impairment loss must be recognized.[7] Assume that goodwill has a fair value of $25,000 at the end of the year, which represents an impairment loss of $28,000 minus $25,000, which equals $3,000. The equity method subtracts this amount from investment income, while the consolidation method displays it as an impairment loss. We add both the extra depreciation and the impairment loss to "other expenses."

Investment income begins with 80 percent of Serpentino's income, which equals 80 percent of $10,000, or $8,000. From this quantity the accountant subtracts out the extra depreciation and the impairment loss, so investment income comes to $8,000 minus $2,400 minus $3,000, which equals $2,600. Note that this amount is shown in the income statement of Publius in Exhibit 3.3.

In a consolidated income statement, we also need to compute what is called *minority interest net income (MINI)*. The MINI is computed as the minority shareholders' interest in the subsidiary's income. In this example, MINI equals 20 percent of $10,000, or $2,000. The consolidated income eliminates the parent's investment income account and recognizes the extra depreciation, the impairment loss, and MINI. All other items are merely added together. Sales, for example, become $100,000 plus $40,000, or $140,000. Keep in mind that the account "Other expenses" not only combines those of the two firms but also includes the extra depreciation and the impairment loss.

An important corollary of this discussion is that consolidated net income always equals the parent's net income. The equity method is designed to make this result occur. Because of this effect, consolidated retained earnings will always match the parent's retained earnings.

The balance sheet proceeds pretty much as before, bearing in mind that buildings must be increased by the extra $24,000 and accumulated depreciation by the $2,400 and that goodwill now has a fair value of $25,000. Also note that minority interest is 20 percent of the subsidiary's equity of $65,000, or $13,000. The parent's investment account and the subsidiary's stockholders' equity accounts are eliminated. Finally, all remaining accounts are combined.

The first key point is that the consolidated net income always equals the parent's net income. Even so, return metrics such as return on assets or return on sales usually differ because assets and sales are not the same under these two formats. However, even though consolidated net income equals the parent's net income, having two formats can interfere with an analyst's or an investor's assessment of the growth rate in sales or operating expenses.

The second key point, as before, is that the equity method understates the financial leverage of the business enterprise. The equity method nets out the subsidiary's liabilities, so these liabilities are not part of the corporate debt. The consolidated method, however, correctly includes these liabilities in the balance sheet; so financial ratios computed on these numbers properly reveal the hidden financial risk. For our hypothetical illustration, the results are:

Financial Ratio	Equity Method	Consolidated #1	Consolidated #2
Debt/total assets	.40	.44	.47
Debt/equity	.68	.80	.90
Long-term debt/equity	.38	.48	.48

As before, two columns are shown for the consolidated method, depending on one's viewpoint about minority interest. Again, the equity method understates the financial leverage of the enterprise, because this method omits from the balance sheet the liabilities of the subsidiary. This is why the equity method belongs to that class of accounting tricks called off-balance sheet financing.

HIDING DEBT WITH THE EQUITY METHOD

Enough hypotheticals—let us turn our attention to some examples in practice. I shall examine the procedures applied by Elan, Coca-Cola, and WorldCom, with the greatest attention on Coca-Cola.

Elan

Managers at Elan[8] either did not learn the lessons from Boston Chicken or they learned the wrong lessons. Elan, the New York Stock Exchange (NYSE) pharmaceutical company from Ireland, invented a number of joint ventures and chose to account for them with the equity method. By itself that might be proper, for a number of these joint ventures are structured so that Elan has less than a majority stake in them. The problem, however, is that many of the contracts contain option clauses that allow Elan to obtain additional equity in the joint ventures so that it is conceivable, even likely, that Elan controls the operating, investing, and financing decisions of these joint ventures.

The SEC first started investigating Elan in 1999 because of these joint ventures with call options. Interestingly, the SEC returned to this issue in July 2002 because Elan continues to apply this rule in a ridiculous manner.

More specifically, footnote 4 of the 1998 financial statements stated that Elan had an equity venture with Axogen Limited and NeuroLab and that Elan had the option to purchase the rest of Axogen's shares and NeuroLab's shares. Apparently Elan's management team ignored the existence of the option when they performed their accounting tasks. Why? I could not find separate financial statements for Axogen or for NeuroLab, but my bet is that Elan loaded them up with debt and hoped to keep these items off the balance sheet, at least for a while.

The accounting profession did not have a rule on how to handle accounting for investments when call options are part of the contract, but does the profession really have to regulate every possible human action? Some common sense along with a duty to pursue fair reporting to the investment community and a commitment to "substance over form" would seem more than enough to tip the scales toward recognizing the economic truth in this case. Clearly, Elan ran the show for these joint ventures and controlled their every move. The company should consolidate these joint ventures.

Coca-Cola

Coca-Cola has referred to its product as the real thing, but what about its balance sheet? Is it the real thing? Critics often have complained about the firm's strategy to devise affiliates with just under 50 percent ownership but completely under the control of the parent company.[9] This strategy allows Coke to apply the equity method for its investments in affiliates instead of consolidating their results with the mother firm.

I shall attempt to unpack what is really going on by consolidating the results of Coca-Cola Enterprises, one of the main bottlers for the group. Unfortunately, I do not have enough data to consolidate the other bottlers and franchisees and various affiliates with the parent company. The financial statements for Coca-Cola Enterprises and some data about the intercompany transactions are available so that the results can be consolidated with some degree of reliability.

I do not have fair values of the assets and liabilities of Coca-Cola Enterprises. This is not critical, however, because I shall assume that the fair value differentials (fair value less book value) have been completely depreciated. This seems reasonable given that Coca-Cola has owned these bottlers for several decades. Goodwill, on the other hand, can be estimated as the difference between the carrying amount in the investments account and the book values of the net assets of Coca-Cola Enterprises. I invoke the assumption that goodwill is either unimpaired or that any impairment has been accounted for by the parent corporation.

With these assumptions, we proceed to consolidate Coca-Cola Enterprises with Coca-Cola. Exhibit 3.4 presents the results for these two corporations separately and then for the two combined as one entity for the years 2000 and 2001. Panel A gives the income statements for 2001, even as panel C displays the income statements for 2000. While the consolidated entity shows the same income as Coke by itself, notice that the line items differ remarkably. Operating revenues, cost of goods sold, gross profit, and operating expenses diverge from one another and perhaps could lead readers of the financial statements to interpret the results differently. Notice also that while Coke is bigger than Coca-Cola Enterprises, interest expense for the latter is much bigger than for the parent. This fact suggests that Coke is parking most of the liabilities with the subsidiary.

Panels B and D of Exhibit 3.4 contain the balance sheets for 2001 and 2000. As suggested by the income statements, the most striking feature of the balance sheets crops up in the liability section. In particular, notice that Coca-Cola Enterprises has long-term

Exhibit 3.4   Financial Statements of Coca-Cola (in Millions of $)

Panel A: Income Statement for the Year Ending December 31, 2001

	Coke (Parent)	Bottlers (Subsidiary)	Consolidated Entity
Net Operating Revenues	20,092	15,700	30,663
Cost of Goods Sold	(6,044)	(9,740)	(11,078)
Gross Profit	14,048	5,960	19,585
SG&A Expenses	(8,696)	(5,359)	(13,632)
Operating Income	5,352	601	5,953
Interest Income	325	0	325
Interest Expense	(289)	(753)	(1,042)
Investment Income	152	0	275
Other Income	130	2	132
Minority Interest Net Income	0	0	198
Income before Taxes	5,670	(150)	5,841
Income Taxes	(1,691)	131	1,560
Net Income before Accounting Change	3,979	(19)	4,281
Cumulative Effect of Accounting Change	(10)	(302)	(312)
Net Income	3,969	(321)	3,969

Panel B: Balance Sheet as of December 31, 2001

	Coca-Cola (Parent)	Bottlers (Subsidiary)	Consolidated Entity
Current Assets			
Cash and Marketable Securities	1,934	284	2,218
Trade Accounts Receivable	1,844	1,540	3,384
Amounts Due from Affiliate	38	0	0
Inventories	1,055	690	1,745
Prepaid Expenses and Other Assets	2,300	362	2,592
	7,171	2,876	9,939

Note: Parentheses denote negative numbers.

Exhibit 3.4 *(Continued)*

Panel B: *(Continued)*

	Coca-Cola (Parent)	Bottlers (Subsidiary)	Consolidated Entity
Investments			
Equity Method Investments			
Coca-Cola Enterprises	788	0	0
Coca-Cola Amatil Limited	432	0	432
Other	3,908	0	3,908
Cost Method Investments	294	0	294
Other Assets	2,792	0	2,282
	8,214	0	6,916
Property, Plant, and Equipment (Net)	4,453	6,206	10,659
Intangible Assets (Including Goodwill)	2,579	14,637	16,933
Total Assets	22,417	23,719	44,447
Current Liabilities			
Accounts Payable and Accrued	4,530	2,648	7,140
Debts			
Deferred Cash Payments	0	70	0
Notes Payable and Current Debt	3,899	1,804	5,703
	8,429	4,522	12,843
Noncurrent Liabilities			
Long-Term Debt	1,219	10,365	11,584
Other Noncurrent Liabilities	961	1,166	2,127
Deferred Cash Payments	0	510	0
Deferred Taxes	442	4,336	4,778
	2,622	16,377	18,489
Shareholders' Equity			
Minority Interest	0	0	1,712
Preferred Stock	0	37	37
Common Equity	11,366	2,783	11,366
	11,366	2,820	13,115
Total Liabilities and Equity	22,417	23,719	44,447

Exhibit 3.4 *(Continued)*

Panel C: Income Statement for the Year Ending December 31, 2000

	Coke (Parent)	Bottlers (Subsidiary)	Consolidated Entity
Net Operating Revenues	19,889	14,750	29,727
Cost of Goods Sold	(6,204)	(9,083)	(10,924)
Gross Profit	13,685	5,667	18,803
SG&A Expenses	(9,994)	(4,541)	(13,986)
Operating Income	3,691	1,126	4,817
Interest Income	345	0	345
Interest Expense	(447)	(791)	(1,238)
Investment Income	(289)	0	(386)
Other Income	99	(2)	97
Minority Interest Net Income	0	0	(139)
Income before Taxes	3,399	333	3,496
Income Taxes	1,222	97	1,319
Net Income before Accounting Change	2,177	236	2,177
Cumulative Effect of Accounting Change	0	0	0
Net Income	2,177	236	2,177

Panel D: Balance Sheet as of December 31, 2000

	Coca-Cola (Parent)	Bottlers (Subsidiary)	Consolidated Entity
Current Assets			
Cash and Marketable Securities	1,892	294	2,186
Trade Accounts Receivable	1,757	1,297	3,054
Amounts Due from Affiliate	0	47	0
Inventories	1,066	602	1,668
Prepaid Expenses and Other Assets	1,905	391	2,296
	6,620	2,631	9,204
Investments			
Equity Method Investments			
Coca-Cola Enterprises	707	0	0
Coca-Cola Amatil Limited	617	0	617
Other	3,922	0	3,922

Note: Parentheses denote negative numbers.

Exhibit 3.4 *(Continued)*

Panel D: *(Continued)*

	Coca-Cola (Parent)	Bottlers (Subsidiary)	Consolidated Entity
Cost Method Investments	519	0	519
Other Assets	2,364	0	2,364
	8,129	0	7,422
Property, Plant, and Equipment (Net)	4,168	5,783	9,951
Intangible Assets (Including Goodwill)	1,917	13,748	15,227
Total Assets	20,834	22,162	41,804
Current Liabilities			
Accounts Payable and Accrued Debts	4,505	2,321	6,779
Deferred Cash Payments	0	0	0
Notes Payable and Current Debt	4,816	773	5,589
	9,321	3,094	12,368
Noncurrent Liabilities			
Long-Term Debt	835	10,348	11,183
Other Noncurrent Liabilities	1,004	1,112	2,116
Deferred Cash Payments	0	0	0
Deferred Taxes	358	4,774	5,132
	2,197	16,234	18,431
Shareholders' Equity			
Minority Interest	0	0	1,645
Preferred Stock	0	44	44
Common Equity	9,316	2,790	9,316
	9,316	2,834	11,005
Total Liabilities and Equity	20,834	22,162	41,804

liabilities about seven times the size of the long-term debts of Coke itself. Whereas the parent company has a moderate financial structure, the subsidiary clearly has a more aggressive financial structure.

The financial ratios reveal the discrepancy between the equity method and consolidation. Exhibit 3.5 communicates the financial ratios for the parent when applying the equity method and the consolidated results. Readers cannot help but notice that virtually all ratios are negatively impacted when we move from the equity method to the consolidation method. Financial leverage is the hardest hit. Debt to equity doubles, while debt to tangible equity goes from a positive number to a negative number. Times interest earned shrinks to less than half. Long-term debt to equity and long-term debt to assets mushroom.

The return metrics are also negatively impacted. While the net income of the parent equals consolidated net income, the denominators have increased. Return on sales, return on assets, and return on tangible or total equity show decreases. Both sales and cost of goods sold increase, but the net effect is a decline in the gross margins.

Exhibit 3.5   Financial Ratios of Coca-Cola Equity Method versus Consolidation

Financial Ratios	2001		2000	
	Equity	Consolidated	Equity	Consolidated
Current Ratio	0.85	0.77	0.71	0.74
Debt to Equity	0.97	2.39	1.24	2.80
Debt to Tangible Equity	1.26	(8.21)	1.56	(7.29)
Debt to Assets	0.49	0.70	0.55	0.74
Debt to Tangible Assets	0.56	1.14	0.61	1.16
Gross Profit	0.70	0.64	0.69	0.63
Return on Sales	0.20	0.13	0.11	0.07
Return on Assets	0.18	0.09	0.10	0.05
Return on Tangible Assets	0.20	0.14	0.12	0.08
Return on Equity	0.35	0.30	0.23	0.20
Return on Tangible Equity	0.45	(1.04)	0.29	(.52)
Times Interest Earned	20.62	6.61	8.60	3.82
Inventory Turnover	5.73	6.35	5.82	6.55
Receivables Turnover	10.90	9.06	11.32	9.73
LTD to Equity	0.11	0.88	0.09	1.02
LTD to Assets	0.05	0.26	0.04	0.27

Note: Parentheses denote negative numbers.

Even the current ratio, inventory turnover, and receivables turnover deteriorate.

In short, there is no good news in Coke's consolidated numbers. Accordingly, it is easy to understand why Coke would want to generate a different impression by not consolidating these corporations.

This leads us to the real question: Should Coca-Cola in fact consolidate the results of its bottlers and company-owned franchisees? The firm argues no because the rules say not to. Statement of Financial Accounting Standards (SFAS) No. 94 requires consolidation only when the parent company owns more than 50 percent of the investee. The difficulty of this position is that it is patently unfair to the readers of the financial statements and does not reflect the substance of what is going on. Coca-Cola runs the shop in these investees; it controls everything that matters. If the business enterprise offered financial statements that were fair to the investment community—as Arthur Andersen of old argued should be done (see Chapter 11)—then Coca-Cola would consolidate these operations and quit playing games with investors and creditors.

WorldCom

That paragon of accounting we know as WorldCom apparently has been at it again—with an interesting twist. WorldCom owns 52 percent of the voting stock of Embratel, a Brazilian telecommunications company—and correctly has consolidated the results of Embratel with its own. Managers at WorldCom now argue that this consolidation is inappropriate because they do not own a majority of all the stock, just a majority of the voting stock.[10] In fact, these managers are now arguing that WorldCom owns less than 20 percent of Embratel, so it should apply the equity method instead.

Not only is such a deconsolidation unusual, but also it makes one curious about the real reasons for pursuing such a tack. I do not have the data necessary to contrast the impact of consolidating and not consolidating Embratel with WorldCom, but I have to wonder about the debt level of Embratel. Given the culture of today's managers, my guess is that WorldCom cares little about the accuracy or fairness of the accounting, but again its managers are trying to paint a pretty picture for investors and creditors. Given past actions of managers at this corporation, more data and disclosures should be offered to prove that they are not trying to pull another one on us.

SUMMARY AND CONCLUSION

A number of accounting tricks fall under the umbrella of off-balance sheet accounting, and the equity method is one of them. The equity method hides liabilities because it nets the assets and liabilities of the investee. Since assets are almost always greater than liabilities, this net amount goes on the left-hand side of the balance sheet. This accounting thus hides all of the investee's debts.

When a corporation controls the operations of another company, it should consolidate the operations of both. When the parent applies the equity method instead, we can be sure that it is hiding debt. Where possible, as in the case of Coca-Cola and Coca-Cola Enterprises, readers of financial statements can perform their own analytical adjustments and obtain the consolidated income statement and consolidated balance sheet. Analyzing this adjusted set of statements often reveals more than the actual financial report.

Of course, it would help immensely if managers accounted for these transactions properly and fairly. The investment community does not want a mere meeting the letter of the law but also an attempt to meet the spirit of the accounting standards.

NOTES

1. The purpose here is only to give a brief overview of the accounting for investments. Greater details can be found in: D. E. Kieso, J. J. Weygandt, and T. D. Warfield, *Intermediate Accounting,* 10th ed. (New York: John Wiley & Sons, 2001), pp. 917–970; L. Revsine, D. W. Collins, and W. B. Johnson, *Financial Reporting and Analysis,* 2nd ed. (Upper Saddle River, NJ: Prentice-Hall, 2002), pp. 817–882; and G. I. White, A. C. Sondhi, and D. Fried, *The Analysis and Use of Financial Statements,* 3rd ed. (New York: John Wiley & Sons, 1998), pp. 670–726. The applicable accounting rules are found in Accounting Principles Board, *The Equity Method of Accounting for Investments in Common Stock,* APB Opinion No. 18 (New York: AICPA, 1971); and the Financial Accounting Standards Board, *Accounting for Certain Investments in Debt and Equity Securities,* SFAS No. 115 (Norwalk, CT: FASB,1993). Also to be recommended are: P. R. Delaney, B. J. Epstein, J. A. Adler, and M. F. Foran, *GAAP 2000: Interpretation and Application of Generally Accepted Accounting Principles 2000* (New York: John Wiley & Sons, 2000), pp. 357–398; G. Georgiades, *Miller GAAP Financial Statement Disclosures Manual* (New York: Aspen, 2001), section 35.01; and B. D. Jarnagin, *2001 U.S. Master GAAP Guide* (Chicago: CCH, 2000), pp. 321–330.

2. The face value of the debt is how much the investor receives at maturity, ignoring interest. At the issuance date, debt can have fair values above or below this face value because the coupon rate on the debt differs from the market interest rate for securities with similar risk. The investment community calls the difference a *premium* when the fair value exceeds the face value and a *discount* when the face value is greater than the fair value. Accountants amortize (reduce over time eventually to a zero balance) the premium or discount, which affects the computation of interest revenue and interest expense. "Amortized cost" of a held-to-maturity debt security is the face value of the security plus (minus) the unamortized premium (discount).

3. The firm would report the unrealized gain in the statement of comprehensive income. For details, see Kieso et al., *Intermediate Accounting,* pp. 929–930.

4. See A. Bedipo-Memba, "Boston Chicken Files for Protection, Lays Off 500, Shuts 178 Restaurants," *Wall Street Journal,* October 6, 1998; and J. E. Ketz, "Is There an Epidemic of Underauditing?" *Journal of Corporate Accounting and Finance* (Fall 1998): 25–35.

5. Statement of Financial Accounting Standards No. 115 was published in 1993, the same year that Boston Chicken went public. It is not clear why Boston Chicken reported its investments at cost instead of at fair value.

6. Notice that minority interest is computed on the book value of the net assets of Serpentino (20 percent of $60,000) whereas the majority position is based on the fair value of the net assets of Serpentino (80 percent of $90,000). Why the accounting profession measures the parent's share at fair value and the minority's share at historical cost is beyond me.

7. Financial Accounting Standards Board, *Goodwill and Other Intangible Assets,* FASB No. 142 (Norwalk, CT: FASB, 2001).

8. J. E. Ketz and P. B. W. Miller, "Elan Managers Play the Market for a Sucker," *Accounting Today,* November 22–December 12, 1999, pp. 14, 17.
9. B. McKay, "Coca-Cola: Real Thing Can Be Hard to Measure," *Wall Street Journal,* January 23, 2002, p. C16; and White et al., *Analysis and Use of Financial Statements,* pp. 722–726.
10. S. Pulliam and J. Sandberg, "New WorldCom Report to SEC Will Acknowledge More Flaws," *Wall Street Journal,* September 19, 2002.

CHAPTER FOUR

How to Hide Debt
with Lease Accounting

Lease accounting has been a disaster for a very long time. Leases, of course, involve a *lessor* who legally owns some property and a *lessee* who would like to utilize that property. The lessor agrees to lend the property to the lessee, while the lessee agrees to make certain payments. Because of this work's focus on hiding liabilities from the balance sheet, I shall concentrate on the accounting by lessees and downplay issues of concern about lessors. As shall be seen, corporate managers can deceive investors and creditors by reporting leases as operating leases and pretend that they do not have any lease obligations. Similar issues will pop up in Chapter 6 with synthetic leases.

When leases first evolved, managers quickly advocated treating them as what are called today operating leases. *Operating leases* essentially are rentals. The argument continues that accounting for these operating leases involves a simple recognition of rental expense and the payment of the cash or recognition of a payable. While this method appears acceptable when one rents something for a short period of time, such as a day, a week, or even a month, it stretches credulity to make this argument when the rental period extends for a substantial time.

I shall not reconstruct the tortured history of what happened next.[1] Suffice it to say that the Financial Accounting Standards Board (FASB) issued Statement No. 13 in 1976, and there have been dozens of modifications and interpretations since. This accounting rule was clearly superior to its predecessors since it required more leases to be capitalized than had been previously. *Capital leases* are those leases that in substance are really purchases of the property. The lease contract serves merely as a legal mechanism by which the transaction is effected. In other words, leasing is simply one way of financing the purchase of the piece of property. Accounting for capital leases proves straightforward inasmuch as the property is treated as belonging to the lessee and the liability is considered to be assumed by the lessee. And, in the words of Shakespeare, there's the rub. Managers do not like to show these liabilities, especially when they become huge. So managers expend much time and effort in an attempt to keep these liabilities off the balance sheet.

Actually, we do not have to presume that the leasing activity is de facto a purchase of the leased item. Instead, we could invoke a property rights argument. The essence of this approach is to observe that a lease gives the lessee a right to employ the property any way desired, constrained only by the contract made with the lessor. The lessee obtains an intangible asset that gives it the right to use certain property for a specified period of time, and this asset should appear on the balance sheet. Likewise the lessee makes a firm commitment to pay for this lease, and this obligation should be recorded on its books. Leases involve transactions that obtain property rights in exchange for a commitment to pay cash for a specified period of time.

Unfortunately, too many leases are still off the balance sheet. The mission in this chapter is to put them back on the balance sheet via analytical adjustments. Recall from Chapter 3 that an analytical adjustment entails taking the reported numbers and adjusting them for economic reality—for the truth. Financial statement readers then analyze the corporation in terms of these adjusted numbers rather than the reported numbers that appear in the financial statements. In this case, investors or creditors should ignore financial reports of those companies using operating leases and should replace those reported numbers with those that would occur if the business enterprise correctly accounted for them as capitalized leases. Investors or creditors could then compute financial ratios with these adjusted numbers and thereby obtain a better—and more accurate—picture of the corporate health than if they calculated these ratios with the reported numbers.

This chapter investigates lease accounting and describes how corporate managers try to argue that their leases are operating leases for the purpose of hiding lease liabilities from investors and creditors. The first section covers the concept of present value. The second section summarizes lease accounting with a relatively straightforward illustration. The third section depicts some common and easy ways for managers to thwart FASB's intentions in Statement No. 13. The fourth section describes an elementary way to adjust these reported numbers into more useful numbers that yield a more truthful representation of a firm's financial activities, including the assumptions required for conducting this type of analysis. I illustrate this process with Delta Airlines. The next section introduces the rest of the airline industry, discusses the considerable number of operating leases that exist in it, and considers why this industry maintains so many operating leases. Then I carry out the analytical adjustment process explained earlier, revealing the results when analytical adjustments are made for airline corporations and contrasting these results with the reported numbers.

PRESENT VALUE

Readers familiar with the topic of the time value of money and who can calculate future and present value can skip this section. Here I explain these notions and give some details about computing present value so that we can value a lease obligation. These ideas will also help in later chapters dealing with pension accounting, securitizations, borrowings with special-purpose entities (SPEs), and synthetic leases.

A dollar is not always worth one dollar if a time difference exists for when the dollar is obtained. One dollar received today is worth more than one dollar received some time in the future because an individual can place the dollar received today into a savings account and earn interest on that dollar. The dollar received today grows into a larger amount than the dollar received in the future by the amount of interest earned on the original dollar; this concept is known as the *time value of money.*

Interest, of course, is the price of credit. Interest is the return that a lender obtains by allowing someone to rent his or her money; alternatively, interest is the cost that a borrower pays to rent someone's money. *Principal* is the amount on which interest is determined. *Simple interest* is the interest on a constant principal. By definition, interest is computed with the formula:

$$I = PRT$$

where I stands for interest, P stands for principal, R stands for the rate of interest, and T stands for the amount of time. The rate of interest and time must be measured in the same units of time.

Compound interest is the interest in those situations in which the principal varies. This situation takes place, for example, when a consumer does not pay off a previous loan balance. Any unpaid past interest is added to the old principal to obtain a new, higher principal. Thus, interest is paid on the original principal plus all unpaid past interest. Again, the rate of interest and time must be measured in the same units of time.

When analyzing a set of cash flows, we frequently desire to know its equivalent amount in terms of today or some time in the future. The former is referred to as the *present value* of the cash flows and the latter as the *future value* of the cash flows.

An *annuity* is a set of cash flows of equal amounts (called *rents*[2]) and occurring at equal intervals of time. An *ordinary annuity* is an annuity in which the cash flows occur at the end of the period (e.g., mortgages). An *annuity due* has the cash flows occurring at the beginning of the period (e.g., apartment leases).

With these definitions in mind, we can focus on the main aspects of future and present value. Exhibit 4.1 encompasses these concepts by providing diagrams of the different situations, a formula for each one, and a discussion of how to compute the amounts in practice with tables or financial calculators or Excel (or a similar spreadsheet package).

Future Value of a Single Sum

Suppose we have $1,000 and want to put it in the bank at a rate of interest of 8 percent per year. We want to know how much it will be worth in three years when we hope to use the money to make some purchase. The principal of $1,000 grows in this way.

Year	Amount at Beginning	Interest	Amount at End
1	$1,000.00	$80.00	$1,080.00
2	1,080.00	86.40	1,166.40
3	1,166.40	93.31	1,259.71

The interest for the first year is computed as $1,000 times 8 percent times one year for $80. The interest is added to the amount at the beginning so we have $1,080 at the end of the year. This amount, of course, becomes the amount at the beginning of the next year. The interest in the second year equals the new principal, $1,080, times 8 percent times one year for $86.40. When we add the interest to $1,080, the balance now becomes $1,166.40. Repeating the process for year 3, we find the interest is $93.31 and the ending balance is $1,259.71, which is the answer to the original question.

Panel A in Exhibit 4.1 provides a diagram of this example. There is only one cash flow, and we want to find the balance if we leave the amount in the bank account for three years. An alternative way to solve the problem is to use the formula:

$$FVSS = X\,(1 + r)^n$$

where *FVSS* denotes the future value of a single sum, *X* denotes the cash flow, *r* denotes the interest rate, and *n* denotes the number of periods over which the cash accumulates. The future value equals $1,000 times $(1 + .08)^3$, which is $1,000 times 1.25971, which is $1,259.71. If we have a financial calculator or a spreadsheet at our disposal, we merely enter $X = \$1,000$, $n = 3$, and $r = 8$ percent. (Specifics obviously depend on the machine and software.)

Exhibit 4.1   Future and Present Value Concepts

Panel A: Future Value of a Single Sum

Diagram of cash flows

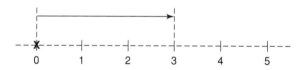

Formula

Let $X =$ some cash flow that occurs now and assume that the interest rate is r. Then the future value at time n of the single sum is: $FVSS = X\,(1 + r)^n$.

Tables and Calculators and Spreadsheets

In practice a table can be employed that has calculated the future value interest factor, that is, $(1 + r)^n$; simply find the number in the interest rate column and the time period row. Then multiply this interest factor by X to obtain the future value.

A financial calculator or a spreadsheet package such as Excel can be used (apply the function FV). Just plug in X, r, and n, and the calculator or spreadsheet spits out the future value of a single sum. The trick for both financial calculators and spreadsheets is to understand that they are constructed to allow computations for either single sums or annuities. For a single sum, tell the financial calculator or the spreadsheet program that the "payment" is zero (i.e., it is not an annuity) and the "present value" is the cash flow.

Exhibit 4.1   *(Continued)*

A caveat! In all situations, n and r must be compatible—in other words, they must use the same time frame. If stated in different time units, they must be adjusted and put into the same time units before using the formula or future value tables or calculator or spreadsheet.

Panel B: Present Value of a Single Sum

Diagram of cash flows

Formula

Let X = some cash flow that occurs at time n and assume that the interest rate is r. Then the present value of the single sum is: $PVSS = X (1 + r)^{-n}$.

Note: The interest factor for present value of a single sum $(1 + r)^{-n}$ is the reciprocal of the interest factor for future value of a single sum $(1 + r)^{n}$.

Tables, Calculators, and Spreadsheets

In practice, a table can be employed that has calculated the present value interest factor, that is, $(1 + r)^{-n}$; simply find the number in the interest rate column and the time period row. Then multiply this interest factor by X to obtain the present value.

A financial calculator or a spreadsheet package such as Excel can be used (apply the function PV). Just plug in X, r, and n, and the calculator or spreadsheet spits out the present value of a single sum. The trick for both financial calculators and spreadsheets is to understand that they are constructed to allow computations for either single sums or annuities. For a single sum, tell the financial calculator or the spreadsheet program that the "payment" is zero (i.e., it is not an annuity) and the "future value" is the cash flow.

A caveat! In all situations, n and r must be compatible—in other words, they must use the same time frame. If stated in different time units, they must be adjusted and put into the same time units before using the formula or future value tables or calculator or spreadsheet.

Panel C: Future Value of an Ordinary Annuity

Diagram of cash flows

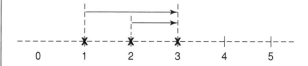

Exhibit 4.1 *(Continued)*

Panel C: *(Continued)*

Formula

$FVOA = X \{[(1 + r)^n - 1] / r\}$. With annuities, the cash flows X are called the rents.

Tables and Calculators and Spreadsheets

In practice a table can be employed that has calculated the future value interest factor; simply find the number in the interest rate column and the time period row. Then multiply this interest factor by X to obtain the future value of the ordinary annuity.

A financial calculator or a spreadsheet package such as Excel can be used (apply the function FV). Just plug in X, r, and n, and the calculator or spreadsheet spits out the future value of an ordinary annuity. The trick for both financial calculators and spreadsheets is to understand that they are constructed to allow computations for either single sums or annuities. For an annuity, tell the financial calculator or the spreadsheet program that the "payment" is the rent (i.e., it *is* an annuity) and the "present value" is zero.

Financial calculators and spreadsheets programs typically assume that the annuity is an ordinary annuity. If it is annuity due, then change one variable or button and the package will do the rest.

A caveat! In all situations, n and r must be compatible—in other words, they must use the same time frame. If stated in different time units, they must be adjusted and put into the same time units before using the formula or future value tables or calculator or spreadsheet.

Panel D: Present Value of an Ordinary Annuity

Diagram of cash flows

Formula

$$PVOA = X \{[1 - (1 + r)^{-n}] / r\}.$$

Note: If a *perpetuity* (i.e., the rents go on forever), then PVOA = X / r.

Tables and Calculators and Spreadsheets

In practice, a table can be employed that has calculated the present value interest factor; simply find the number in the interest rate column and the time period row. Then multiply this interest factor by X to obtain the present value of the ordinary annuity.

Exhibit 4.1 *(Continued)*

A financial calculator or a spreadsheet package such as Excel can be used (apply the function PV). Just plug in X, r, and n, and the calculator or spreadsheet spits out the present value of an ordinary annuity. The trick for both financial calculators and spreadsheets is to understand that they are constructed to allow computations for either single sums or annuities. For an annuity, tell the financial calculator or the spreadsheet program that the "payment" is the rent (i.e., it *is* an annuity) and the "future value" is zero.

Financial calculators and spreadsheets programs typically assume that the annuity is an ordinary annuity. If it is an annuity due, then change one variable or button and the package will do the rest.

A caveat! In all situations, n and r must be compatible—in other words, they must use the same time frame. If stated in different time units, they must be adjusted and put into the same time units before using the formula or future value tables or calculator or spreadsheet.

Panel E: Present Value of an Annuity Due

Diagram of cash flows

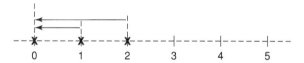

Formula

$$PVAD = X \{\{[1 - (1 + r)^{-n+1}] / r\} + 1\}.$$

Tables and Calculators

In practice, a table can be employed that has calculated the present value interest factor; simply find the number in the interest rate column and the time period row. Then multiply this interest factor by X to obtain the future value of the ordinary annuity.

A financial calculator or a spreadsheet package such as Excel can be used (apply the function PV). Just plug in X, r, and n, and the calculator or spreadsheet spits out the present value of an annuity due. The trick for both financial calculators and spreadsheets is to understand that they are constructed to allow computations for either single sums or annuities. For an annuity, tell the financial calculator or the spreadsheet program that the "payment" is the rent (i.e., it *is* an annuity) and the "future value" is zero.

Financial calculators and spreadsheets programs typically assume that the annuity is an ordinary annuity. Since this is an annuity due, change one variable or button and the package will do the rest. In Excel, the variable is called "type." If "type" equals zero or is omitted, then the program takes the cash flows as forming an ordinary annuity. To tell Excel that an annuity is due, make "type" equal to one.

A caveat! In all situations, n and r must be compatible—in other words, they must use the same time frame. If stated in different time units, they must be adjusted and put into the same time units before using the formula or future value tables or calculator or spreadsheet.

Present Value of a Single Sum

Suppose instead we have a lump sum of money that will come to us in three years and want to know its value in today's terms. Because of the time value of money, the lump sum will be worth less in today's terms, the difference being the interest over the three-year period. For example, suppose we will receive $1,259.71 three years from now. What is it worth today? What is its present value? We can use the same chart as we did with the future value of a single sum and work backward. Accordingly, the present value of $1,259.71 discounted back one, two, or three years is, respectively, $1,166.40, $1,080, and $1,000. The answer to the original question is that the $1,259.71 to be received in three years is worth $1,000 today, given an interest rate of 8 percent.

Panel B of Exhibit 4.1 describes the present value of a single sum. Notice in the diagram that there is only one cash flow that takes place in three years, and we want to know its value in today's terms. Compare and contrast the diagrams in panels A and B. There is only one cash flow in each, reflecting our assumption of a single flow. The difference is that in panel A, the cash flow occurs at time zero and we are looking for the value in the future, whereas in panel B the cash flow occurs at time equal to three and we are searching for the value today. The distinction in the two diagrams demonstrates the difference between future value and present value.

An alternative way to solve the problem is to use the formula:

$$PVSS = X (1 + r)^{-n}$$

where $PVSS$ stands for the present value of a single sum, X stands for the cash flow, r stands for the interest rate, and n stands for the number of periods. The present value equals $1,259.71 times $(1 + .08)^{-3}$ or $1,259.71 times .793832241, which is $1,000. If we have a financial calculator or a spreadsheet at our disposal, we merely enter $X = $1,259.71$, $n = 3$, and $r = 8$ percent and solve for the present value.

Future Value of an Ordinary Annuity

Often in practice there is not just one cash flow but several. These problems can be solved by taking the present or future value, as the case may be, of each cash flow and then adding up the results. If the cash flows are of the same amount and occur periodically, then a shortcut is possible, which we explore here.

For example, assume that the rent equals $1,000 and the rate of interest is 8 percent per year and cash flows occur at the end of the year. How much will be in the account at the end of three years?

Year	Amount at Beginning	Interest	Amount at End
1	$ 0.00	$ 0.00	$1,000.00
2	1,000.00	80.00	2,080.00
3	2,080.00	166.40	3,246.40

Since cash flows take place at the end of the year, there is no cash at the beginning of year one and no interest. The cash at the end of year one is the first installment of cash flows, $1,000. This amount earns $80 interest during the second year. The amount in the account at the end of year two is the beginning amount $1,000 plus the interest of $80 plus the second installment of cash $1,000, for a total of $2,080. This amount earns $166.40 interest during the third year, so the amount at the end of year three is the beginning amount $2,080 plus the interest of $166.40 plus the third and last installment of cash $1,000, for a total of $3,246.40.

As stated earlier, an annuity is just a group of single sums. We can solve this example by summing the future values of each cash flow. When we do this, we achieve the same answer.

Year	Future Value of Separate Single Sums
1	$1{,}000 \times (1 + .08)^2 = \$1{,}166.40$
2	$1{,}000 \times (1 + .08)^1 = \ \ 1{,}080.00$
3	$1{,}000 \times (1 + .08)^0 = \ \ \underline{1{,}000.00}$
	$\overline{\underline{\$3{,}246.40}}$

Panel C of Exhibit 4.1 discloses information about the future value of an ordinary annuity. There are three cash flows at the end of years one, two, and three. We take each of them forward to the end of year three so that we can obtain the future value of this set of cash flows at this point in time.

To solve the question directly, we can make use of the formula:

$$FVOA = X \left\{ [(1 + r)^n - 1] / r \right\}$$

where *FVOA* is the future value of an ordinary annuity, *X* is the rent (the equal and periodic cash flows), *r* is the interest rate, and *n* is the number of periods (and the number of cash flows). In our example, the formula yields:

$$FVOA = 1{,}000 \times \frac{(1 + .08)^3 - 1}{0.08}$$

which gives the answer $3,246.40. If we have a financial calculator or a spreadsheet at our disposal, we merely enter $X = \$1{,}000$, $n = 3$, and $r = 8$ percent and solve for the future value of the ordinary annuity.

Some problems have the cash flows taking place at the beginning of the period, and we could modify these statements to account for the future value of an annuity due. We do not cover that possibility, for we never encounter this scenario in this book.

Present Value of an Ordinary Annuity

Let us draw on the same illustration, in which the rent equals $1,000 and the rate of interest is 8 percent per year and cash flows occur at the end of the year. Instead of asking how much will be in the account at the end of three years, let us now ask what this ordinary annuity is worth today. What is its present value?

Since an annuity is just a group of single sums, we solve this inquiry by finding the present value of each separate cash flow and then add them up. When we do this, we learn that the present value is $2,577.10.

Year	Present Value of Separate Single Sums
1	$1{,}000 \times (1 + .08)^{-1} = \$\ 925.93$
2	$1{,}000 \times (1 + .08)^{-2} = \quad 857.34$
3	$1{,}000 \times (1 + .08)^{-3} = \quad 793.83$
	$\$2{,}577.10$

A diagram for present value of ordinary annuity is displayed in panel D of Exhibit 4.1. There are three cash flows that take place at time one, two, and three. Each of them is "discounted back" to the present; that is, we find the present value of each of the cash flows.

We can solve the question directly by applying the formula:

$$PVOA = X \left\{ [1 - (1 + r)^{-n}] / r \right\}$$

where $PVOA$ denotes the present value of an ordinary annuity, X denotes the rent (the equal and periodic cash flows), r denotes the interest rate, and n denotes the number of periods (and the number of cash flows). In our example, the formula gives:

$$PVOA = 1{,}000 \times \frac{1 - (1 + .08)^{-3}}{.08}$$

which gives the answer $2,577.10. If we have a financial calculator or a spreadsheet, we plug in X of $1,000, n of 3, and r of 8 percent and solve for the present value of the ordinary annuity.

If the cash flows occur forever, they form what is called a *perpetuity*. The present value of a perpetuity is $PVOA = X / r$. We make use of this fact in the chapter on pension accounting.

Present Value of an Annuity Due

Leases typically have the cash flows occurring at the beginning of the period, so these cash flows constitute an annuity due. They are treated in a manner quite similar to the previous case of finding the present value of an ordinary annuity. Once again we assume that the rent equals $1,000 and the rate of interest is 8 percent per year, but now cash flows occur at the beginning of the year. What is this annuity due worth today? What is its present value?

As before, we note that an annuity is just a group of single sums, so we solve this question by computing the present value of each cash flow and then adding up the present values. It turns out that the present value is $2,783.27.

Year	Present Value of Separate Single Sums
1	$1{,}000 \times (1 + .08)^{-0} = \$1{,}000.00$
2	$1{,}000 \times (1 + .08)^{-1} = \quad 925.93$
3	$1{,}000 \times (1 + .08)^{-2} = \quad 857.34$
	$\$2{,}783.27$

A diagram for present value of an annuity due is contained in Exhibit 4.1, panel E. Like panel D, there are three cash flows. Unlike panel D, these three cash flows occur at time zero, one, and two. To solve the problem, calculate the present value of each of the cash flows.

We can solve the question directly by applying the formula:

$$PVAD = X \{\{[1 - (1 + r)^{-n+1}] / r\} + 1\}$$

where *PVAD* represents the present value of an annuity due, *X* represents the rent (the equal and periodic cash flows), *r* represents the interest rate, and *n* represents the number of periods (and the number of cash flows). In this instance the formula returns:

$$PVAD = 1000 \times \left[\frac{1 - (1 + .08)^{-3+1}}{.08} + 1 \right]$$

which gives the answer $2,783.27. With a financial calculator or a spreadsheet, we would insert *X* of $1,000, *n* of 3, and *r* of 8 percent and solve for the present value of the annuity due.

BRIEF OVERVIEW OF LEASE ACCOUNTING[3]

Accounting for lessees, as stated earlier, breaks down into two categories. Either the leases are operating leases or they are capital leases. We account for operating leases by recognizing a rental expense and either a cash payment or a current liability. Accountants treat capital leases in a manner similar to that of a long-term asset by putting an asset on the balance sheet as well as the long-term liability. Periodically, accountants would recognize interest on the long-term liability, and they depreciate the leased asset. On the income statement, we show rental expense for an operating lease versus interest expense plus depreciation for a capital lease. The balance sheet difference is starker—there is no asset or liability for an operating lease, while a capital lease would report a leased asset (less its amortization or depreciation) and a lease obligation.

Before I illustrate these disparities, let me first demonstrate the similarity between accounting for the purchase of an asset, which is financed by a notes payable (or some other financial instrument), and accounting for a capital lease. Assume that on January 1, 2003, van der Wink, Inc., obtains an automobile. In the first case, the corporation buys the automobile and finances it with a car loan. The automobile costs $60,560, has a life of five years, and has a salvage value of zero. The loan calls for five equal annual payments of $15,000, payable at the beginning of the year. (Of course, in practice such loans are typically monthly. The assumption of annual payments greatly reduces the arithmetic but has no impact on the points to be made.) Exhibit 4.2 contains the details of this transaction and its accounting.

The repayment schedule, also termed a *loan amortization schedule*, can be found in panel A of Exhibit 4.2. In the business world, a cash payment or receipt first attends to the interest component; any residual amount is then applied to reduce the outstanding balance. The first payment occurs at the very beginning, so there is no interest, and the entire $15,000 reduces the principal, which becomes $60,560 minus $15,000, or $45,560.

Interest accrues on this amount, computed with the usual formula $I = PRT = \$45,560$ times 12 percent times one year, for an amount of \$5,467. This is added to the balance, making the outstanding debt \$51,027. (Alternatively, the accountant may record it as interest payable. The key thing is to note that the full liability includes the principal of \$45,560 and the interest of \$5,467.) On January 1, 2004, the lessee pays \$15,000, which covers the interest and a portion of the principal (\$9,533). The balance becomes \$36,027, which equals \$45,560 minus \$9,533. Interest accrues on this to the tune of \$4,324, so the outstanding debt at the end of the second year is \$40,351. The process continues until the loan is paid off.

Panel B of Exhibit 4.2 compares the journal entries for a purchase financed with notes payable versus a capital lease. As can be seen, the entries essentially are the same for all periods. They chronicle the same amount of interest expense and the same amount of depreciation in each of the five years. Further, as panel C shows, they divulge the same amount of total liabilities on the balance sheet. The point is this: Recording a lease as a capital lease makes it look like a purchase with debt financing of some sort.

Exhibit 4.2   Comparison of Purchase and Lease Financing

Assume that on January 1 van der Wink Inc. purchases or leases an automobile for five years from Golan Inc. The car costs \$60,560 and will be financed by five annual payments of \$15,000, each at the beginning of the year. The interest rate implicit in the lease is 12 percent.

We verify this is the situation by noting that

$$\frac{15,000}{1.00} + \frac{15,000}{1.12} + \frac{15,000}{(1.12)^2} + \frac{15,000}{(1.12)^3} + \frac{15,000}{(1.12)^4} = 60,560$$

Panel A: The Repayment Schedule

Payment January 1 in Year	Cash Payment	Principal Reduction	Obligation at Beginning of Year (after Payment)	Interest Expense	Obligation at End of Year
2003	\$15,000	\$15,000	\$45,560	\$5,467	\$51,027
2004	15,000	9,533	36,027	4,324	40,351
2005	15,000	10,676	25,351	3,042	28,393
2006	15,000	11,958	13,393	1,607	15,000
2007	15,000	13,393	0	0	0

Exhibit 4.2 *(Continued)*

Panel B: Comparison of Journal Entries for Purchase and Lease Financing

Purchase Financing			Lease Financing		
Car	$60,560		Car	$60,560	
Notes Payable		$60,560	Lease Payable		$60,560
Notes Payable	$15,000		Lease Payable	$15,000	
Cash		$15,000	Cash		$15,000
Depreciation	$12,112		Depreciation	$12,112	
Accumulated Depreciation		$12,112	Accumulated Depreciation		$12,112
Notes Payable	$ 9,533		Lease Payable	$ 9,533	
Interest Expense	$ 5,467		Interest Expense	$ 5,467	
Cash		$15,000	Cash		$15,000
Depreciation	$12,112		Depreciation	$12,112	
Accumulated Depreciation		$12,112	Accumulated Depreciation		$12,112
Notes Payable	$10,676		Lease Payable	$10,676	
Interest Expense	$ 4,324		Interest Expense	$ 4,324	
Cash		$15,000	Cash		$15,000
Depreciation	$12,112		Depreciation	$12,112	
Accumulated Depreciation		$12,112	Accumulated Depreciation		$12,112
Notes Payable	$11,958		Lease Payable	$11,958	
Interest Expense	$ 3,042		Interest Expense	$ 3,042	
Cash		$15,000	Cash		$15,000
Depreciation	$12,112		Depreciation	$12,112	
Accumulated Depreciation		$12,112	Accumulated Depreciation		$12,112
Notes Payable	$13,393		Lease Payable	$13,393	
Interest Expense	$ 1,607		Interest Expense	$ 1,607	
Cash		$15,000	Cash		$15,000
Depreciation	$12,112		Depreciation	$12,112	
Accumulated Depreciation		$12,112	Accumulated Depreciation		$12,112

Exhibit 4.2   *(Continued)*

Panel C: Comparison of Balance Sheet—Liability Effects

	Notes Payable	Lease Payable
December 31, 2003	$51,027	$51,027
December 31, 2004	40,351	40,351
December 31, 2005	28,393	28,393
December 31, 2006	15,000	15,000
December 31, 2007	0	0

Exhibit 4.3 contrasts the accounting for a capital lease and an operating lease. The case remains the same, so panel A's repayment schedule is unaffected. Note, however, the acute disparity in the bookkeeping and in the effects shown on the income statement and the balance sheet in panels B and C of Exhibit 4.3. Treating the lease as an operating lease involves annual rent expense of $15,000 but does not disclose the property rights the corporation has in the lease or any of its financial commitments. As before, treating the lease as a capital lease results in depreciation expense each year of $12,112 and a varying amount of interest expense. Panel D depicts the amount of liability shown on the balance sheet for a capital lease.

Investors and creditors think long-term leases (say, anything over one year in duration) are capital leases for three reasons.

1. Virtually all long-term leases look like and smell like purchases. There is little difference between them economically speaking.

2. The lessee possesses significant control over the property during the lease period, and this control is quite similar to the rights an owner of the property has.

3. When the lessee signs the contract, the entity commits itself to a particular set of cash payments over the life of the lease. This commitment looks like and smells like debt.

For these reasons, investors and creditors often argue that all long-term leases should be capitalized.[4]

Exhibit 4.3 helps us to understand why some managers prefer treating long-term leases as operating leases. While the two methods recognize the same total expenses over the life of the lease, the two differ in when they show them. If the lease is recorded as an operating lease, then the firm incurs $75,000 expense over the five years, all of it rental expense of $15,000 annually. If the lease is recorded as a capital lease, the corporation would show depreciation expense of $60,560 (annual amount of $12,112) and interest expense of $14,440, so it too adds up to $75,000. The interest expense declines over time, starting at $5,467 in 2003 and reaching zero in 2007. In other words, capital leases show higher expenses in the early years of the lease and lower expenses in the

Exhibit 4.3   Contrast between Capital and Operating Lease Accounting

Assume that on January 1 van der Wink Inc. purchases or leases an automobile for five years from Golan Inc. The car costs $60,560 and will be financed by five annual payments of $15,000, each at the beginning of the year. The interest rate implicit in the lease is 12 percent.

We verify this is the situation by noting that

$$\frac{15,000}{1.00} + \frac{15,000}{1.12} + \frac{15,000}{(1.12)^2} + \frac{15,000}{(1.12)^3} + \frac{15,000}{(1.12)^4} = 60,560$$

Panel A: The repayment schedule

Payment January 1 in Year	Cash Payment	Principal Reduction	Obligation at Beginning of Year (after Payment)	Interest Expense	Obligation at End of Year
2003	$15,000	$15,000	$45,560	$5,467	$51,027
2004	15,000	9,533	36,027	4,324	40,351
2005	15,000	10,676	25,351	3,042	28,393
2006	15,000	11,958	13,393	1,607	15,000
2007	15,000	13,393	0	0	0

Panel B: Comparison of Journal Entries for Purchase and Lease Financing

Operating Lease		Lease Financing		
		Car	$60,560	
		Lease Payable		$60,560
Rent Expense	$15,000	Lease Payable	$15,000	
Cash	$15,000	Cash		$15,000
		Depreciation	$12,112	
		Accumulated Depreciation		$12,112
Rent Expense	$15,000	Lease Payable	$ 9,533	
Cash	$15,000	Interest Expense	$ 5,467	
		Cash		$15,000
		Depreciation	$12,112	
		Accumulated Depreciation		$12,112

Exhibit 4.3 *(Continued)*

Panel B: *(Continued)*

Operating Lease		Lease Financing		
Rent Expense	$15,000	Lease Payable	$10,676	
Cash	$15,000	Interest Expense	$ 4,324	
		Cash		$15,000
		Depreciation	$12,112	
		Accumulated Depreciation		$12,112
Rent Expense	$15,000	Lease Payable	$11,958	
Cash	$15,000	Interest Expense	$ 3,042	
		Cash		$15,000
		Depreciation	$12,112	
		Accumulated Depreciation		$12,112
Rent Expense	$15,000	Lease Payable	$13,393	
Cash	$15,000	Interest Expense	$ 1,067	
		Cash		$15,000
		Depreciation	$12,112	
		Accumulated Depreciation		$12,112

Panel C: Comparison of Balance Sheet—Liability Effects

	Operating Lease	Lease Payable
December 31, 2003	$0	$51,027
December 31, 2004	0	40,351
December 31, 2005	0	28,393
December 31, 2006	0	15,000
December 31, 2007	0	0

latter years. Since managers often prefer to show lower expenses in the early years, they prefer operating leases. In addition, because operating leases show no assets on the books, the company will have higher returns on assets. Most important of all, the corporation discloses no liabilities for operating leases, but if it reported a capital lease, it might have to show some large additions to the financial structure of the firm.

When the FASB issued Statement No. 13, it improved financial reporting significantly over what it had been; nonetheless, it still compromised on reporting fully and completely the financial commitments of corporate entities. It invented four criteria for the recognition of a lease as a capital lease. If any one of the following criteria is met, then the business enterprise must account for the lease as a capital lease.

For easy reference, these criteria are listed in Exhibit 4.4.

The reason for the first criterion is obvious—a purchase in fact does occur in the future, and there seems no good reason for not recognizing the transaction today. The second concerning an option by the lessee to purchase the property at a very low price is likewise easy to understand. If the lessor, at the end of the lease term, offers the lessee the property at an unreasonably low price, such as $1, then we may assume that the lessee is rational and will exercise the option and purchase the property. This makes the lease a de facto purchase. The third criterion says that if the lessee obtains property rights for most of the life of the property, then the lessee has in essence purchased the item. The FASB uses as the cutoff 75 percent of the resource's life. Last, the FASB claims that if the lessee pays virtually the same price as a purchase price, then the transaction by the lessee is equivalent to a purchase. The FASB applies as the cutoff 90 percent of the property's fair value. Clearly, the two cutoff points are arbitrary, but they serve as a means to classify some leases as capital leases.

Efforts by the FASB to distinguish operating from capital leases have been an improvement over the old rules; however, they serve as fodder for managers to manipulate. For example, there are many leases in practice in which the present value of the minimum lease payments is 89.99 percent of the property's assets values. Certified public accountants (CPAs) and lawyers design the contracts to avoid classification as a capital lease, and in doing so they throw out any sense of decency. While they may meet the technical rules, obviously they have no intention of providing investors and creditors with useful information. More tricks are available, as we shall discover when we look at leases in more depth.

Exhibit 4.4   Lease Criteria

Criteria for a capital lease (any one):

1. Passage of title to the lessee
2. Bargain purchase option
3. Lease term equals or is greater than 75 percent of the useful life of the asset
4. Present value of the minimum lease payments equals or is greater than 90 percent of the fair value of the property

If any one of these criteria is met, then the lease is treated as a capital lease.

If all four criteria fail, then the lease is treated as an operating lease.

MORE DETAILS ABOUT LEASE ACCOUNTING

Lease accounting is rich in nuances, so this text cannot investigate every aspect of leases. I shall, however, delve into three major details about lease accounting that illustrate how lessees can hide debt with lease accounting. These details concern:

1. The interest rate used to discount the cash flows when performing the 90 percent test
2. The role of residual values
3. Contingencies

When a lessor issues a lease, it knows the fair value of the property and the rate of return required on the investment. Armed with these data, the lessor can then determine the monthly rentals that will generate this rate of return.[5] This rate of return is referred to as the *implicit rate of return.*

When a lessee signs a contract with the lessor, the lessee may or may not have knowledge of the implicit rate of return embedded in the lease. Because lessees may be ignorant of this rate, the FASB introduces the concept of the *borrower's incremental borrowing rate*, which is the rate of interest that the lessee would have incurred to borrow over a similar time period the funds necessary to purchase the property. Then the FASB says that if the lessee does not know the implicit rate, the lessee will discount the minimum lease payments at the incremental borrowing rate; if the lessee does know the implicit rate, then the lessee will discount the minimum lease payments at the lower of the implicit interest rate or the lessee's incremental borrowing rate.

Since lower rates imply higher present values, the consequence of the latter rule is to make it more likely that the 90 percent rule is met. Returning to the example in Exhibit 4.3, we can recompute the present values at other interest rates to see what happens. Here is a sample.

Interest Rate	Present Value
6%	$66,976
9%	63,596
12%	60,560
15%	57,825
18%	55,351
21%	53,107

Now let us think like a manager. Keep in mind that the incremental borrowing rate often is higher than the implicit rate, although not always. To make the example more concrete, assume that the incremental borrowing rate is 21 percent. If we do not want this lease capitalized, what can we do? The most obvious thing is to tell the lessor that we do not want to know what the implicit rate is (recall that the implicit rate is 12 percent as shown in Exhibits 4.2 and 4.3); in fact, if the lessor tells us, then the deal is off. Ignorance allows us to discount the cash flows at 21 percent, and this gives us a present value ($53,107) that is only 88 percent of the fair value of $60,560. Voilà! Ignorance allows us to avoid capitalization and not disclose the financial commitment to investors and creditors.

A second detail of lease accounting concerns the residuals. Like the salvage value used when computing depreciation expense, the *residual value* is the estimated value of the property at the end of the lease term. These residual values may or may not be guaranteed and uncreatively are termed *guaranteed residual values* and *unguaranteed residual values*. These ideas are relevant to the process because the FASB considers guaranteed residual values part of the minimum lease payments; after all, with the existence of a guaranteed residual value, either the lessee returns the property with a value at or greater than the residual value or it must pay for any deficiencies. Unguaranteed residual values, though, never require a payment from the lessee, so the FASB says that they are not part of the minimum lease payments.

Suppose we have a lease that has an implicit rate of 12 percent and has $15,000 of annual payments on January 1 of each year for four years with a residual value of $15,000 at the end of the four-year lease term. The fair value again is $60,560, for the lessor expects to receive the residual value, and includes the residual value in its computation of the present value. To the lessee, however, there is a major difference between what happens if the residual is guaranteed or not. If guaranteed, then the present value equals $60,560, which is 100 percent of the fair value, so the lease is capitalized. If unguaranteed, then the present value is $51,027, which is only 84 percent of the fair value. The lease is not capitalized. By not guaranteeing the residual value, the lessee unearths yet another way to avoid capitalization and not disclose the financial commitment to investors and creditors.[6]

The third and last detail we shall entertain involves contingencies. Think of a firm that leases floor space in a mall and that has average sales of $1 million per month. Given the nature of the business, the sales are relatively stable from month to month. The lessor wants to charge $50,000 per month for use of the store, but the lessee wants to avoid capitalization of the lease and offers the following counterproposal. The lease will require payment of $10,000 per month plus 4 percent of the sales. According to the accounting rules, contingent rental fees are excluded from the minimum lease payments, so this clause would reduce the minimum lease payment per month from $50,000 to $10,000 and substantially reduce the present value of this stream of cash flows. In this way managers of this business enterprise can avoid reporting its financial commitments from leasing activities.

There are other ways to avoid lease capitalization, but these three ways are dominant and relatively easy to implement. By using the incremental borrowing rate, by not guaranteeing the residual value, and by employing contingent rental fees, a lessee probably can account for the lease as an operating lease.

ADJUSTING OPERATING LEASES INTO CAPITAL LEASES

As with the equity method in Chapter 3, operating leases accompanied by good disclosures allow knowledgeable investors and financial analysts the opportunity to adjust the reported numbers to numbers that are more meaningful. These analytical adjustments will transform the reported numbers by assuming that the operating leases are in fact capital leases and adjusting, as appropriate, various balance sheet and income statement accounts. Investors and financial analysts can construct these adjustments because the FASB and the Securities and Exchange Commission (SEC) require certain disclosures by those entities that have operating leases. If we assume these disclosures are proper and if we make some other assumptions about asset lives, tax rates, and cash flow patterns, we can generate these more useful numbers.[7]

I have chosen the airline industry to illustrate these analytical adjustments. The industry is good for this purpose because it has regularly attempted to avoid reporting its financial commitments under leasing arrangements. The results from 2001, however, will be somewhat skewed as a result of the September 11 attack on the World Trade Center. The industry leases most of its aircraft from others, in part because financial institutions can purchase aircraft on more favorable terms than the airline companies. As a result of FASB Statement No. 13 and its amendments, some of these leases are capitalized, but a significant portion are not. These operating leases constitute a significant amount of unrecognized debt, and I shall demonstrate how financial statements can be adjusted to take this into account. I illustrate this method with Delta Air Lines and then discuss what these adjustments reveal for six major firms in the industry.

Analytical Adjustments of Delta Air Lines

Like other enterprises in the airline business, Delta leases many of its airplanes and associated pieces of equipment. Delta capitalizes some of these leases and treats others as operating leases. I begin with the reported numbers (the units are millions of dollars) in the financial statements, given in Exhibits 4.5 and 4.6, and proceed with the adjustment process. This process consists of seven steps:

1. Find the lease cash payments.
2. Choose an appropriate interest rate.
3. Compute the leased assets and the lease obligations as the present value of the lease cash payments using an appropriate interest rate.
4. Choose an appropriate life for the leased assets and estimate their present age. With these assumptions, calculate the depreciation expense and the accumulated depreciation.
5. Estimate the interest expense.
6. Estimate the change in the income tax expense and deferred income taxes.
7. Obtain the adjusted income statement and the adjusted balance sheet.

The FASB requires those that employ operating leases to disclose the future cash commitments; specifically, the company should reveal the amounts of the cash flows for each of the next five years and then give a cumulative number for the remaining cash

Exhibit 4.5   Delta Air Lines Balance Sheets (in Millions of Dollars for Period Ended December)

	2001	2000
Current Assets:		
Cash and Cash Equivalents	2,210	1,364
Short-Term Investments	5	243
Accounts Receivable, Net	368	406
Expendable Parts and Supplies Inventories, Net	181	170
Deferred Income Taxes	518	345
Fuel Hedge Contracts, at Fair Market Value	55	319
Prepaid Expenses and Other	230	358
Total Current Assets	3,567	3,205
Property and Equipment:		
Flight Equipment	19,427	17,371
Less: Accumulated Depreciation	5,730	5,139
Flight Equipment, Net	13,697	12,232
Flight Equipment under Capital Leases	382	484
Less: Accumulated Amortization	262	324
Flight Equipment under Capital Leases, Net	120	160
Ground Property and Equipment	4,412	4,357
Less: Accumulated Depreciation	2,355	2,313
Ground Property and Equipment, Net	2,057	2,058
Advance Payments for Equipment	223	390
Total Property and Equipment, Net	16,097	14,840
Other Assets:		
Investments in Debt and Equity Securities	96	339
Investments in Associated Companies	180	222
Cost in Excess of Net Assets Acquired, Net	2,092	2,149
Operating Rights and Other Intangibles, Net	94	102
Restricted Investments for Boston Airport Terminal Project	475	0
Other Noncurrent Assets	1,004	1,074
Total Other Assets	3,941	3,886
Total Assets	23,605	21,931

Exhibit 4.5 *(Continued)*

	2001	2000
Current Liabilities:		
Current Maturities of Long-Term Debt	260	62
Short-Term Obligations	765	0
Current Obligations under Capital Leases	31	40
Accounts Payable and Miscellaneous Accrued Liabilities	1,617	1,634
Air Traffic Liability	1,224	1,442
Income and Excise Taxes Payable	1,049	614
Accrued Salaries and Related Benefits	1,121	1,170
Accrued Rent	336	283
Total Current Liabilities	6,403	5,245
Noncurrent Liabilities:		
Long-Term Debt	7,781	5,797
Long-Term Debt Issued by Massachusetts Port Authority	498	0
Capital Leases	68	99
Postretirement Benefits	2,292	2,026
Accrued Rent	781	721
Deferred Income Taxes	465	1,220
Other	464	388
Total Noncurrent Liabilities	12,349	10,251
Deferred Credits:		
Deferred Gains on Sale and Leaseback Transactions	519	568
Manufacturers' and Other Credits	310	290
Total Deferred Credits	829	858
Series B ESOP Convertible Preferred Stock	452	460
Unearned Compensation under ESOP	(197)	(226)
Total Employee Stock Ownership Plan Preferred Stock	255	234
Shareowners' Equity:		
Common Stock	271	271
Additional Paid-in Capital	3,267	3,264
Retained Earnings	2,930	4,176
Accumulated Other Comprehensive Income	25	360
Treasury Stock at Cost	(2,724)	(2,728)
Total Shareowners' Equity	3,769	5,343
Total Liabilities and Shareowners' Equity	23,605	21,931

Note: Parentheses denote negative numbers.

Exhibit 4.6   Delta Air Lines Income Statements (in Millions of Dollars for Period Ended December)

	2001	2000	1999
Operating Revenues:			
Passenger	12,964	15,657	13,949
Cargo	506	583	561
Other, Net	409	501	373
Total Operating Revenues	13,879	16,741	14,883
Operating Expenses:			
Salaries and Related Costs	6,124	5,971	5,194
Aircraft Fuel	1,817	1,969	1,421
Depreciation and Amortization	1,283	1,187	1,057
Other Selling Expenses	616	688	626
Passenger Commissions	540	661	784
Contracted Services	1,016	966	824
Landing Fees and Other Rents	780	771	723
Aircraft Rent	737	741	622
Aircraft Maintenance Materials and Outside Repairs	801	723	594
Passenger Service	466	470	498
Asset Writedowns and Other Nonrecurring Items	1,119	108	469
Stabilization Act Compensation	(634)	0	0
Other	816	849	753
Total Operating Expenses	15,481	15,104	13,565
Operating Income (Loss)	(1,602)	1,637	1,318
Other Income (Expense):			
Interest Expense, Net	(410)	(257)	(126)
Net Gain from Sale of Investments	127	301	927
Miscellaneous Income (Expense), Net	(47)	27	(26)
Fair Value Adjustments of SFAS 133 Derivatives	68	(159)	0
Total Other Income (Expense)	(262)	(88)	775
Income (Loss) before Income Taxes and Accounting Change	(1,864)	1,549	2,093
Income Tax Benefit (Provision)	648	(621)	(831)
Net Income (Loss) before Accounting Change	(1,216)	928	1,262
Cumulative Effect of Accounting Change	0	(100)	(54)
Net Income (Loss)	(1,216)	828	1,208

Note: Parentheses denote negative numbers.

flows. Delta provides these data in footnote 10 of its 2001 annual report. In that footnote, we learn that the minimum rental commitments are:

Year	Cash Flow
2002	$1,271
2003	1,238
2004	1,197
2005	1,177
2006	1,144
After 2006	8,068

We assume that the cash flows after 2006 occur at the same level as 2006 until a residual remains; that amount goes in the last year. Accordingly, the future cash flows are:

Year	Cash Flow
2002	$1,271
2003	1,238
2004	1,197
2005	1,177
2006	1,144
2007	1,144
2008	1,144
2009	1,144
2010	1,144
2011	1,144
2012	1,144
2013	1,144
2014	60

Notice that the cash flows in the seven years from 2007 to 2013 are seven times $1,144, or $8,008. That leaves only $60 as a cash flow in the year 2014.

The second step in this adjustment process is to ascertain an interest rate with which to discount these cash flows. If the managers tell us the rate for discounting the capital leases, then that would be a good rate to use. Otherwise, we need to search the footnotes for a description of the firm's debts and the interest rates and attempt to find a comparable financial risk, using the interest rate associated with that debt. Delta does not inform us of the rate used in discounting the cash flows in its capital leases, so we go to footnote 8, which describes its debt. After reading that footnote, we shall assume that an appropriate rate is 7.5 percent.

From step 1, we have the cash flows, and from step 2, we have an approximate interest rate. We shall assume that the cash flows occur annually at the end of the year. Discounting the cash flows of the operating leases at 7.5 percent, we obtain a present value of $10,439 as the capitalized value. We use this capitalized value as the value of the property and the value of the total lease obligation. The latter can be partitioned into the current and noncurrent portions by looking at next year's (2002) cash payment, which will be $1,271. The present value of $1,271 equals $1,182, and this becomes the incremental current liability. The rest of the obligation is $10,439 less $1,182, or $9,257, and it represents the addition to long-term liabilities.

We shall assume a life of 15 years for the aircraft, which seems consistent with the firm's depreciation policy. That means straight-line depreciation will be $10,439 divided by 15 years, for $696 per annum. These are not new leases, by assumption, so we guess how old they are. The easiest way to compute the average age of the assets is to divide the cost of the property and equipment already on the books by their depreciation. Using this ratio, we calculate the average age of Delta's aircraft as 5.17 years, so accumulated depreciation is 5.17 times $696, or $3,597. The analyst adds this year's depreciation of $696 to the income statement; the incremental depreciation will also affect retained earnings. The rest of the accumulated depreciation ($3,597 less $696 equals $2,901) reflects depreciation from previous years and will require an adjustment to deferred income taxes; we discuss this modification when we talk about what happens to income tax expense.

While we take out rental expense of $1,300 and add in depreciation expense of $696, we also have to estimate the interest expense. This fifth step is a bit trickier since it requires knowing the beginning balance in leases, but no one can figure this out without knowing what leases have terminated and begun during the year. We overcome this problem by assuming that all of the leases were in operation at the beginning of the year and are continuing after this year. With this assumption, the only thing that can affect the lease balance would be interest expense (which adds to the balance) and cash payments (which naturally reduce the amount owed.) Thus,

$$\text{Lease obligation}_{BOY} + .075 \text{ Lease obligation}_{BOY} - \text{cash payment} = \text{Lease obligation}_{EOY}$$

where BOY denotes "beginning of the year" and EOY "end of the year." Substituting into this equation the cash payment of $1,300 and the end-of-year balance in the lease obligation of $10,439, we compute the beginning-of-the-year balance as $10,920. Now we can estimate interest expense as 7.5 percent of $10,920, or $819.

Step 6 concerns income tax expense. From the adjustments made thus far, the impact on earnings before taxes is to increase it $1,300 for rent expense and decrease it $696 for depreciation and $819 for interest. The net impact on earnings before taxes is thus a decrease of $215. The tax rate is about 35 percent, which we glean from the tax footnote, so the change in income tax expense is a decrease of 35 percent of $215, or $75. Even though income tax expense varies, nothing here modifies the tax liabilities to the federal, state, local, and international authorities; therefore, the decrease in income tax expense of $75 corresponds with a decrease of $75 in deferred income taxes. In addition, the change in previous years' depreciation must also affect deferred taxes. Since we increase old depreciation by $2,901, we have a further decrease in deferred income taxes of 35 percent of $2,901, or $1,015.

Putting this together, net income in 2001 lowers by $140, computed as (parentheses denote a decrease in the account):

Rent expense	$ (1,300)
Interest expense	819
Depreciation expense	696
Income tax expense	(75)
Net income	$ (140)

The assets of Delta Air Lines increase by $6,842:

Leased assets	$10,439
Accumulated depreciation	3,597
	$ 6,842

Liabilities and stockholders also change by $6,842.

Current liabilities	$ 1,182
Long-term liabilities	9,257
Deferred income taxes	(1,090)
Total liabilities	$ 9,349
Retained earnings (plug)	(2,507)
Debt plus equities	$ 6,842

These effects are summarized in Exhibit 4.7. In addition, we adjust Delta's numbers for 2000 and report them in the exhibit.

Whew! What a lot of work! Admittedly, we had to make a number of assumptions to get to this point, but at least we are including the effects of all of the leasing financial commitments contracted by Delta Air Lines. If the managers would do this in the first

Exhibit 4.7   Adjustments to Delta's Financial Statements (Capitalizing All Leases) (in Millions of Dollars for Period Ended December)

	As Reported		Adjusted	
	2001	**2000**	**2001**	**2000**
Total Assets	23,605	21,931	30,447	28,528
Current Debts	6,403	5,245	7,585	6,454
Long-Term Debts	12,349	10,251	20,523	18,460
Total Debts	19,581	16,354	28,930	25,772
Stockholders' Equity	4,024	5,577	1,517	3,197
Interest Expense (Revenue)	(410)	(257)	409	602
Net Income	(1,216)	828	(1,356)	652

place, investors and financial analysts would not have to guess these details. While some of these assumptions may be incorrect, we are at least in the ballpark when all leases are capitalized. More precise models exist for adjusting leases, but they are even more complex. The real question is whether these analytical adjustments have been worth the work. Have they provided any new insights into Delta?

Results of Capitalizing Leases

The process of adjusting operating leases as if the firm had applied capital lease accounting was conducted for 2001 and 2000 for American Airlines, Continental, Delta, Northwest, Southwest, and United. The results are contained in Exhibit 4.8. This exhibit reports several financial ratios calculated with the reported numbers and with the adjusted numbers.

As can be observed, the current ratio declines in all cases. This is understandable since current assets stay constant for each company while current liabilities increase as a consequence of the additional lease obligation.

Return on assets generally shows little change. Return on equity sometimes reveals small changes, as with Southwest, but at other times shows bigger changes, as with American Airlines in 2001. Interestingly, some adjusted return-on-equity values show increases, such as Continental in 2000. This increase occurs because the equity is reduced to a rather small number.

Exhibit 4.8   Results of Capitalizing Leases for Six Airline Companies

	As Reported		Adjusted	
	2001	2000	2001	2000
American Airlines				
Current Ratio	0.90	0.65	0.77	0.53
Return on Assets	−0.06	0.03	−0.04	0.02
Return on Equity	−0.43	0.15	−1.18	0.17
Debt to Equity	6.95	3.21	25.31	9.69
Debt to Common Equity	N/A	72.41	N/A	N/A
Debt to Total Capital	0.82	0.72	0.93	0.88
Continental Airlines				
Current Ratio	0.67	0.83	0.53	0.65
Return on Assets	−0.03	0.02	−0.01	0.02
Return on Equity	−0.07	0.30	−0.58	0.46
Debt to Equity	7.43	6.54	40.02	48.20
Debt to Common Equity	7.43	6.54	40.02	48.20
Debt to Total Capital	0.88	0.83	0.99	0.96

Exhibit 4.8 *(Continued)*

	As Reported		Adjusted	
	2001	2000	2001	2000
Delta Air Lines				
Current Ratio	0.56	0.61	0.47	0.50
Return on Assets	−0.06	0.03	−0.04	0.03
Return on Equity	−0.31	0.15	−0.69	0.20
Debt to Equity	4.87	2.93	14.54	8.06
Debt to Common Equity	5.20	3.06	16.67	8.70
Debt to Total Capital	0.83	0.75	0.95	0.90
Northwest Airlines				
Current Ratio	0.91	0.57	0.79	0.49
Return on Assets	−0.01	0.04	−0.02	0.02
Return on Equity	−1.47	0.25	N/A	N/A
Debt to Equity	43.98	9.65	N/A	N/A
Debt to Common Equity	N/A	42.67	N/A	N/A
Debt to Total Capital	0.98	0.91	1.05	1.01
Southwest Airlines				
Current Ratio	1.13	0.64	1.00	0.51
Return on Assets	0.06	0.10	0.06	0.08
Return on Equity	0.13	0.18	0.14	0.20
Debt to Equity	1.24	0.93	1.84	1.67
Debt to Common Equity	1.24	0.93	1.84	1.67
Debt to Total Capital	0.55	0.48	0.66	0.64
United Airlines				
Current Ratio	0.63	0.73	0.53	0.61
Return on Assets	−0.07	0.01	−0.06	0.00
Return on Equity	−0.67	0.01	−3.02	−0.14
Debt to Equity	6.85	3.16	43.07	11.23
Debt to Common Equity	7.25	3.39	53.82	12.92
Debt to Total Capital	0.87	0.76	0.99	0.93

Debt-to-equity ratios generally display increases, but some values are not meaningful. For instance, observe the Northwest panel in Exhibit 4.8. Equity turns negative once the analytical adjustments are completed. Once that happens, the ratio does not take on any meaningful value.

The last ratio in Exhibit 4.8 is perhaps the most telling, given the purposes of this book. In all cases, the debt-to-total capital (or total assets) ratio goes up. Southwest has the lowest debt/total assets on both reported and adjusted numbers. Northwest, however, has the highest debt/total assets on both sets of numbers. While Northwest's values are very high to begin with, the adjusted values unambiguously demonstrate that the airline is technically insolvent.

We can also discern that changes in the debt-to-total capital ratio range from 10 to 15 percentage points (except for Northwest, which already possesses incredibly high amounts of debt in its financial structure). By employing analytical adjustments, however, we have uncovered the true economic picture and have discovered the legerdemain. While a lot of work, these analytical adjustments prove useful in perceiving what is really going on.

United Airlines declared corporate bankruptcy on December 9, 2002.[8] The ratios in Exhibit 4.8 tell us why—United has very little equity and has been heading in the wrong direction, even before September 11. The adjusted debt-to-total capital ratio shows that equity makes up only 1 percent of the firm's financial structure. By the time United managers filed for Chapter 11, the true equity was probably negative. US Airways filed for bankruptcy on August 11[9]; it too was overladen with debt. In the meantime, most of the remaining firms in the industry are trying to restructure their business, for example, by asking workers to delay pay raises.[10]

SUMMARY AND CONCLUSION

Lease obligations matter. Because debt is important to investors and creditors, many managers of business enterprises have engaged in schemes to underreport the truth. The FASB attempted to deal with lease accounting but left many opportunities for creative accounting. The good news is that if the managers report the truth in the footnotes, investors and creditors and their agents can transform the financial statements into a set of numbers that are more accurate and more revealing. Doing so requires making a number of assumptions and clearly takes some work, but the adjusted data are usually worth it.

Use of operating lease accounting "gains" the managers an understatement of their firm's financial structure by 10 to 15 percentage points. Given that investors and creditors and their analysts can unravel this truth, it seems likely that the investment community charges the airline industry for the costs necessary to transform reported numbers into the truth and for the risks that something might be missing that would help in the unraveling process. Appropriately, investors and creditors charge a premium for the financial reporting risk. The cost of capital goes up and stock prices and bond prices go down.

Meeting the spirit of Statement No. 13 and not merely the mangled letter of the law would be very refreshing. Are any managers willing to quit playing games with lease accounting? Are any directors, general counsel, and auditors willing to assist them?

NOTES

1. A short history of lease accounting is given by H. I. Wolk, J. R. Francis, and M. G. Tearney, *Accounting Theory: A Conceptual and Institutional Approach,* 3rd ed. (Cincinnati, OH: South-Western Publishing,1992), pp. 510–544.

2. These cash flows are called rents because the major application when these formulas were first conceived was in the renting or leasing business. Renters or lessees would pay (say) monthly cash flows, and these were called rents. So today the cash flows are called rents, whether the application is renting or something else.

3. Details about lease accounting can be found in: D. E. Kieso, J. J. Weygandt, and T. D. Warfield, *Intermediate Accounting,* 10th ed. (New York: John Wiley & Sons, 2001), pp. 1189–1252; L. Revsine, D. W. Collins, and W. B. Johnson, *Financial Reporting and Analysis,* 2nd ed. (Upper Saddle River, NJ: Prentice-Hall, 2002), pp. 575–628; and G. I. White, A. C. Sondhi, and D. Fried, *The Analysis and Use of Financial Statements,* 2nd ed. (New York: John Wiley & Sons, 1998), pp. 531–547. Also worth reading are P. R. Delaney, B. J. Epstein, J. A. Adler, and M. F. Foran, *GAAP 2000: Interpretation and Application of Generally Accepted Accounting Principles 2000* (New York: John Wiley & Sons, 2000), pp. 515–572; G. Georgiades, *Miller GAAP Financial Statement Disclosures Manual* (New York: Aspen, 2001), section 17.01; and B. D. Jarnagin, *2001 U.S. Master GAAP Guide* (Chicago: CCH, 2000), pp. 739–870.

4. The Association for Investment Management and Research (AIMR) is a professional organization of chartered financial analysts. The AIMR promotes the capitalization of all leases: *Financial Reporting in the 1990s and Beyond* (Charlottesville, VA: AIMR, 1993), pp. 49–50.

5. In Excel, this monthly (or quarterly or whatever) rental is easily found by applying the PPMT function. Financial calculators also can solve for the monthly rental by inputting the fair value of the property (which is the present value), the interest rate, and the number of periods in the lease.

6. Lessors like guaranteed residual values, for the guarantees provide some protection against abuse from lessees. Lessees, as stated, prefer not to have guaranteed residual values. Both parties can be satisfied by hiring third parties to come in and insure the residual value to the lessor. It is incredible to what lengths some managers will go just for the sake of deceiving investors and creditors about the extent of their financial structure.

7. In *Analysis and Use of Financial Statements,* 2nd ed., White, Sondhi, and Fried discuss one process for making these analytical adjustments, though they restrict themselves only to obtaining the present value of the operating leases (pp. 541–547). We extend their technique by considering distributive effects as well by including the value of the leased property less its accumulated depreciation in the assets section of the balance sheet, dividing the present value of the operating leases into a current and a long-term portion in the liabilities section, replacing rent expense with interest expense and depreciation on the income statement, and considering the changes to income tax expense and deferred income taxes.

8. "UAL Files for Creditor Shield But Vows to Keep Flying," *Wall Street Journal,* December 9, 2002.

9. C. H. Sieroty, "US Airways Files for Chapter 11," *Washington Times,* August 11, 2002; M. Maynard, "US Airways to Cut Costs $1.8 Billion a Year," *New York Times,* December 22, 2002.

10. S. McCartney, "American Air Asks Workers to Forgo Pay Raises in 2003," *Wall Street Journal,* December 9, 2002.

CHAPTER FIVE

How to Hide Debt with Pension Accounting

Pensions involve promises made to employees that if they work for the company over some minimum period of time, then they will receive cash payments during their retirement years. As such, pensions serve as additional compensation for employees. At the same time, however, the business enterprise enters into financial commitments that financial statement users need to perceive if they are going to analyze the firm properly and accurately.

Pension accounting takes credit for being one of the most difficult segments of financial accounting to master. We can clearly see its importance by examining corporate financial reports and noticing how large these items can be. What becomes critical is to understand how much larger pension liabilities can be if netting were not allowed. In addition, the Financial Accounting Standards Board (FASB) has introduced unwarranted smoothing into the accounting process, which distorts the income statement; proper analysis requires unsmoothing these items. Presumably, the FASB introduced these compromises to pacify some objectors to truthful reporting in the pension area.

For years, most pension liabilities did not appear on the balance sheets. The FASB tried to improve the situation, for some firms were committing millions and even billions of dollars to these pension plans, and the FASB correctly believed that these amounts should appear in the financial statements. Pension accounting hit the scene in 1985, when the FASB issued Statements No. 87 and 88. The idea under both is that the employer should report what it owes its employees, in present value terms, and it should report the fair value of the assets held in the pension plan. Among other things, displaying these two items allows readers to comprehend whether the pension plan is overfunded or underfunded and by how much. Statement No. 87 deals with how the corporation accounts for the pension plan, and I shall concentrate on the basics of that statement. FASB Statement No. 88 handles curtailments and terminations of pension plans, which, although important, I shall not discuss in this chapter. While these statements have been major improvements of previous accounting rules, they still contain large loopholes.[1]

Pension accounting affects the income statement, the balance sheet, and the cash flow statement. Because of the emphasis on hiding liabilities from the balance sheet, I shall concentrate on the balance sheet disclosure of pension obligations and pension assets. Similar to the equity method, which allows investee liabilities to be netted against investee assets, I will show that the FASB allows business enterprises to net pension assets against pension liabilities. This is inappropriate inasmuch as corporate managers have some discretion to remove assets from the pension plan. The netting gives people the illusion that the assets will be there to cover the pension liabilities, but that is not necessarily true.

I should also point out that pension plans are a type of special-purpose entity (SPE), even though many observers do not think of them as such. The FASB's definition of SPEs, which is covered in the next chapter, would include pension plans except for their specific exclusion. When a corporation has a pension plan, it creates this special entity and has significant control over its operations, despite the fact that the federal and state governments have many laws that prescribe and proscribe various activities in an attempt to protect the workers. The pension entity itself has a specific function to carry out, it has only certain types of assets, and it has only certain kinds of debt. As such, the pension plan looks like and smells like an SPE. I say more about this in Chapter 6.

In addition to pensions, business enterprises sometimes promise *other postemployment benefits,* such as health plans. In accounting lingo, these other postemployment benefits are termed *OPEBs.* In Statement No. 106, issued in 1990, the FASB requires firms to account for these OPEBs. Operationally, there are some significant differences between pension plans and OPEBs, but the FASB mandates essentially the same type of accounting for both. I shall discuss accounting for these items as well, although the emphasis will be on pension plans.

As stated earlier, the accounting for pensions and OPEBs is like the equity method in that the FASB allows corporations to net the relevant assets against the relevant liabilities. Consistent with discussions in the previous two chapters, I propose some analytical adjustments that will present a clearer picture of the firm's economic condition.

Standard & Poor's (S&P's) provides testimony that the FASB pronouncements are deficient.[2] Since it seems that the FASB and the Securities and Exchange Commission (SEC) will not take action, S&P's decided that it would make some analytical adjustments on its own. Recently it began computing what it terms "core earnings" to get around the shenanigans played by so many managers. One of the adjustments made by S&P's is to use the actual pension fund returns instead of the expected returns. This simple adjustment helps investors and creditors obtain a more accurate picture of corporate performance, and it underscores the absolute necessity for investors and creditors to understand pension accounting—unless they once again desire to be Enronized.

This chapter investigates how corporations account for pension plans and other postretirement benefits, including how managers lower their reported financial structures. The first section defines some terms, especially differentiating between defined benefit plans and defined contribution plans. The next section covers some basic pension computations that depend heavily on present value concepts (readers in need of a brush-up should review that material in Chapter 4). The next section describes a few important complications. Then I demonstrate an easy way to disentangle the numbers and obtain a better representation of the firm, illustrating this process with General Mills. The last section of this chapter reports the results from performing analytical adjustments on a variety of entities. The conclusion is that some firms have little change in their financial structures, while others show significant differences.

DEFINITIONS AND CONCEPTS UNDERLYING PENSION PLANS

Players

A *pension plan* is an agreement between the employer and the employees such that, under prespecified conditions, the employer provides for cash payments to the employees when they retire. Because of abuses against workers, Congress passed the Employee Retirement Income Security Act (ERISA) in 1974. In turn, ERISA created the Pension Benefit Guaranty Corporation (PBGC), which oversees certain aspects of pension plans; for example, it ensures that corporations with certain types of pension plans contribute at least minimum amounts to those plans. The OPEBs address other benefits—in practice, these benefits primarily involve health plans—but there is no law governing corporate use of OPEBs in the way that ERISA impacts pension plans.

Exhibit 5.1 displays a schematic for a typical pension plan. The business enterprise constructs a plan with its employees and lays out the details with them. The employees may be organized in a union, in which case the pension plan likely results from a negotiation process between the business enterprise and the union.[3] Here we assume that the plan has been approved between the two parties.

The employer or business enterprise carries out two main functions. The recording function determines in the aggregate the amount of the pension expense, the pension assets, and the pension liabilities. Once these items are computed, the firm records some of them in its books and reports them in the financial statements. The company also decides how much cash to contribute to the pension plan. Keep in mind that the corporation does not directly pay the employees; rather, the entity contributes cash to the pension plan, which in turn pays the retired workers whatever the agreement says. The PBGC and ERISA specify the minimum amount that the corporation must contribute to

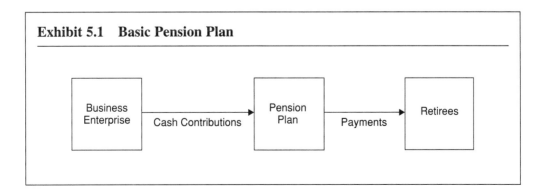

Exhibit 5.1   Basic Pension Plan

the pension plan. Of course, the corporation records the cash flow to the pension plan in its own books.

The pension plan is itself a business entity. It receives cash from the employer, and it invests this money in stocks and bonds and other investments. ERISA requires these investments to be placed into low-risk assets so that employee pension funds will be protected.[4] Earnings from these investments are added to the pension assets. The pension fund also has the responsibility to pay out funds to retirees. Of course, the plan must account for these transactions between itself and the employer, its investments and its returns on the investments, and those transactions between itself and the qualified former employees. Reports of many pension plans must be filed with the SEC.[5]

The retirees, of course, receive the cash benefits from the pension plan. As stated before, the corporation establishes these amounts in the terms of the pension contract.

Healthcare plans and other OPEBs usually are not structured like the pension plan in Exhibit 5.1. Instead, the firm either determines and makes the payments to the employees, or it outsources this activity to some independent firm, such as an insurance firm. There are no special reporting requirements for healthcare plans.

Types of Pension Plans

Employees become *vested* in a pension plan when they earn the right to receive funds from the company upon retirement. If the plan does not require the employees to ante up money into the pension fund, the plan is *noncontributory*. Those plans that require some payment by the employees are termed *contributory* plans. In a *funded* retirement plan, the employer sends money to an independent entity, which then handles the investments and the disbursements of funds to employees. If the employer keeps control over the pension funds, the plan is called *unfunded*. Note that these latter terms should not be confused with *funding policy*, which refers to the employer's decisions about the amounts and the timing of disbursing funds to the pension plan. The plan is *overfunded* if the pension assets exceed the pension liabilities but *underfunded* when the reverse is true.

There are two major types of pension plans: defined contribution plans and defined benefit plans. In a *defined contribution plan,* the employer (and sometimes the employee as well) promises to contribute so much money into the pension fund, the amounts and the timing determined by the arrangement between employer and employees. The pension plan uses the funds to make investments until the employee retires. How much money the employee receives upon retirement depends on how much money the employer contributed to the plan and how well the plan managed its investments. There is no guaranteed amount of money to be received by the retiree.

Accounting for and reporting on defined contribution plans are easy. The accountant ascertains how much the employer needs to contribute to the plan and records this short-term payable. The firm then pays this cash to the pension plan, and the accountant records the cash outflow and the reduction in the short-term payable. The key point is that the business enterprise has no long-term payable for how much the retired employees deserve, for the firm has incurred no such obligation.

Exhibit 5.2 shows the disclosure by Starbucks about its defined contribution plan. Starbucks supplies a brief description about the mechanics of the pension plan and

---

Exhibit 5.2   Defined Contribution Plan Disclosure (from Starbucks 10K Dated September 30, 2001)

Defined Contribution Plans

Starbucks maintains voluntary defined contribution plans covering eligible employees as defined in the plan documents. Participating employees may elect to defer and contribute a percentage of their compensation to the plan, not to exceed the dollar amount set by law. For certain plans, the Company matches 25 percent of each employee's eligible contribution up to a maximum of the first 4 percent of each employee's compensation.

The Company's matching contributions to the plans were approximately $1.6 million, $1.1 million, and $0.9 million for fiscal 2001, 2000, and 1999, respectively.

---

reveals the amounts of the cash contributions to the pension plan. That tells the whole story under a defined contribution plan. Because these plans do not involve hidden debt, I say little more about them.

A *defined benefit plan* is one in which the employer promises to pay so much when employees retire, the amounts determined by the arrangement between the employer and the employees. The employer has considerable flexibility in deciding how much and when the cash contributions are paid to the pension plan, of course subject to the requirements of ERISA and PGBC. Unlike defined contribution plans, defined benefit plans encumber employers with long-term liabilities because they are in fact promising to pay their employees certain guaranteed amounts. Measuring this liability and the year-to-year costs is a major challenge to accountants. Appreciating this pension debt is critical to investors and creditors, who also need to comprehend some of the arbitrary rules concerning pension costs and concerning the inappropriate netting of pension assets and pension liabilities.

To quickly grasp the enormous difference between defined contribution plans and defined benefit plans, read the disclosure by General Mills in Exhibit 5.3. Note the complexity of this disclosure versus the simple disclosure by Starbucks in Exhibit 5.2. In this footnote to its annual report (10K), General Mills describes briefly its defined benefit plan. Afterward, it divulges the fair value of the pension assets and the projected benefit obligation, including their components, and then nets them to what is called the "funding status" of the pension plan. General Mills then provides three line items unrecognized in the accounts. Later it discloses the assumptions it made when computing these various components. Last, the firm states what it recognizes as pension cost, showing the various details behind that calculation.

Accounting for OPEBs is virtually the same as the accounting for defined benefit pension plans. Most U.S. companies do not set aside cash for these healthcare and other plans, so the fair value of the assets is zero; General Mills is an exception to this observation. Exhibit 5.3 also contains a typical set of disclosures. Notice that since the accounting for OPEBs is so much like that of defined benefit pension plans, the two can be reported together in the footnote schedules.

The fundamental difference between these two types of plans is who bears the risks of not having enough assets in the plan when workers retire. In defined benefit plans, the corporation bears the risk. If there is a shortfall, the employer must make up the difference. In defined contribution plans, the employees bear the risk. When there is a shortfall, then the workers obtain less cash during their retirement years.

Exhibit 5.3 Defined-Benefit Plan Disclosure (from General Mills 10K Dated May 25, 2002)

14. Retirement and Other Postretirement Benefit Plans

We have defined-benefit retirement plans covering most employees. Benefits for salaried employees are based on length of service and final average compensation. The hourly plans include various monthly amounts for each year of credited service. Our funding policy is consistent with the requirements of federal law. Our principal retirement plan covering salaried employees has a provision that any excess pension assets would vest in plan participants if the plan is terminated within five years of a change in control.

We sponsor plans that provide health-care benefits to the majority of our retirees. The salaried health-care benefit plan is contributory, with retiree contributions based on years of service. We fund related trusts for certain employees and retirees on an annual basis.

Trust assets related to the above plans consist principally of listed equity securities, corporate obligations and U.S. government securities.

Reconciliation of the funded status of the plans and the amounts included in the balance sheet are as follows:

	Pension Plans		Postretirement Benefit Plans	
In Millions	**2002**	**2001**	**2002**	**2001**
Fair Value of Plan Assets				
Beginning fair value	$1,606	$1,578	$237	$230
Actual return on assets	(2)	83	(10)	(2)
Acquisition	1,167	—	—	—
Company contributions	7	11	29	28
Plan participant contributions	—	—	5	2
Benefits paid from plan assets	(107)	(66)	(28)	(21)
Ending Fair Value	$2,671	$1,606	$233	$237

Note: Parentheses denote negative numbers.

Exhibit 5.3 *(Continued)*

In Millions	Pension Plans		Postretirement Benefit Plans	
	2002	2001	2002	2001
Projected Benefit Obligation				
Beginning obligations	$1,077	$958	$286	$231
Service cost	34	18	11	6
Interest cost	122	79	33	21
Plan amendment	21	1	(13)	—
Curtailment	5	—	2	—
Plan participant contributions	—	—	5	2
Actuarial loss (gain)	(15)	87	72	42
Acquisition	963	—	248	—
Actual benefits paid	(107)	(66)	(33)	(16)
Ending Obligations	$2,100	$1,077	$611	$286
Funded Status of Plans	$571	$529	$(378)	$(49)
Unrecognized actuarial loss	334	106	154	59
Unrecognized prior service				
Costs (credits)	49	36	(17)	(5)
Unrecognized transition asset	(3)	(18)	—	—
Net Amount Recognized	$951	$653	$(241)	$5
Amounts Recognized on Balance Sheets				
Prepaid asset	$1,001	$677	$82	$75
Accrued liability	(62)	(44)	(323)	(70)
Intangible asset	—	1	—	—
Minimum liability adjustment in equity	12	19		
Net Amount Recognized	$951	$653	$(241)	$5

Assumptions as of year-end are:

	Pension Plans		Postretirement Benefit Plans	
	2002	2001	2002	2001
Discount rate	7.50%	7.75%	7.50%	7.75%
Rate of return on plan assets	10.4	10.4	10.0	10.0
Salary increases	4.4	4.4	—	—
Annual increase in cost of benefits	—	—	8.3	6.6

Exhibit 5.3 *(Continued)*

The annual increase in cost of postretirement benefits is assumed to decrease gradually in future years, reaching an ultimate rate of 5.2 percent in the year 2007.

Components of net benefit (income) or expense each year are as follows:

In Millions	Pension Plans			Postretirement Benefit Plans		
	2002	2001	2000	2002	2001	2000
Service cost	$34	$18	$20	$11	$6	$6
Interest cost	122	79	69	33	21	17
Expected return on plan assets	(241)	(159)	(142)	(23)	(23)	(22)
Amortization of transition asset	(15)	(15)	(14)	—	—	—
Amortization of (gains) losses	2	2	1	3	1	1
Amortization of prior service costs (credits)	8	6	6	(1)	(2)	(2)
Settlement or curtailment losses	5	—	—	2	—	—
(Income) expense	$(85)	$(69)	$(60)	$25	$3	$—

Assumed trend rates for health-care costs have an important effect on the amounts reported for the postretirement benefit plans. If the health-care cost trend rate increased by 1 percentage point in each future year, the aggregate of the service and interest cost components of postretirement expense would increase for 2002 by $5 million, and the postretirement accumulated benefit obligation as of May 26, 2002, would increase by $51 million. If the health-care cost trend rate decreased by 1 percentage point in each future year, the aggregate of the service and interest cost components of postretirement expense would decrease for 2002 by $4 million, and the postretirement accumulated benefit obligation as of May 26, 2002, would decrease by $44 million.

Corporate Pension Highlights

These remarks help us understand recent corporate events with respect to pensions and OPEBs. As I discuss in more detail later in this chapter, pension costs are a function of what the firm promises to its employees, the interest rate, and changes to the pension plan. In addition, as the pension fund generates returns, these gains reduce the pension cost. (Losses, of course, would increase the pension cost.) A few months ago, Northwest Airlines reported that its pension costs would exceed $700 million in the fourth quarter.[6] Chevron Texaco will take a pension hit of $500 million.[7] In particular, the weak financial markets will depress earnings by pension funds and thus boost pension costs. Cassell Bryan-Low maintains that this fragility by pension funds will have a major impact on AMR, Delta Air Lines, Avaya, Goodyear, General Motors, Delphi, Navistar, and Ford.[8]

The balance sheets are also under attack. The PBGC states that unfunded pension liabilities increased from $26 billion in 2000 to $111 billion in 2001.[9] This fourfold increase in pension debts foreshadows some potentially dramatic problems in corporate America and on Wall Street unless either business enterprises can pump cash into the pension plans or the economy rebounds sufficiently to produce good returns on the pension assets.

The cash flow statement can be severely impacted as well, as General Motors recently added $2.6 billion into its pension fund.[10] IBM has contributed close to $4 billion, Ford will put up almost $1 billion, and many other corporations will have to make up the shortfalls.

These ideas also help us understand why so many companies in recent years have modified their pension plans. For example, IBM announced in 2000 that it would shift from its traditional defined benefit pension plan to a cash-balance plan.[11] Recently Delta Air Lines did the same.[12] Traditional defined benefit plans determine the pensions as a function of the employees' last years of work, while cash-balance plans compute the pension payments on the basis of the average salary earned over the employee's entire career with the firm. This change reduces the benefits to the workers and so reduces pension costs to the firms.

Yet another tactic is tapping an underfunded pension plan by selling it the firm's stock, which Navistar recently did.[13] This is an interesting way of taking a weak pension plan and making it weaker. Not only does management take cash out of the pension plan so less cash is available to the retirees, but also the pension plan is left with the less valuable and undiversified stock of the company.

BRIEF OVERVIEW OF PENSION ACCOUNTING[14]

Basic Example

This section continues to focus on defined benefit plans, and I develop the concepts through an example. Nittany Fireworks begins operations with one employee named Red. Management offers Red suitable compensation plus a defined benefit pension package. The firm estimates that Red will work for five years, retire, and then live another five years. These projections have to be made so that the company can estimate how much it will owe him for the promised pension and estimate the cost to the business enterprise.[15]

For each year of work Red will receive $1,000 at the end of each year during retirement.[16] Further, Nittany Fireworks estimates an interest rate on pension obligations of 6 percent and that it can earn 10 percent on its pension assets. The funding policy of Nittany Fireworks is to contribute $2,000 at the end of each year that Red works for the company.

The *service cost* is the cost to the employer incurred as the result of the employee's working for the firm and earning pension benefits upon retirement. In the case of Nittany Fireworks, for each year that Red works, the company must pay him $1,000 per year during retirement, which we assume lasts five years. These cash flows are diagrammed in Exhibit 5.4. This diagram runs from time $t = -5$ (read "five years until

111

Exhibit 5.4 Present Value of Pension Payments

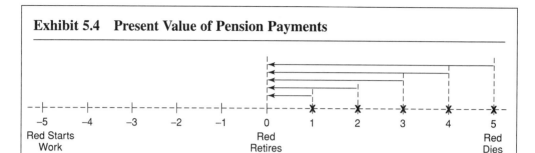

By agreement, for each year of work the pension pays the employee $1,000 at the end of each year during retirement. This forms an ordinary annuity where the rent is $1,000. With an interest rate of 6 percent, the present value of this ordinary annuity at $t = 0$ is $4,212.

To obtain the service cost for a particular year, discount this amount to the end of that year. For Red's first year of work, from $t = -5$ to $t = -4$, we discount $4,212 back four more years and the present value is $3,337. Likewise, we can discount the amount for each of the other years he works as well. We determine the service cost to be:

After first year of work:	$3,337
After second year of work:	3,537
After third year of work:	3,749
After fourth year of work:	3,974
After fifth year of work:	4,212

retirement"), when the employee begins working for the firm, until time $t = 5$ ("five years after retirement"), when the employee will die.[17]

As shown in Exhibit 5.4, there are five cash flows, one for each year during retirement. These cash flows constitute an ordinary annuity. With an interest rate of 6 percent, Nittany Fireworks would compute this present value as $4,212. But this present value is as of the date Red retires, when time $t = 0$. When Nittany Fireworks prepares its income statement for the year ending at $t = -4$, it will need to discount this amount back another four years. Treat the $4,212 as a single sum and discount it back four years at 6 percent, and the present value is $3,337; this is the service cost for that year. When Red works a second year, he will earn another pension benefit of a second $1,000 each year during retirement. To obtain the service cost for the next year, Nittany Fireworks will discount the $4,212 back to the year ending at $t = -3$, so the present value is $3,537. In like manner, Nittany Fireworks establishes that the service cost for Red's third, fourth, and fifth years of work is $3,749, $3,974, and $4,212.

The *projected benefit obligation* measures how much the business enterprise will have to pay out for the employee's pension in today's terms.[18] Projected benefit obligation and service cost are similar inasmuch as the entity determines the present value of the ordinary annuity at the date of retirement and then the present value of this amount for both constructs. The projected benefit obligation differs from the service cost because service cost quantifies the effects of only that year's impact on the pension commitments, while the projected obligation assesses the cumulative effect from all the years worked by the employees. Consider Red's second year of work. The service cost measures the present value of the incremental $1,000 per year he will receive during retirement, and this service cost is $3,537. To measure the projected benefit obligation, we must realize that Red will get $2,000 per year during retirement since he has worked two years for Nittany Fireworks, each year earning him $1,000 per year during retirement. The projected benefit obligation is a present value of $2,000 per year for five years, and this present value is $8,424 at time $t = 0$. Discounting this back for the financial statements ending time $t = -3$, the projected benefit obligation is $7,074. An easy shortcut for computing this is to multiply the numbers of years worked by the current year's service cost (2 times $3,537 equals $7,074). Similarly, the projected benefit obligation for the next three years is $11,247, $15,896, and $21,062, respectively.

Let us complete this basic pension example by adding other components, as depicted in Exhibit 5.5. We have already computed the service costs and the projected benefit obligations, and we copy them to the service cost column and to the projected benefit obligation column in this exhibit. The *interest cost* is the interest rate multiplied by the projected benefit obligation at the beginning of the year. In this case, it is 6 percent times these amounts. For example, for the second year, the interest cost is $3,337 times 6 percent for $200. The *expected return on plan assets* is 10 percent times the plan assets at the beginning of the year. For Nittany Fireworks' second year, the amount is 10 percent of $2,000, or $200. (That the service cost and the return on plan assets are equal is an artifact of this example—do not read anything special into this.) The *net pension cost* is the service cost for the year plus the interest cost minus the expected return on plan assets. For example, in the second year, the net pension cost is $3,537 plus $200 minus $200, for $3,537. This amount is shown on the income statement.

The *funding* is $2,000 in this example by assumption. In practice, managers can contribute anything they want as long as it is at least as much as ERISA requires.[19] The *prepaid pension cost* (an asset account) or *accrued pension cost* (a liability account) is the previous balance minus the net pension cost plus the funding. It is prepaid pension cost if this amount is positive but accrued pension cost if the amount is negative. We obtain $(2,874) in the second year as the previous balance of $(1,337) minus the net pension cost of $3,537 plus the funding of $2,000. Since this amount is shown on the balance sheet as an asset when positive and as a liability when negative, Nittany Fireworks has a liability of $2,874.

The *plan assets* equal the previous balance plus the expected return on plan assets plus any additional funding. For the second year, we have the previous balance of $2,000 plus the return of $200 plus additional funding of $2,000, for a new balance of $4,200. At this point, there is an internal check on our computations. The prepaid pension cost or accrued pension cost should equal the plan assets minus the projected benefit obligation.

While these items are important to comprehend pension accounting, only two of them go on the financial statements. The net pension cost or pension expense goes on the income statement, although its components are disclosed in the footnotes. If there is a

Exhibit 5.5 Basic Pension Example

End of Year	Service Cost	Interest Cost	Expected Return on Plan Assets	Net Pension Cost or Pension Expense	Funding	Prepaid Cost Pension Cost/Accrued Pension Cost	Projected Benefit Obligation	Plan Assets
First	3,337	0	0	3,337	2,000	(1,337)	3,337	2,000
Second	3,537	200	200	3,537	2,000	(2,874)	7,074	4,200
Third	3,749	424	420	3,753	2,000	(4,627)	11,247	6,620
Fourth	3,974	675	662	3,987	2,000	(6,614)	15,896	9,282
Fifth	4,212	954	928	4,238	2,000	(8,852)	21,062	12,210

Service cost computation is given in Exhibit 5.4.

Interest cost is 6 percent of the projected benefit obligation at the end of the previous year.

Expected return on plan assets is 10 percent of the plan assets at the end of the previous year.

Net pension cost equals the service cost plus the interest cost minus the expected return on the plan assets.

The prepaid or accrued pension cost equals the previous balance plus the net pension cost minus the funding.

Projected benefit obligation is the present value of all pension cash flows.

The plan assets equal the previous balance plus the expected return on plan assets plus the funding.

prepaid pension cost, it goes on the asset section of the balance sheet; if there is an accrued pension cost, it reaches the liability section of the balance sheet. The constituents of this asset or liability are also revealed in the footnotes.

Prior Service Cost

Often real-world pension plans are started after the corporation has been in existence for a while. The corporation might decide to grant employees some pension benefits based on their prior years' working for the enterprise. The cost for this generosity is termed the *prior service cost.*

Continuing with the above illustration, assume that Red has worked three years prior to the pension plan. Nittany Fireworks grants him three years toward his pension plan, so he will receive $3,000 per year ($1,000 for each year) during his retirement. Because of this prior service cost, the managers increase the yearly funding up to $4,000. All other assumptions remain the same, so this $3,000 each year for five years represents an ordinary annuity, which yields a present value at the date of retirement of $12,637. We discount this single sum back to time $t = -5$, and the present value is $9,443. This becomes the initial projected benefit obligation at the beginning of this year.

The new question is when to inject this prior service cost into the income statement. While it should go into the income statement in the year that this prior service commitment is made because that is when the cost is incurred, the FASB appeased managers by allowing them to add this cost into the income statement gradually over time. We shall amortize this amount on a straight-line basis over the rest of the period that the employee works for the firm, which is five years. Therefore, the amortization cost equals one-fifth of $9,443, or $1,889 per year. With these computations, we create a new pension schedule that is shown in Exhibit 5.6. As can be seen, this schedule is similar to that in Exhibit 5.5.

Nothing changes with respect to the service cost, so that column stays the same. The interest cost is computed the same as before. The numbers in this column are bigger than those in the previous exhibit since this example begins with a larger projected benefit obligation. The expected return on plan assets in Exhibit 5.6 is computed in the same way as in Exhibit 5.5. As explained, the amortization of the prior service cost is a constant $1,889. We amend the net pension cost, so that now it is the service cost plus the interest cost minus the expected return on plan assets plus the amortization of prior service cost. The funding is $4,000 per annum by assumption. The prepaid pension cost or accrued pension cost is the previous balance plus the funding minus the net pension cost. Both the projected benefit obligation and the plan assets are calculated in the same manner, making allowances for changes in the demonstration. Again, a built-in check exists, for the prepaid pension cost or accrued pension cost must equal the plan assets plus the unrecognized portion of the prior service cost minus the projected benefit obligation. Exhibit 5.6 also presents the unrecognized prior service cost, that is, the amount not yet admitted into pension expense.[20]

As before, only two of these constructs go on the financial statements. The net pension cost or pension expense goes on the income statement, and the prepaid pension cost or accrued pension cost enters the balance sheet. The other ingredients of this pension

Exhibit 5.6   Pension Example with Prior Service Cost

End of Year	Service Cost	Interest Cost	Return on Plan Assets	Amortization of Prior Service Cost	Net Pension Cost or Pension Expense	Funding	Prepaid Pension Cost/Accrued Pension Cost	Projected Benefit Obligation	Plan Assets	Unrecognized Prior Service Cost
								9,433	0	9,443
First	3,337	567	0	1,889	5,792	4,000	(1,792)	13,346	4,000	7,555
Second	3,537	801	400	1,889	5,826	4,000	(3,618)	17,684	8,400	5,666
Third	3,749	1,061	840	1,889	5,859	4,000	(5,477)	22,494	13,240	3,777
Fourth	3,974	1,350	1,324	1,889	5,888	4,000	(7,365)	27,817	18,564	1,889
Fifth	4,212	1,669	1,856	1,889	5,914	4,000	(9,279)	33,699	24,420	0

Notice that the prior service cost is $9,433 at the beginning of the first year, which is the initial projected benefit obligation.

Service cost computation is given in Exhibit 5.4.

Interest cost is 6 percent of the projected benefit obligation at the end of the previous year.

Expected return on plan assets is 10 percent of the plan assets at the end of the previous year.

The amortization of prior service cost is ⅕ of $9,433 or $1,889 per year.

Net pension cost equals the service cost plus the interest cost minus the expected return on the plan assets plus the amortization of the prior service cost.

The prepaid or accrued pension cost equals the previous balance plus the net pension cost minus the funding.

Projected benefit obligation is the previous balance plus the service cost plus the interest.

The plan assets equal the previous balance plus the expected return on plan assets plus the funding.

The unrecognized prior service cost is the previous amount less the current year's amortization of $1,889.

recipe can be found in the footnotes, including the unrecognized prior service cost. Exhibit 5.3 shows these accounts and others for General Mills.

Financial Statement Effects

The income statement for the basic example makes sense, but the amortization of the prior service cost does not. A more accurate view of what is going on requires investors and creditors and their analysts to adjust the reported numbers and place the entire quantity in the year of adoption. The smoothing that the FASB allows is arbitrary and irrational, for the amortization expense relates to nothing in those later years.

A second thing to notice on the income statement is the net pension cost includes the *expected* return on plan assets. It would seem that the actual return should be reported, as the actual numbers are purportedly used elsewhere in the financial report instead of some fantasy amounts. What the FASB did in SFAS No. 87 was permit entities to report the expected return as part of the pension expense and then compute pension gains or losses as the difference between the expected and actual returns on the plan assets. It gets worse, however, because the FASB permits business enterprises to amortize these gains and losses over a long period of time, thus obfuscating any bad news when it incurs pension losses.[21] In short, we cannot believe the pension costs that most corporations report, for the FASB engages in some fairy-tale magic. This fact also explains why I applaud S&P's use of actual returns when it determines core earnings of business entities.

The netting of the projected benefit obligation against the plan assets is likewise silly. Given that managers have some discretion for removing some of the assets from the pension plan, the netting is improper. A correct balance sheet would report these two accounts separately, as I shall illustrate later in the chapter.

Finally, the unamortized prior service cost is not recognized in any account. The entire prior service cost represents a commitment made by the managers of the corporation. Given that the firm has an obligation, the ethical thing to do is to report the debt rather than conceal it.

While the discussion has concentrated on pension accounting, the points generally apply to OPEBs as well. Some of the terminology differs between them, but the computations and the methods are the same. This fact becomes obvious by looking at the General Mills footnote in Exhibit 5.3 and observing that both pension plans and postretirement benefit plans can be put into the same schedule.

ADJUSTING PENSION ASSETS AND LIABILITIES

To obtain a better view of the business enterprise, readers should employ analytical adjustments. In this case, we shall adjust the balance sheet and ignore the effects on the income statement, except to the extent they affect stockholders' equity.[22] Unlike the equity method in Chapter 3 and accounting by lessees in Chapter 4, these adjustments may improve the reported numbers. Whether they in fact do this depends on whether the corporation is hiding pension gains or losses and amortization expenses.

Interest Rate Assumption

As the company performs the pension calculations, it must make some estimate of the interest rate on the projected benefit obligation and of the expected return on plan assets. The interest rate on the projected benefit obligation should be the rate that a third party would charge the company to settle the pension debt. In other words, if the business enterprise would pay another entity to take over its pension debt, the interest rate that would be embedded in that contract is the interest rate that the firm should use when computing the pension expense. This settlement could be accomplished by buying an annuity contract from an insurance company. The expected return on the plan assets ought to be the long-run return from interest, dividends, and capital appreciation.

Investors and creditors and financial analysts grasp the fact that managers have incentives to "cook" these rates. Managers look better if they overstate the interest rate on the projected benefit obligation, because lower interest rates result in higher projected benefit obligations while higher interest rates result in lower liabilities. To hide its pension debts, managers can choose higher interest rates. This masquerade often carries a cost to the managers; namely, they usually report higher interest expenses because of the higher rate. But this higher rate is multiplied by the lower projected benefit obligation, so the interest cost can be either lower or higher. In the early years of a pension plan, the interest rate tends to be lower, but in the later years, it can become quite large. But the managers might themselves be retired by then.

Managers also can play with the expected return on plan assets. In this case they unambiguously prefer higher rates, which reduce the accrued pension liability shown on the balance sheet and decrease the net pension cost. Because of these incentives, investors and creditors and their agents must investigate the interest rate assumptions made by a business enterprise.

If financial statement users do not like the interest rate reckoned by managers, they can formulate a simple adjustment. Let us assume that the pension cash flows are constant and that they constitute a perpetuity, that is, the cash flows go forever. Given that pensions actually cover a long period of time, say 40 to 50 years, this assumption does not introduce very much error. As stated in Chapter 4, the present value of a perpetuity is the cash flow divided by the interest rate. In this context, the value of the projected benefit obligation is the present value of the annuity. Statement users can take the reported projected benefit obligation and multiply by the assumed interest rate to arrive at the presumed cash flows ("rents" as defined in Chapter 4), then take this presumed annual cash flow and divide by the interest rate they think is proper. The answer is the suitable projected benefit obligation.

As an example, let us reconsider the pensions of General Mills, as reported in Exhibit 5.3. In 2002 General Mills had a projected benefit obligation of $2.1 billion under a discount rate of 7.5 percent. Suppose one thinks that a more appropriate rate is 6 percent. One would then compute the implied annual cash flow as $2.1 billion multiplied by .075 for $157.5 million, then divide this rent by .06 to obtain a projected benefit obligation of $2.6 billion. Notice how such a simple assumption increases the liabilities by

$500 million. These assumptions therefore are critical to a proper analysis of a firm's economic well-being.

Similar calculations can be conducted for the plan assets and for OPEBs.

Eliminating the Netting and the Amortizations

As explained, it is improper to net the projected benefit obligation and the pension plan assets, and it is foolish not to include the prior service cost in the pension cost and the projected benefit obligation. Now we shall make two analytical adjustments to discover the more accurate balance sheet. The first adjustment unnets the projected benefit obligation and the pension assets. The pension assets are placed in the assets section of the balance sheet, whereas the pension debts are situated in the liabilities section of the balance sheet. Since the prepaid pension cost/accrued pension cost equals the difference between those two accounts, the balance sheet will stay in balance.

The second adjustment puts all of the unrecognized prior service cost and any other unrecognized items into both the pension expense and the projected benefit obligation. Since revenues and expenses are transferred into retained earnings, that is where we shall put them. Keep in mind that some of these unrecognized items might be unrecognized pension gains, so this adjustment could decrease the debt levels of some organizations.

We shall again use General Mills as an example, and we report the process in Exhibit 5.7. We obtain the assets, the tangible assets (assets minus the intangible assets), debts, equities (including minority interest), and tangible equities (equities minus the intangible assets) from the 10K. Panel A reveals these reported numbers and computes four indicators of the financial structure of General Mills. (The assets are so much bigger in 2002 than in 2001 because of acquisitions that General Mills made during the year.)

Panel B of Exhibit 5.7 gives the three numbers needed for the adjustments for unrecognized items, plan assets, and projected benefit obligations. (They also appear in Exhibit 5.3.) These quantities apply for both pensions and OPEBs. We then adjust the reported numbers in panel A utilizing these items in panel B. We add plan assets to the reported assets, and we subtract the unrecognized items from stockholders' equity. Since the balance sheet has to balance, we calculate adjusted liabilities as the adjusted assets minus the adjusted equities. Alternatively, the adjusted liabilities equal the reported debts minus the accrued pension costs (not shown in the exhibit) plus the projected benefit obligation plus the unrecognized items.

Panel C of Exhibit 5.7 shows the resulting accounts along with the subsequent ratios. Notice that all of the debt ratios deteriorate, thus disclosing the effects of the hidden debts. For example, the debt-to-assets ratio increases in 2002 from 0.77 to 0.81 and in 2001 from 0.99 to 1.02.

Exhibit 5.8 depicts the results of these analytical adjustments to a random sample of corporations. Some companies, such as Conseco, show little change. Some companies, such as Nicor and AK Steel, experience large modifications in the ratios. The debt ratios of a few companies, such as the Washington Post, improve.

These analytical adjustments serve as a way to better assess the financial structure of a business enterprise. The unnetting of the pension asset and the pension liability and the recognition of the items not recognized in the financial statements are important steps in understanding company performance.

119

Exhibit 5.7 Pension Analytical Adjustments for General Mills

Panel A: Reported Numbers (in Millions of Dollars) and Ratios

	2002	2001
Assets	16,540	5,091
Tangible Assets	7,977	4,221
Debts	12,811	5,039
Equities	3,729	52
Tangible Equities	(4,834)	(818)
Debt/Equity	3.43	96.90
Debt/Tangible Equity	(2.65)	(6.16)
Debt/Assets	0.77	0.99
Debt/Tangible Assets	1.61	1.19

Panel B: Adjustments

	2002	2001
Unrecognized Items	517	174
Pension Assets	2,904	1,843
Projected Benefit Obligation	2,711	1,363

Panel C: Adjusted Numbers and Ratios

	2002	2001
Assets	17,057	6,934
Tangible Assets	8,494	6,064
Debts	13,845	7,056
Equities	3,212	(122)
Tangible Equities	(5,351)	(992)
Debt/Equity	4.31	(57.84)
Debt/Tangible Equity	(2.59)	(7.11)
Debt/Assets	0.81	1.02
Debt/Tangible Assets	1.63	1.16

Note: Parentheses denote negative numbers.

Exhibit 5.8   Analytical Adjustment with a Sample of Firms

Company	Ratio	2001		2000	
		Original	Adjusted	Original	Adjusted
Conseco, Inc.					
	Debt to Equity	11.51	11.51	11.84	11.82
	Debt to Tangible Equity	51.74	51.62	90.33	88.90
	Debt to Assets	0.89	0.89	0.88	0.88
	Debt to Tangible Asset	0.95	0.95	0.95	0.95
Sprint Corporation					
	Debt to Equity	2.61	2.93	2.12	2.22
	Debt to Tangible Equity	4.18	4.77	3.24	3.32
	Debt to Assets	0.72	0.74	0.68	0.69
	Debt to Tangible Asset	0.80	0.82	0.76	0.76
Reader's Digest Association					
	Debt to Equity	2.50	3.14	2.66	2.38
	Debt to Tangible Equity	14.40	10.08	24.42	5.13
	Debt to Assets	0.71	0.76	0.73	0.70
	Debt to Tangible Asset	0.94	0.91	0.96	0.84
Nicor, Inc.					
	Debt to Equity	1.18	1.53	1.72	1.80
	Debt to Tangible Equity	1.18	1.53	1.72	1.80
	Debt to Assets	0.54	0.61	0.63	0.64
	Debt to Tangible Asset	0.54	0.61	0.63	0.64
American Greetings Corporation					
	Debt to Equity	1.90	2.20	1.59	1.80
	Debt to Tangible Equity	2.44	2.87	2.04	2.34
	Debt to Assets	0.65	0.69	0.61	0.64
	Debt to Tangible Asset	2.44	2.87	2.04	2.34
AK Steel Holding Corporation					
	Debt to Equity	4.06	15.70	2.97	4.38
	Debt to Tangible Equity	5.17	28.55	3.27	4.73
	Debt to Assets	0.80	0.94	0.75	0.81
	Debt to Tangible Asset	0.84	0.97	0.77	0.83

Exhibit 5.8   *(Continued)*

Company	Ratio	2001 Original	2001 Adjusted	2000 Original	2000 Adjusted
Kmart Corporation					
	Debt to Equity	2.29	1.39	2.72	1.13
	Debt to Tangible Equity	2.43	2.89	1.22	1.49
	Debt to Assets	0.70	0.58	0.73	0.53
	Debt to Tangible Asset	0.71	0.74	0.55	0.60
H J Heinz Corporation					
	Debt to Equity	4.98	6.68	5.58	6.57
	Debt to Tangible Equity	4.83	5.08	5.50	6.55
	Debt to Assets	0.83	0.87	0.85	0.87
	Debt to Tangible Asset	1.26	1.24	1.22	1.18
AGCO Corporation					
	Debt to Equity	1.72	2.49	1.66	2.25
	Debt to Tangible Equity	3.56	5.83	2.61	3.55
	Debt to Assets	0.63	0.71	0.62	0.69
	Debt to Tangible Asset	0.78	0.85	0.72	0.78
Washington Post					
	Debt to Equity	1.10	1.00	1.14	0.99
	Debt to Tangible Equity	3.79	2.13	3.51	1.92
	Debt to Assets	0.52	0.50	0.53	0.50
	Debt to Tangible Asset	0.79	0.68	0.78	0.66
Key Corporation					
	Debt to Equity	12.15	12.76	12.18	12.21
	Debt to Tangible Equity	14.89	15.77	15.35	15.82
	Debt to Assets	0.92	0.93	0.92	0.93
	Debt to Tangible Asset	0.94	0.94	0.94	0.94

SUMMARY AND CONCLUSION

Debt matters, and that includes pension debt. Given the huge amounts of money that are involved in pensions, it behooves the investment community to obtain a right understanding of what pension accounting is about. Pension expense includes the service cost plus the interest on the projected benefit obligation minus the expected return on plan assets plus the amortization of various unrecognized items, such as the unrecognized prior service cost. The only item found on the balance sheet is the prepaid pension asset or the accrued pension cost, which in turn equals the pension assets minus the projected benefit obligation minus various unrecognized items.

While the FASB made great strides over existing practice when it issued SFAS No. 87 and related statements, interpretations, and amendments, it still falls short of what is correct and appropriate. The netting of the projected benefit obligation and the pension assets is wrong; consequently, investors and creditors and financial analysts must unnet them to gain a better understanding of what is really going on. Additionally, the lack of recognition of the prior service cost and the actual gains and losses on the plan assets and other items is incorrect; investors and creditors and financial analysts must add these items to the pension liability and remove them from stockholders' equity. These analytical adjustments will help financial statement readers to discover the effects of this hidden debt.

Last, managers' interest rate assumptions can greatly influence the reported numbers. The investment community should examine these interest rates carefully and assess whether they are appropriate. By assuming that the cash flows form a perpetuity, investors and others can easily adjust the values for other interest rates.

NOTES

1. A short history of pension accounting is given by H. I. Wolk, J. R. Francis, and M. G. Tearney, *Accounting Theory: A Conceptual and Institutional Approach,* 3rd ed. (Cincinnati, OH: South-Western Publishing, 1992), pp. 476–509. As to still-existing loopholes, analysts are beginning to cover this topic with much fervor. As examples, read: J. Doherty, "Pay Me Later? An Increase in Underfunded Pension Plans Could Pose Trouble for Companies and Shareholders." *Barron's,* October 21, 2002; D. Kansas, "Plain Talk: Pension Liabilities a Big Concern," *Dow Jones News Service,* October 1, 2002; J. Revell, "Beware the Pension Monster," *Fortune,* December 9, 2002; and B. Tunick, "The Looming Pension Liability: Analysts Focus on Problem that FASB Rules Ignore," *Investment Dealers Digest,* October 14, 2002.

2. C. Bryan-Low, "Heard on the Street: Pension Funds Take Spotlight—Numbers Released by S&P Bring Attention to Issue of Accounting for Costs," *Wall Street Journal,* October 25, 2002.

3. An obvious question to raise is what is a good or fair pension plan. Accounting can answer questions about cost and can even assist in devising incentives to motivate employees to act in ways beneficial to the firm, but it can do little else with respect to determining what a fair price of labor is.

4. As is well known now, a number of pension plans lost big because they invested a lot of funds in Enron or WorldCom.

5. The FASB (1980) has set accounting and reporting rules for pension plans in Statement No. 35.

6. *Dow Jones Newswires,* "Northwest Will Take a Charge of $700 Million for Pensions," November 6, 2002.

7. Burke, 2002.

8. C. Bryan-Low, "SEC May Take Tougher Tone on Accountants in Bad Audits," *Wall Street Journal,* November 17, 2002.

9. K. Chen, "Unfunded Pension Liabilities Soared in 2001 to $111 Billion," *Wall Street Journal,* July 26, 2002.

10. M. W. Walsh, "Companies Fight Shortfalls in Pension Funds," *New York Times,* January 13, 2003.

11. CBS News, "IBM Workers: Pension Change Hurts," *CBS News,* April 25, 2000.

12. M. Brannigan and N. Harris, "Delta Air Changes Pension Plan to Slash Costs over Five Years," *Wall Street Journal,* November 19, 2002.

13. F. Norris, "Using a Weak Pension Plan as a Cash Cow," *New York Times*, December 20, 2002.

14. For more details about accounting for pensions and OPEBs, see: P. R. Delaney, B. J. Epstein, J. A. Adler, and M. F. Foran, *GAAP 2000: Interpretation and Application of Generally Accepted Accounting Principles 2000* (New York: John Wiley & Sons, 2000), pp. 635–667; G. Georgiades, *Miller GAAP Financial Statement Disclosures Manual* (New York: Aspen, 2001), section 22-24; B. D. Jarnagin, *2001 U.S. Master GAAP Guide* (Chicago: CCH, 2000), pp. 871–1068; D. E. Kieso, J. J. Weygandt, and T. D. Warfield, *Intermediate Accounting,* 10th ed. (New York: John Wiley & Sons, 2001), pp. 778–848; L. Revsine, D. W. Collins, and W. B. Johnson, *Financial Reporting and Analysis,* 2nd ed. (Upper Saddle River, NJ: Prentice-Hall, 2002), pp. 689–757; and G. I. White, A. C. Sondhi, and D. Fried, *The Analysis and Use of Financial Statements,* 2nd ed. (New York: John Wiley & Sons, 1997), pp. 591–670. FASB's SFAS No. 132 standardizes pension disclosures; see Financial Accounting Standards Board, *Employers' Disclosures about Pensions and Other Postretirement Benefits: An Amendment of FASB Statements No. 87, 88, and 106,* SFAS No. 132 (Norwalk, CT: FASB, 1998).

15. These calculations require present value tools. To brush up on how to compute a present value, read about this topic in Chapter 4.

16. Of course, in practice pensions are typically monthly payments. I assume annual payments to simplify the arithmetic at no loss of generality.

17. Trying to estimate when one person will die has obvious measurement error, but if the corporation has hundreds or thousands of employees, this error becomes much smaller as some people die before and some after their life expectancy, and the errors begin to cancel out.

18. A related concept is *accumulated benefit obligation.* The two concepts are the same, except that accumulated benefit obligation ignores future salary raises, but projected benefit obligation includes them. Since accumulated benefit obligations enter the picture only in the determination of minimum pension liability, we ignore them.

19. The movie *Wall Street* reminds us that managers usually do not want to put too many funds into the pension plan because it sets up the firm as a potential takeover target.

20. There are several other components of net pension cost, including amortization of effects of amendments and the transition to adoption of SFAS No. 87 (and SFAS No. 106). These details are omitted here, but they are treated in a manner similar to the prior service cost.

21. Actually the FASB creates a complicated method termed the *corridor approach*, which creates certain boundaries. The firm must show gains and losses that exceed these limits. For details, see Delaney et al., *GAAP 2000,* pp. 635–667; Georgiades, *Miller GAAP Financial Statement Disclosures Manual,* section 22–24; and Jarnagin, *2001 U.S. Master GAAP Guide,* pp. 871–1068.

22. White, Sondhi, and Fried discuss one process for making these income statement analytical adjustments; see *Analysis and Use of Financial Statements,* 2nd ed., pp. 541–547.

CHAPTER SIX

How to Hide Debt with Special-Purpose Entities

Debt matters. Managers can magnify returns to shareholders as they add debt to the financial structure and obtain good returns on corporate assets, but managers also can magnify losses when returns on assets become less than the cost of debt. Because of this double-edged sword, investors and creditors scrutinize the financial leverage of any institution. As discussed in Chapter 2, when the ratio of debt to equity gets too high, investors and creditors increase the cost of capital to protect themselves. Managers frequently counter that move by not reporting the liabilities of the business enterprise.

This chapter ends the four-chapter set in techniques managers employ to understate their firm's liability level. Chapter 3 covered the equity method, Chapter 4 described lease accounting, while Chapter 5 delved into pension accounting. By applying analytical adjustments, investors could correctly restate the debts of the business enterprise and better ascertain the condition of the company. This chapter examines special-purpose entities (SPEs) to conceal the corporation's obligations. Unfortunately, analytical adjustments do not solve the problem of making hidden SPE debts appear, for corporations rarely disclose enough to make any adjustments. In addition, contingencies often exist that prove hard to measure.

Structured finance and derivatives both strike at the heart of financial accounting inasmuch as bookkeeping methods are not designed to capture their effects in a timely and informative manner. Fair value accounting for the assets and liabilities helps, along with full and complete consolidation. However, even these treatments prove ineffective when a contingent risk deemed of very small probability explodes on the scene one day. That is why disclosure plays a critical role with respect to both of these types of activities.

Structured finance covers a multitude of transactions; I shall limit the discussion to securitizations and synthetic leases. This coverage will be sufficient to present the fundamental issues at stake and to discuss how managers could properly report these activities. I shall omit derivatives since discussing them would require us to spend considerable time covering a number of institutional issues.[1] Interestingly, many of the crucial points are the same for both topics, and the accounting for both sets of endeavors will be improved with fair value reporting, consolidation, and disclosure.

This chapter examines how business enterprises hide debts with SPEs. The first section provides a general explanation of SPEs, what they are, how they are organized, and how they are employed. The next section will cover securitizations, while the third section discusses synthetic leases. The fourth section discusses the response by the Financial Accounting Standards Board (FASB), the new rules that have been put into motion, and the invention of variable interest entities. The final section looks at corporate responses to Enron, the public's suspicion of SPEs, and the new accounting rule.

SPECIAL-PURPOSE ENTITY LANDSCAPE

Special-purpose entities come in so many shapes and sizes and colors that they are hard to define. While they have captured the imagination of the public in the last couple of years, they have been around since 1970, when the Government National Mortgage Association (Ginnie Mae) securitized government-insured mortgages. Banks started using them a few years later, and they became enormously popular by the early 1980s. Originally, their purpose was to convert receivables into cash by converting them into a set of securities; thus the name *securitization*. Today corporations use them in many fashions.

General Comments about Special-Purpose Entities

A *special-purpose entity*, sometimes called a special-purpose vehicle, can be defined as an entity created to carry out a specific or limited purpose.[2] The creator of the SPE is called the *sponsor*. The SPE can take any organizational form, so the sponsor can set it up as a corporation, partnership, trust, or joint venture. The organizational form facilitates the particular purpose or goal of the particular SPE.

Firms have used SPEs to do a number of things. Some of the more common things SPEs are used for include selling or transferring assets to the SPE, all sorts of leasing activities, borrowing money, issuing one type of equity to the SPE that is converted into another type of security, creating research and development vehicles, and as hedging devices.[3] This chapter is most concerned with securitizations and synthetic leases.

While SPEs assume many shapes for many different activities and goals, Exhibit 6.1 shows a generic SPE. Assume that the firm or business enterprise acts as the sponsor and creates the SPE. At its genesis, the SPE receives some assets from the corporation. Simultaneously, the SPE receives cash from a set of investors and passes some or all of this cash on to the business enterprise. In turn, the investors receive *asset-backed securities* (ABS), which are securities that are backed by the assets of the SPE. In other words, the asset passed by the company to the SPE acts as collateral to cover any losses sustained by the investors.

Investors become interested in the SPE because it provides a well-defined set of cash flows to them. The business enterprise usually provides a variety of *credit enhancements* that make the investment very safe. The firm typically writes the contract in such a way that if it declares corporate bankruptcy, the assets in the SPE cannot be used to pay the firm's debts. Doing this obviously protects the investors in the SPE because they

Exhibit 6.1   Generic Special-Purpose Entity

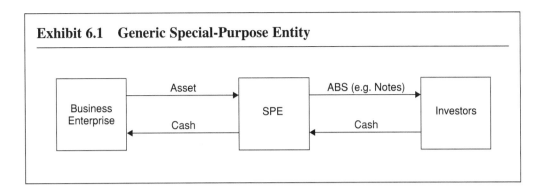

will not lose any funds if such a dire circumstance unfolds. Another credit enhancement is for the firm to include more assets in the SPE than cash received. For example, if the investors put up $1 million cash, then the business enterprise might put up $1.3 million receivables. In this way, if some of the receivables become uncollectible, it is hoped that there will be enough receivables left to pay off the amount of the investment plus some amount of return to them. Of course, if there are some receivables left over after the investors' claims are satisfied, the contract must specify who gets the residual cash. A third credit enhancement comes in the form of guarantees. If something happens, such as a souring of the economy that causes the credit risk of the receivables to increase, then the firm might have to ante up more money to the investors. These credit enhancements make the SPE an attractive vehicle in which to invest.

Most of the investors in the SPE take a creditor relationship vis-à-vis the SPE. For example, many SPEs will issue notes to these investors, specifying some interest rate that the SPE will pay them.

What is in it for the business enterprise? After all, the firm could just as easily sell the assets outright or borrow money putting the assets up as collateral. The first legitimate reason for utilizing an SPE is that the firm obtains credit at a cheaper price. The credit enhancements reduce the riskiness of the investment, so the interest rate required by the creditors is less than it otherwise would be. An example, discussed more fully later, concerns *securitizations*, which involve amassing certain (usually financial) assets and creating securities that are paid off with cash flows produced by the pool of assets. What the business enterprise gains from a securitization that makes use of an SPE is a lower interest rate on the debt.

A second legitimate application of SPEs deals with corporate tax planning. With certain types of arrangements, a business enterprise will be able to decrease its income tax liability. A *synthetic lease*, which is described more fully later in the chapter, provides a mechanism that allows business enterprises to treat leases as operating leases for financial reporting purposes but as capital leases for tax purposes. The former treatment raises all of the problems mentioned in Chapter 4 because managers hide the lease obligation from financial statement readers. Regarding leases as capital leases for tax purposes, however, permits firms to deduct depreciation expense on their tax forms and thereby increase their tax deductions. Thus, the synthetic lease helps managers to reduce the taxes that the business entity owes the government.

A third but illegitimate reason for employing SPEs is that managers think they do not have to include them in the balance sheet. Managers will claim that the debts are the debts of the SPE, not the business enterprise. Thus, the whole area of structured finance becomes tainted in an effort to deceive the investment community as managers engage in "financial engineering."[4] The argument is frequently silly, for the corporation often has control over what the SPE does.

Notice from this brief discussion that pension funds can be considered SPEs. By comparing Exhibit 5.1 with Exhibit 6.1, the reader will note much similarity. As the accounting issues diverge between pension funds and other types of SPEs, the FASB and the Securities and Exchange Commission (SEC) often exclude pension funds from SPE accounting considerations.

Governments, including the United States, frequently employ SPE arrangements. For example, the government's pension fund known as social security is a massive SPE that the federal government maintains for the express purpose of hiding the debts from its citizens. The United States owes billions and billions of dollars to its retirees over the next several decades, but no one in Washington wants to disclose the true numbers. Just as Enron attempted to deceive investors about the levels of debt it maintained, the United States government engages in the same type of fraud.[5]

Fraudulent Uses of Special-Purpose Entities

Of course, Enron's schemes and swindles have made everybody interested in SPEs, even though they have been around for decades.[6] The difficulty, though, rests with Enron's inappropriate application of the SPEs, its deceptions in the financial accounting and reporting of these transactions and events, and Arthur Andersen's approval of the financial statements and the associated footnotes and schedules. In similar fashion, Dynegy recently paid a $3 million fine to the SEC because of its misuse of SPEs.[7]

The Internal Revenue Service (IRS) does not permit taxpayers to create some entity for the sole purpose of avoiding taxes; any manager who engages in this activity may be charged with tax fraud. Correspondingly, financial executives who set up an SPE for the sole purpose of misrepresenting corporate liabilities on the balance sheet may be accused of fraud. Lynn Turner, former SEC Chief Accountant, provides some questions to raise when considering this issue. He suggests asking:

- "Does the transaction have a legitimate business purpose other than avoiding presenting the financing as bank debt on the balance sheet?
- "Does the SPE engage in normal business operations?
- "Does the SPE have more than nominal capitalization? . . . Could it operate on its own?
- "Does the SPE have officers and directors who function as they would in any normal trading company?
- "Does the sponsor of the SPE or the entity it enters into transactions with have all the risks and rewards of the transactions or does the SPE have them? Is there any economic substance to the SPE . . . ?

- "Do the transactions between [the business enterprise], an SPE, and the bank actually transfer risk from or to [the business enterprise], the SPE or bank?

- "Are the transactions linked in such a manner that risks or the ultimate obligations to repay financings are not really transferred?"[8]

This list serves as a good checklist for auditors as they examine the pursuits of an SPE. It also provides managers and directors a list to help them understand what is going on with respect to the SPE. Given the similarity of this series of questions to the issue of setting up dummy corporations and tax fraud, an issue that has been around a long time, the managers, directors, and auditors should be very familiar with these points.

The remainder of the chapter assumes that the SPE itself is a legitimate business entity. We still have many issues to clarify with respect to accounting.

Introduction to the Accounting Issues

Stephen Ryan pinpoints the major issues with respect to accounting for SPEs, as he views SPEs as a nexus of various contracts.[9] The SPE itself takes the assets from the business enterprise and transforms the risks and the rewards of the assets to the various parties to the SPE. Each party to the SPE has contractual rights and contractual obligations. To understand an SPE fully requires one to understand each party's rights and obligations. Accounting has difficulties with SPEs because it has problems in accounting for these various rights and obligations. Ryan specifically points out four difficulties:

1. Executory contracts

2. Guarantees

3. The lack of applying fair value accounting to many financial instruments

4. The lack of consolidation

Executory contracts involve a promise for a promise. For example, I promise to give you so many barrels of oil by a certain date and you promise to give me certain assets by a certain date. Executory contracts have been around a long time, and the traditional way of dealing with them is to ignore them. Ignoring them causes problems for investors and creditors who do not know of their existence or do not fully understand the implications.[10]

An example is a *take-or-pay contract,* which is common in the oil and gas business.[11] One firm agrees to provide some raw materials during a time period, and the other agrees to buy some minimum amount of these resources. These contracts are important to the distributors because they can be used at banks as collateral for a loan. In other words, the take-or-pay contract establishes a guarantee by the purchasing firm to procure a minimum amount of the resource. Such commitments typically were ignored until the FASB issued Statement No. 47 in 1981, which requires disclosure of the financial commitments made. Gerald White, Ashwinpaul Sondhi, and Dov Fried mention that financial analysts should use this disclosure to analytically adjust the purchaser's balance sheet for the obligation.[12]

Guarantees are often part of these SPE packages, as they reduce the risk involved in investing in the SPE. In the past, accounting has not processed these guarantees very well, so investors and creditors of the business enterprise were often left in the dark. The FASB has required firms to disclose the nature of these guarantees and the losses that may be incurred under some situations. In 2002, the FASB issued Interpretation No. 45, which requires firms to value these guarantees and report them as liabilities.

Financial instruments involve contracts that give rights or responsibilities to companies to receive or pay cash or contracts leading to a cash settlement. Many financial instruments that appear on the asset side of the balance sheet are valued at fair value—what the market would pay for them. But many financial instruments that appear as liabilities on the balance sheet are measured at amortized cost, which equals the historical cost of the debt plus or minus some amortizations. The key point is that the FASB has built an asymmetry between the assets and the liabilities. This hurts banks, for example, because they rely on the natural hedging of assets and liabilities but must account for them differently. The contractual rights and liabilities in SPEs, including the debts arising from the transactions, are best accounted for in terms of their fair values.

More important, these debts often are omitted from the balance sheet. Firms engineer the transactions so they think that they do not have to record the liabilities. Consolidation becomes an important consideration. If a business enterprise controls the SPE or has a residual interest in the SPE, it seems logical that the firm ought to consolidate the results of the SPE with those of the firm.[13] The arguments for consolidation run much the same as those presented in Chapter 3. These issues will come up as we discuss securitizations and synthetic leases.

Principles-based Accounting

Lately, the press has reported on proposals for principles-based accounting that has been advocated by Harvey Pitt, former chairman of the SEC, Walter Wriston, former chairman of Citicorp, David Tweedie, chairman of the International Accounting Standards Board, and even the FASB itself. The idea behind these proposals is that rules generally promulgated by the FASB focus on minutia and are dense, picky, and sometimes impenetrable. If the rules concentrate instead on broad-based principles, then the rules themselves can be stated rather easily. The process becomes simpler for everyone and managers will choose good methods rather than game the system.

Chapter 9 critiques this proposal in detail. Suffice it for now to say that managers, directors, and their auditors had a chance to account for SPEs using good principles of accounting. As mentioned, SPEs have been in existence since the 1970s, and rules about SPEs have been introduced only in the last dozen years or so. In such a climate, managers could have chosen the high road, accounted for the SPEs in some reasonable fashion, and provided much-needed disclosures. They flunked the test since they typically hid the debt and did not say anything even in the footnotes until prodded by the SEC and by the FASB. In fact, the whole area of SPEs has been seen as a colossal way of engineering the balance sheet. The case of Enron has revealed not only the specific frauds by Jeff Skilling, Kenneth Lay, Andy Fastow, and others, but it also has exposed the reality that corporate disclosures about most SPEs stink. Managers failed this exam badly, and so did their auditors, so I have significant reservations about principles-based accounting.

SECURITIZATIONS

Securitizations take a pool of more or less homogeneous assets and turn them into securities.[14] As Exhibit 6.1 shows, the idea is to borrow money from investors, who in turn are repaid by the cash manufactured by the asset pool. This process began with mortgages, credit card receivables, and accounts receivable; for example, by General Motors Acceptance Corporation, Goodyear Tire, and Willis Lease Finance Corporation.[15] Today securitizations have expanded to include all kinds of assets, including transportation equipment, timberlands fixed-price energy contracts, and studio movies.[16] It is even possible to securitize whole businesses, such as water utilities.[17]

Securitizations are big business. Securitized lending has reached $6 trillion in the U.S. economy; Citigroup has $204 billion of asset-backed securities, and J.P. Morgan has $75 billion.[18] Clearly, when $6 trillion does not appear on anyone's balance sheet, the accounts do not reflect the financial risks of the economy.

This section will fill in more details about securitizations in general. This characterization is necessarily generic for a great many variations take place in practice.

Setup and Operation

Exhibit 6.2 takes the generic graphic in Exhibit 6.1 and adds details for securitizations. Panel A shows the transfers that take place when the SPE is created. Panel B depicts the transactions that occur after the initial setup.

Panel A of Exhibit 6.2 is quite similar to Exhibit 6.1. The corporation creates the SPE for some specific purpose, such as processing mortgages. The SPE issues asset-backed securities to investors and receives cash from the investors. These asset-backed securities usually assume the form of debt. Once the SPE receives the cash, it transmits the cash to the business enterprise, which in turn transfers the assets to the SPE. The specific amounts are determined contractually by a sponsor, the business enterprise, and the investors. At the same time, someone guarantees that the investors will receive their principal and interest. Typically, the guarantee comes in the form of guaranteeing the value of the assets transferred by the firm to the SPE.

Panel B of Exhibit 6.2 portrays the processing of transactions by the various parties to the securitization. The customers repay their debt by sending the funds to the SPE. The SPE uses the cash to pay off the investors, both the principal and the interest. The SPE often also will pay the guarantor some fee for the guarantee and the business enterprise for whatever services the firm provides the SPE.

The SPE continues until the customers pay off their debts and until the SPE pays off the investors of the SPE. Some assets may remain in the SPE at this point; the contract must specify what is to be done with this residual equity.

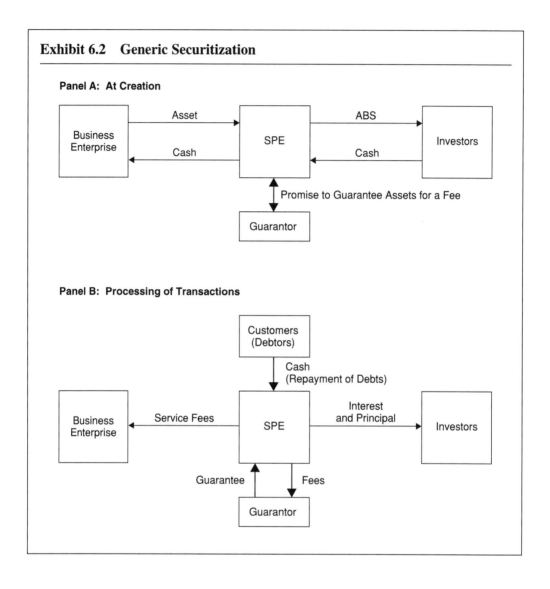

Exhibit 6.2   Generic Securitization

Let us add some specificity with an illustration, one that will not only assist us to understand the nature of securitizations, but also to elicit the major accounting issues with respect to securitizations. A simple example appears in Exhibit 6.3. Consider a car dealer named CarSales. It sells $100,000 of automobiles in a certain time period, with the customers disbursing $5,000 as down payments on these cars. To keep things simple, let us assume that the car loans were offered at no interest. Because it wants cash now, the business enterprise decides to securitize these auto loans. Notice, therefore, that securitizations are fancy instruments by which the company borrows money at cheap interest rates. These rates are lower than conventional loans because of the credit enhancements provided by the SPE.

CarSales creates Wash-and-Rinse as an SPE to securitize these receivables. Creditors lend $80,000 to the SPE in return for asset-backed securities. In this case, the

---

Exhibit 6.3   Easy Car-Dealer Example of a Securitization

Suppose that CarSales, Inc. sells $100,000 of cars in a month. Customers provide a down payment of $5,000, leaving accounts receivable of $95,000. These receivables are interest-free.

An SPE is created and called Wash-and-Rinse. CarSales transfers all of the receivables to Wash-and-Rinse and receives $80,000. At the same time, investors pony up $80,000 cash and receive notes that specify an interest rate of 10 percent.

At creation, Wash-and-Rinse obtains $80,000 from its creditors; it then transfers this cash to CarSales.

Subsequently, Wash-and-Rinse receives money from the original automobile purchasers.

Scenario 1: Suppose Wash-and-Rinse receives $94,000 from the debtors one year later.
   The creditors receive $80,000 (principal) + $8,000 (interest) = $88,000.
   Who receives the residual amount of $6,000?

Scenario 2: Suppose Wash-and-Rinse receives $85,000 from the debtors one year later.
   The creditors receive $80,000 (principal) + $8,000 (interest) = $88,000.
   Who bears the risk of default and loses $3,000?

---

loan is secured by the auto loans. Let us assume that these asset-backed securities pay 10 percent on the principal.

Simultaneously, on the day of creation, the SPE sends $80,000 to CarSales in return for $95,000 of auto loans. CarSales accepts less cash than the value of the receivables for two reasons. The first reason is the time value of money. CarSales can receive the money from its customers as they remit their monthly cash payments, but these cash flows occur in the future. The value of these cash flows today is less than their future value, as discussed in Chapter 4. The second reason is that some customers will skip their payments. Maybe they lose their jobs, maybe their families suffer major health problems, or maybe some of them are deadbeats. Whatever the reason for the customers' inability or unwillingness to pay their debts, we expect some of them to miss the payments. The firm enhances the value of these assets by putting more of them into the pool that is transmitted to the SPE than it hopes is necessary.[19]

After the construction of the SPE, Wash-and-Rinse will receive cash from the customers and then disburse these funds to the investors. This process continues until the receivables generate enough money to discharge the obligation to the investors. Exhibit 6.3 then raises two possible scenarios. In the good scenario, most of the customers pay off their loans to produce the cash to pay the principal and the interest of the SPE's creditors. The question arises as to who will receive the residual interest in the SPE. In the bad scenario, there is a shortfall in cash. The SPE Wash-and-Rinse still fulfills its obligation to the creditors by giving them the principal plus interest, but the original customers do not contribute enough cash. The question in this case is who bears the risk of the loss. After these transactions, the SPE is dissolved, though of course the business enterprise may create new SPEs.

Accounting Issues in Securitizations

One possible issue with securitizations occurs when the SPE involves related parties, such as when an executive from the business enterprise also manages the SPE (such as Andy Fastow for Enron). Investors should be alerted to related party transactions because they involve transactions between the business enterprise and another party that is somehow related to it. Because the firm might not engage in transactions with related parties that are not competitive (e.g., transferring receivables to the SPE at unusually high or low values), the FASB requires the company to disclose any related party transactions, including the dollar amounts involved.[20]

Another possible issue focuses on contingencies. If the firm bears the risk of default, then it might have losses in the future from its SPE transactions. Statement No. 5 by the FASB applies in this case, and the accounting rule is outlined in Exhibit 6.4. The FASB begins by defining contingencies as possible future transactions. The board then concentrates on losses that might occur from contingencies and dismisses any concern about gain contingencies.

How to account for loss contingencies depends on the probability that the contingency will take place. If the probability is remote—that is, if the probability is small—then the corporation does not have to report anything. If the event or transaction is probable, then the firm needs to book the loss on the income statement and the liability on the balance sheet. This action assumes that the accountant can measure the amount of the probable loss. If the accountant cannot do so or if the transaction is reasonably possible (i.e., between probable and remote), then no journal entry is made on the books. Instead, the firm should disclose the nature of the contingency and provide some estimate of possible losses or explain why it cannot estimate these losses.

While Statement No. 5 provides a powerful solution to many situations, it is not entirely satisfactory. Even if the probability of a loss contingency is remote, firms should still disclose their possible losses. With the speed of today's economy, what is remote one day might become probable some time thereafter.

The remaining accounting issue was addressed by the FASB in Statement No. 140.[21] The major issue focuses on whether the issuing firm retains control over any financial interests in the assets. If it does, the corporation must recognize the borrowings as its liabilities. In other words, the series of transactions is accounted for as a secured borrowing. If the firm severs all control and all residual interest in the assets, then it can recognize the gain or loss on the transfer of the assets to the SPE. And, significantly, the business entity does not recognize any of the liabilities.[22]

Statement No. 140 seems reasonable, though unfortunately it does not address the accounting of all securitizations, much less all transactions dealing with SPEs.

Exhibit 6.4 Accounting Requirements for Disclosing Contingent Liabilities (SFAS No. 5)

A *contingency* involves some type of uncertainty. For example, a debt materializes only under a certain set of circumstances.

Gain contingencies are never recognized.

Loss contingencies are recognized sometimes, as developed below.

Three levels of probability exist:
- *Probable:* The future event is likely to occur.
- *Reasonably possible:* The chance of the future event's occurring is greater than remote but less than probable.
- *Remote:* The probability the future event will occur is small.

Accounting for contingent losses:
- If a probable loss will occur in the future and if it can be estimated, the entity must accrue the loss in the income statement and report the liability in the balance sheet.
- If a probable loss cannot be estimated or if a loss is reasonably possible, the entity must disclose the situation. This disclosure should explain the nature of the contingency and provide an estimate of the possible loss or a range of loss, if possible; otherwise, the entity should explain that an estimate is not possible.

Douglas Skipworth studied how corporate concerns implemented the requirements of Statement No. 140.[23] Financial institutions mostly did a reasonable job, but other companies typically failed to meet their reporting obligations. For example, one of the disclosures asks issuing companies to report the effects from adverse changes on the retained interests in the SPE. Such a sensitivity analysis goes a long way in helping investors and creditors perceive the effects of remote disasters on the firm. Most financial institutions complied with this requirement, but many others did not.[24]

An example of a securitization disclosure by Lear Corporation is given in Exhibit 6.5. The first paragraph of the disclosure mentions that it transferred $4.1 billion of receivables to the SPE and nominally received $4.084 billion in cash ($4.1 billion–$16.2 million), but see below. Lear describes that three of its customers are experiencing troubles that have reduced their credit ratings. Apparently, this securitization arrangement protects the investors of the SPE by requiring adjustments whenever the customers have decreases in their credit ratings.[25] Lear does not tell us how it modified the contract, but it could have required a cash payment to the SPE or a transfer of additional receivables.

The second paragraph of this disclosure mentions the issuance of commercial paper by the banks to fund the SPE. It says that Lear receives 1 percent of the sold receivables in terms of servicing fees. Lear states that it has residual interests in the

Exhibit 6.5   Example of Securitization Disclosure (Lear, from 2001 10-K)

Asset-backed Securitization Agreement

In November 2000, the Company and several of its U.S. subsidiaries, through a special purpose corporation, entered into a receivables-backed receivables purchase facility (collectively, the "ABS facility"). The ABS facility originally provided for a 364-day committed facility and maximum purchases of adjusted accounts receivable of $300 million. In November 2001, the ABS facility was amended to extend the termination date to November 2002 and to accommodate the reduction in the credit ratings of the Company's three largest customers, whose receivables are transferred to the ABS facility, as well as recent declines in automotive production volumes. As a result, the Company's utilization of the ABS facility in the future may be lower than in prior periods. In addition, should the Company's customers experience further reductions in their credit ratings, the Company may be unable to utilize the ABS facility in the future. Should this occur, the Company would seek to utilize other available credit facilities to replace the funding currently provided by the ABS facility. During the year ended December 31, 2001, the Company and its subsidiaries, through the special purpose corporation, sold adjusted accounts receivable totaling $4.1 billion under the ABS facility and recognized a discount of $16.2 million, which is reflected as other expense, net in the consolidated statement of income for the year ended December 31, 2001.

The special purpose corporation purchases the receivables from the Company and several of its U.S. subsidiaries and then simultaneously transfers undivided interests in the receivables to certain bank conduits, which fund their purchases through the issuance of commercial paper. The Company continues to service the transferred receivables and receives an annual servicing fee of 1.0% of the sold receivables. The conduit investors and the special purpose corporation have no recourse to the Company's or its subsidiaries' other assets for the failure of the accounts receivable obligors to timely pay on the accounts receivable. With respect to the sold receivables, the Company's retained interest is subordinated to the bank conduits' undivided purchased interests. The sold receivables servicing portfolio amounted to $566.9 million as of December 31, 2001.

The following table summarized certain cash flows received from and paid to the special purpose corporation (in millions):

Year Ended December 31, 2001	
Proceeds from new securitizations	$ 260.7
Proceeds from collections reinvested in securitizations	3,656.3
Servicing fees received	5.1

sold receivables, which seems incompatible with SFAS No. 140. The explanation may rest with the effective date of SFAS No. 140 being later than the creation of this SPE.

Lear next presents a table of the cash inflows it has received in fiscal year 2001. The huge cash flows are a result of amending the original SPE arrangement and the new transfer of the $4.1 billion of receivables. Lear collected proceeds of $3.917 billion, which is a bit different from our calculation of $4.084 billion. Apparently, the corporation incurred some additional expenses that explain the difference.

Lear does not provide the sensitivity analysis required by Statement No. 140. These data could prove important if the customers experience a further erosion of their credit ratings.

SYNTHETIC LEASES

Synthetic leases constitute a technique by which firms can assert that they have capital leases for tax purposes but operating leases for financial reporting purposes. They form a way for companies to decrease income taxes without admitting any debt on corporate balance sheets.

Like securitizations, synthetic leases are big business. Some estimate "the size of the synthetic lease market at $6 billion to $8 billion per year."[26] Cisco has synthetic leases measured at about $1.6 billion.[27] US Airways possesses synthetic leases to the tune of approximately $1.1 billion.[28]

Because of the size of these omitted liabilities, it would be natural for financial analysts to attempt to include them in their investigations and assessments. Fitch, for example, recently discussed its rating of A− for a new debt issue by Constellation Energy Group.[29] As Fitch described why it rated the debt as it did, it indicated that it adjusted the numbers of Constellation Energy Group to reflect its synthetic lease obligation. In a manner similar to the process explained in Chapter 4, Fitch added the debt back into the balance sheet.

In recent days, synthetic leases have come under attack. Much of the criticism is directed to the noninclusion of the liabilities on the balance sheet.[30] Not only is this technique some accountant's legerdemain to produce results that corporate executives want for tax purposes and for financial reporting purposes, but the footnotes on synthetic disclosures have become wonderful exercises in using a lot of words to say very little.[31] It is virtually impossible to decode some of these so-called disclosures.

Krispy Kreme recently took the high road with respect to synthetic leases.[32] After getting hammered at a shareholders' meeting about its synthetic leases, management decided to eliminate them. Clearly management wants to assuage shareholders of any doubts about its integrity.

The remainder of this section sketches a typical synthetic lease and discusses the accounting issues further.

Setup and Operation

Exhibit 6.6 takes the generic graphic in Exhibit 6.1 and offers some additional details for synthetic leases.[33] Panel A illustrates the transactions that take place upon creation of the SPE. Panel B displays the transactions that occur after the initial setup. Exhibit 6.2 and 6.6 clearly have many similarities.

Look first at Panel A of Exhibit 6.6. The business enterprise engineers the SPE to handle the lease operation. In practice, many of these deals have a life of only five or

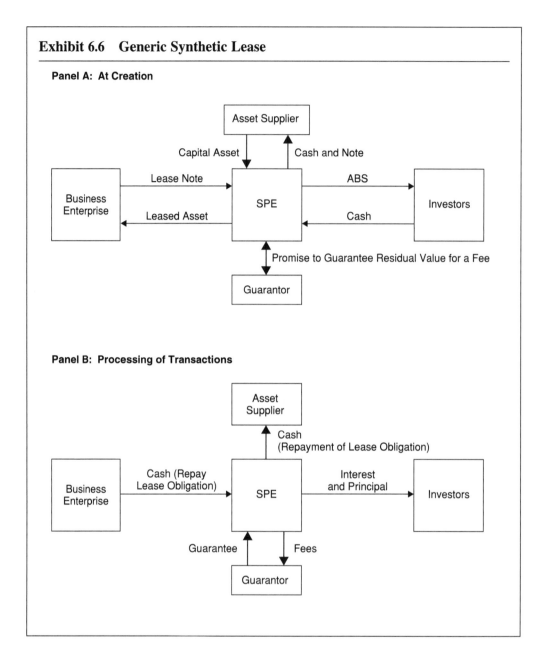

Exhibit 6.6   Generic Synthetic Lease

Panel A: At Creation

Panel B: Processing of Transactions

six years and involve a balloon payment at the end. The SPE issues asset-backed securities, usually notes, to the investors; it receives cash from them. As typical with most SPEs, this security probably is debt rather than equity. The SPE then purchases the property or plant or equipment from the supplier of the capital asset. In turn, the SPE pays cash and signs a note to pay the rest. The SPE now becomes a lessor by leasing this property or plant or equipment to the corporation. The leased asset is transferred to the firm, and the firm signs a lease contract (and sometimes provides a down payment). The residual value of the leased asset tends to be large. For reasons explicated in

Chapter 4, the residual value almost always is unguaranteed. Some third party joins the arrangement and, for a fee, promises to guarantee the residual value.[34]

Exhibit 6.6 Panel B graphs what happens afterward. The business enterprise makes its payments to the SPE. The SPE uses this cash to pay off the liability to the capital asset supplier and to repay the investors of the SPE their principal and pay interest on the principal. As necessary, the SPE will pay the guarantor its fees.

The SPE continues until the last payment is made (frequently a balloon payment). This payment by the business enterprise satisfies the lease obligation. The SPE then pays off the asset supplier, thus discharging that liability. If necessary, the sponsor of the SPE makes sure that any guarantee is paid. Finally, the SPE pays the investors.

As a demonstration of a synthetic lease, consider the simple example listed in Exhibit 6.7. Suppose that Wheeler-Dealer, Inc., wants to obtain the use of an automobile and desires to do this with a synthetic lease. The car has a price tag of $60,560 and will be financed by four annual payments of $15,000, each at the beginning of the year. We estimate that the residual value, which is unguaranteed, will be $15,000. This example is a variation of the illustration contained in Exhibits 4.2 and 4.3. Recall from Chapter 4 that if this last $15,000 comes in the form of another cash payment or a guaranteed residual value, then the lease falls in the category of capital lease and the debt must be recognized. By the lessee's not guaranteeing the residual value, however, the present value of the cash flows flunks the 90 percent rule (along with the other three criteria) and the liability need not be recognized in the balance sheet.

Wheeler-Dealer creates an SPE that we shall call WD Leasing. The SPE issues notes to the investors after receiving their $60,560. WD Leasing takes the cash and buys the automobile. It then leases the vehicle to Wheeler-Dealer. Again, the residual value is unguaranteed by Wheeler-Dealer, so WD Leasing finds a third party to provide such a guarantee.

Exhibit 6.7 Easy Wheeler-Dealer Example of a Synthetic Lease

Suppose that Wheeler-Dealer, Inc. wants to lease an automobile from CarSales. The car costs $60,560 and will be financed by four annual payments of $15,000, each at the beginning of the year. The residual value is $15,000. We know that a traditional arrangement requires Wheeler-Dealer to capitalize the lease if the residual value is guaranteed but as an operating lease if unguaranteed. But CarSales insists on a guaranteed residual value.

An SPE can be created; let us call it WD Leasing. Investors give WD Leasing $60,560, while WD Leasing signs notes with them. WD Leasing leases (or buys) the auto from CarSales. WD Leasing transfers the car to Wheeler-Dealer. Also, WD Leasing, for a fee, gets an insurance company to guarantee the residual value.

Subsequently, Wheeler-Dealer makes payments to WD Leasing. WD Leasing transfers cash to the investors. If it leased instead of bought the car, it also remits cash to CarSales.

Issue: While Wheeler-Dealer has made a financial commitment, must it report a lease obligation on its financial statements?

Over time Wheeler Dealer makes lease payments to WD Leasing; specifically, Wheeler Dealer pays $15,000 at the beginning of each lease term. WD Leasing then takes the money and pays the creditors of the SPE.

The deal, of course, is great for Wheeler-Dealer, Inc., because it obtains the depreciation expense as a tax deduction and it does not show any lease obligation on the balance sheet. The only losers are the investors and creditors of Wheeler-Dealer since they are deceived about the firm's true level of financial structure. Of course, if the business enterprise provides sufficient disclosures, the investment community can make analytical adjustments and obtain the true picture.

Exhibit 6.8 contains a real-world example of a synthetic lease disclosure. In this note, Qwest explains that it leases "corporate offices, network operations centers, and CyberCenters." The second paragraph of the disclosure mentions that the corporation has borrowed $177 million from the SPE, but it is silent with respect to the interest rate, the term of the loan, covenants, guarantees, and the impact on annual cash flows.

The first paragraph also declares that Qwest no longer has a liability for its guarantees of certain residual values. This revelation is surprising since most synthetic leases employ third parties to guarantee these residual values. In particular, the firm does not explain how it could avoid capitalization while guaranteeing the residual values.

Exhibit 6.8   Example of Synthetic Lease Disclosure (Qwest, from 2001 10-K)

Included in the operating lease amounts in the first table and in the guarantees in the second table [not shown here] are amounts relating to structured finance transactions under which Qwest agreed to lease from unrelated parties certain real estate properties, including corporate offices, network operations centers, and CyberCenters. These are referred to as synthetic lease facilities. These leases, which had lease terms of six years, were accounted for as operating leases and represent $67 million of the total operating lease payments and all of the guarantee amounts. In March 2002, the Company paid the full amount necessary to acquire all properties subject to the synthetic lease agreements and terminated these agreements. The purchase price of all such properties was approximately $255 million. As a result of the payments, the loan commitments totaling $382 million were terminated and the Company is no longer liable for its residual value guarantees of up to $228 million that were applicable if the leases expired at the end of their term.

During 2001, the Company entered into an operating lease arrangement ("synthetic lease") under which the Company had the option to purchase the leased real estate properties at any time during the lease term. This synthetic lease facility had a capacity of approximately $305 million, although only approximately $177 million had been utilized at December 31, 2001. This synthetic lease, in combination with approximately $77 million of previously existing synthetic leases, had certain financial covenants. The total debt held by these lessors related to the property leased to Qwest was $254 million at December 31, 2001.

ACCOUNTING FOR SPECIAL-PURPOSE ENTITIES

Senator Everett Dirksen commented that "[a] billion dollars here and a billion dollars there—pretty soon you're talking about real money." With securitized lending and synthetic leasing estimated in the trillions of dollars, clearly we are talking about real money in the eyes of any quipster. As we learn that almost all of this debt is not recognized on anyone's balance sheet, we realize that the U.S. economy has an incredibly high degree of financial risk. And seemingly everyone wants to keep hiding this debt and pretending that it does not exist!

The cascading scandals of yesteryear put enormous pressure on the FASB to clean up the abuses of SPEs.[35] The major issue centers on consolidation. What is at stake, as discussed in Chapter 3, is whether the liabilities are booked in the financial statements or whether they continue to be swept into some virtual dustbin.

The old rule, such as it was, stated that if the SPE had at least 3 percent of its total capital from some outside source, then the business enterprise did not have to consolidate the SPE with its own affairs. The Emerging Issues Task Force (EITF), an organization under the auspices of the FASB, published this old rule and labeled it EITF 90-15, which indicates that this rule was its fifteenth rule during 1990. While EITF 90-15 originally applied to certain leasing activities, business managers quickly applied it to all sorts of SPEs. The threshold was so low that managers found it an easy way to keep SPE debt off the balance sheet.

Because of recent condemnation, the FASB proposed requiring consolidation unless outsiders contributed at least 10 percent of the capital to the SPE and this capital is at risk.[36] One of the criticisms was that 3 percent equity does not really put the equity at risk. It takes more equity and less debt in the SPE to really put the equity stakeholders at risk; moreover, the FASB clearly stated in its proposal that the equity has to be at risk. To me that implies that the equity must be subordinated to the debt in terms of the returns and in terms of any distributions in bankruptcy. Sure, the 10 percent cutoff remains arbitrary, but it clarifies the situation for all participants. Many managers complained because they perceived that billions of dollars would be added to the corporate balance sheet.[37] Apparently the appeals had some effect, for the FASB modified the final rule to allow an exception to this 10 percent dividing line.

The FASB in 2003 issued Interpretation No. 46, which deals with the accounting of a subset of SPEs.[38] The FASB set up two criteria so that if either is met, then the SPE is subject to consolidation. The two criteria are:

1. "The total equity investment at risk is not sufficient to permit the entity to finance its activities without additional subordinated financial support from other parties. That is, the equity investment at risk is not greater than the expected losses of the entity."

2. "As a group the holders of the equity investment at risk lack any one of the following three characteristics of a controlling financial interest:

    a. The direct or indirect ability to make decisions about an entity's activities through voting rights or similar rights . . . .

  b. The obligation to absorb the expected losses of the entity if they occur . . . .

  c. The right to receive the expected residual returns of the entity if they occur . . . ."

Paragraph 9 of this interpretation mentions the 10 percent threshold. However, the FASB says that this bright line can be ignored if the SPE can prove that it can finance its operations without further "subordinated financial support," the SPE has as much equity as similar organizations, or its equity is greater than the estimated expected losses.

I think the FASB waffled greatly in this promulgation. Tying the issue of consolidation to expected losses is absurd for two reasons. First, the conceptual error by the FASB is that the issue of whether to consolidate depends on whether the debt of the SPE is seen as the debt of the combined grouping. It has nothing to do with expected losses. I believe that the debt of an SPE is like the debt of a subsidiary. If the FASB thinks that SPE debt does not have to be consolidated, it might as well announce that parent companies no longer have to show the liabilities of their subsidiaries. Second, the implementation error of the paragraph 9 exception is that the corporate managers will make those judgments while their auditors will attest to these decisions. Given the ethical failures of both managers and auditors, I predict that many SPEs will have equity that exceeds their estimated expected losses.

I speculate that someone in the banking industry or in government privately asked the FASB members to consider what would happen if suddenly several trillion dollars of liabilities were added to corporate balance sheets.[39] Some, maybe many, banks would be in violation of their capital requirements. Further, the economy already is struggling to get out of a recession. What would happen to the recovery if the truth were known?

Financial accounting rules should reinforce the desire to tell the truth. If our society drops this imperative from the purposes of accounting standards setting, then we might as well tell business enterprises that they can report anything they like. Trying to engineer results for an industry or for the economy overall eventually sabotages the whole system as investors and creditors learn that financial statements are not worth the electronic pages on which they are virtually printed.

PRELIMINARY CORPORATE RESPONSES
ABOUT SPECIAL-PURPOSE ENTITY ACCOUNTING

Firms have been revising their accounting practices with respect to SPEs for the past year or so. In part, they were anticipating what the FASB and the SEC might do. In part, they were proclaiming that they are not the next accounting scandal. Now that the FASB has issued Interpretation No. 46, that pressure will diminish. Instead of worrying about what the new rules could do to them, managers and auditors will decide strategies for overcoming any consolidation of SPE liabilities. The more important force is the continued dismay and cynicism of the public, although it may not last much longer.

FleetBoston Financial Corporation reported the consolidation of $6 billion of previously off-the-books SPE debts.[40] Boeing proposed putting $1.2 billion of such liabilities on its books.[41] Krispy Kreme nullified a synthetic lease to erase any perception of deception. On the other hand, El Paso Corporation continues to make deals that would challenge a financial Einstein to understand them, although the net effect seems to be the hiding of $2.5 billion of debt.[42] The Federal Reserve Board has taken the unusual stand of forcing PNC Financial Group to consolidate $762 million of debt that it wrongfully concealed. The SEC also issued a cease-and-desist order against PNC because of its treatment of SPEs.[43]

In a recent survey, 80 percent of the respondents said they have no intention of consolidating any of the SPE debts.[44] Interestingly, many of them admitted that they guaranteed the investments of outsiders against any losses. Perhaps now that the new FASB rule is out, they will attempt to obtain multiple-party guarantees so that no one has a majority interest in them and therefore no one will have to consolidate the SPEs.[45]

Investment bankers are concerned about what impact Interpretation No. 46 will have on their business.[46] Rather than worrying about reporting the truth, their anxiety is inwardly focused on how they can engineer new deals in the future.

Homer unabashedly reports one expert's stance that "almost every synthetic lease has been counted as debt."[47] Reading a bit further, we find out what he really means: "But the lenders know all about it; it's not going to bust the balance sheet." If he really believes in the latter point, he should have no objection to the consolidation of SPEs. More important, his initial premise likely is untrue, so it underscores the solution that we must consolidate all SPEs.

SUMMARY AND CONCLUSION

Special-purpose entity debt matters. With trillions of dollars of SPE debts off the books, of course it matters! Only those blind to ethical considerations can claim otherwise.

Recall the typical structure of a securitization or of a synthetic lease in Exhibits 6.2 and 6.6. Since the SPE has nothing else to do other than process the transactions related to the securitization or to the synthetic lease, it is apparent that the SPE is working at the beck and call of the business enterprise. Legally, securitizations and other arrangements may be constructed so as to protect the investors in case of bankruptcy, but the accounting profession has long held the view that accounting statements should reflect the economic substance of what is taking place rather than the legal form. Form over substance should become the rallying cry yet again.

The FASB issued a disappointing ruling with its Interpretation No. 46. While keeping the 10 percent threshold in its statement, it created three loopholes to allow business entities a way out. It will be interesting to see how many SPEs actually get consolidated in the future. I predict many fibs as financial executives continue to hide debts with SPEs.

Because of these continued deceptions, I offer the following investment tip. Consider investing only in those companies that consolidate their SPE debts, such as FleetBoston, Boeing, and Krispy Kreme. Do not invest in those that play games, such as PNC, or those that refuse to recognize the liabilities in their statements, such as El Paso Corporation.

This pathetic scenario reveals deep cracks and crevices in the world of accounting. Before these disappointments ever get resolved, we shall have to understand what mistakes have been made. The failures of managers and directors are examined in the next chapter; the failures of auditors are covered in Chapter 8; the failures of regulators, including the FASB, are discussed in Chapter 9; and the failures of investors are assessed in Chapter 10. We shall continue to experience lousy accounting until we acknowledge these failures and look for solutions.[48]

NOTES

1. For a basic treatment of derivatives, see F. K. Reilly and K. C. Brown, *Investment Analysis and Portfolio Management,* 6th ed. (New York: Dryden, 2000); for advanced coverage, see R. W. Kolb, *Futures, Options, and Swaps,* 3rd ed. (London: Blackwell, 1999).

2. Financial Executives International, "Special Purpose Entities: Understanding the Guidelines," *FEI Issues Alert* (January 2002); A. L. Hartgraves and G. J. Benston, "The Evolving Accounting Standards for Special Purpose Entities and Consolidations," *Accounting Horizons* (September 2002): 245–258; and K. Merx, "Off the Books, Not Off the Wall: Off-Balance Sheet Financing Makes Some Squirm, But It's Legit and Common," *Crain's Detroit Business,* May 13, 2002.

3. Financial Executives International, "Special Purpose Entities"; Hartgraves and Benston, "The Evolving Accounting Standards for Special Purpose Entities and Consolidations"; S. G. Ryan, *Financial Instruments and Institutions: Accounting and Disclosure Rules* (Hoboken, NJ: John Wiley & Sons, 2002).

4. See, for example, K. Eichenwald, "Enron Ruling Leaves Corporate Advisers Open to Lawsuits," *New York Times,* December 23, 2002.

5. W. Lambert, A. Galloni, and P. Dvorak, "A Global Journal Report: Enron Uproar Focuses a More Critical Eye on Accounting Abroad—Off-Balance Sheet Financing Clouds Economic Health of Certain Nations—Japan Is Among Those Using 'Tricks,'" *Asian Wall Street Journal,* July 15, 2002, p. A1; and P. Lemieux, "Our Government: The Ultimate Enron," *National Post,* June 25, 2002.

6. See: D. Ackman, "Andrew Fastow, Fall Guy," *Forbes,* October 3, 2002; A. Barrionuevo, J. Weil, and J. R. Wilke, "Enron's Fastow Charged with Fraud—Complaint by U.S. Signals Peril for Other Ex-Officials: Merrill Lynch Role is Cited," *Wall Street Journal,* October 3, 2002, p. A3; P. Beckett and J. Sapsford, "Energy Deals Made $200 Million in Fees for Citigroup, J. P. Morgan," *Wall Street Journal,* July 24, 2002; P. Behr and A. Witt: "Visionary's Dream Led to Risky Business," July 28, and "Dream Job Turns into a Nightmare," *Washington Post,* July 29, 2002; O. Bilodeau, "Lawyers Fingered in Enron Report," *Fulton County Daily Report,* October 11, 2002; R. Bryce, *Pipe Dreams: Greed, Ego, and the Death of Enron* (Cambridge, MA: Perseus Book Group, 2002; L. Fox, *Enron: The Rise and Fall* (Hoboken, NJ: John Wiley & Sons, 2003); D. Q. Mills, *Buy, Lie, and Sell High: How Investors Lost Out on Enron and the Internet Bubble* (Upper Saddle River, NJ: Prentice-Hall, 2002); W. Powers, S. Troubh, and H. S.Winokur Jr., *Report of Investigation by the Special Investigative Committee of the Board of Directors of Enron Corp.,* February 1, 2002; A. Raghunathan, "Interim CEO Must Simplify Enron to Save It," *Dallas Morning News,* August 18, 2002; and J. Sapsford and P. Beckett, "Citigroup Deals Helped Enron to Disguise Its Debts as Trades," *Wall Street Journal,* July 22, 2002.

7. D. Barboza, "Dynegy to Pay $3 Million in Settlement with S.E.C.," *New York Times,* September 25, 2002.

8. L. Turner, "Financial Institutions and Collapse of Enron." Congressional Testimony before the Committee on Senate Governmental Affairs, July 23, 2002.

9. S. G. Ryan, *Financial Instruments and Institutions: Accounting and Disclosure Rules* (Hoboken, NJ: John Wiley & Sons, 2002).

10. Y. Ijiri, *Recognition of Contractual Rights and Obligations.* Research Report (Stamford, CT: FASB, 1980).

11. G. I. White, A. C. Sondhi, D. Fried, *The Analysis and Use of Financial Statements* New York: John Wiley & Sons, 1997), pp. 548–549.

12. Ibid.

13. Sometimes managers fool themselves. When they remove the debts from the balance sheet, they might forget that the risks do not go away and must still be managed. See F. L. Ayres and D. E. Logue, "Risk Management in the Shadow of Enron," *Journal of Business Strategy* (July-August 2002).

14. Ryan's *Financial Instruments and Institutions* provides an excellent narrative of securitizations. A simpler and readable treatment is found in G. I. White, A. C. Sondhi, and D. Fried, *The Analysis and Use of Financial Statements,* 3rd ed. (New York: John Wiley & Sons, 2003). While much of the discussion in this section is applicable to all sorts of securitizations, I restrict the examples to securitizations of receivables. For a taste of the smorgasbord of topics, see: EIU Viewsware, "USA Finance—Commercial Paper Chase," *CFO Magazine,* June 27, 2002, on commercial paper conduits; J. R. Butler Jr. and J. E. Steiner, "New Rules of Engagement for Workouts: REMICs and Distressed Real Estate Loans," *Real Estate Issues,* January 1, 2001, on real estate mortgage investment conduits (REMICs); P. Townsend, "Asset-Backed Securities Market Feels the Pinch," *eFinancial News,* June 12, 2002, on collateralized debt obligations (CDOs); and C. A. Stone and A. Zissu, "Synthetic Collateralized Loan Obligations: Olan Enterprises, PLC," *Journal of Derivatives,* March 22, 2002, on synthetic collateralized loan obligations. Truly, the variation and the complexity of securitizations are staggering.

15. Dow Jones Corporate Filings Alert, "General Motors Details Use of Special Purpose Entities," *Dow Jones,* February 25, 2002; Dow Jones Corporate Filings Alert, "Goodyear Tire Had $339.2M Invested in SPE at June 30," *Dow Jones,* August 7, 2002; Business Wire, "Willis Lease Finance Closes New, Increased Warehouse Credit Facility and Announces Partners for Planned Securitization," *Business Wire,* September 17, 2002.

16. S. T. Whelan, "Operating Assets: The Latest Securitization Niche," *Equipment Leasing Today,* August 1, 2002; PRNewswire, "S&P: Timber Securitizations Unique Among ABS Transactions," *PRNewswire,* June 6, 2002; C. Cummins and A. Barrionuevo, "El Paso Investors Question Booking of Power Contracts," *Wall Street Journal,* July 23, 2002; C. M. O'Connor, "How Dreamworks Works: Anatomy of Movie-Backed Deals," *Asset Securitization Report,* November 4, 2002.

17. P. Townsend, "Asset-Backed Securities Market Feels the Pinch."

18. R. Lenzner and M. Swibel, "Warning: Credit Crunch; Regulators Want $1 Trillion or More of Hidden Corporate Debt Moved into Plain View. The Reform Could Stifle the Credit-Driven Economy," *Forbes,* August 12, 2002.

19. Alternatives exist. These receivables can be placed into the SPE with or without recourse. *With recourse* means that if the customer's account becomes uncollectible, then the firm must make it up. *Without recourse* implies that if the customer's account becomes uncollectible, then the firm does nothing. The credit risk involved in these accounts receivables lies with

the business enterprise in the first instance, but with the investors in the SPE in the latter case. Of course, some third party might guarantee these assets for the SPE investors.

20. Financial Accounting Standards Board, *Related Party Disclosures,* SFAS No. 57 (Stamford, CT: FASB, 1982).

21. Statement No. 140 is restricted to securitizations that involve financial assets.

22. The FASB standard is actually much more complicated. The FASB covers the possibility that a firm retains partial control over the assets, in which it accounts for the transactions as part of secured borrowing and part selling of the assets. It effects this partial treatment via what the FASB calls the "financial components concept." See: Financial Accounting Standards Board, *Accounting for Transfers and Servicing of Financial Assets and Extinguishments of Liabilities,* SFAS No. 140 (Norwalk, CT: FASB, 2000).

23. D. Skipworth, *Statement 140—A Study of Securitization Disclosures.* Research Report (Norwalk, CT: FASB, 2001).

24. This lack of compliance begs the question of why the firm's auditors are signing off when the enterprise does not meet the requirements of Statement No. 140. Perhaps the effects are immaterial, but in this post-Enron age, it conjures up alternative explanations.

25. General Electric reports that it would encounter adjustments to its SPEs whenever the credit rating of GE Capital drops. Its SPEs hold $43 billion of assets, and they are secured by a variety of assets, mostly receivables. If the credit rating of GE Capital falls too low, then it must supply additional "credit support" or liquidate the SPEs. Dow Jones Business News, "GE Sees 1st-Quarter Charge of About $1 Billion from Goodwill Elimination," *Dow Jones,* March 8, 2002; and A. Elstein, "GE Sheds Light on Its Finances—in Its Annual Report, Conglomerate Provides More Detailed Profit Figures—Company Tries to Reassure Investors in the Wake of Enron's Collapse," *Asian Wall Street Journal,* March 11, 2002.

26. S. Bergsman, "Scrutinizing Synthetic Leases," *Shopping Center World,* July 1, 2002. This estimate, however, appears very low. It probably reflects only new synthetic leases and only the amount of funds provided by investors in the SPE, which frequently is much smaller than the lease obligation.

27. P. Loftus, "Cisco Details Synthetic Leases Worth at Least $1.6B," *Dow Jones News Service.* March 11, 2002.

28. "US Airways Awash in Problems Despite Guarantee," *Airline Financial News,* July 15, 2002.

29. "Fitch Rates Constellation Energy's $500MM Senior Notes 'A–,'" *Business Wire,* August 27, 2002.

30. S. Bergsman, "Serious Questions about Synthetic Leases," *National Real Estate Investor,* May 1, 2002; E. MacDonald, "False Front," *Forbes.* October 14, 2002; S. Muto, "Firms Use Synthetic Leases Despite Criticism—Some Charge Leases Hide Potential Liabilities from the Balance Sheet," *Wall Street Journal,* February 20, 2002; and S. Muto, "'Synthetic Lease' Arrangements Thrive in U.S. Despite Scrutiny—Critics Say Financing Method Hides Potential Liabilities from Balance Sheet—Account Maneuver Can Be Used to Boost Earnings per Share," February 22, 2002.

31. T. Sickinger, "In Search of the Bottom Line," *The Oregonian,* March 31, 2002.

32. C. Byron, "Krispy Kreme Bites," *New York Post,* February 11, 2002.

33. R. L. Nessen, "The Appropriate Solution—Synthetic Leases vs. Bond Net Lease," *www.crico.com/articles,* 2002; Ryan, *Financial Instruments and Institutions.*

34. Schwab says that it "has provided a residual value guarantee of approximately $200 million to one of its lessors in the event the leased property is sold and the proceeds on the sale are

below the guarantee"; G. F. Ceron, "Schwab Annual Report Spells Out Synthetic Lease Details," *Dow Jones Newswires*. May 2, 2002.

35. Hartgraves and Benston furnish the history of accounting for SPEs; see "The Evolving Accounting Standards for Special Purpose Entities and Consolidations."

36. Financial Accounting Standards Board, *Consolidation of Certain Special-Purpose Entities.* Proposed Interpretation (Norwalk, CT: FASB, June 28, 2002).

37. C. Bryan-Low and C. Mollenkamp, "'Off the Books' Cleanup Turns Out to Be Tough," *Wall Street Journal,* January 13, 2003; D. L. Coallier, "Buyer Beware of Off-the-Books Funding: An Enron-Inspired Accounting Change Would Force Acquirers to Determine Whether They Have Bought a Live Time Bomb," *Mergers and Acquisitions Journal,* October 1, 2002; R. Garver, "FASB Proposes Special-Entity Asset Pullback," *American Banker,* July 2, 2002; F. Norris, "Accounting Reform Takes Step Backward," *New York Times,* June 9, 2002; and C. S. Remond, "FASB Mulls Excluding Some SPEs from Consolidation Rules," *Dow Jones News Service,* May 8, 2002.

38. F. Norris, "Accounting Rules Changed to Bar Tactics Used by Enron," *New York Times,* January 16, 2003.

39. Compare Garver, "FASB Proposes Special-Entity Asset Pullback," and B. Nelson, "FASB Puts Banks in a Bind," *Forbes,* January 1, 2003.

40. S. B. Nelson, "FleetBoston May Have to Hike Its Reserves by Up to $600 Million," August 27, 2002, and "FleetBoston Financial Changes Accounting of 'Special Purpose Entities,'" *Boston Globe,* August 28, 2002.

41. A. Keeton, "Boeing CEO Assures Investors on Special Purpose Entity," *Dow Jones News Service,* March 19, 2002.

42. D. Barboza, "Dynegy to Pay $3 Million in Settlement with S.E.C.," *New York Times,* September 25, 2002, p. C6; and M. Davis, "Questions Raised about El Paso Corp.'s Bond Deal, Trading Liabilities," *Houston Chronicle,* July 11, 2002.

43. J. N. DiStefano, "SEC Makes Allegations about PNC Financial's Accounting Reports," *Philadelphia Inquirer,* July 19, 2002; R. Julavits, "PNC Leadership Changes May Be Far from Over," *American Banker,* August 19, 2002; M. P. Oliver, "Off-Balance Sheet Representations/Warranties," *Hoosier Banker,* August 1, 2002; and G. Silverman, "Second Bank Falls Foul of Regulators," *Financial Times,* July 19, 2002.

44. R. Fink, "The Fear of All Sums: To Restore Investor Trust, Many Companies Are Disclosing More Information, According to a CFO Survey. But It May Not Be Enough," *CFO Magazine,* August 1, 2002.

45. Norris, "Accounting Rules Changed to Bar Tactics Used by Enron."

46. See: "How Scrutiny of SPEs Will Affect Financing in the Middle Market," *Bank and Lender Liability Litigation Reporter,* August 29, 2002; J. Chang, "Wall Street Sharpens Focus on Off-Balance Sheet Items: Impact on Chemical Industry Has Been Negligible as Companies Have Provided Reasonable Disclosures," *Chemical Market Reporter,* April 8, 2002; T. Davenport, "In Focus: SEC Proposal Could Cloud Off-Balance Sheet Picture," *American Banker,* November 4, 2002; A. Hill and A. Michaels, "Hostile Terrain," *Financial Times,* August 13, 2002; E. Homer, "Sale/Leaseback Flow to Swell as FASB Prepares to Drain Synthetic Leases," *Private Placement Letter,* June 17, 2002; E. Homer, "Synthetic Leases: Extinct, or Just Evolving?" *Asset Securitization Report,* July 8, 2002; E. Homer, "Synthetic Intelligence: How Will FASB Decisions Truly Affect Synthetic Issues?" *Private Placement Letter,* July 8, 2002; E. Homer, "Synthetic Leases—One Hundred, Fifty-four Million Dollars," *Asset Securitization Report,* September 9, 2002; E. Homer, "Lease Pros Come Out

Swinging at Synthetic Lease/CTL Conference," *Private Placement Letter,* November 4, 2002); J. Keegan and B. Tunick, "Shell Shocked," *Investment Dealers Digest,* July 8, 2002; Lenzner and Swibel, "Warning: Credit Crunch; Regulators Want $1 Trillion or More of Hidden Corporate Debt Moved into Plain View. The Reform Could Stifle the Credit-Driven Economy," *Forbes*, August 12, 2002; P. Thangavelu, "SPE Controversy Having Impact on Commercial MBS Market," *American Banker,* August 19, 2002; and Townsend, "Asset-Backed Securities Market Feels the Pinch."

47. E. Homer, "Lease Pros Come Out Swinging at Synthetic Lease/CTL Conference."

48. Because generally accepted accounting principles frequently serve as a means for legalized fraud, Briloff termed them "cleverly rigged accounting ploys." The acronym is fitting. As I tell my MBA students, "GAAP is CRAP!"

More energetic investors should consider using their inspection rights if firms do not consolidate their SPEs, especially if they are incorporated in Delaware; C. Reese, "Avoiding the Next Enron," *Fortune,* April 15, 2002, p. 358. If business enterprises will not disclose the information, investors have the right to inspect corporate documents that should provide the data. If the firms say this cannot be done or ignore investors, petition the Chancery Court for a summary order against the corporation. The Chancery Court is supportive of investor rights, and we should exercise these rights when managers do not disclose the true level of debt in their firms.

Part III

Failures that
Led to Deceptions

CHAPTER SEVEN

Failure of Managers and Directors

Financial events in the last two years have raised questions about the role of modern-day managers and the board of directors. It feels as if we have been watching a Woody Allen movie in which the purpose of management has become the transfer of wealth from shareholders and creditors to managers, and the board of directors agrees to this brave new corporate world. If so, perhaps now is the time to exit the theater and ask for a refund. We must reaffirm the orthodox belief that managers are stewards of the business enterprise and that directors should see that they behave as good stewards for the owners.

Some managers are responsible for the accounting frauds of the last few years; after all, they committed the frauds. Likewise, some directors are undoubtedly responsible for not taking the appropriate steps in investigating management behavior and providing the oversight necessary to keep managers in check. Just as clearly, not all managers and not all directors perpetrate acts of dishonesty; many maintain high standards of professionalism and ethics. Consciously or unconsciously, however, many of these managers are engaging in activities that potentially could lead them down a destructive path, so it is important to look at these dysfunctional aspects of corporate culture.

Despite the appearance of strength and endurance, accounting is fragile; despite the look of science and exactness, accounting is imprecise; despite the rigid face of arithmetic, accounting is soft and malleable; and despite the outline of mechanical perfection, accounting is sandcastles and soap bubbles. Accounting can turn a history of transactions and events into discrete statistics, but whether these numbers have meaning depends on the transformation process. If treated with professional care, accounting can inform thousands about the well-being of a corporation. When abused and scorned, accounting becomes a monster of unimaginable proportions.

Chapters 7 to 10 look at the collective failure of the American economic system. Chapter 7 tackles the failure of corporate governance, Chapter 8 scrutinizes the failure of the auditing profession, Chapter 9 investigates the failure of regulation, and Chapter 10 considers the failure of investors to protect themselves.

The first two sections of this chapter examine the failure of managers and the failure of the board of directors and investigate the concept of corporate governance, including a critique of the Preliminary Report by the American Bar Association. The next section looks at the recent nascent interest in business ethics, wondering whether it is for show or for real. The final section of the chapter studies how to restore confidence to the economic system by refocusing and reinvigorating corporate culture and by appropriate measures of enforcement.

FAILURE OF MANAGERS

Chapter 1 has already discussed a number of highly visible financial failures in recent years. Managers have engaged in a number of scams and swindles (see again Exhibit 1.1); even more have toyed with accounting numbers, bending them in all sorts of shapes in an attempt to make themselves look good and perhaps also to increase the value of their stock options. Because of the failures at Enron and WorldCom and elsewhere, some new attention has been given to these financial disclosures, and as a result corporations have churned out a flood of accounting restatements, as shown in Exhibit 1.2. The sheer volume of restatements implies a variety of serious problems with financial reporting if not a high amount of fraud.

Michael Young, head of Willkie Farr & Gallagher's Accounting Irregularities Practice Group, reminds us that managers typically do not awake one morning and ask whom they might defraud that day.[1] Instead, managers face temptations in the form of pressure from the chief executive officer (CEO) or the board of directors or externally, perhaps from the need to meet analyst forecasts. Because of these pressures and because managers want to be team players or perhaps worry that their jobs or promotions or salary increases are on the line, the managers' ethical stance becomes softened. Usually managers try the direct approach of meeting analyst forecasts by working longer or harder and trying to increase sales or decrease expenses, but there comes a point at which this effort turns unfruitful, and it becomes very difficult or impossible to improve the situation. At that point managers might look at the reporting system. Because of the many ambiguities in accounting and the many areas that require professional judgment, an opportunity presents itself for improvement.[2] The managers then say "yes" to this opportunity, rationalizing that the change is small, or it will happen only this once, or it is for a good cause, or it falls within that acceptable range of generally accepted accounting principles (GAAP), which we might rename "generally ambiguous accounting possibilities." Unfortunately, new pressures arise and the managers continue to employ the opportunity to tweak the financial reporting system. They dig a bigger hole and eventually have no way to extract themselves from the mess. Sooner or later, investors and creditors find out the truth, and the jig is up.

Exhibit 7.1 depicts a simple schematic of this process, which we shall call the Young model. Pressures to perform mount until they become unbearable, then the manager grasps the opportunity to cook the books, and the fraud begins. Little does the manager realize the snag in this "solution"—the problem frequently escalates and requires further exaggerations and manipulations. The process continues until either something great happens for the corporation that allows the managers to hide their deceptions or the fraud becomes public knowledge.

Consider the case of Sensormatic Electronics, described in Chapter 1. Managers of Sensormatic Electronics changed the computer clock to treat some of the sales of the following period as if they were sales of the current period. For example, suppose that

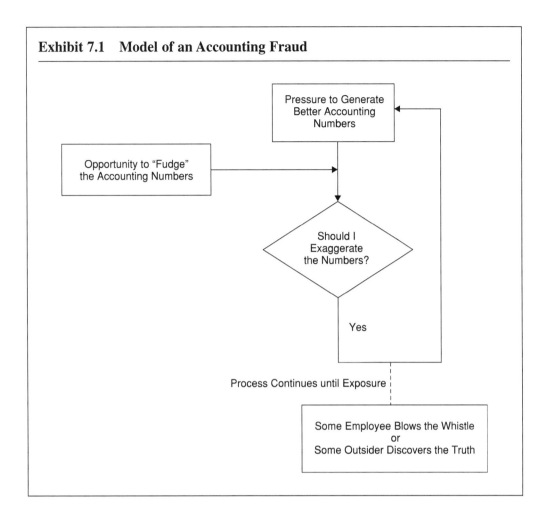

Exhibit 7.1   Model of an Accounting Fraud

we feel the pressure to record $100 million sales in the current quarter but have only $95 million in revenues. We remedy the problem by moving $5 million of quarter 2 sales into quarter 1 and thereby achieve our goal in the first quarter. But a day of reckoning comes. Suppose we now need $100 million of sales in the second quarter but have only $95 million. First, we have to make up the $5 million "loan" to the first quarter, so we are only showing $90 million sales despite actually having $95 million in sales. To make the numbers, managers transfer $10 million of third-quarter sales to the second quarter. And the problem escalates. Of course, if a banner quarter takes place, the corporate managers might get out of the seemingly infinite loop. Otherwise, the discrepancies grow until eventually the executives get caught. When an employee with conscience pangs decides to expose the dishonesty or an outsider stumbles across the facts, the press broadcasts the truth around the world and everyone realizes that the firm, its managers, and its directors are tainted.

Arthur Levitt delivered a simple but valuable speech at the New York University Center for Law and Business on September 28, 1998. Entitled "The 'Numbers' Game,"

Levitt's discourse bore down on this problem of earnings management. His basic premise states that "the motivation to meet Wall Street earnings expectations may be overriding common sense business practices. Too many corporate managers, auditors, and analysts are participants in a game of nods and winks. In the zeal to satisfy consensus earnings estimates and project a smooth earnings path, wishful thinking may be winning the day over faithful representation."[3]

Little did he know how prophetic that statement would be!

Levitt continued in his speech to discuss five methods of accounting hocus pocus (restructuring charges, in-process research and development, cookie jar reserves, misuse of the materiality principles, and premature recognition of revenue). Then he unveiled an action plan for dealing with these problems. These recommendations involved tactical, short-term solutions to the five accounting issues that Levitt raised. At the end of his speech, the former Securities and Exchange Commission (SEC) chairman looked at the broad spectrum and returned to the fundamental problem—a culture that encourages accounting fictions in the name of earnings management. More precisely, Levitt called for "nothing less than a cultural change. . . . While the temptations are great, and the pressures strong, illusions in numbers are only that—ephemeral, and ultimately self-destructive."

To demonstrate its resolve, the SEC celebrated the one-year anniversary of this speech by issuing 30 enforcement releases that alleged accounting abuses.[4] These improper applications of accounting mostly entailed embellishing revenues, but included some cases of understating liabilities. Schroeder and MacDonald pointed out that these cases targeted smaller companies, hypothesizing that the SEC was reluctant to take on large companies who had the resources to fight the "understaffed agency."[5] If Schroeder and MacDonald are correct, it might explain why Enron, WorldCom, and others apparently were not much influenced by these SEC enforcement actions. The SEC and federal prosecutors need to aim their guns at the large corporations, their directors, and their advisers for major changes to occur.

Levitt continued his campaign against accounting misrepresentations in another speech at New York University's Center for Law and Business, which was titled "Renewing the Covenant with Investors."[6] On one hand, Levitt said he was encouraged how audit committees seemed "revitalized," but on the other hand, he remained concerned about the "game playing" with accounting numbers. Upon reflection, the former chairman returned to the theme of corporate culture. He not only emphasized his apprehension over managers' short-run focus on Wall Street, but also how analysts were being judged on their contributions to selling rather than scrutinizing firm performance and how auditors were evaluated on their bringing in new business rather than on how well they audited a firm. While he spent most of the rest of the speech exhorting the accounting profession to return to basics and deliver independent, thorough, and hard-hitting audits, he continued to say that the system has to keep the investment community in mind and meet their needs.

The Powers report echoed many of these topics when it tried to determine what happened at Enron.[7] The tone at the top was to deliver results using any methods necessary. Ethics apparently meant little to Ken Lay and Jeff Skilling (and the directors for that matter) as they dismissed the code of ethics whenever it got in the way of what they wanted to do. Enron's managers had a short-run focus to deliver increased earnings every quarter. As Andy Fastow invented the infamous LJM2 special-purpose entity (SPE) to "hedge" the Rhythms NetConnections $300 million gain, Lay, Skilling, and the directors paid little attention to whether the hedge was an effective one or whether the deal made any business sense. Likewise, Lay and Skilling did not care whether Fastow and others followed the accounting rules correctly; they just wanted results. Worst of all, Lay, Skilling, and the directors were insensitive to the horrendous conflicts of interest that they created by having Fastow, an Enron employee, head up the LJM2 business. The pressure to perform came from Lay and Skilling, and when it came time for publishing the financial reports, the other players distorted accounting numbers until they told the story that Enron wanted the world to hear. Unfortunately, they could not get out of this seemingly infinite loop on their own because one lie required a couple of more lies to sustain the original deception. The process grew until the house of cards fell down.[8]

The failure of Enron managers begins with Wall Street's undue pressure for results and the focus on short-term results. At Enron, these pressures combined with an attitude that investors and creditors are unimportant at best and troublemakers at worst. Their disdain was perhaps most noticeable when Enron executives refused to answer investor questions about their accounting practices. Further evidence of a corrupt corporate culture at Enron is seen in how they dealt with accounting standards. Rather than trying to meet the needs of the corporate community, Enron executives would attempt to cajole and pressure the Financial Accounting Standards Board (FASB) to relent and, when profitable, to run to Congress for help. Of course, Enron would dole out campaign contributions to get senators and representatives to help out. In short, the culture at Enron ruined the firm long before it actually declared bankruptcy.

FAILURE OF DIRECTORS

Much of what has been laid at the feet of managers in terms of the Young model applies to directors as well. When the directors were not on the golf course, they focused on short-term results, particularly with an eye toward the firm's stock prices. They pressured managers or at least refused to assuage the pressures that top management placed on others. Besides, they too had little respect for investors and creditors and little regard for accurate and truthful reporting.

Enron, of course, is the classic case.[9] The 2002 Powers report provides some important details about the actions of Enron managers, the Arthur Andersen auditors, and the Vinson and Elkins lawyers. It gives many examples of how managers engaged in fraudulent activities and how auditors and lawyers did not supply useful evaluations of management's plans and business deals. What remains fascinating, however, is that the report incriminates the directors because it clearly demonstrates how they did not oversee what managers did. The directors merely listened to the discussions of Lay, Skilling, and others and then nodded assent. Even when proposed actions broke the firm's code of ethics, the directors did not challenge the endeavors. Maybe some directors think that they discharge their responsibilities by showing up for the meetings and agreeing with the CEO, but society demands more than that.[10]

WorldCom provides another instance. When a dozen or so employees or former employees blew the whistle on the fraud at WorldCom, the directors turned their attention to other matters.[11] It appears that they did not bother to investigate the charges leveled by these whistle-blowers.

To illustrate these issues, let us examine the failure of directors in dealing with management compensation and their failure to build strong audit committees. We then turn our attention to recommendations made by the American Bar Association.

Stock Options

So much has been written recently about the expensing of stock options that people may miss the more important issue—are stock options worthwhile in motivating managers to perform their best? We address the financial reporting issue after tackling the question of whether options are efficacious.

Do stock options align the interests of managers with the interests of the owners? I submit the answer is no.[12] While stock options allow the holder to enjoy gains as the stock price increases, it spares the holder of any pain from stock price decreases. Managers with stock options do not face any downside risk. Also, if stock prices do not move in such a way to allow managers a wealth increment, then business entities often reload the stock options. In other words, managers typically face little risk that the stock options will run dry because compensation committees react by lowering the strike price to some figure more likely to allow the managers a chance to exercise the options. Shareholders, on the other hand, experience any losses very dearly and very personally, and they have no opportunity to reload and buy the stock at lower prices than they originally paid. Stock options do not align the interests of managers and shareholders.

Even if compensation contracts could be written that better align these divergent interests, stock options are still deficient because many times they are not distributed on the basis of performance. In addition, the principal determinant in the movement of a firm's stock price is the movement in the overall market. Typical stock option plans do not distinguish between the performance of the overall stock market and the performance by company executives, so the real value of the stock option is driven by macroeconomic or industry forces. At the margin, managerial performance has little impact on the value of stock options.

Typical corporate stock option plans encourage managers to think of themselves as above the investors and creditors. If compensation committees really want to motivate managers, they probably should design bonus packages that distribute cash based on managerial performance, and they should make a very concerted effort to adjust the numbers for macroeconomic and industry movements. The trick is to isolate and assess corporate behavior itself. The metrics that measure and evaluate this performance should be long run in nature, so that managers do not have incentives to play games by making suboptimal short-run operating decisions or manipulating the financial reporting system.

Now, as we consider how to account for the stock option, the answer of course is to account for it as compensation expense. After all, if it is not compensation, then why do so many managers care so much about their stock options? The FASB presents a clear definition of expenses. According to FASB's Concepts No. 6, "Expenses are outflows or other using up of assets or incurrences of liabilities . . . from delivering or producing goods, rendering services, or carrying out other activities that constitute the entity's ongoing major or central operations."[13] Since the definition does not require cash outlays for some outflow to be an expense, arguments against expensing stock options because there are no cash outlays turn into pointless rhetoric. Stock options have value to the recipients, and they are given as part of the compensation package for work that is clearly an ongoing central operation. Finally, stock options eventually use up assets in either of two ways. Many business enterprises take cash to purchase treasury stock and then transfer the certificates to the managers. Alternatively, the entity could issue new stock to the employees, but this action deprives the corporation of assets it otherwise would receive when the firm issues stock. Either way, the company has consumed assets. Therefore, stock-based compensation ought to be expensed.

Corporate executives, especially those in the high-tech industry, have long argued that these options should not be expensed for the sole purpose of overstating net income.[14] Fortunately some sanity has returned to the corporate boardrooms, and firms are starting to switch to the expensing alternative of FASB Statement No. 123. Investors should pay close attention to who expenses these stock options and who does not. With the release of Statement No. 123, the issue no longer rests with whether outsiders have the knowledge of what the firm is doing, because the nonexpensers must disclose the data in their footnotes. Investors and financial analysts can easily prepare analytical adjustments as discussed in Chapters 3 to 5 to obtain superior information about the business enterprise.

As an example, consider Cisco's footnote 10 from its 2002 10-K, which is duplicated in Exhibit 7.2. Among other things, the footnote reveals the difference in net income with a proper inclusion of the stock-based compensation and with an improper exclusion. To put these numbers in perspective, let us look at the return metrics for Cisco Systems. These ratios clearly indicate that Cisco has consistently overstated income by 200 to 400 percent by not expensing its stock options.

	2000		2001	
	Reported	Adjusted	Reported	Adjusted
Return on Assets	.050	.010	(.028)	(.076)
Return on Equity	.066	.013	(.037)	(.100)
Return on Sales	.100	.020	(.045)	(.121)

Today the issue is whether the company cares about the investment community and whether it desires to keep investors and creditors informed. Better corporations will provide the information, and they will provide it in an easy-to-find and easy-to-analyze manner, such as on the income statement itself.[15] Given that the investment community reads the nonexpensing of stock options as a signal that correlates with firms that do not

---

Exhibit 7.2   Cisco System's Disclosure about Stock Options

Pro forma information under SFAS No. 123 is as follows (in millions, except per-share amounts)

Years Ended	July 27, 2002	July 28, 2001	July 29, 2000
Net Income (Loss)—as Reported	**$1,893**	$(1,014)	$2,668
Stock Option Compensation Expense, Net of Tax	**(1,520)**	(1,691)	(1,119)
Net Income (Loss)—Pro Forma	**$ 373**	$(2,705)	$1,549
Basic Net Income (Loss) per Share—as Reported	**$ 0.26**	$ (0.14)	$ 0.39
Diluted Net Income (Loss) per Share—as Reported	**$ 0.25**	$ (0.14)	$ 0.36
Basic Net Income (Loss) per Share—Pro Forma	**$ 0.05**	$ (0.38)	$ 0.22
Diluted Net Income (Loss) per Share—Pro Forma	**$ 0.05**	$ (0.38)	$ 0.21

---

care about reporting their financial statements accurately, directors should urge their managers to join the move toward higher-quality financial reporting.

Audit Committees

Audit committees function as subcommittees of the board of directors. They should act as a liaison between management and the external auditor; they ought to oversee the company's internal audit activities; and they must be a contact point for whistle-blowers. With respect to the external accountant, the audit committee must investigate whether the auditors are independent of their firm, including an assessment of the consulting fees that have been paid by the business enterprise. Exhibit 7.3 presents an example of the audit committee report of St. Paul Companies.

Daniel Sorid correctly reports that the disclaimers contained in such reports have "come under fire."[16] Notice that the audit report in Exhibit 7.3 provides three qualifications of what the committee has done. Members claim that they do not have professional expertise and competence. If so, they should resign from the committee, and the board should find people who do have the skill and judgment to sit on the audit committee. While the committee does not have to contain certified public accountants (although ironically Enron's did), the members need to have enough savvy to deal with managers and external auditors in a judicious manner. Otherwise, what is the point of having an audit committee? Exhibit 7.3 also contains the disclaimer that the audit com-

Exhibit 7.3   St. Paul Companies' Audit Committee Report

The role of the audit committee is to assist the Board of Directors in its oversight of the Company's financial reporting process. All members of the committee are "independent," as required by applicable listing standards of the New York Stock Exchange. The committee operates pursuant to a charter, which is reviewed annually by the committee. A brief listing of the primary responsibilities of the committee is included in this Proxy Statement under the discussion of "Board Committees." As set forth in the charter, management of the Company is responsible for the preparation, presentation, and integrity of the Company's financial statements, the Company's accounting and financial reporting principles, and internal controls and procedures designed to assure compliance with accounting standards and applicable laws and regulations. The independent auditors are responsible for auditing the Company's financial statements and expressing an opinion as to their conformity with generally accepted accounting principles.

In the performance of its oversight function, the committee has considered and discussed the audited financial statements with management and the independent auditors. The committee has also discussed with the independent auditors the matters required to be discussed by Statement on Auditing Standards No. 61, *Communication with Audit Committees*, as currently in effect. Finally, the committee has received the written disclosures and the letter from the independent auditors required by Independence Standards Board Standard No. 1, *Independence Discussions with Audit Committees*, as currently in effect, and written confirmations from management with respect to information technology consulting services relating to financial information systems design and implementation and other non-audit services provided by the auditors, has considered whether the provision of information technology consulting services relating to financial information systems design and implementation and other non-audit services by the independent auditors to the Company is compatible with maintaining the auditors' independence and has discussed with the auditors the auditors' independence.

The members of the audit committee are not professionally engaged in the practice of auditing or accounting and are not experts in the fields of accounting or auditing. Members of the committee rely, without independent verification, on the information provided to them and on the representations made by management and the independent auditors. Accordingly, the audit committee's oversight does not provide an independent basis to determine that management has maintained appropriate accounting and financial reporting principles or appropriate internal controls and procedures designed to assure compliance with accounting standards and applicable laws and regulations. Furthermore, the audit committee's considerations and discussions referred to above do not assure that the audit of the Company's financial statements has been carried out in accordance with generally accepted auditing standards, that the financial statements are presented in accordance with generally accepted accounting principles, or that the Company's auditors are in fact "independent."

Based upon the reports and discussions described in this report, and subject to the limitations on the role and responsibilities of the committee referred to above and in the charter,

159

Exhibit 7.3 *(Continued)*

---

the committee recommended to the Board that the audited financial statements be included in the Company's Annual Report on Form 10-K for the year ended December 31, 2001 to be filed with the Securities and Exchange Commission.

Submitted by the audit committee of the Company's Board of Directors:
David G. John (Chairman), H. Furlong Baldwin, Carolyn H. Byrd, John H. Dasburg, Thomas R. Hodgson, and Bruce K. MacLaury.
March 15, 2002

---

mittee relies on the representations of management and the audit firm. Up to a point, this dependence necessarily exists, but the committee must examine the big issues and provide some evidence that things are proceeding as they should. For example, it is the audit committee's responsibility to verify that the external auditor is independent of the firm and remains so. The committee needs to conduct some inquiries to verify that this is the case and must not rely on management's representations. In addition, the audit report in Exhibit 7.3 asserts that the audit committee cannot assure that the audit firm has conducted an audit properly. While I accept this premise for the most part, I still feel that the audit committee can ask some tough questions and follow through with its own investigations that a thorough audit has been carried out. Among other things, the audit committee can direct the internal auditors to check some aspects of the firm's operations and compare their notes with those of the external auditor. The audit committee is not helpless, so it should quit issuing these meaningless disclaimers.

American Bar Association Task Force Recommendations[17]

The American Bar Association (ABA) recently created a Task Force on Corporate Responsibility, which issued its preliminary report in 2002.[18] The report asserts that "most executive officers, directors and professional advisers act honestly and in good faith." While probably correct, I think the public regards this statement as more a matter of faith than fact. Given the number and the severity of accounting and business scandals in the last few years, and given the hundreds and hundreds of accounting restatements, it seems rational for an observer to hold the opposite viewpoint. At the very least, the burden of proof rests with the managers, directors, and professional advisers.

The Task Force on Corporate Responsibility spends much time in the preliminary report discussing the board of directors. It recommends such things as requiring a substantial majority of the directors be independent of management and that the audit committee[19] be composed of independent directors. However, Enron met many of these recommendations; a majority of Enron directors supposedly were independent of management, and the audit committee was composed of people with great expertise, including a former dean of Stanford's business school. It was not enough to stop the downfall at Enron.

I am skeptical that rules about organizational architecture will prove sufficient in deterring accounting frauds. Chief executive officers have great power and will always have some minimal influence over the choice of directors. Directors also know that usually they can ask only so many probing questions before they lose the chance of getting reappointed. The fact that CEOs often sit on each other's boards also complicates matters as this leads to inherent conflicts. The task force does not address the director-politician nexus as exhibited by Enron's Wendy Gramm, the wife of Senator Phil Gramm.[20] For example, did Ms. Gramm ever sweet-talk her husband into advocating favorable treatment for Enron? If she did, was she acting in the interests of managers or in the interests of the shareholders? Further, the task force does not adequately address the qualifications of the directors. For example, O. J. Simpson served as an auditor for Infinity Broadcasting; he even served on its audit committee.[21] It seems likely that Infinity Broadcasting hired Simpson for name recognition as a great football player and as an actor instead of any accounting prowess. If so, Simpson could offer little substantive help to the board of directors. Nor does the task force speak to the problem of overworked directors. Vernon Jordan, for example, currently sits on 12 boards in addition to holding down jobs at an investment bank and a law firm. Who is naïve enough to believe that Mr. Jordan can serve as independent director and have enough time to ferret out what is really going on at these dozen corporations and can guarantee that there is no accounting hanky-panky? It is humanly impossible.

Having independent directors is better than having managers as directors, but it is no guarantee of truthful accounting. Rather than worrying about organizational architecture, a better solution would focus on the directors' responsibilities. Increasing their exposure to civil liability and criminal charges would do more to change their behavior. Consider the indictment against Frank Walsh, a former Tyco director, and his subsequent guilty plea and restitution of $20 million and fine of $2.5 million.[22] Walsh did not tell other Tyco board members about his finder's fee for Tyco's acquisition of CIT. His indictment will serve as an example that directors cannot do whatever they wish with impunity.[23]

BUSINESS ETHICS: AS OXYMORONIC AS CORPORATE GOVERNANCE[24]?

Need to Get Real

After the financial disasters of the early 21st century, everyone has found religion. Corporations parade their ethics programs, the business press publishes many articles about the topic, and business schools claim that they have been teaching ethics for decades. The public, however, persists in its skepticism.[25] Many people remain wary and suspicious about corporate ethics training[26]; indeed, many wonder whether ethics can ever coexist with the business spirit.[27] Corporate failures have led several people to question what business schools are accomplishing.[28] Paul Williams takes the stance further by insisting that accounting is an ethical discipline.[29] He criticizes the modern academic transformation of accounting from its moral roots to its presumed technical foundations as a measurement science. Williams argues that university professors by and large have quit discussing the "ought" for the "is" and view accounting merely as a tool for maximizing profit.[30] If he is correct, then the education system is fundamentally involved with the decline of ethics in the accounting and business community. Worse, without deep-seated change, there will be more Enrons, WorldComs, and Global Crossings.

I offer a two-pronged treatment for improvement. The business world desperately needs to grasp ethics and not merely employ it as a public relations tool. Ethics by itself is quite fragile, so we need to address the culture of the business community and how attitudes and thought processes must become more investor focused.

Gough Model

General Norman Schwarzkopf has remarked that "[t]he truth of the matter is that you always know the right thing to do. The hard part is doing it." While we might quibble with the word "always," we would agree with the general and argue that, for the most part, his aphorism can be extended to business.[31] New managers and new professional advisers have to learn their professional responsibilities and the social nuances of various business situations, but, once they have done that, they too usually know what is good behavior and what is unacceptable. The difference in which they choose has more to do with whether they have the will and the courage to do the right thing.

In a recent book Gough makes the same point.[32] Gough claims that everything in life has an ethical dimension and that we are all responsible for our behavior. Accordingly, he exhorts people to practice good behavior. Living virtuously helps individuals to live a good life and to make good ethical decisions in the future.

Gough later develops a simple schema for making good ethical decisions: right thinking leads to right actions, which in turn lead to good habits when making ethical decisions and ultimately lead to a strong character.[33] It begins with right thinking about our lives, including our professional lives. Right thinking leads to good acts, however small and seemingly insignificant. These lesser, almost routine decisions have importance, because they help us to make a habit of right decision making. When we develop a habit of ethical decision making, then we build character and obtain a position from which it becomes easier to make right decisions when confronting large ethical problems. Besides, as Young pointed out, most business frauds begin with small mistakes in ethical decision making.[34]

Gough sums up his book with an ethics checklist, which is adapted in Exhibit 7.4.[35] The first set of questions deals with compliance issues: Does the planned action meet the law and any applicable rules? Gough correctly points out that this step constitutes merely a starting point and should never be considered an ending point. Meeting the rules does not make any action ethical.

The second collection of queries gets to the heart of the matter: Is the action fair to everyone concerned? In particular, does the accounting meet the needs and concerns of investors, creditors, employees, and the public? Given that accounting is inherently subjective, are managers presenting the information in a way that describes as accurately and as completely as possible what the business enterprise has done and what it has accomplished during the period? If managers have difficulty envisioning what is fair to

---

Exhibit 7.4   An Ethics Checklist for Managers

---

1. Is it in compliance with the law or any written rules?
   - Federal or state securities law?
   - Company or institutional policies?
   - Company code of ethics?
   - NYSE or other exchange's rules?
   - Professional rules?
   - Other rules?

2. Is it fair to everyone involved?
   - To my employer?
   - To my directors?
   - To my auditors and other professional advisers?
   - To my colleagues?
   - To my subordinates?
   - To the employees?
   - To the stockholders?
   - To the creditors?
   - To the community?

3. Would my ethical role model do it?
   - Who *is* my ethical role model?
   - How would that person feel about me if I did it?
   - How would I feel about that person if he or she did it?
   - Do I have time to get that person's advice first?
   - Do I have the courage to do what that person would do?

From *Character Is Destiny: The Value of Personal Ethics in Everyday Life* by Russell W. Gough, copyright (c) 1998 by Russell Wayne Gough. Used by permission of Prima Publishing, a division of Random House, Inc.

---

others, perhaps they should invoke the golden rule and do as they would like others to do to them. In other words, what types of disclosures would they want if they were the investors or creditors?

Since objectivity may be difficult to achieve in practice, Gough recommends that each person have a role model or mentor. Individuals should ask the person for his or her advice and evaluate whether various courses of action are ethical or not. This mentor can act as a strong buffer against making bad choices.

With this three-pronged arrangement of compliance-fairness-mentor, individuals within a corporate setting can think and act in an ethical manner. Ethical managers will then produce an ethical firm that tells the truth to the investment community and acts as a good citizen in society.

CULTURE

Much of this material sounds like pie-in-the sky bravado, for managers can act as if they are following much of Gough's formula and still act unethically. The key for managers is to quit pretending and start doing these things for real. Levitt's comments should be heeded, because a new culture for business enterprises is critical to restoring credibility to accounting numbers and financial reports. Corporations need to have a good ethics education program, including education in how to read and interpret financial numbers, but they also need to socialize their employees that these values really and truly are important.[36] These values go to the core of the entity's existence. Corporations also need to reinforce good behaviors and punish bad behaviors so that better ethical decisions result. To the extent that the corporate culture has good health, we may expect managers to practice good ethics.

Attributes of an Ethical Firm

What would a firm look like that followed good financial reporting ethics? What would be its ethos? Such organizations exist today; Berkshire Hathaway and TIAA-CREF are two examples. In my judgment these firms possess seven characteristics, as shown in Exhibit 7.5.

The first attribute of a company that achieves good accounting ethics is that it practices active ethics in all aspects from the top down.[37] As Gough and others have said, people find it difficult to apply moral principles in one area of their lives while ignoring ethical principles in other areas. For example, it is easier for a person not to lie to the investment community when he or she honors the truth in other aspects of business affairs. When deception is approved of with (say) the suppliers or the customers, it is easy to lie to investors and creditors as well. It is critical for the top managers to tell the

---

Exhibit 7.5   Aspects of a Good Corporate Culture (with Respect to Accounting and Reporting Issues)

1. Practice active ethics in all aspects from the top down.
2. Respect investors and creditors and financial analysts.
3. Disclose, disclose, and disclose.
4. Maintain a long-run focus on the business.
5. Let auditors do their job.
6. Encourage whistle-blowers to come forward.
7. Support the FASB and the SEC.

---

truth to the investment community. Employees often follow the tendencies of their superiors, so the tone at the top is important.

Assuming that the organization attempts to follow ethical practices, then the second attribute of a good culture with respect to accounting and reporting issues is for the managers to respect investors and creditors and their agents, including financial analysts. Alex Berenson provides an example of what not to do.[38] After forecasting a decline in "free cash flow,"[39] Tyco's fourth-quarter 2002 free cash flow showed a healthy increase. This improvement did not result from operating or corporate enhancements, but rather from a redefinition of the term *free cash flow*. In particular, Tyco removed cash from selling or buying receivables from its definition because the item turned sour. Just as managers have invented EBITDA (earnings before interest and taxes and depreciation and amortization) or other strange mutations of earnings to disguise the bad stuff, Tyco has contorted free cash flow so that it excludes the bad stuff. This is not the way to win the hearts of the investment community or to demonstrate a moral turnaround.

Another example of what not to do is when corporations lobbied against a proposal by the FASB for firms to disclose "comprehensive income."[40] Instead of using substantive arguments, corporate executives merely asserted that financial analysts are dumb and that they would not understand the disclosures. That tack proved strange and disingenuous since the investment community indicated its desire for these disclosures. If managers truly are worried about how their disclosures will be understood, I suggest that they educate investors and creditors about the meaning of the numbers and the disclosures rather than attempting to ban the materials.

Firms that purposefully apply incorrect accounting and claim they can do so because it is "immaterial" also mistreat shareholders and others in the investment community. This usage turns the materiality principle on its head. The original force behind the idea was that proper accounting for some items involved too much bookkeeping costs, such as the depreciation of a waste can. The item might cost a few dollars and have a life of five years. The depreciation amounts are so small that expensing the waste can immediately would hurt nobody. This application is a conservative one; it recognizes expenses earlier than is proper. In recent years firms have been known to front-load revenues quite aggressively. I strongly urge managers to stop pushing the envelope and auditors to stop allowing them to misuse the materiality principle.

Financial executives also need to quit blaming the media for the accounting scandals. When CEOs go on CNBC, CNN, or MSNBC and assert that the scandals are overstated by the media, they look like idiots. Recall from Chapter 1 that in the last few years alone, the American society has experienced at least 50 accounting frauds and almost 1,000 accounting restatements. Not only is it virtually impossible for the press to embellish these facts, but also we have to keep in mind who caused the problems—corporate managers. Sometimes reporters do get carried away, since their careers get a boost when they discover a problem, but these indiscretions shrink in comparison to the accounting frauds of the past few years.

Managers need to bring investors and creditors into the business relationship, just as they have embraced customers and suppliers, and provide them with as much information as they need.[41] This leads us to the third aspect of a good culture with respect to accounting and reporting issues. Managers should disclose all of the information that is necessary to inform financial statement readers of what they are doing. The Accounting Principles Board (APB), the predecessor of the FASB, called this the *disclosure principle*. The judge in the famous Continental Vending case, more fully described in Chapter 11, called on corporations and their accountants to inform the investment community of what was going on and quit hiding behind the rules. The adage "Do for others as you would like them to do for you" would help in this case. Chief executive officers and chief financial officers should ask themselves what knowledge they would like to have if they changed places with the investors.

The fourth principle is to focus on the long-run aspects of the business. Wall Street financial analysts acted silly when trying to discover each and every nuance of the almost daily activities of a firm. Real value creation takes time, so investors need to concentrate on what the entity is doing over the long haul. McKay and Brown report that managers of Coke have decided to quit worrying about meeting somebody else's quarterly forecasts and start centering their attention on their long-term goals.[42] I think that is a great move for Coca-Cola and hope that other business enterprises will follow suit. Besides liberating the firm from a slavish addiction to short-term myopic decisions, it frees them from abusive uses of accounting. Accounting numbers lose their power when reporting over short intervals, but prove more reliable and more accurate when reporting over long intervals.

The fifth attribute of a good accounting culture is to let the external auditors do their jobs. Too many managers have abused their powers with respect to the independent auditors, arguing unconvincingly that audits provided little or no value. Today we know that assertion is ridiculous. If the auditors had performed their tasks with true professionalism, a number of these frauds would have been caught earlier and the damages would have been smaller. Managers also should quit dangling consulting fees before auditors and just pay them for external audits. The audit committee must step up to the plate and play a more active role: Help the auditors do their work and resist the efforts of those managers who do not want any checks or balances.

The sixth characteristic of a good corporate culture concerns the protection of whistle-blowers.[43] No way has yet been found to encourage those in the know to speak out on corporate fraud without penalty from their employers. With respect to Enron, many commentators have focused on the testimony of Sharron Watkins, but her whistle-blowing occurred late in the game, when it was impossible to avert disaster. I find it much more interesting to consider the role of Vince Kaminsky, Enron's former executive in charge of risk management. When Skilling first approached Kaminsky in 1999 about the LJM SPE to protect the $300 million gain in Rhythms NetConnections, Kaminsky and others laughed because they realized that the hedge was bogus. Skilling rewarded Kaminsky's blunt honesty with a demotion. What incentives and protections can we put into place to encourage someone in Kaminsky's position to report such "irregularities" to the board of directors, external auditors, SEC, or federal prosecutors? If such incentives and protections had existed, Kaminsky might have blown the whistle when there was plenty of time to stop the fraud and avert financial disaster. I realize that the Sarbanes-Oxley Act includes a provision to protect whistle-blowers, but I doubt that is enough to encourage people to speak up. Every firm needs to provide a culture that promotes such activity.

The last attribute is for managers to support the FASB and the SEC. Just as too many managers dishonor and scorn investors, many have the same attitude toward the FASB and the SEC because they realize that the FASB stands for improved accounting practices. The FASB wants business enterprises to provide more accurate and more meaningful measures and disclosures rather than obfuscating the reports.

Similarly, managers and auditors should support the SEC and its mission to protect investors and creditors.[44] A strong, effective SEC would root out the "bad guys," leaving the "good guys" to carry on with business. Such a powerful organization would add credibility to managers, corporations, and their financial reports. People would have confidence again in the system, and that restored credibility would provide economic benefits to all, including the managers who played by the rules.

Achieving the Right Culture

Putting these attributes into play will prove tricky. Corporations need strong and ethical leaders to have a vision that includes telling the truth to shareholders. Such individuals do exist in the financial community. They need the courage to take the reins of their organizations and promote active ethics and practice quality financial reporting.

Unfortunately, too many managers and directors still do not get it. External pressures must turn the tide against them, so we shall continue to rely on enforcement by the SEC and federal prosecutors and on civil complaints by plaintiffs' attorneys. With enough diligence, some of these managers and directors can be put behind bars and the rest dismissed from their current positions. With new leadership, there comes hope for a brighter culture.

SUMMARY AND CONCLUSION

As stated before, debt matters and so does lying about debt. This chapter confronted the liars themselves and their trusted advisers.

The Young model offers a simple but powerful explanation of accounting frauds. Managers who commit such accounting misrepresentations begin by being pressured to make their numbers. Seeing an opportunity to twist and turn accounting numbers, they seize the opportunity, give in to the temptation, and commit the sin of deceiving the investment community and the public.

The recent Boies report about Tyco provides a fitting end to this chapter.[45] The firm took an additional $382 million charge for the fiscal year ending September 30, 2002, for accounting errors. The Boies report states that Tyco managers engaged in "aggressive accounting" but found no evidence of "significant or systemic fraud." This finding is peculiar for two reasons. The report admits that the authors did not closely examine the accounts; it is curious that they could conclude that there was no "significant or systemic fraud"? The authors could have testified that they did not find evidence of such fraud rather than saying there was no fraud. More important, fraud consists of doing or saying something to entice others to do something that they otherwise would not do in order to obtain some advantage. Tyco's previous management (and let us hope that it stops there) used very, very aggressive accounting procedures in its financial statement in an effort to entice investors and creditors to bid up the company's stock prices. Managers apparently benefited by the increased value of their stock shares and their stock options, which some sold at lofty profits. While I am not a lawyer, that sounds like it could be considered accounting fraud. Just as the accounting profession learned that when negligence becomes so egregious it constitutes fraud,[46] hopefully managers one day will learn that overly aggressive accounting procedures plus inadequate and misleading disclosures should meet the definition of fraud, especially when managers busily sell their stocks when simultaneously telling shareholders about a brighter tomorrow. After the events of the last two years, it might be quite easy to find a jury that will understand these facts and arrive at a just verdict.

Levitt clearly is correct that there must be a change in corporate culture. Managers must become ethical in how they treat financial reports and how they treat the investment community. While external forces are required to put pressures on managers and directors, the best returns will occur when corporate governors embrace a partnership with shareholders and actively practice telling "the truth, the whole truth, and nothing but the truth." President Bush echoed the same sentiments in his speech on July 9, 2002.[47] In his words, we need "a new ethic of personal responsibility in the business community."

Finally, lest we think the problems are behind us, accounting lapses in 2003 have surfaced at Ahold, AOL (again!), HealthSouth, Medco, and Sprint. Unethical or illegal practices at these entities inform us that the accounting failures of 2001–2002 were not episodic. Until society changes its ethics and its culture, more accounting scandals will surface this year and in the future.

NOTES

1. M. R. Young, ed., *Accounting Irregularities and Financial Fraud,* 2nd ed. (San Diego: Harcourt Professional Publishing, 2002), pp. 11–13. Concerning pressures to meet analyst forecasts, see A. Berenson, *The Number: How the Drive for Quarterly Earnings Corrupted Wall Street and Corporate America* (New York: Random House, 2003).

2. Briloff, Mulford and Comiskey, and Schilit explain many ways in which accounting provides various alternatives, is ambiguous, entails estimates, or requires professional judgment. See: A. J. Briloff, *Unaccountable Accounting* (New York: Harper & Row, 1972), *More Debits than Credits* (New York: Harper & Row, 1976), and *The Truth about Corporate Accounting* (New York: Harper & Row, 1981); C. W. Mulford and E. E. Comiskey, *The Financial Numbers Game: Detecting Creative Accounting Practices* (New York: John Wiley & Sons, 2002); H. Schilit, *Financial Shenanigans: How to Detect Accounting Gimmicks and Fraud in Financial Reports* (New York: McGraw-Hill, 2002).

3. A. Levitt, "The Numbers Game." Remarks by Chairman Arthur Levitt, presented at the NYU Center for Law and Business, New York, September 28, 1998; see: *www.sec.gov/news/speech/speecharchive.shtml.* See also A. Levitt, *Take on the Street: What Wall Street and Corporate America Don't Want You to Know: What You Can Do to Fight Back* (New York: Pantheon Books, 2002), pp. 204–235. Compare A. Berenson, *The Number*.

4. Securities and Exchange Commission, "Details of the 30 Enforcement Actions," September 28, 1998; see *www.sec.gov/news/extra/finfrds.html.*

5. M. Schroeder and E. MacDonald, "SEC Enforcement Actions Target Accounting Fraud," *Wall Street Journal,* September 29, 1999.

6. A. Levitt, "Renewing the Covenant with Investors." Remarks by Chairman Arthur Levitt, presented at the NYU Center for Law and Business, New York, May 10, 2000; see: *www.sec.gov/news/speech/speecharchive.shtml.*

7. W. Powers, R. S. Troubh, and H. S. Winokur Jr., *Report of Investigation by the Special Investigative Committee of the Board of Directors of Enron Corp.,* February 1, 2002.

8. P. Behr and A. Witt, "Dream Job Turns into a Nightmare," *Washington Post,* July 29, 2002, p. A01; A. L. Berkowitz, *Enron: A Professional's Guide to the Events, Ethical Issues, and Proposed Reforms* (Chicago: Commerce Clearing House, 2002); R. Bryce, *Pipe Dreams: Greed, Ego, and the Death of Enron* (Cambridge, MA: Perseus Book Group, 2002); B. Cruver, *Anatomy of Greed: The Unshredded Truth from an Enron Insider* (New York: Carroll and Graff, 2002); L. Fox, *Enron: The Rise and Fall* (Hoboken, NJ: John Wiley & Sons, 2003); D. Q. Mills, *Buy, Lie, and Sell High: How Investors Lost Out on Enron and the Internet Bubble* (Upper Saddle River, NJ: Prentice-Hall, 2002); and M. Swartz and S. Watkins, *Power Failure: The Inside Story of the Collapse of Enron* (New York: Doubleday, 2003).

9. Ibid.

10. J. Beauprez, "Reforming Corporate Boards on Agenda: Directors too Close to Execs, Critics Say," *Denver Post,* June 9, 2002.

11. A. Weinberg, "Asleep at the Switch," *Forbes,* July 22, 2002.

12. See W. Buffett, "Stock Options, the Megabucks Battle," *Mercury News,* April 15, 2002, and his letters to the shareholders of Berkshire Hathaway, especially the one in 1998, at: *www.berkshirehathaway.com/letters.* Also recommended are: R. P. Miles and T. Osborne, *The Warren Buffett CEO: Secrets of the Berkshire Hathaway Managers* (New York: John Wiley & Sons, 2001); and H. I. Wolk, M. G. Tearney, and J. L. Dodd, *Accounting Theory: A Conceptual and Institutional Approach,* 5th ed. (Cincinnati: South-Western Publishing, 2001), pp. 362–366. Cf. J. Balsi, D. Kruse, and A. Bernstein, *In the Company of Owners: The Truth about Stock Options (And Why Every Employee Should Have Them)* (New York: Basic Books, 2003).

13. Financial Accounting Standards Board, *Elements of Financial Statements,* SFAC No. 6 (Stamford, CT: FASB, 1985).

14. TechNet, "Stock Option Accounting," 2002; see: *www.technet.org/issues/stock.html.*

15. See A. Borrus and P. Dwyer, "To Expense or Not to Expense," *Business Week,* July 29, 2002. Some companies that have recently switched to the expensing of stock options include: American Express, Bank One, Coca-Cola, Conoco Phillips, Du Pont, Tupperware, and the Washington Post.

16. D. Sorid, "Audit Committee Disclaimer Comes Under Fire," *Forbes,* December 24, 2002.

17. These comments are taken from my 2002 and 2003 essays in *Accounting Today*: "Why Didn't the Private-Sector Watchdogs Bark?"; "What Happens When Government Is of the CEO, by the CEO, and for the CEO?"; and "Corporate Governance: As Oxymoronic as Business Ethics"; see *www.SmartPros.com.* Also see Levitt, *Take on the Street,* pp. 204–235; P. Plitch, "Independent Directors May Not Be Cure-all," *Associated Press Newswires,* August 30, 2002; J. Weil, "Heard on the Street: Board Members Draw Scrutiny for Roles at Other Companies," *Wall Street Journal,* December 9, 2002; and "Volcker Calls for Non-Exec Board Structure in Large Corporations," November 5, 2002.

18. American Bar Association, *Preliminary Report of the American Bar Association Task Force on Corporate Responsibility,"* July 16, 2002; see: *www.abanet.org/buslaw/corporateresponsibility/preliminary_report.pdf.*

19. Much good can come from audit committees, as evidenced by J. V. Carcello, D. R. Hermanson, and T. L. Neal, "Disclosures in Audit Committee Charters and Reports," *Accounting Horizons* (December 2002): 291–304, among others. The trick is to move from the potential to the actual.

20. Fox, *Enron,* p. 48; A. Huffington, *Pigs at the Trough: How Corporate Greed and Political Corruption Are Undermining America* (New York: Crown Publishers, 2003).

21. J. Nocera et al., "System Failure: Corporate America Has Lost Its Way. Here's a Road Map for Restoring Confidence," *Fortune,* June 24, 2002.

22. G. Levine, "Ex-Tyco Exec Walsh: I Did It, I'll Pay; Ebbers Cronies Quit WorldCom," *Forbes* (December 2002).

23. Recently a federal judge ruled that Enron's professional advisers are subject to liability for their actions and inactions. See K. Eichenwald, "Enron Ruling Leaves Corporate Advisers Open to Lawsuits," *New York Times,* December 23, 2002. Perhaps this judge or another judge will issue a similar ruling concerning Enron's directors. Conversely, the Supreme Court ruled in *Central Bank of Denver v. First Interstate Bank of Denver* that professional advisers who knowingly aid and abet securities fraud are not liable to victims. See W. S. Lerach, "The Chickens Have Come Home to Roost: How Wall Street, the Big Accounting Firms and Corporate Interests Chloroformed Congress and Cost America's Investors Trillions," 2002; see *www.milberg.com/pdf/news/chickens.pdf.* I wonder how the courts will sort out these conflicting judgments and how Congress will deal with these issues.

24. The accounting and business literature is replete with articles on accounting and business ethics: M. B. Armstrong, *Ethics and Professionalism for CPAs* (Cincinnati: Southwestern, 1993); M. Bebeau, "Influencing the Moral Dimension of Dental Practice," in J. Rest and D. Varvaez, eds., *Moral Development in the Professions* (Hillsdale, NJ: Lawrence Earlbaum Associates, 1994); L. Brooks, *Professional Ethics for Accountants,* 2nd ed. (Minneapolis: West Publishing, 2000); D. DeMarco, *The Heart of Virtue: Lessons from Life and Literature Illustrating the Beauty and Value of Moral Character* (San Francisco: Ignatius Press, 1996); M. Dirsmith and J. E. Ketz, "A Fifty-Cent Test: An Approach to Teaching Integrity," *Advances in Accounting* (1987), pp. 129–141; J. Dobson and M. B. Armstrong, "Applications of Virtue Ethics Theory: A Lesson from Architecture," *Research on Accounting Ethics* (1995), pp. 187–202; M. J. Epstein and A. D. Spalding Jr., *The Accountant's Guide to Legal Liability and Ethics* (Homewood, IL: Irwin, 1993); L. Kohlberg, *The Psychology of Moral Development,* 2nd ed. (San Francisco: Harper & Row, 1984); H. T. Magill and G. J. Previtts, *CPA Professional Responsibilities: An Introduction* (Cincinnati: Southwestern, 1991); S. M. Mintz, "Virtue Ethics and Accounting Education," *Issues in Accounting Education* (Fall 1995), pp. 247–267; E. Pincoffs, *Quandaries and Virtues* (Lawrence: University Press of Kansas, 1986); L. A. Ponemon and A. Glazer, "Accounting Education and Ethical Development: The Influence of Liberal Learning on Students and Alumni in Accounting Practice," *Issues in Accounting Education* (Fall 1990), pp. 195–208; J. Rest, *Moral Development: Advances in Research and Theory* (New York: Praeger, 1986); J. Rest, D. Varvaez, M. J. Bebeau, and S. T. Thomas, *Postconventional Moral Thinking: A Neo-Kohlbergian Approach* (Hillsdale, NJ: Lawrence Erlbaum Associates, 1999); M. Shaub, "Limits to the Effectiveness of Accounting Ethics Education," *Business and Professional Ethics Journal* (1994), pp. 129–145; S. Sisaye, "An Overview of the Institutional Approach to Accounting Ethics Education," *Research on*

Accounting Ethics (1997), pp. 233–244; I. Stewart, "Teaching Accounting Ethics: The Power of Narrative," *Accounting Education: A Journal of Theory, Practice, and Research* (1997), pp. 173–184; L. Thorne, "The Role of Virtue in Auditors' Ethical Decision Making: An Integration of Cognitive-Developmental and Virtue-Ethics Perspectives," *Research on Accounting Ethics* (1998), pp. 291–308; F. W. Windal, *Ethics and the Accountant: Text and Cases* (Englewood Cliffs, NJ: Prentice-Hall, 1991); and F. W. Windal and R. N. Corley, *The Accounting Professional: Ethics, Responsibility, and Liability* (Englewood Cliffs, NJ: Prentice-Hall, 1980). Given the events of the past few years, however, it appears that collectively these writings have had virtually no impact on practice. Perhaps the theories have defects; perhaps the authors have sound theories that are hard to implement; perhaps they have useful ideas that have been ignored by the business community.

25. "Faith in Corporate Ethics Not Yet Restored," December 9, 2002; see: *www.SmartPros.com*; A. Wheat, "Keeping the Eye on Corporate America," *Fortune,* November 25, 2002, pp. 44–46.

26. R. B. Schmitt, "Companies Add Ethics Training: Will It Work?" *Wall Street Journal,* November 4, 2002, p. B1.

27. J. Hughes, "Ethics in a Culture of Greed," *Christian Science Monitor,* July 3, 2002; C. J. Loomis, "Whatever It Takes," *Fortune,* November 25, 2002, p. 74.

28. C. Duhigg, "Ethicists at the Gate: Can Harvard Business School Make Its Graduates Behave?" *Boston Globe,* December 8, 2002; A. Etzioni, "When It Comes to Ethics, B-Schools Get an F," *Washington Post,* August 4, 2002, p. B4; F. E. Greenman, "Business School Ethics—An Overlooked Topic," *Business and Society Review* (Summer 1999), pp. 171–176; and R. Prentice, "An Ethics Lesson for Business Schools," *New York Times,* August 20, 2002.

29. P. Williams, "Accounting Involves Ethics, Not Just Technical Issues," *Strategic Finance* (September 2002). Compare A. Bloom, *The Closing of the American Mind: How Higher Education Has Failed Democracy and Impoverished the Souls of Today's Students* (New York: Simon & Schuster, 1987), especially his comments about MBA programs.

30. Robert Sterling makes a similar point when he bemoans the transition of academic accounting from an accounting measurement focus to what he called accounting anthropology and what I would call financial economics of accounting; see Sterling: "Accounting Power," *Journal of Accountancy* (January 1973), pp. 61–67; "Accounting Research, Education and Practice," *Journal of Accountancy* (September 1973), pp. 44–52; *Toward a Science of Accounting* (Houston: Scholars Book Co., 1970); compare American Accounting Association, *Statement on Accounting Theory and Theory Acceptance,* Report of Committee on Concepts and Standards for External Financial Reports (Sarasota, FL: AAA, 1977). The point is that the academic community has shunned making "value judgments" to pursue a "scientific" understanding of accounting. The conundrum, of course, is that one cannot do ethics without value judgments. This elevation of the so-called scientific method carried along with it the implied statement to students that ethics is unimportant. Accounting academics obviously need to do some soul searching.

31. C. S. Lewis maintained that humans instinctively have some notion of right and wrong, as seen when people claim that others are not treating them fairly. Our impediment lies not in understanding fairness, but in applying the standard to others—for example, for managers to be fair to investors and creditors; see Lewis, *Mere Christianity,* 2nd ed. (New York: Macmillan, 1952), pp. 3–7.

32. R. W. Gough, *Character Is Destiny: The Value of Personal Ethics in Everyday Life* (Rocklin, CA: Prima Publishing, 1998); compare M. B. Armstrong, J. E. Ketz, and D. Owsen, "Ethics

Education in Accounting: Moving Towards Ethical Motivation and Ethical Behavior," *Journal of Accounting Education* (2003).

33. Gough, *Character Is Destiny*, p. 142.

34. Young, *Accounting Irregularities and Financial Fraud*, 2nd ed.

35. Gough, *Character Is Destiny*, p. 161.

36. B. Deener, "Corporate Directors Return to School for Training Seminars," *Dallas Morning News*, June 10, 2002; Swartz and Watkins, *Power Failure*.

37. Berkowitz, *Enron*; A. Hill and A. Hill, *Just Business: Christian Ethics for the Marketplace* (Downers Grove, IL: Intervarsity Press, 1997); R. M. Kidder, *How Good People Make Tough Choices: Resolving the Dilemmas of Ethical Living* (New York: Fireside, 1996); L. J. Rittenhouse, *Do Business with People You Can Trust: Balancing Profits and Principles* (New York: AndBEYOND Communications, 2002); and L. K. Trevino and K. A. Nelson, *Managing Business Ethics: Straight Talk About How to Do It Right*, 2nd ed. (New York: John Wiley & Sons, 1999). Also see the article "Communicating Trustworthiness," *International Accounting Bulletin*, June 14, 2002.

38. A. Berenson, "Changing the Definition of Cash Flow Helped Tyco," *New York Times*, December 31, 2002.

39. Free cash flow is not well defined, and neither the SEC nor the FASB has addressed the issue. This construct attempts to measure how much cash flowed into corporate coffers after deducting all necessary expenditures, including operating items, investing items such as replacing the firm's infrastructure, and financing items such as dividends. There are many variations in how to measure free cash flow, as discussed by R. C. Higgins, *Analysis for Financial Management* (New York: Irwin, 2000); F. K. Reilly and K. C. Brown, *Investment Analysis and Portfolio Management* (New York: Dryden, 2000); and G. I. White, A. C. Sondhi, and D. Fried, *The Analysis and Use of Financial Statements*, 2nd ed. (New York: John Wiley & Sons, 1998). I discuss free cash flow in Chapter 10.

40. See J. E. Ketz and P. B. W. Miller, "Time to Stop Pfooling Around," *Accounting Today*, September 22–October 5, 1997, pp. 28, 31; L. Revsine, D. W. Collins, and W. B. Johnson, *Financial Reporting and Analysis*, 2nd ed. (Upper Saddle River, NJ: Prentice-Hall, 2002), pp. 63–66, 543, 822, 845; and White et al., *Analysis and Use of Financial Statements*, 2nd ed. pp. 18, 958–959). I also briefly touched on the topic in the notes for Chapters 3 and 5.

41. P. B. W. Miller and P. R. Bahnson, *Quality Financial Reporting* (New York: McGraw-Hill, 2002).

42. B. McKay and K. Brown, "Coke to Abandon Forecasts to Focus on Long-term Goals," *Wall Street Journal*, December 16, 2002; compare S. Galbraith, "With Guidance Like This . . . ," *Wall Street Journal*, January 7, 2003.

43. D. Ivanovich, "Economist Raised Doubts about Partnerships/Enron Researcher Raised Issue in '99," *Houston Chronicle*, March 19, 2002.

44. D. Akst, "Why Business Needs a More Powerful S.E.C.," *New York Times*, November 3, 2002.

45. Tyco International Ltd., Form 8-K, December 30, 2002; compare P. Eavis, "Many Numbers Still Don't Add Up at Tyco," December 31, 2002; see: *www.TheStreet.com*; F. Norris, "Should Tyco's Auditors Have Told More?" *New York Times*, January 3, 2003; A. R. Sorkin, "Tyco, After the Glitter and the Agile Math," *New York Times*, January 1, 2003; and A. Weinberg, "Tyco Counts Sheep, But Can Investors Sleep?" *Forbes*, December 31, 2002.

46. Judge Cardozo said as much in his ruling in the 1931 Ultramares case.

47. G. W. Bush, "Speech in New York City, July 9," *Wall Street Journal*, July 9, 2002.

CHAPTER EIGHT

Failure of the Auditing Profession

Many commentators as well as investors and creditors have wondered about the recent meltdown of the financial markets, asking not only how it happened, but how it could have happened in such short order. Chapter 7 examined the failure of the management process, including the failure of corporate governance. The next two chapters investigate the failure of the regulators and the investors themselves. In this chapter, the focus rests with the external auditors.

Managers must be primarily responsible for the financial lies and exaggerations of the last decade, for they are the ones who distorted and misdirected the investment community when they issued deficient financial reports. Auditors brought themselves into the circle of blame because in too many cases they instructed managers how to hide the bad stuff and approved reports that had defective accounting applications. Society gave auditors a very important responsibility, but the accounting profession fumbled the ball.

Several tensions exist. The investment community and the auditing profession are at odds because investors and creditors think that auditors should discover and ferret out fraud, while auditors continue to try to circumscribe their responsibilities. Congress questions the certified public accountants (CPAs) about what happened, but the profession ducks behind its literature and its "generally accepted" accounting and auditing rules. The biggest tension lies with management and its auditors. Management hires someone to perform an audit, something that many managers claim is non-value adding, which reflects how little they know, and the auditor attempts to meet its professional obligations while at the same time profiting financially from the engagement. Compounding all these problems is the mistaken belief by auditors that their client is management instead of the shareholders.

Terence Johnson describes the accounting profession in terms of a *patronage system*.[1] By this Johnson means that large corporations have a need for accountants, but they retain significant influence over what the accountants do. Corporations—large and independent and powerful—act like patrons in doling out funds for various services. Accountants, as recipients of the funds, must recognize that these patrons are the sources of those funds and kowtow to their whims. While performing the attest function, auditors remain loath to cut off their source of revenues.

Robert Sterling provides a different take, though it ends with nearly the same conclusion.[2] He examines the most famous accountant of all—Bob Cratchit—and deduces that, like Cratchit, today's accountants have low power. They might try to do the right thing, but the system is against them. Having little power vis-à-vis managers, external auditors tend to do what their Scrooges want instead of what they should. Short of a revolution, CPAs will remain enslaved to their corporate masters.

Abraham Briloff and Eli Mason remain the most virulent opponents of consulting of any type by the external auditors.[3] In addition, they frequently chide them for their lack of independence when performing the attest function. Given the numerous instances of fraudulent accounting plus the hundreds and hundreds of accounting restatements in the last couple of years, it appears that history has proven the correctness of Briloff's and Mason's charges.

David Duncan was the Arthur Andersen auditor in charge of the Enron account. Whether Duncan felt that he was a servant of Enron or that he had little power or even recognized that he had lost his independence, the fact is that when the struggle for accounting truth was waged, he surrendered rather easily to the corporation.[4] Duncan did not hinder Enron in its rape of the financial markets, nor did top echelons of Arthur Andersen oversee and overturn his actions. Carl Bass was one of the few people in Andersen who tried to right the situation, but others in the organization muffled his cries of outrage.

After Enron, Global Crossing, WorldCom, Adelphia, Tyco, and Peregrine Systems, to name but a few of the extant problems, we should ask what is being done to minimize future occurrences of accounting fraud. Until those issues are dealt with adequately, I believe that these breakdowns will come to pass again and again. Since most of the real issues have cultural and institutional causes, we must change the culture and the institutions.

The first section of this chapter looks at the auditing profession in relation to the creation of the securities laws. The next section studies the evolution of what I term *underauditing,* including a look at the changing nature of big auditing firms. Then the chapter investigates the polemic *Serving the Public Interest*, a document that provides compelling evidence that the leadership of the profession has lost its moral compass. The next section reviews the Arthur Andersen verdict, and the final section revisits the Young model and adapts it for the auditing profession.

SECURITIES LAWS AND THE AUDITING PROFESSION[5]

American accountants held relatively low social status during the early and middle 19th century, but the confluence of a number of events elevated the profession into the elite category in the late 19th and early 20th centuries. The growth of railroads and their regulation by the Interstate Commerce Commission, enactment of laws including a constitutional amendment allowing taxation on personal and corporate income, regulation by the New York Stock Exchange that required audited financial statements by listed companies, and the federal government's need for financial expertise during World War I contributed to the rise of the accounting profession. The biggest boost, however, came during the early 1930s, when Congress passed the Securities Act of 1933 and the Securities Exchange Act of 1934. Collectively these statutes required business enterprises that wanted to issue securities to the public to publish audited financial reports in certain Securities and Exchange Commission (SEC) filings. Such documents, of course, call for independent external auditors, though it was up for grabs whether these auditors would be government or private sector accountants.

The goals of the two securities acts embrace the concepts of "fair play" and "full and fair" disclosure. Besides condemning various abuses, such as wash sales and other schemes designed to manipulate stock prices, these acts require corporations that issue stocks or bonds to the general public to provide accounting information in registration statements, 10-Ks, 10-Qs, and other schedules that must be filed with the SEC. The idea, of course, is to give investors and creditors complete and accurate information so they can make informed investment and credit decisions.

A contributing factor to passage of these acts by Congress includes the case of Kreuger and Toll, Inc.—the 1920s version of Enron and WorldCom.[6] Kreuger and Toll generated much excitement in its securities because it paid high dividends and provided fairly high and stable stock returns. Unfortunately, Ivar Kreuger was the 1920s prototype for Ken Lay, Jeff Skilling, and Bernard Ebbers. He published deceitful financial statements by which he defrauded many investors, proving that deceptions are limited to no era. When the legerdemain was up, the value of the stock plummeted and many investors lost a ton of money. As Enron and WorldCom played significant roles in motivating Congress to pass the Sarbanes-Oxley bill, Kreuger and Toll did its part to stimulate action by Congress in the 1930s.

The SEC does not designate any security as a good or poor investment; instead, its accounting-related purpose is to regulate corporations to ensure that they furnish pertinent, truthful, and complete information so that the investor has the knowledge to make rational decisions. A key component of this institutional arrangement includes the SEC's requirement that the 10-Ks submitted by registrants contain an audit report by an independent, external auditor. The idea is simple: This external auditor, who possesses (or should possess) independence and objectivity, will provide greater assurance to the investment community that the information in the 10-K is reliable. Such independence and objectivity would restore and maintain investor confidence in the stock market.

As Congress and the Roosevelt administration drafted the legislation that eventually became the securities acts of 1933 and 1934, they considered utilizing government employees to perform the external audit, probably those working for the Federal Trade Commission. The accounting profession initiated a campaign to change this proposal and have third-party, private sector accountants serve as external auditors. An oft-quoted passage during the congressional hearings proceeds in this way (Colonel Carter represented the public accountants):

Senator Barkley: You audit the controllers?
Colonel Carter: Yes, the public accountant audits the controller's account.
Senator Barkley: Who audits you?
Colonel Carter: Our conscience.

In the end, the auditing profession convinced Congress and President Roosevelt that it had the conscience to do the job, so they relinquished their original notion of government auditors.

The hearings in the early 1930s established several elementary statements of purpose and of high-level strategy. Congress wanted an audit of corporate affairs to ensure the fairness and accuracy of financial statements, and this goal presumes an investigation to provide reasonable assurance that fraud by management did not take place. In other words, the financial statements would contain no taint of management fraud. For its part, the accounting profession accepted the challenge, for they did not want government auditors to assume the jobs. It not only said that it would perform this function, but that it would maintain clear consciences that would enable it to constrain management misbehavior. This social contract is captured in Exhibit 8.1. The U.S. society conferred exclusive rights to the accounting profession—specifically to those licensed as certified public accountants—to audit public companies. In return, society hoped not to have the problems that it experienced during the 1920s.[7]

This social transaction explains why the investment community feels that the external auditor should discover material fraud by managers when it occurs. At that time the accounting profession agreed to ferret out problems such as those that happened during the 1920s. Since then, however, the profession has changed its collective mind.

While no one should expect auditors to detect all fraud, until recently the profession has acted as if it has little or no responsibility in discovering management misconduct. While CPA firms have fought this duty for many decades, the SEC clearly has expected some minimum threshold by which the CPA would detect and warn investors of sizable irregularities, intentional or otherwise. Statement on Auditing Standards (SAS) No. 82, issued by the American Institute of Certified Public Accountants (AICPA) in 1997, grudgingly acknowledges some responsibility for accountants to uncover fraud or error, if material. It also provides guidance about what to look for, how to document problems, and how and to whom to communicate the infractions. The bottom line is simple: When management frauds are as massive as those at Enron, Global Crossing, Adelphia, Tyco, and WorldCom, the auditor ought to find them. There is no excuse not to.[8]

Exhibit 8.1   Social Contract with External Auditors

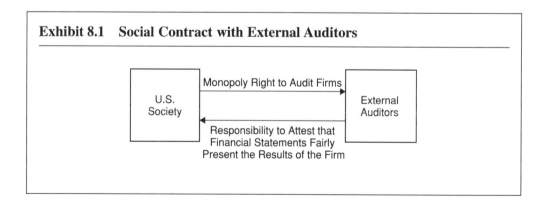

From the beginning, Congress expected the public accounting profession to watch over management and attempt to prevent corporate managers from engaging in the accounting abuses of the 1920s unearthed in the congressional hearings or from engaging in any new fraudulent schemes. Further, Congress expected that when the independent external auditor could not forestall managerial manipulations, it would at least blow the whistle on those managers who willfully issued inaccurate financial statements. With this and other institutional arrangements, Congress hoped to curb managers' temptations to distort accounting truth.

The major irony that arose out of these hearings is the further institutionalization of the audit arrangement by which corporate managers hire and fire those who audit them. While personnel for the large accounting firms and many academic accountants defend this practice, a bit of common sense would suggest that this social convention takes the form of corporate patronage, as pointed out by Terence Johnson and Robert Sterling.[9] It is the patron who decides what is audited and to what extent. In other words, auditors have little power relative to corporate managers, and little has been done since the 1930s to amend this power relationship. Because of this unequal affiliation, there have always been managers who committed accounting fraud and there have always been auditors who have looked the other way or neglected to examine some important evidence or not maintained a degree of "skepticism."[10]

The current environment, however, presents a strange set of circumstances. A large number of accounting irregularities exist, as noted in Exhibits 1.1 and 1.2. The accounting profession continues to contract through mergers and seems indifferent, even bored, with external auditing and keenly energized with respect to consulting opportunities. Putting the two together raises the question of whether we have entered a period in which auditing firms render the least amount of auditing that they can get by with so that they can concentrate on moneymaking activities. Given the number of irregularities that have arisen in the past year or two, it is questionable whether this minimal auditing suffices.[11]

With the historical setting of the 1929 crash and the enactment of the Securities Act of 1933 and the Securities Exchange Act of 1934, there exists a natural link between the CPA and the corporation. Congress in the early 1930s clearly expected external auditors to help prevent management frauds and to report those that they discovered. In today's environment, the large accounting firms have changed course and started looking for other opportunities. Let us move to an exploration of the interests and the concerns of managers and accountants who find themselves in this new institutional setting of underauditing.

EVOLUTION OF UNDERAUDITING

Despite the ubiquitous existence of some corrupt managers and auditors, the past decade or so has ushered in a plethora of accounting abuses and the absence of auditor involvement either to stop the frauds or to report them once they occurred. In addition to the big bangs of Enron, Global Crossing, and WorldCom, recall the bad accounting at Boston Chicken, Cendant, MicroStrategy, Rite Aid, Sunbeam, Waste Management, W. R. Grace, and Xerox. Also recall Arthur Levitt's piercing and incisive "Numbers

Game" speech and how the SEC celebrated the one-year anniversary of the speech by issuing administrative proceedings or litigation releases against 30 corporations and their managers for accounting frauds.[12] Levitt repeated his concerns in his speech "Renewing the Covenant with Investors."[13] While others in the field try to rationalize the many accounting frauds in recent years and approximately 1,000 accounting restatements, I submit these examples constitute a very strong prima facie case against corporate managers and their auditors. Too many managers are lying in financial statements, and too many presumably independent external auditors are allowing them to do so, in part because they do not have sufficient power to withstand corporate caprice.

I think that large accounting firms are not auditing the corporations to the extent or depth that Congress originally envisioned, that the courts have expected, or that the investment community has desired; I call this practice *underauditing*. Their planning models are even set up in ways that explicitly attempt to minimize the cost of the audit. These models go further by specifying that it is permissible to accept certain amounts of audit failure. While realizing that perfect audits do not exist in the real world, this orientation distorts the view of the profession so much that many accountants have a difficult time keeping the purpose of the audit in mind.[14]

Unintended Consequences of Federal Trade Commission Actions

I hypothesize several reasons for this increase in accounting fraud and the contemporaneous development of underauditing. The first cause concerns the attack by the Federal Trade Commission (FTC) on AICPA Rules of Conduct Rule 302, which prohibited members from accepting contingent fees; on Rule 502, which prohibited advertising and other forms of solicitation; and on Rule 503, which prohibited members from accepting any commission or referral fee. The AICPA reached an agreement with the FTC in 1990 whereby the AICPA stated that it would not enforce Rule 502 unless the member lied or deceived another; it also consented to modify Rules 302 and 503. While the FTC seems to have had the admirable goal of eliminating arrangements leading to restraint of trade, the 1990 compromise led to deleterious effects for the accounting world. Large accounting firms increased their competition for audit clients not only by advertising and by permitting contingent fees and commissions in certain instances, but also by cutting audit prices so much so that various parties within the profession started speaking of auditing as a "loss leader." To make money, auditing firms have to hold down costs on audit engagements, and they need to obtain consulting contracts. These activities lead to audits that are less than optimal.

Transformation of Large Accounting Firms

A related explanation for the increase in accounting fraud and the concurrent development of underauditing is the metamorphosis of the large accounting practice. In the past, such firms mostly did audit work and some tax work; today they mostly do consulting and some auditing and tax. In the past, these entities hired mostly accountants, and everyone knew they made up an accounting partnership; today they hire many types of professionals and have evolved into professional organizations. Such movements are aided and abetted by the AICPA, whose leadership seems determined to remove the word *accountant* from CPA, replacing it with the word *adviser*, and wants to push accountants into other realms of the business world. Those leaders have also organized committees to redefine *independence* to allow a number of activities previously thought incongruent for external auditors and to rationalize consulting as merely a way of helping the client corporation. Enormous tension arises between the senior partners and those in the trenches. Most auditors in the field know the problems and risks of their clients and attempt to examine financial weaknesses of the corporation. Yet the only message they hear from their bosses is that they must generate profits. The tone at the top is unambiguous but misguided, for those on the firing line need support when they confront managers who want to push the limits of accounting truth and propriety. Clearly, this metamorphosis has triggered a confusion of roles, and many accountants do not have a grasp of their fundamental responsibilities to the public. The next section addresses this issue in greater detail.

So-Called Litigation Reform

A third hypothesized explanation for the increase in accounting abuses and underauditing rests with litigation reform. In 1995 Congress passed the Securities Litigation Reform Act, which had the purposes of making it more difficult for plaintiffs to file a class action suit against business enterprises, corporate managers, and public auditors and of curbing the awards when plaintiffs won. Litigation attorneys naturally turned to the state courts, but this strategy was thwarted in 1998 when Congress passed the Securities Litigation Uniform Standards Act, which requires class action lawsuits brought because of accounting issues to be filed in federal court. Since audit effort is directly related to the penalties from audit failures and to the probability of losing the case, the natural consequence is a lessening of audit effort. Why incur the incremental costs to audit a firm when the expected value of losing money in a court case becomes less significant (smaller probability of losing multiplied by a smaller penalty)?

Management Succumbs to Analyst Pressures

A fourth reason for the higher incidence of accounting abuses is the incredible pressure by financial analysts for firms to meet the analyst forecasts and the managers' consent to partake in this dance. What started out as a useful service to society by analysts when they collect and study the financial statements and other news about a corporation's welfare to predict its future earnings has become an insane escapade.[15] Accounting is simply not precise enough to allow people to predict that a company is going to have quarterly earnings of (say) $1.23 per share and then actually expect the firm to meet the number exactly. Given the limitations of accounting, I cannot understand why anyone becomes troubled if the earnings number actually turns out to be (say) $1.22 or $1.21 per share. But investors do react to a firm's missing its forecast even by one penny by punishing the company with a big drop in the stock price. It makes me wonder how much accounting these investors and analysts really understand. Unfortunately, managers have observed this stock behavior, and they understand the importance of meeting earnings forecasts. Given that so much real money is riding on meeting these fore-casts, it is easy to understand (but not accept) why some managers lie about actual cor-porate results. These managers pressure auditors to allow them to account for events and transactions as the managers see fit.

You Scratch My Back . . .

The fifth and perhaps most pervasive cause of the greater number of accounting manip-ulations rests with how auditing firms are compensated. As long as corporate managers pay auditors for their stamp of approval, managers will wield an enormous amount of power. Combine the method of payment with corporate powers to hire and fire auditors, and trouble results. Add in a pinch of consulting fees, and we have a recipe for disaster. Money corrupts; and lots of money corrupts in lots of ways. This variation of an old adage hit home recently as I talked with an AICPA official about conflicts of interest when auditors also provide consulting services. He responded that there had been so many debates about conflicts of interest that he could no longer recognize when a con-flict existed. No wonder accountants as bright as David Duncan do not even realize the hold that $25 million of revenue per year has on them.

Maybe a football analogy would help. When Penn State played at Michigan during the 2002 football season, the referees made several questionable calls. Later, fans learned that two of the officials lived in Michigan's backyard. Joe Paterno made a fuss when he went public with his speculations about the conflicts of interest when home-town "good old boys" make the calls. Whether Coach Paterno is correct about the ques-tionable calls or about going public with his concerns is immaterial. What is interesting is that everyone on ESPN understood exactly what conflicts of interest might exist, and no one disagreed that hometown officials created at least the perception of a conflict of interest. In the same way, accountants should quit ignoring the corrupting influence of a lot of money, especially since the large accounting firms reward their partners on the basis of how much new revenue they bring in.

With these factors at work today in the financial world, there should be little surprise at the number and the extent of accounting irregularities found in American financial statements. These factors affect both the big and the small; in the case of Enron, we now realize that even very large entities can commit these transgressions.

CHANGING NATURE OF THE BIG, INDEPENDENT AUDITOR

An observer of the accounting world cannot help notice dramatic changes during the last few years. Mergers, sellouts to large nonaccounting firms, litigation reform, growth of assurance services and other consulting activities, and the creation of the Independence Standards Board serve as beacons toward uncharted seas. These alter-ations come as the profession's leaders claim that the audit market is declining, and ironically the signs all indicate that auditors are pursuing fields and activities other than auditing. Perhaps it is time to change the refrain to "Where are the auditors going?"

Metamorphosis of the Large Accounting Firms (à la Kafka)

Mergers, such as the recent creation of PricewaterhouseCoopers, and the elimination of Arthur Andersen as an external auditor provide solid evidence that change is hitting the profession. The obvious impact of these activities is less competition among the remaining four firms. What this implies is less clear because the resulting structural relationships can be positive or negative. The positive contribution occurs if accounting firms can grow in power vis-à-vis the companies they audit. For example, CPAs might find it easier to say no to bookkeeping tomfoolery, for corporations have fewer substitute firms from which to choose. Whether CPAs will exercise such power is another question, since they do not want to lose any consulting dollars or audit fees. The negative impact comes from a possible further diminishing of auditing, because the merged firms could consolidate the auditing work while expanding the consulting activities. A less likely but very negative effect could result from a dropout of another firm from the audit business, whether by another bankruptcy or by choice. This situation would lead to an unacceptably high level of concentration in the industry.

The internal transformation of these firms has been impressive. These accounting firms used to hire accountants to perform auditing, tax, and accounting-related consulting. Now they hire people with all kinds of skills that have little or nothing to do with accounting, and they perform many types of services. This demographic shift raises the question of whether these firms are still accounting firms. Certainly if the transformation continues, accounting and auditing will not be the main function of the Big Four.[16]

Another shift, though not quite as recent as these other changes, concerns the top administrators of the accounting firms. In times past, heads of these firms had stature in the area of accounting theory. They developed and debated what they thought was good policy for the firm and for the profession; examples include Arthur Andersen's Leonard Spacek and Harvey Kapnick. Today the top managers of the large accounting firms do not possess theoretical bents; instead they have marketing and selling savvy. They know how to make money. A good example was Arthur Andersen's Joseph Berandino. This orientation raises concerns about the priority of accounting and auditing within the Big Four.

Another change concerns the expectations of audit partners. Anthony Rider, a former partner at Ernst & Young, states that his superiors recently added a new requirement when they asked him to bring in $3 million of new business per year.[17] When he did not meet his quota initially, his salary was reduced; later he was fired. Apparently, Ernst & Young was not nearly as interested in Rider's audit abilities as they were his talents to sell, sell, sell.

American Institute of Certified Public Accountants

While the AICPA claims to represent the interests of all CPAs, clearly the institute's leadership has goals and aspirations more consonant with the Big Four than with the small practitioner. This fact becomes evident in comments by Stu Kessler, past chairman of the AICPA, when he claims that we ought to redefine CPA to mean "certified professional adviser."[18] This incredible proposal replaces "public" with "professional," which indicates that AICPA leaders seek to reduce if not abandon the organization's mission to the public. Most states granted CPAs exclusive right to perform public audits, but in return they expected external auditors to bring to their work a high level of competence, objectivity, and integrity, thereby promoting the general welfare of the state. Kessler apparently is willing to nix this covenant.

Kessler's proposition also replaces "accountant" with "adviser." He defends this recommendation by asserting that accountants do more than just accounting work, but the public perception of accounting is still riveted on green eyeshades. By changing the word "accountant" to "adviser," Kessler argues that the profession can convince the public of the burgeoning skills that CPAs possess. This reasoning is faulty, for it assumes that an advertising campaign that educates the public about the accountant's new skills cannot succeed, whereas a name change will. The real reason for the proposal rests with the desire to certify nonaccountants as CPAs. The Big Four might like this, given the metamorphosis of their firms, but the general effect will enervate the accounting profession.

In addition, Barry Melancon, AICPA president and chief executive, has made the astonishing statement that the profession's public orientation can be realized in the marketplace.[19] In other words, satisfying the consumer's needs by providing appropriate professional services discharges the CPA's public interest responsibilities. This crass commercial equation turns "public interest" on its head. For decades accountants have understood that the public interest requires CPAs to perform their duties in such a way as to instill confidence in society in general and in the marketplace in particular. Born in the 1930s, this idea meant that the accountant's integrity had priority over the profit incentive so that investors could trust the audit opinion and in turn, if the opinion was unqualified, the financial statements. If Melancon's proposal is followed, the transformation of the profession will be dramatic, and further erosion of public confidence in financial reports is likely.

Whither Independence?

Recently the concept of independence has entered the spotlight again. The large accounting firms have engaged in activities that some question with respect to independence. As a result of these grumblings, including concerns raised by the SEC, a new organization was created in 1998, called the Independence Standards Board (ISB), but it did not last long.[20] The ISB never engaged in anything profound because half of the board members were heads of the large accounting firms. As stated earlier, these men have great skills at administration and entrepreneurship, but they are theoreticians neither in accounting nor in auditing. Even if they were, this organization had the impossible task of creating rules that would have governed itself. Given the changing nature of the business, the most likely result would have been pronouncements that rationalized the new goals of the Big Four. Anyone ready for colleges to hire hometown referees?

In December 1997 the SEC announced that it had begun an administrative proceeding against KPMG Peat Marwick. In January 1995 KPMG Peat Marwick created KPMG BayMark, which essentially acted as an investment banker. KPMG audited Porta, which in turn had several business transactions with KPMG BayMark, including a loan to Porta's president. The SEC argued that transactions between Porta and

BayMark imply that Peat Marwick lost its independence. KPMG vigorously fought this allegation, claiming that it had established organizational firewalls between the audit side of the firm and BayMark and that the transactions were immaterial; nonetheless, KPMG dissolved BayMark.[21] That KPMG even created BayMark in the first place is significant inasmuch as it pushes the envelope on the concept of independence. This action seems to suggest that, with respect to independence, the Big Four will take aggressive stances in the future as they develop new businesses.

The large accounting firms continue to market the benefits to corporations of outsourcing their internal audit. This action has been debated for years. Those who oppose this outsourcing to the external auditor claim that they are merely auditing their own work, as, for example, when Arthur Andersen audited its own internal auditing of Enron. Those supporting the practice claim that the firm can employ different teams of auditors and that it will make the process more efficient. The debate continues, though it is interesting that a number of corporations that have tried outsourcing, such as Disney, have reinstated the internal audit staff, because they incurred greater theft and fraud when internal auditing was outsourced.

Serving the Public Interest, which is discussed later in this chapter, presents more evidence of a problem.

Political Action Committees

Not too long ago, each of the large accounting firms and the AICPA created political action committees (PACs) to influence Congress. These PACs raised huge amounts of money, but they generated large returns as Congress passed litigation reform. Among other things, this reform makes it harder to sue external auditors and places caps on the penalties. As stated earlier, while this bill helps CPAs, it may have detrimental effects on others. Audit effort is a function of the size of the corporation receiving the audit, its complexity, its control system, the probability of becoming sued for a bad audit, and the costs of an audit failure. Litigation reform affects the last two variables. The probability of lawsuit became smaller and the costs of an audit failure are less; therefore, audit effort can be reduced. This result benefits auditors since they can curtail audit costs. It hurts others because the chance of finding accounting irregularities decreases, and it is more difficult to redress any problems.

More recently, the PACs of the industry influenced President Bush and the Senate to nominate and to approve Harvey Pitt as chairman of the SEC. Pitt proved a disaster not only because of his tone deafness with respect to politics, but also and more important because he was so much an advocate for the accounting industry that he could not grasp the significance of Enron's bankruptcy. One clear piece of evidence is Pitt's op-ed piece in the *Wall Street Journal*, in which he argued that our system needs to be "modernized."[22] It was not until WorldCom collapsed that Pitt would even acknowledge an ethics problem in the world of accounting and finance. SEC commissioners need a much better appreciation of the social contracts that exist between Wall Street and Main Street and a keener sense of business ethics. For the accountants' part, if they wish to suggest future candidates for positions important to them, I propose that they put forward individuals who clearly espouse principles of fairness to the investment community.

Accountants previously took neutral stands with respect to politics, at least from an industry viewpoint. During the last decade, however, the profession has become one of the most politically active groups in the country, raising millions of dollars in an attempt to influence Congress. The First Amendment may give accountants the right to raise campaign funds, but doing so has cheapened the profession. The money provided returns in the so-called litigation reforms and in the appointment of Harvey Pitt as SEC chair. The profession is now bearing the costs of the PAC donations, for the drama of the accounting scandals have turned on darker and gloomier stage lights.

How Audits Are Conducted

With megabucks in consulting, it is no wonder that audits have been treated as if they were loss leaders. The Big Four currently utilizes them as a vehicle to generate consulting business. Small profits or even losses on audit engagements become acceptable as long as the consulting business provides enough profits to make the total service contract lucrative. The difficulty with this approach is that it gives incentives to auditors to cut audit costs wherever they can. Being a loss leader is one thing; having big losses is another. Such incentives might reduce audit effort.

One way of saving money is to employ cheap, inexperienced labor. Audit firms have always done this, and the practice provides excellent training to junior accountants. With the growing complexity of the business world, there is concern whether these junior accountants have enough smarts to detect accounting irregularities. Quality audits may require utilization of more seasoned auditors.

Statistical sampling yields an objective sample size to control risk at acceptable levels. Interestingly, many audit firms have rejected statistical sampling, claiming that it yields too high a sample size. In other words, they would rather use professional judgment and use a smaller audit size and save money.

Firms have designed analytical reviews to help them assess the corporation overall and obtain some degree of assurance on the total picture without spending much time or money on lots of audit procedures.[23] The idea is to ascertain whether there are any blips and, if there are, to investigate them. For example, the return on sales could be computed to determine whether the enterprise has had any major changes. The fallacy of analytical reviews is that finding no blip may actually be a cause for concern. Can anyone say WorldCom?

Audit firms have increased their reliance on computers when conducting audits. While this may save money, it is effective only if the computer programs can detect whatever accounting irregularities exist. Unfortunately, corporations have created programs that anticipate what the auditor will do. One executive told me that his auditor insisted that all inventory over six months old be classified as obsolete. He bragged that he had his staff write a computer program that flagged all inventory when it was five months old so he could have it moved to a different location. The auditor's program did not catch the interfirm transfer and thought that the inventory was new. The point is that these cost-saving techniques may be lowering audit effectiveness, especially with inexperienced accountants on the job.

SERVING THE PUBLIC INTEREST

In 1997 the AICPA issued a so-called White Paper entitled *Serving the Public Interest: A New Conceptual Framework for Auditor Independence* and submitted the document to the Independence Standards Board on October 20, 1997.[24] In it the AICPA sought to redefine and reinterpret independence to allow outsourcing of internal audits and many other activities traditionally deemed inconsistent with independence. Exhibit 8.2 furnishes a brief outline of this text. Interestingly, the AICPA decided to publish the volume only in electronic form by placing the document on its website. Another fascinating point is that the AICPA hired Harvey Pitt and David Birenbaum from the law firm of Fried, Frank, Harris, Shriver, and Jacobson to write the document. This fact is useful, for the book not only gives us a glimpse into the thinking of the AICPA, but also into that of Harvey Pitt, the former SEC chairman.

Mike Sutton, at the time chief accountant at the SEC, wrote a letter on December 11, 1997, to the ISB and copied the AICPA.[25] This letter was accompanied by a SEC staff analysis that strenuously objected to the White Paper.[26] Sutton and his staff enumerated many problems with the document, but the most serious centered on the purpose of

---

Exhibit 8.2   Outline of *Serving the Public Interest* (Except for Appendixes, Written by Harvey Pitt and David Birenbaum)

I.   Introduction and Executive Summary

II. Historical and Institutional Framework

III. Economic and Other Determinants of Auditor Independence

IV. Regulatory Policy Considerations

V.   Proposal for a New Conceptual Framework

VI. Conclusion

Appendix A.   The Appearance Standard for Auditor Independence: What We Know and Should Know (Gary Orren)

Appendix B.   An Economic Analysis of Auditor Independence from a Multi-Client, Multi-Service Public Accounting Firm (Rick Antle, Paul Griffin, David Teece, and Oliver Williamson)

Appendix C.   Auditor Independence: An Organizational Psychology Perspective (Warner Burke)

Appendix D.   Auditor Independence Through Self-Regulation and Professional Ethics (Gary Edwards)

---

auditing. They objected that the White Paper adopts the auditor's viewpoint, which ignores the historical origins of the SEC and misses the whole point of why the SEC requires its registrants to have audits. To meet societal expectations, the investor's viewpoint is the only correct perspective. This staff analysis is so central to my thesis that I duplicate the letter and the staff analysis in the appendix to this chapter.[27]

The AICPA report begins with a definition of independence as "an absence of interests that create an unacceptable risk of bias with respect to the quality or context of information that is the subject of an audit engagement." Readers learn later that the unacceptable risk of bias is the unacceptable risk to the auditor, because in a microeconomic model, the auditor will maximize its profits where the marginal costs from these unacceptable risks equals the marginal revenues from the auditing and the consulting engagements. As the argument develops, readers notice that the client is the corporate firm and that the degree of risk is put entirely in terms of the economics of the accounting firm. The AICPA then proposes that each firm be allowed to develop its own independence rules, which would be enforced via the peer review process.

As Sutton and his staff point out, the fundamental error in the report is that it treats the investor with contempt. The AICPA argues for profit maximization for the auditor without regard to its effects on investors, creditors, employees, or the public. In other words, AICPA leaders ask us to forget 1929 and the reason why Congress created the SEC. In its place, the organization asks us to enable the auditing profession to do what it wants and allow firms to find their own points of equilibrium. The most the report says about the investment community is that investors and creditors can use the courts to protect themselves—of course, this report was written after the accounting firms successfully convinced Congress to pass litigation reform.

Despite its title, the White Paper shows no concern for the public interest. The authors apparently accepted Melancon's notion that serving the public interest is equivalent to serving the client, though now the client has shifted from the investor to the managers of the corporation. The redefinition of independence is designed to allow auditors to meet the client's needs while making a handsome profit. The AICPA and the Big Four merely want to find some way to rationalize and justify the auditor's providing various types of consulting services and, it is hoped, mitigate the SEC's prior conception of independence.

The risks discussed in the document seemingly are the risks of litigation. There is no mention of what investors and creditors might lose from an audit failure, or the risks to the economic system if no one trusts the numbers and the disclosures in financial reports. Clearly, *Serving the Public Interest* is one of the most self-serving documents ever written by the profession.

The proposal that firms should be allowed to develop their own independence rules is preposterous. Rules are developed by governmental institutions so that all parties know what the rules are; then investors and creditors can know what to fairly expect from auditors and auditors will know what their responsibilities are. When each firm makes its own rules, financial statement users would have to study the rules and the enforcement of each of the firms to determine what is going on and whom they can trust. To restore credibility to the current system requires a reenergized SEC with full enforcement powers. To restore trust in a system in which accounting firms determine their own rules requires investors and creditors to put hope not in one organization but in many. Of course, after the last two years, we know that we cannot trust the accounting profession.

Peer review will not help either. If peer review were worthwhile, then the peer reviews of Arthur Andersen would have surfaced structural and functional and cultural areas of concern. Then someone at Arthur Andersen or the SEC would have done something about those problems. Given that peer reviews did not prevent Arthur Andersen from shoddy audits at numerous companies, we can rest assured that peer reviews are smoke and mirrors.

My reading of the White Paper convinces me that Arthur Andersen and the remaining Big Four and the AICPA have had a culture change so radical that they do not really understand their purpose in society. Perhaps the infamous malfunctions at Enron, Global Crossing, WorldCom, and others will wake them up so they again will support the public interest. Only time will tell us whether this will happen.

As a footnote to this quite public chastening from the SEC, the AICPA removed the White Paper from its website.[28]

ANDERSEN VERDICT

The case against Arthur Andersen was peculiar on a number of fronts. Why did the jury members take so long to make a decision? In a lot of ways it did not matter whether they found the firm guilty, not guilty, or became a hung jury—Andersen's demise was all but certain. The firm's poor auditing and the poor public relations campaign led to Andersen's losing clients and incurring a brain drain of its human resources before the trial commenced. As the firm looked more and more guilty, it was natural for clients and employees to look for cleaner pastures.

I believe the auditors were guilty of obstruction of justice.[29] The key issue in the case is Nancy Temple's e-mail reminding Andersen personnel about the company's shredding policy. If this e-mail were as innocent as Andersen's attorney Rusty Hardin claimed, it seems that Andersen lawyers and administrators would have sent out such reminders before, including to employees auditing other corporations. As this activity would form a beautiful defense against the charges, Hardin would have provided such evidence if it existed. Alas, he presented no such proof, so we have to presume that none exists. Corroborating this conclusion is the fact that several Andersen witnesses testified that they did not know that the firm even had a policy concerning the shredding of documents. The only logical inference is that Temple's e-mail contained the message to shred as many documents as possible before the SEC inquiry turned into an official SEC investigation.

Having said this, however, I wonder about the penalty. With a guilty verdict, what more can or should be done to the firm? The Department of Justice drove Arthur Andersen to the brink of bankruptcy before the firm ever received a fair hearing. In addition, there clearly are innocent people at Andersen. Why did they have to suffer for the crimes of others? Could not the Department of Justice have indicted the individuals who obstructed justice, such as Nancy Temple, without indicting everyone?

On the other hand, I am not going to cry for Andersen or its employees. The fiasco at WorldCom prevents me from shedding a single tear. The mishaps at Boston Chicken, Waste Management, Sunbeam, Baptist Foundation, Enron, and WorldCom tell me that Arthur Andersen had a culture of underauditing its clients and deceiving the readers of financial statements.

The case against Arthur Andersen dredged up a lot of accounting filth. Andersen practically allowed Enron officials to dictate the audits by telling Andersen employees what they could and could not do. Any Andersen accountant who tried to do the right thing was removed from the audit. Anyone who disapproved of the special-purpose entities or how they were accounted for got drowned out by others. Unfortunately, a number of Andersen employees acted unprofessionally throughout their long tenure with Enron.

These observations lead to my last major question: Are things really different at the other public accounting firms? What exists in the fabric of their cultures that will prevent them from underauditing? Reactions by the remaining Big Four are telling: They viewed Andersen's downfall as a yard sale in which clients and personnel can be acquired at cheap prices. Additionally, they are lobbying Congress hard not to implement any rules detrimental to them and lobbying the SEC and the new oversight board to do little more than peer reviews. I see no movement for reform within these organizations or even an acknowledgment that the profession is in trouble.

The state of affairs in the accounting profession appears worse than I thought. It may be much worse. As I view Arthur Andersen on its deathbed, I have the eerie feeling that I am also witnessing the disintegration of private sector auditing. Perhaps our consciences are not enough to audit us. Perhaps we do need government auditors.

YOUNG MODEL: A REPRISE

As covered in the last chapter, Michael Young reminds us that managers typically do not awake one morning and ask whom they might defraud that day.[30] In the same way, the vast majority of auditors do not wake up one day with the idea that they will automatically approve whatever their clients (unfortunately, auditors still think that their clients are the CEOs and other managers instead of the shareholders) propose. Rather, auditors face temptations from both their clients to "go along" with what they want and from their superiors who want to bring in extra revenues. At some point, the auditor wants to be a team player and have a successful career and can do so by expanding the accounting rules to include something managers covet or by attenuating the rules to exclude something managers want to avoid. Because of the many ambiguities in accounting standards and the many areas that require professional judgment, an opportunity presents itself for improvement. The auditor says "yes" to this opportunity, rationalizing that the change is immaterial, or it will happen only this once, or it is for a good cause, or it falls within an acceptable range of generally accepted accounting principles. As new pressures arise, the auditor continues to employ such opportunities to tweak the financial reporting system until he or she digs such a big hole that there is no way out. Sooner or later, investors and creditors stumble on to the truth.

Exhibit 8.3 displays the version of the Young model that is applicable to audit frauds. Pressures to sign off combined with an opportunity to bend the accounting rules leads the auditor to decide whether to approve something inappropriate. As he or she grasps the opportunity to cook the books, the fraud begins. It typically continues until something great happens for the corporation that allows managers and auditors to hide their deceptions or the fraud becomes public knowledge.

We shall never eliminate the pressures to approve something questionable or the opportunities to bend the accounting rules. To minimize the number of times that auditors commit fraud, we need to change the culture, we need to increase the power of accountants, and we need to increase enforcement of the rules.

Exhibit 8.3   Model of an Auditing Fraud

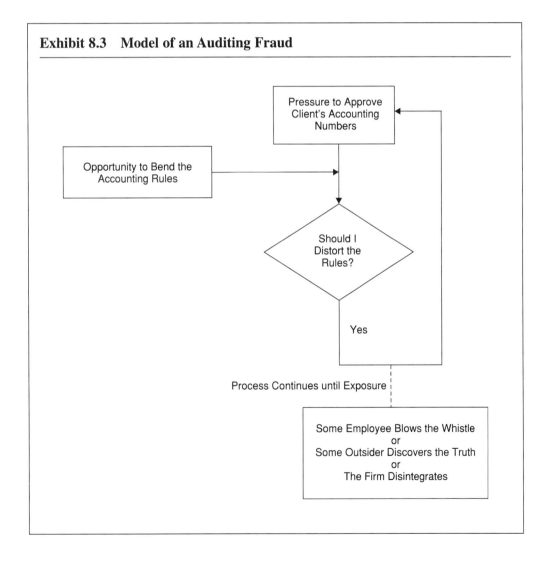

SUMMARY AND CONCLUSION

A few years ago the General Accounting Office (GAO) studied the accounting profession and found significant weaknesses in the areas of auditor independence and auditor responsibility for detecting fraud.[31] Today that GAO analysis seems prescient.

People today still remember the market crash of 1929 and the Great Depression, though thankfully most of us did not live through it. While the recent market failures have not been that bad, they have been bad enough. It is important for us to recall those days and the remedies that Congress established. Certified public accountants should recall those times and renew their vows with the public about their mission. Auditors in the early 1930s knew that vigorous and thorough audits of business enterprises would help to restore public confidence in the economic system. Today's auditors need to capture that vision if we are ever to trust accounting numbers again.[32]

Most auditors I know are very moral and upright people. Their ethics are impeccable. Yet the vast majority of them have no inkling about the conflicts of interest they face, the additional conflicts they would face if the proposals in the White Paper *Serving the Public Interest* were ever adopted, and about the incredible if unconscious effects that large amounts of money have on people.[33] Perhaps one of the first things that needs to be done is for accountants to realize and acknowledge the pressures they face and the slanted actions they are adopting, perhaps unawares. By making these items conscious, the profession might actually begin to address the root problems.

Given the difficulty individuals have in noticing conflicts of interest and possible ethical violations, accounting firms must create the internal controls to check one another. Each person needs to be accountable to others so that high professional values can be maintained. More important, firms must create a culture that values and embraces investors and creditors, with a true desire to provide them complete and accurate information so that rational investment and other economic decisions can be made. Firms need to create a culture that values independence and auditing and does not make these institutions subordinate to other activities.

Firms and the profession should address conflicts of interest. Most consulting activities create problems, so they likely should be disallowed. To make money, audit prices have to go up substantially, and agencies such as the Federal Trade Commission should not worry about the price increases. They are needed to attract and retain talent in the audit profession. Other items should be considered, such as rotation of partners or firms. The point is that the number of conflicts of interest needs to be reduced. Further, for those conflicts that cannot be eliminated, the accounting firms need to invent ways to address them and ensure ethical behavior on the part of individual accountants and accounting firms.

The SEC needs to offer the profession a "carrot" and encourage it through education efforts with accountants. At the same time, the SEC, federal prosecutors, and the civil courts need to provide a "stick" to bring along the recalcitrant accountants who have not yet captured the vision of true service to the public. Greater enforcement must be exercised if real reforms are to take place.[34]

Early signs are not too good. As Floyd Norris has noted, it appears that the accounting industry is fighting real reform all the way.[35] The Big Four opposed Sarbanes-Oxley and any other bill that Congress entertained. (I do not argue that the bills were good;

rather, the accounting firms displayed a bad attitude in their opposition. It is one thing to oppose bad reforms, but quite another to stand in the way of good and decent improvements in the system.) They disputed the nomination of John Biggs to head the Public Company Accounting Oversight Board, discussed further in the next chapter. They are lobbying heavily for this board to do little more than "peer reviews" that accomplish nothing. In short, the leadership of the Big Four appears to be doing great public relations work while privately attempting to sabotage anything that substantively would reform the industry.

This may be a critical juncture for the profession. If the public accountants do not answer the call for improvement, society might have to reexamine the desirability of government auditors. Undoubtedly there are substantial disadvantages in employing government workers as auditors, but there are some gains as well. Before going that route, however, we should give the profession another chance, for significant improvement in the public accounting profession is possible. If only the leaders of the Big Four would show signs of true leadership.

PricewaterhouseCoopers says that it will take the challenge and perform "more thorough and more detailed audits."[36] If so, it would be a welcome sign of leadership in the profession. I suggest that the firm begin with Tyco. Norris has pointed out that Tyco has not made any significant changes to its past reporting, relying on the analysis by David Boies to justify no change.[37] At best this is a reflection of what is wrong in the business world; it indicates that financial executives and auditors may not even recognize significant and systemic fraud. They have a blind spot. At worst, Tyco is attempting a massive cover-up to resist any momentous transformation in its mode of operations. We now must ask whether PricewaterhouseCoopers' goal of "more thorough and more detailed audits" is a sham or whether it is for real. The public eye is on the company to see what it does with respect to Tyco; that holds the answer to whether we can trust the new PricewaterhouseCoopers.

NOTES

1. T. J. Johnson, *Professions and Power* (London: Macmillan, 1972). Also see R. Dingwall and P. Lewis, eds., *The Sociology of the Professions: Lawyers, Doctors and Others* (London: Macmillan, 1983); E. Friedson, *Professional Powers: A Study of the Institutionalization of Formal Knowledge* (Chicago: University of Chicago Press, 1986); and M. S. Larson, *The Rise of Professionalism: A Sociological Analysis* (Los Angeles: University of California Press, 1977).

2. R. R. Sterling, "Accounting Power," *Journal of Accountancy* (January, 1973), pp. 61–67.

3. A. J. Briloff: *Unaccountable Accounting* (New York: Harper & Row, 1972); *More Debits than Credits* (New York: Harper & Row, 1976); and *The Truth about Corporate Accounting* (New York: Harper & Row, 1981); and E. Mason, *Random Thoughts: The Writings of Eli Mason* (New York: Eli Mason, 1998).

4. The Powers report provides much detail about Duncan's activities and describes how Arthur Andersen failed in performing its attest function. W. Powers, R. S. Troubh, and H. S. Winokur Jr., *Report of Investigation by the Special Investigative Committee of the Board of Directors of Enron Corp.*, February 1, 2002; compare R. R. Reynolds, "Enron Held Too Much Influence over Andersen, Partner Says," *Dow Jones Business News,* May 31, 2002.

5. These sections are adapted from my essays in the *Journal of Corporate Accounting and Finance* entitled "Is There an Epidemic of Underauditing?" (Fall 2002), pp. 25–35; and "Can We Prevent Future Enrons?" (May–June 2002), pp. 3–11. For more details about the history of the accounting profession, see E. S. Hendriksen, *Accounting Theory,* 2nd ed. (Homewood, IL: Irwin, 1970), pp. 22–91); G. J. Previtts and B. D. Merino, *A History of Accountancy in the United States: The Cultural Significance of Accounting* (Columbus: Ohio State University Press, 1998); M. Stevens: *The Big Eight* (New York: Macmillan, 1981), and *The Big Six: The Selling Out of America's Top Accounting Firms* (New York: Simon & Schuster, 1991); R. K. Storey, *The Search for Accounting Principles—Today's Problems in Perspective* (New York: AICPA, 1964); H. I. Wolk, J. R. Francis, and M. G. Tearney, *Accounting Theory: A Conceptual and Institutional Approach,* 5th ed. (Cincinnati, OH: South-Western Publishing, 1992), pp. 49–76; and S. A. Zeff, *Forging Accounting Principles in Five Countries* (Champaign, IL: Stipes Publishing, 1971), pp.110–268. For a more sociological flavor, see P. D. Montagna, *Certified Public Accounting: A Sociological View of a Profession in Change* (Houston: Scholars Book Co., 1974); and R. R. Sterling, ed., *Institutional Issues in Public Accounting* (Lawrence, KS: Scholars Book Co., 1974).

6. D. L. Flesher and T. K. Flesher, "Ivar Kreuger's Contribution to U.S. Financial Reporting," *The Accounting Review* (July 1986), pp. 421–434.

7. M. E. Hussein and J. E. Ketz: "Ruling Elites of the FASB: A Study of the Big Eight," *Journal of Accounting Auditing and Finance* (Summer 1980), pp. 354–367, and "Accounting Standards-Setting in the U.S.: An Analysis of Power and Social Exchange," *Journal of Accounting Auditing and Finance* (Spring 1991), pp. 59–81; compare B. Lev, "Toward a Theory of Equitable and Efficient Accounting Policy," *The Accounting Review* (January 1988), pp. 1–22.

8. Typical reactions from the accounting profession can be found in various auditing textbooks and supplements, such as: F. W. Windal and R. N. Corley, *The Accounting Professional: Ethics, Responsibility, and Liability* (Englewood Cliffs, NJ: Prentice-Hall, 1980); and V. M. O'Reilly et al., *Montgomery's Auditing,* 12th ed. (New York: John Wiley & Sons, 1998).

9. Johnson, *Professions and Power*; and R. R. Sterling, "Accounting Power."

10. Compare E. Mason, "SAS 99: A View from a Skeptic," *Accounting Today,* December 16–January 5, 2003, pp. 6–7.

11. A. Levitt, "Renewing the Covenant with Investors." Remarks by Chairman Arthur Levitt, presented at the NYU Center for Law and Business, New York, May 10, 2000; see: *www.sec.gov/news/speech/speecharchive.shtml.*

12. A. Levitt, "The Numbers Game." Remarks by Chairman Arthur Levitt, presented at the NYU Center for Law and Business, New York, September 28, 1998; see: *www.sec.gov.news/speech/speecharchive.shtml.*

13. Levitt, "Renewing the Covenant with Investors."

14. While the details of the arguments might change, others have also come to the conclusion that auditors as a group are not meeting societal expectations. See: M. Brewster, *Unaccountable: How the Accounting Profession Forfeited a Public Trust* (Hoboken, NJ: John Wiley & Sons, 2003); A. Briloff: *Unaccountable Accounting, More Debits than Credits,* and *The Truth about Corporate Accounting*; General Accounting Office, *The Accounting Profession: Major Issues: Progress and Concerns.* Report to the Chairman, Committee on Commerce, U.S. House of Representatives (Washington, DC: GAO, 1996); D. S. Hilzenrath, "Big Four Firms Face Post-Enron Scrutiny," *Washington Post,* June 7, 2002; S. Liesman, J. Weil, and M. Schroeder, "Accounting Profession Faces a Credibility Crisis," *College Journal from the*

Wall Street Journal, 2002; see: *www.collegejournal.com*; M. Maremont and L. P. Cohen, "Probe of Tyco Is Expanded to Include Its Auditor PwC," *Wall Street Journal,* September 30, 2002; E. Mason, *Random Thoughts* (1998); P. B. W. Miller and P. R. Bahnson, *Quality Financial Reporting* (New York: McGraw-Hill, 2002); S. P. Pizzo, "Making Accounting Add Up," *Forbes,* February 26, 2002; Stevens, *The Big Eight* and *The Big Six*; and U.S. Senate: *The Accounting Establishment.* Report of the Staff to the Senate Subcommittee on Reports, Accounting, and Management, Committee on Government Operations (Washington, DC: U.S. Senate, December 1976); and *Financial Oversight of Enron: The SEC and Private-Sector Watchdogs.* Report of the Staff to the Senate Committee on Governmental Affairs (Washington, DC: U.S. Senate, October 8, 2002).

15. Levitt, among others, reminds us that the analysts are in bed with the sales staff, so their motivations are far from pure; see A. Levitt, *Take on the Street: What Wall Street and Corporate America Don't Want You to Know: What You Can Do to Fight Back* (New York: Pantheon Books, 2002). Also see A. Berenson, *The Number: How the Drive for Quarterly Earnings Corrupted Wall Street and Corporate America* (New York: Random House, 2003).

16. While many commentators employ the tag "Final Four," I prefer the label "Big Four" because of Agatha Christie's novel with the same title. That book deals with corporate intrigue, so it seems fitting.

17. I. J. Dugan, "A Decade of Greed Undid a Once-Proud Profession," *College Journal from the Wall Street Journal,* 2002; see: *www.collegejournal.com.*

18. J. Von Brachel, "Professional Issues: New AICPA Chairman: Creating a Future," *Journal of Accountancy* (November 1997).

19. B. C. Melancon, "The Changing Strategy for the Profession, the CPA, and the AICPA: What This Means for the Education Community," *Accounting Horizons* (December 1998), pp. 397–406.

20. The Independence Standards Board was created in 1998 with SEC approval in FRR No. 50, but it was dissolved in 2001; see Securities and Exchange Commission, "SEC Statement of Policy on the Establishment and Improvement of Standards Related to Auditor Independence," Financial Reporting Release No. 50, 1998. Glazer and Jaenicke bemoan the termination of the ISB prior to an issuance of a conceptual framework on auditing and particularly focused on independence; see A. S. Glazer and H. R. Jaenicke, "A Pathology of the Independence Standards Board's Conceptual Framework Project," *Accounting Horizons* (December 2002), pp. 329–352. While Glazer and Jaenicke might be correct, I view the construction of the ISB as an attempt by leaders within the profession to hijack independence and mold this institution in a way that they preferred; the White Paper discussed later in the chapter is my evidence. I view the annihilation of the ISB as a recognition that Sutton and others at the SEC were going to block such efforts.

21. KPMG's challenge of the cease-and-desist order from the SEC was argued before the United States Court of Appeals for the District of Columbia Circuit on February 15, 2002, and decided on May 14, 2002. KPMG asserted that the SEC lacks authority on certain aspects of the proceedings and that the cease-and-desist order was "overbroad and vague." The court held that "although KPMG did not have fair notice . . . , the Commission properly could use a negligence standard to enforce violations . . . ." Further, the court held that there is "no ambiguity" and so denied the petition.

22. Harvey L. Pitt, "How to Prevent Future Enrons," *Wall Street Journal,* December 11, 2001.

23. K. Brown, "Heard on the Street: Auditors' Methods Make It Hard to Uncover Fraud by Executives," *Wall Street Journal,* July 8, 2002.

24. American Institute of Certified Public Accountants, *Serving the Public Interest: A New Conceptual Framework for Auditor Independence.* Submitted to the Independence Standards Board on October 20, 1997, written by H. L. Pitt and D. E. Birenbaum.

25. M. H. Sutton, Unpublished letter to W. T. Allen, Chairman of the Independence Standards Board, December 11, 1997.

26. Securities and Exchange Commission, "Staff Analysis of AICPA White Paper: A New Conceptual Framework for Auditor Independence," December 11, 1997.

27. The foundation for the SEC's case is found in Securities and Exchange Commission, "Staff Report on Auditor Independence," prepared by the Office of the Chief Accountant, March 1994. Also see the critiques by J. E. Ketz and P. B. W. Miller, "Looking at a White Paper Through Rose-Colored Glasses," *Accounting Today,* May 25–June 7, 1998, pp. 14, 17; and E. Mason, "White Paper or Whitewash?" *Accounting Today* (January 5-25, 1998).

28. While that confiscation removes a piece of trash from the world of ideas, it also removes the evidence of wrong thinking by the leaders of the accounting profession. Fortunately, I downloaded a copy before the AICPA eviscerated its copies. If anyone wants a copy, e-mail me at *edketz@psu.edu* and I shall forward you a copy of *Serving the Public Interest.*

29. This material is gleaned from my July 15, 2002, essay, "The Andersen Verdict: Questions Worth Asking"; see: *www.SmartPros.com.* Also see D. Ivanovich and S. Brewer, "The Andersen Verdict: Verdict May Aid Government's Case Against Enron," *Houston Chronicle,* June 16, 2002; and R. R. Reynolds: "Enron Held Too Much Influence over Andersen, Partner Says," and "WRAP: Jury Finds Andersen Guilty on Obstruction Charge," *Dow Jones Energy Service,* June 15, 2002. For a discussion of the corrupt culture at Andersen, see B. L. Toffler, *Final Accounting: Ambition, Greed, and the Fall of Arthur Andersen* (New York: Broadway Books, 2003).

30. M. R. Young, ed., *Accounting Irregularities and Financial Fraud* (San Diego: Harcourt Professional Publishing, 2002), pp. 11–13.

31. General Accounting Office, *The Accounting Profession.*

32. In a recent paper, Sutton claims that external auditors must do three things:

    (a) "embrace a role that is fully consistent with high public expectations"

    (b) "tackle fraudulent financial reporting as a distinct issue with a distinct goal—zero tolerance" and

    (c) "accept and support necessary regulatory processes that give comfort to investors and the public that the profession is doing all that it can do to prevent future episodes of failed financial reporting."

    See: M. H. Sutton, "Financial Reporting at a Crossroads," *Accounting Horizons* (December 2002), pp. 319–328.

33. M. H. Bazerman, G. Loewenstein, and D. A. Moore, "Why Good Accountants Do Bad Audits," *Harvard Business Review* (November 2002); and A. B. Crenshaw and B. D. Fromson, "A Conflict for CPAs?" *Washington Post,* March 28, 1998, p. H1.

34. C. Bryan-Low, "SEC May Take Tougher Tone on Accountants in Bad Audits," *Wall Street Journal*, December 13, 2002.

35. F. Norris, "Will Auditing Reform Die Before It Begins?" *New York Times*, December 27, 2002.

36. J. D. Glater, "Pricewaterhouse Taking a Stand, and a Big Risk," *New York Times,* January 1, 2003.

37. F. Norris, "Should Tyco's Auditors Have Told More?" *New York Times,* January 3, 2003.

Sutton's Critique of
Serving the Public Interest

United States
SECURITIES AND EXCHANGE COMMISSION
Washington, DC 20549

December 11, 1997

William T. Allen, Chairman
Independence Standards Board
1211 Avenue of the Americas
New York, New York 10012

Dear Chairman Allen:

The staff of the Securities and Exchange Commission (the "staff") is pleased to respond to your request that we review the report presented to the Board on October 20 by the American Institute of Certified Public Accountants (the "AICPA"), entitled *Serving the Public Interest: A New Conceptual Framework for Auditor Independence* (the "White Paper") and provide our commentary to the Board. I understand that the Board will be discussing the White Paper at its December 15 meeting. Those observations are presented in the attached Appendix.

   The White Paper articulates well an argument for a particular approach and a particular model that would provide for greater professional self-regulation. The staff's understanding and expectation, however, is that the Board intends to deliberate and solicit input on the issues from many points of view. In the staff's view, the White Paper does not present the balanced exposition of the issues that will be essential for the Board's deliberations and for soliciting public input. Consistent with that expectation, the staff believes that the Board should consider developing a more neutral document that presents the full range of issues and views before soliciting public input. The approach used by the Financial Accounting Standards Board for preparing discussion memoranda might be a useful model for the Board.

The staff's observations presented in the Appendix reflect the Commission's overarching concern for maintaining investor confidence in the independent audit and the capital markets. The role of the independent audit in public capital markets is to enhance the credibility of financial reports, thereby providing investors with a degree of comfort that they will be treated fairly. While many factors arguably affect the efficient functioning of capital markets, it seems obvious that those markets will not function unless the information used for making investment decisions has credibility. Thus, the independent audit's significant role in providing credibility must be first and foremost on the Board's agenda.

As the Board takes up the issues that lie ahead, expectations demand that the investor's point of view be kept sharply in focus. As it considers the issues, the Board's important decisions must be guided by the answers to the most basic questions— whether a reasonable investor, with full knowledge of all the facts and circumstances, would have confidence that the independent auditor would put the interests of investors first and that those interests would not be compromised by an conflicting interest of the auditor or the auditor's client. Only affirmative answers to those kinds of questions will assure the market credibility that is so essential.

The staff agrees that framing the discussion in the context of the changing business and professional environment is useful. Clearly, the application of some guidance that worked well decades ago is less clear today. Conversely, some more recent and important issues are not addressed in the guidance at all. The Board will be expected to fill those gaps.

Although investors' expectations of the independent audit have been the focus of the Commission's rule-making from the beginning, it is clear that all could, and should, learn more. The White Paper suggests that the Board may want to sponsor research in certain areas. The staff believes that the Board will need wide-ranging research focused on identifying and gaining a better understanding of the issues that affect investors' confidence in financial reports.

The staff recognizes that thoughtful consideration of these important issues will take time. The White Paper, as I mentioned earlier, proposes one approach and model, presented from the point of view of the practicing profession. But there are other, important considerations, and judging the issues will take objective analysis, deliberation, and substantial public dialogue. The staff is committed to assisting you in those efforts.

From the Commission's perspective, the goals of strengthening the quality and independence of audits are clear and unambiguous—it's all about maintaining investor confidence in the fairness and honesty of our securities markets. That was the objective of the securities laws that require an independent audit, and it is the fundamental focus of the Commission today.

Thank you very much for providing this opportunity for the staff to share its views with the Board.

Sincerely,
Michael H. Sutton
Chief Accountant

SEC STAFF ANALYSIS

AICPA WHITE PAPER: A NEW CONCEPTUAL FRAMEWORK FOR AUDITOR INDEPENDENCE

The staff of the SEC concurs with the overarching imperative stated in the White Paper of serving the public interest in assuring auditor independence. This is consistent with the view expressed by the Supreme Court that clarifies the auditor's "ultimate allegiance to a corporation's creditors and stockholders, as well as to the investing public" and that the auditor's "public watchdog" function "demands that the accountant maintain total independence from the audit client at all times and requires complete fidelity to the public trust." *United States v. Arthur Young*, 465 US 805, 817 (1984). With that goal in mind the following analysis is respectfully submitted. {Footnote 1: The comments that follow are those of the staff of the SEC and do not necessarily represent the views of the Commission.}

I. THE WHITE PAPER ILLUSTRATES THAT MORE STUDY IN THIS AREA IS NEEDED.

The principal conclusion reached by the White Paper is that the existing regulatory system should be replaced with a principles-based model. The White Paper further states that the new model would have the ISB establish core principles of independence, establish safeguards, and challenge firms to design effective independence codes.

To understand whether, and if so how, the existing system may be improved, it is important to consider how the present system evolved and operates. That consideration necessarily involves understanding, among other things: 1) the procedures and guidance that firms have in place to deal with independence issues that arise; and 2) how the firms interact with the AICPA, the SEC, and other regulatory bodies. Most firms already have guidance or "codes" of independence, and these documents could provide the ISB with an excellent source of educational material in order to understand the issues.

It also would be helpful to further explore the notion of whether the existing system is a "command and control" regulatory system or merely the natural evolution of any system that would involve implementing principles of independence. It appears that the AICPA, which is not a regulatory body, developed a very similar system to the SEC's with respect to addressing independence issues and experienced the same result. First, the SEC developed, overtime, certain underlying guidelines or principles of independence. (See Rule 2-01 of Regulation S-X.) Those underlying guidelines state that the auditor should not enter into relationships that a reasonable investor would perceive as placing the auditor in the position of having either mutual or conflicting interests with the audit client. Those relationships would include, among other things, situations in which the auditor would audit his or her own work, act in the capacity of management or an employee of the audit client, act as an advocate or attorney or broker/dealer for the client, or have a financial interest in the client.

Similarly, the AICPA developed broad guidelines based on the same notion that an auditor must be independent in fact and appearance. Both the SEC and the AICPA developed an extensive base of "interpretations" of their respective basic notions or principles of independence that address fact-specific independence questions. In each case, the broad notions and specific interpretations were developed over a long period of time, with input from knowledgeable practitioners and regulators, and after consideration of administrative and court cases. In this sense, instead of "command and control" regulation, it has been a participatory "question and answer" form of regulation.

After substantial consideration of the White Paper, the staff believes that significant additional research is needed before the ISB may decide which regulatory approaches would best serve the public interest by promoting investors' confidence in the credibility of financial reporting and the markets.

It appears that in certain areas new, updated research is needed—focusing on investors' confidence in the audit process and in the markets—before the ISB considers whether to abandon approaches that have been in place for 60 years. The current system, although it may be in need of repair, has worked. For example, an article co-authored by a CPA and a lawyer in the July 1993 edition of *The CPA Journal* noted that independence issues have been somewhat mitigated because both the profession and the SEC strengthened the rules over the years. Brown and Carmichael, "An Analysis of SEC Disciplinary Proceedings," *The CPA Journal*, 54 (July 1993). This system, therefore, should not be dismissed lightly.

A research approach similar to that discussed on pages 46 through 48 of the White Paper might be appropriate, provided it is focused on investors. This research, which could assist the Board's evaluation of various independence models, could cover a range of issues such as:

Who are the investors the independence requirement is intended to protect? (in view of the "resurgence" of small investors, it may be appropriate to define a "reasonable investor" in terms of small investors having sufficient confidence in the markets to continue investing directly or through mutual funds),

Are investors concerned about the current regulatory structure, and if so, why? (the White Paper seems to suggest that investor confidence in the audit process is high; this may imply that the current auditor independence regulatory system is working; and, that investors may believe that the SEC will not permit an auditor to engage in any activity that creates a mutuality of interest),

What should the conceptual underpinnings for auditor independence be?

What nonaudit services are firms providing to SEC audit clients today, and are investors aware of these services? Would disclosure of the services provided to public companies be helpful in improving investor understanding?

What nonaudit services or business relationships, between auditors and their SEC audit clients do investors consider important? (note that in the October 20, 1997 ISB meeting, the analyst group observed that, if they perceive an independence problem, they simply "walk away from the stock"),

What nonaudit services would the firms provide to SEC audit clients and what business relationships would be entered into if the AICPA White Paper approach were adopted? How would investors react to those services and relationships?

Does an investor's perception of an independence problem change when a significant financial reporting problem or financial fraud has gone undetected by the auditor?

How would investors react to leaving it to each firm to determine its own independence code, subject only to broad guidelines?

What are the countervailing pressures on individual auditors and firms between providing investor confidence in the audit process and expanding nonaudit services?

II. THE POINT OF VIEW OF THE INVESTOR

It is of utmost importance to keep the mission of the ISB sharply in focus. Article 1, paragraph 1, of the ISB's Operating Policies, states that the mission of the ISB is "to establish independence standards applicable to audits of public entities in order to serve the public interest and to protect and promote investors' confidence in the securities markets." The point of view of the investor and the investor's view of the process, therefore, are key elements in addressing auditor independence issues.

The SEC historically has maintained that the requirement for an independent audit is to assure investor confidence in the audit process and in the markets; accordingly, it has stressed the need to view independence issues from the investors', not the auditors', point of view (auditing standards, the US Supreme Court, and others agree with this view by stressing the need for auditors not only to be independent but also to appear to be independent; see Part IV of the staff outline distributed at the October 20, 1997 ISB meeting, which quotes portions of *United States v. Arthur Young*, 465 US 805, 819 n. 15 (1984) for the proposition that auditors must not only be independent but also be perceived as independent).

The White Paper does not fully explore the recommended change in the system from the investors' point of view. Rather, the White Paper appears to be written from the point of view that if the auditor believes he or she is acting with integrity and objectivity in performing an audit, then whether a relationship, service, or event impairs independence should focus on a "balancing of risks and benefits in the public interest." The Paper indicates that the auditor's view of the independence issue is significant because "participants in the regulated profession possess detailed knowledge not available to the regulators and standards-setters." (page 6) The White Paper further reflects this point of view by defining "independence" as "an absence of interests that create an unacceptable risk of bias with respect to the quality or context of information that is the subject of an audit engagement." (pages 7 and 14) The Paper also emphasizes that, as a general rule, firms should be able to perform almost any service provided "safe-guards" are in place to protect the public. (pages 128-130 and elsewhere)

The White Paper similarly stresses the auditors' views as opposed to investors' views when it emphasizes that the firms are "best positioned to recognize the risks and threats [to auditor independence], and . . . also possess the incentives to achieve an appropriate solution. (page 8) The White Paper also notes that firms should exercise "front-line responsibility" for interpreting independence requirements. (page 15)

None would deny that auditor involvement in the independence process is essential; however, when considering new auditor independence codes, the firms would seem to be subject to conflicting interests. As a result, a public body, rather than the firms, would seem to be in a better position to focus full attention on the most fundamental issue— investor confidence in the independent audit—and to craft appropriate solutions to significant independence issues.

In addition, advocates of the White Paper approach emphasize that a firm would be motivated by ISB review of the codes and market forces for audit services to have an independence code that "enhances the independence of the firm and the audit partner." (page 8) A thorough analysis of the market incentives, however, should include consideration of whether clients and potential clients would be attracted to firms with high independence standards that may restrict the amount or type of services the firm may provide to the client, or to a firm that emphasizes "economy of scales" in providing a variety services over independence.

III. ADDITIONAL QUESTIONS RAISED BY THE WHITE PAPER

A. Need for Interpretative Guidance

The White Paper criticizes practice as a "command and control" system because it is detailed and cumbersome. It is true that the current body of SEC and AICPA guidance regarding independence consists primarily of "case law" in the form of ad hoc interpretive guidance issued over the years. As noted earlier; however, there is the possibility that the proposal in the White Paper for a short list of auditor independence principles, and the issuance of general guidelines for firm codes, could follow the same path and might result in an even more extensive, and more complex, body of interpretive guidance than exists today. This result could occur because the ISB's interpretations would have to address multiple firm codes as well as the SEC's and AICPA's regulations.

It has been the staff's experience that firms often want assurance of their independence before they enter into engagements or conduct audits that could expose their SEC audit clients to either a delay in having a registration statement become effective or the risk of a reaudit because of a question arising on an independence issue. It is not clear how the proposal in the White Paper would eliminate that need for interpretive advice.

The proposal in the White Paper would result in a system in which approximately a thousand firms would adopt independence codes (although the Paper expresses a hope that many of these will be duplicates, it also indicates that each firm will be encouraged to adjust the ISB's model codes to the firm's particular circumstances, resulting in hundreds of codes with both dramatic and subtle, but important, differences). Interpretive responses would have to focus on both the common language and the differences in the firms' codes. Further, it has been suggested that if firms do not participate in the program outlined in that Paper, those firms (domestic and foreign) will remain subject to the current regulatory requirements. The current body of SEC interpretations, therefore, would have to remain intact.

With the ISB staff being asked to interpret both a variety of firm codes and the existing SEC regulations, it will be extremely difficult for the ISB staff to maintain a set of interpretive guidance that is logically consistent and useful to practitioners. In short, the proposal in the White Paper very well could lead us back to the current situation with a set of detailed, fact-specific interpretations.

B. Need to remain focused on investor confidence

The White Paper presents a variety of issues and arguments that could lead the reader away from the central goal of constructing auditor independence guidance that assures investor confidence in the independent audit and in the securities markets. These issues and arguments are discussed below.

TECHNICAL SKILLS. The White Paper stresses that a broad range of technical skills within he firms improves the quality of audits. The issue, however, is not whether the firms should have a variety of technical skills and disciplines; it is generally understood that they should. The question is whether the firm that provides a particular nonaudit service to a public company should be the same firm that audits the company's financial statements. To answer this question, the staff currently considers whether providing the particular nonaudit service to an SEC audit client would, or would appear to a reasonable investor to, (1) involve the auditor too directly in the management of that client or as an employee of that client, (2) align the financial and business interests of the auditor too closely with those of management, or (3) result in the auditor auditing his/her own work.

FIRM'S ECONOMIC INTERESTS. The in-depth discussion in the White Paper of the economic interest of firms in their reputation ("reputational capital") and a firm's economy of scale in providing several services to one client (the "quasi-rents" and "productive capital" discussions on page 60 and elsewhere) overstates significantly the relevance of these issues to an investor's analysis of auditor independence.

In this regard, the White Paper indicates that a new approach to addressing independence issues is necessary because "the current approach fails to serve the public interest because it is inefficient, inflexible and imposes social costs without compensating benefits." (page 10) the White Paper also argues that incidents that would impair independence in a single client context (e.g., that the auditor cannot obtain a return on its "productive capital" invested in a client without retaining that client (pages 60 and 61) or that the auditor receives a significant portion of its revenues from one client (page 65)) should not impair the independence of firms with multiple clients. The Paper indicates that the need for the firm to protect its aggregate revenues is not tied to one client but to all of its clients and, therefore, regardless of how much the firm has invested in one client or how much revenue it receives from one client, the firm would rather walk away from that client than damage its reputation and risk a loss of many clients.

In considering an auditor independence issue, however, the primary focus should be on whether the conduct is reasonable in the eyes of the investors, rather than the cost-benefit analysis done by a firm to see if providing a service to an SEC audit client is worth the cost or whether there is any potential harm to the firm's reputation. There is a profound social benefit, which is not developed in the White Paper, in having investors maintain confidence in the audit process and in the integrity of the securities markets. This benefit cannot be quantified, but it is real nonetheless.

The ISB also should consider the other side of the economy of scale issue, that is, the practice of some firms to underprice audit fees in competing for the audit engagement with an expectation that other, more profitable, nonaudit services and business relationships would follow. These practices have raised concerns for both the quality and independence of audits.

A related issue which the ISB may consider is the impact of conflicting or mutual interests on the audit partner's (as opposed to the firm's) decisions regarding the audit. The audit partner's reputation and career may be impacted if one significant client is lost.

AUDIT QUALITY. The White Paper advocates the expansion of nonaudit services as a means to enhance audit quality. Audit quality, however, is not the issue; everyone supports high quality audits. It should be the auditors' obligation to serve the public and their duty to act with professional skepticism that assures a quality audit rather than a multi-service relationship with the client.

Arguments that more knowledge of the client increases the quality of the audit (page 68 and elsewhere), taken to the extreme, would have the auditor keeping the books and preparing the financial statements. Once a firm has worked closely with a client to improve the client's operations or reporting systems, it would appear that the firm would have difficulty in providing a "critical second look" at those operations and systems. Also, there is little evidence that the individuals performing nonaudit services (such as computer engineers) recognize information significant to the audit.

Arguments in the White Paper that having a firm other than the auditor provide nonaudit services impairs the auditor's access to client information (page 73 n. 187 and elsewhere) are disturbing. If the auditor does not receive all the information necessary to conduct a thorough audit and full cooperation from the client, the Commission expects the auditor to indicate that there is a "scope limitation" on the audit and appropriately qualify the audit report. Thus, it is the independent auditor's obligation to conduct a professional audit that assures the integrity of the financial markets, not an array of services provided to the client. See *United States v. Arthur Young, supra*, at 818–819.

Two common concerns regarding the effect of nonaudit services on audit quality are (1) whether the emphasis on nonaudit services—because of their profitability—could cause a firm to assign a lower priority to audit services, and (2) whether, or at what point, the increasing complexities of the professional and business environment could threaten the fact and appearance of auditor independence. These concerns should be the focus of the ISB's research and deliberations.

FREE RIDING. The White Paper suggest that auditor independence concerns may be limited to a few individual partners who may be tempted to "free ride" on the firm's reputation by pursuing their self interests. (page 67) In the staff's view, however, the issue is not restricted to the possibility that a few individuals may be "free riding" on the reputation of an accounting firm. In truth, there is no reliable information indicating how many auditors may be disregarding potential auditor independence conflicts when obtaining business or assisting clients. This may be one area where additional research would be helpful.

For example, a study published in the *Journal of Business Ethics* and reported in *The Wall Street Journal* indicated that 47% of the top executives, 41% of the controllers, and 76% of the graduate-level business students participating in an experiment would be willing to commit fraud by understating write-offs that cut into their company's profits. *The Wall Street Journal*, at C1 (March 26, 1996); Brief, Dukerich, Brown, Brett, "What's Wrong with the Treadway Commission Report? Experimental Analyses of the Effects of Personal Values and Codes of Conduct on Fraudulent Financial Reporting," 15 *Journal of Business Ethics* 183 (1996).

The issue, however, is not necessarily limited to "rogue auditors," it is how to provide comprehensive and understandable guidance to auditors while giving comfort to the public that the independent audit function remains protective of the interest of investors.

LEGAL LIABILITY—LITIGATION RISKS. Contrary to the arguments in the White Paper (page 82 and elsewhere), potential legal liability in a civil proceedings is not a deterrent to compromising independence. No firm, to the best knowledge of the staff, has paid a judgment or settlement in a private civil proceeding solely as a result a finding of a loss of auditor independence. The arguments and statistics in the White Paper addressing legal liability and litigation costs simply are not relevant to this issue.

The absence of case law addressing auditor independence issues may be attributed to, among other things, (1) the absence of public knowledge of the nature and extent of nonaudit services provided by the firms to audit clients and (2) the fact that a lack of auditor independence may not, by itself, be considered to have caused a plaintiff's damages. *See, e.g., Robbins v. Koger Properties, Inc., Deloitte & Touche, et al.*, 116 F. 3d 1441 (11th Cir. 1997). A lack of independence, however, may be used as evidence of the accounting firm's intent to participate in a fraudulent scheme. *See Lerch v. Citizens First Bancorp. et al.*, [1992–1993 Transfer Binder] Fed. Sec. L. Rep. (CCH) ¶97, 258 (DNJ 1992).

Although private litigation has been limited, the Commission has initiated several enforcement cases in this area. These cases show that a lack of auditor independence can, and does, impact the quality of the audit of a client's financial statements. For example, in some cases, the auditor performed virtually no audit procedures and simply relied on management representations. Many recent enforcement cases are listed in the outline distributed by the staff at the October 20 ISB meeting.

OTHER SELF-REGULATORY EXAMPLES. The regulatory frameworks used by the Nuclear Regulatory Commission, Occupational Safety and Health Administration, bank regulators, the SEC in regulating investment companies and investment advisers, and other regulatory frameworks cited in the White Paper (pages 106–114 and elsewhere), are inapposite to the regulation of auditor independence. Each of the cited regulatory compliance programs relates to heavily regulated industries that include on-site inspections or examinations by government employees to assure the program is being carried out.

The Commission's oversight of the establishment of accounting and auditing standards and expected oversight of the establishment of independence standards by the ISB does not subject the auditing profession to the same degree of government regulation as banks, nuclear power plants, investment companies, investment advisers, or compliance with OSHA and similar regulations. Also, peer review in the auditing profession, although beneficial to the profession and the public, does not equate to the public assurance provided by direct government inspections and examinations.

Also, during the formation of the ISB, the Commission stressed that the auditor independence regulatory program should not be left solely to the auditing profession. The Commission did not endorse the then-existing professional independence body (the AICPA's Ethics Division) as the authoritative source for independence guidance. Instead, the Commission insisted on a new body with public representation, an open and public standard setting process with public commentary on draft standards, and Commission oversight. A strictly "self-regulatory" approach would not be in line with the principles on which the ISB was founded.

ABANDONING THE CURRENT SYSTEM. The current regulatory system is criticized at several points in the White Paper as being a "command and control" approach, overly rigid, detached from "ethical moorings," and so on. (pages 10, 96–102 and elsewhere) While the staff expects the ISB to review and improve that system, it should be done only after full consideration of all reasonable alternatives, including the alternative of simply updating and clarifying that system.

The White Paper states that a lack of auditor independence to date has not been either a substantial factor in audit failures or a serious concern to investors. For example, it cites the study regarding the absence of insurance claims in this area (*but see* the discussion above regarding *Legal Liability—Litigation Risks* that indicates such claims may not be a true indication of independence concerns). (page 56) This acknowledgment may be a strong endorsement that the current system, consisting of the publication of detailed examples and interpretations, is working to protect investors' confidence in the markets.

Many of the arguments in the White Paper for a new regulatory approach focus on the fact that the current regulatory system presents difficulties when firms seek to provide many services to one client. (See the *Firm's Economic Interests* paragraph above.) The auditor independence regulatory system, however, must not lose sight of the primary purpose for having audited financial statements—enhancing investor confidence in the markets—in favor of facilitating the growth of firms' nonaudit services.

Finally, the proposal that the IIC establish best practices or "benchmarks" for auditor independence codes (page 124 and elsewhere) is reminiscent of the IASC's efforts to establish benchmark international accounting standards. These efforts generally were not effective and permitted a wide diversity in accounting practice. The ISB should consider whether a similar result could occur here.

C. Materiality

The White Paper states that "the guidelines [for firm auditor independence codes] would recognize the importance of materiality as a threshold consideration in applying the core principles." (page 8) This point is restated later in the Paper as a presumption, "Immaterial interactions between an auditor or firm and an audit client should be presumed not to impair auditor independence, absent evidence to the contrary." (page 118; emphasis in original) The White Paper also stresses that materiality has both quantitative and qualitative aspects (page 127 n. 333), and that materiality may be assessed on an individual audit partner or audit team level as well as the firm level. (page 127)

As noted in the White Paper, the staff has been reluctant to use firm-level quantitative materiality standard for evaluating independence issues because (1) due to the size of the major firms, no individual client or contract might be material, (2) for smaller firms, a materiality standard may become an absolute bar to entry into a service line or business, and (3) the statutory standard is that auditors must be independent and, with limited exceptions, a firm either is independent or it is not. In this regard, the current regulations recognize that even an immaterial independence violation may raise concerns for investors, such as when the auditor has a mutual interest with the audit client in the client's financial or operating success, when one individual may be able to influence both the company and the auditor, or when the auditor would be confronted with conflicting interests (his/her duty to investors versus the interests of his/her family, former associates, and so on).

The staff also has emphasized that, when evaluating whether a matter is an immaterial business relationship under the current independence regulations, the matter must be immaterial not only to the auditing firm but also to the audit client and other affiliated organizations. *See* letter dated June 20, 1990, from Edmund Coulson, Chief Accountant, to Mr. Robert Mednick.

For these reasons, the staff believes that, as mentioned in the White Paper, any discussion of materiality should include both the qualitative and quantitative aspects of materiality and to whom the materiality standard will be applied (firm, audit partner, audit team, client, affiliates of the firm or audit client, and so on).

D. Profession-Wide Culture

The White Paper states that each firm may adopt an independence code that "reflects its culture, organizational structure, compensation system, practice priorities, quality controls and personnel policies." (page 8) This statement may be in response to the admonition in the Kirk Panel Report that firms should find a way to enhance the unique and overriding importance of the audit function in their multi-service firms. On the other hand, this statement and others in the Paper may suggest that auditors are eroding a profession-wide culture that historically set them apart from other service providers.

E. Legislative Intent

The White Paper suggests that the current regulatory scheme "may be seen as at odds with Congress' original intent" because the current regulations stress maintaining investor confidence in the markets by requiring auditors to be independent in fact and appearance, and provides detailed guidance to auditors on specific, fact-based independence issues. (page 11) The White Paper also takes comfort from the fact that

Congress "expressed no concern about audit firms providing non-audit services to audit clients or the appearance of independence." (page 11)

In truth, there is little legislative history regarding the auditor independence requirements in the securities laws. The principal source of such history consists of testimony at congressional hearings in 1933. *See, e.g.*, Hearings on S. 875 Before the Senate Committee on Banking and Currency, 73d Cong., 1st Sess., at 60 (1933). There is no indication that Congress in 1933 was informed about, or considered, the issue of the provision of nonaudit services to audit clients. The independence requirement, however, clearly was part of the statutory scheme enacted to promote investor confidence in the securities markets.

The role for auditors envisioned by Congress in 1933 might be reflected best in the original language in section 11(c) of the Securities Act of 1933 (the "1933 Act"). The section, as originally adopted, stated that in certifying registrants' financial statements, the "degree of reasonableness" required of auditors in performing audits" shall be that required of a person occupying a fiduciary relationship." *See also* H.R. Rep. No. 85, 73d Cong., 1st Sess., 5 (1933), which states that "the essential characteristic [of the civil liabilities imposed by the 1933 act] consists of a requirement that all those responsible for statements upon the face of which the public is solicited to invest its money shall be held to standards like those imposed by law upon a fiduciary." In 1934, this language was amended to "remove possible uncertainties as to the standard of reasonableness by substituting for the present language the accepted common law definition of the duty of a fiduciary." H.R. Rep. No. 1838, 73rd Cong., 2d Sess., 41 (1934) This concept of the auditor having a fiduciary relationship with purchasers and sellers of securities has continued and is reflected in the *Arthur Young* case noted above, in which the US Supreme Court stressed the auditor's "ultimate allegiance to a corporation's creditors and stockholders, as well as to the investing public" and the "public watchdog" function that "demands that the accountant maintain total independence from the client at all times and requires complete fidelity to the public trust." 465 US at 817–818 As noted elsewhere in this letter, this case also emphasized the requirement that auditors be independent in fact and appearance.

Based on the legislative history and the Court's interpretation of the securities laws, its seems clear that those laws were intended to revive investor confidence in the securities markets, and that instilling auditors with a fiduciary obligation to serve investors and to remain independent from audit clients was part of that effort. The staff, therefore, continues to believe that having auditors maintain the appearance, as well as the fact, of independence, and that providing guidance to auditors on independence issues on request (and making those interpretations available to the public), are consistent with the intent of Congress in enacting the federal securities laws.

F. Disclosure of Nonaudit Services

The White Paper discusses the Commission's prior disclosure requirement regarding the provision of nonaudit services to SEC audit clients and the relative fees for those nonaudit services. The Paper suggests that the withdrawal of that disclosure requirement over 15 years ago indicates that a new, less intrusive requirement for the disclosure of nonaudit services provided by the auditor of a registrant's financial statements (excluding fee disclosures) would not be useful to investors.

For a discussion of the prior disclosure requirement and why it was rescinded, please see pages 27 through 34 of the *Staff Report on Auditor Independence*, published by the Office of the Chief Accountant in March 1994. In sum, one of the principal reasons for withdrawing that disclosure requirement was that boards of directors and managements were considering whether to engage their auditors to perform nonaudit services based on the disclosure of the fees associated with particular services, rather than on the nature of the service and its effect on an auditor's independence. As noted in the White Paper, most of the comments supporting recession were received from public companies (not investors).

It may be that the ISB should initiate discussion of whether public disclosure of nonaudit services provided to registrants by the auditors of their financial statements should be reinstated. Most sources agree that the nature and extent of nonaudit services have evolved significantly over the last 15 years; however, there is little publicity or public knowledge of the services that currently are being performed. As was stressed in the October 20 ISB meeting, it is important for the ISB to have current research based on the current audit environment. Perhaps the best way to facilitate that research and the best way to educate investors, is for the Commission to reinstate a disclosure requirement.

G. Joint Business Ventures

The White Paper suggests that the ISB develop a "pragmatic approach that allows business relationships with audit clients—provided adequate safeguards exist to protect auditor independence." (page 3; *see also* page 94)

In 1988, major accounting firms filed a rulemaking petition with the Commission suggesting that direct business relationships, including prime/subcontractor relationships, would be deemed to impair an auditor's independence only if the relationship was material to either the auditor or the audit client. The Commission response to the petition (at page 4 of the letter dates February 14, 1989 from Jonathan G. Katz to Duane R. Kullberg) states, in part:

> "The Commission has recognized that certain situations, including those in which accountants and their audit clients have joined together in a profit-seeking venture, create a unity of interest between the accountant and the client. In such cases, both the revenue accruing to each party in the prime/subcontractor relationship and the existence of the relationship itself create a situation in which to some degree the auditor's interest is wedded to that of its client. That interdependence impairs the auditor's independence, irrespective of whether the audit was in fact performed in an objective, critical fashion. Where such a unity of interests exists, there is an appearance that the auditor has lost the objectivity and skepticism necessary to take a critical second look at management's representations in the financial statements. The consequence is a loss of confidence in the integrity of the financial statements."

Despite the Commission's clear rejection of the petition, the Commission invited the petitioners to consult with the staff regarding whether "appropriate procedural safeguards and limiting principles" could be developed that would allow auditing firms to enter into certain direct business relationships without impairing their independence. Before meaningful consultations could occur, however, a second petition was filed, which also was not adopted by the Commission.

Prior Commission action on this issue indicates, once again, that significant research may be appropriate before the ISB considers changing the existing regulations. The staff will make the public information regarding these petitions available to the ISB on request.

H. Registrants' Responsibilities

The White Paper states that "the responsibility for maintaining independence rests with individual auditors, their firms, and the accounting profession as a whole." (page 15) No one would deny that the profession plays a major role in this area. It has been recognized, however, that the responsibility under the federal securities laws is on the issuer to obtain an independent audit of its financial statements. If the auditor is not independent, the issuer pays the price of having filed unaudited financial statements and deficient registration statements and reports with the Commission. In addition, management has a serious role to play in the independence arena by deciding which provider will furnish nonaudit services to the issuer. One issue the ISB may wish to address is how to promote the involvement of managements, boards of directors, audit committees, and others, in the development of independence practices and standards.

I. The Appearance of Auditor Independence

There was virtual agreement among the commentators and presenters at the October 20 ISB meeting that the appearance of an auditor's independence is just as critical to investor confidence in the audit process and the markets as whether the auditor is independent in fact. This position is supported and explained in the outline the staff distributed at that meeting and at various points in this analysis.

Also, many of the arguments in the White Paper questioning the need for auditors to maintain the appearance of auditor independence are not new. See the Office of the Chief Accountant's 1994 *Staff Report on Auditor Independence* for a discussion of the history of this and related issues.

The suggestion in the White Paper that the ISB should address "appearance issues" only when there is "an adequate empirical foundation, and a clear need, for such measures" (page 131) may miss the point. As noted at the outset of this analysis, the staff encourages research regarding what services, relationships, and so on, might impact investors' confidence in the audit process and in the markets, and the use of that research by the ISB in revising or creating new auditor independence criteria. If, however, an "empirical foundation" requires a history of enforcement or other actions demonstrating the presence of an independence problem as opposed to a reasoned analysis by the ISB then the damage to investor confidence in the process may occur before the empirical evidence appears. The ISB, after considering the available relevant information, should use its judgment regarding when an act or practice impairs the appearance of auditor independence.

In sum, the staff believes that the goal of the requirement of auditor independence is to foster investor confidence in the securities markets. That sense of investor trust and confidence will endure only so long as auditors not only are in fact independent but also are perceived to be independent.

J. Competition

The White Paper seems to approach the issues from a "big firm" point of view. For example, it discusses independence issues in terms of "multi-disciplinary" firms with "quasi-rents" and reputational and operational capital investments in clients. The paper emphasizes that "multi-disciplinary firms offer access to an existing client base for multiple services" (page 81) and the Paper seeks to facilitate exploitation of a firm's audit client base for the sale of nonaudit services.

The exploitation of an existing base of audit clients to sell nonaudit services and promote additional business ventures could raise questions regarding whether auditors have an unfair competitive advantage in bidding on and providing those services and relationships. Indeed, smaller competent firms (both auditing and consulting firms) may feel they are at a decided disadvantage.

Would the auditor's bidding and "quasi-rents" cost advantage, for example, promote or, in the long run, harm competition for and quality of nonaudit services? Would encouraging fair competition among competent bidders of all sizes and professions provide more innovation in services and a better, broader-based, and stronger economy? For example, it is fairly well recognized that much of the economic growth in this country and many new jobs come from small businesses. The answers to these questions are beyond the scope of this analysis, and may be beyond the scope of the ISB's considerations. They are, however, indicative of the issues that the Commission may consider should it engage in rulemaking to conform its rules to the ISB's standards. *See, e.g.*, section 23(a) of the Exchange Act, section 10b of the National Securities Improvements Act, and the Regulatory Flexibility Act.

In this context, the staff has similar concerns about the application of a materiality standard to auditor independence issues. What may be an insignificant contract to a large firm may be a significant source of revenue to a small one. It could be argued that a materiality standard could foreclose the possibility of a small firm bidding on a contract, reduce the competition faced by large firms for young energetic firms, and solidify the big firms' dominance as multi-service organizations.

If the ISB determines that the independence analysis changes based on the materiality of a contract to the auditor, it should be careful not to inadvertently construct barriers to small firms entering into various service lines.

K. Enforceability of the White Paper Approach

There has been an implication that the Commission could enforce the approach in the White Paper by bringing actions against (1) a firm or individuals in a firm (domestic or foreign) that does not have an ISB approved code if the firm or individual fail to comply with existing SEC independence regulations, or (2) a firm or individual in a firm that has an approved ISB code if the firm or individuals fail to comply with that code. Although the staff has not fully considered the matter, there may be inherent enforcement problems including, among others, that differing codes among the firms potentially could yield substantial inconsistency in determining acceptable or unacceptable conduct.

L. Fire Walls

The White Paper suggests that Fire Walls ("Chinese Walls"), or walling off the audit team from those individuals providing consulting services to the client, may preserve auditor independence. (page 130) Such walls, however, would be contrary to the suggestion in the White Paper that the use of consultants may improve the knowledge base of the auditor and increase the efficiency of the audit. This dichotomy should be addressed.

M. Dependency

The White Paper appropriately states that auditors should not be financially dependent upon an audit client. (page 132) Also important, however, is the expectation that the client should not be dependent on the auditor from a financial or management services standpoint.

Some have argued that a client's dependency on the firm would not affect the firm's judgments regarding the audit of that client's financial statements. Whether this is correct or not, investors would seem to have little confidence that an audit conducted by the firm that is sustaining (financially or otherwise) the operations of the client, would constitute a critical second look at the company's financial statements. Also, if the client is dependent on the auditor, an investor rightly may ask whether he/she is investing in the client based on the capabilities and resources of the client or those of the auditing firm.

N. Managerial Functions

One of the basic notions of auditor independence has been that auditors should not assume management decision making responsibilities. Deciding what are management responsibilities, as opposed to the auditor's responsibilities, however, can be very difficult in practice.

The White Paper indicates that there should not be an independence issue if an auditor provides services to a client "so long as management reviews, understands and bears responsibility for adopting or rejecting the results of those services." (page 137) The staff, however, historically has maintained that (1) having client management approve decisions made by the auditor does not negate the fact that the auditor has assumed a management function, and (2) this approach ignores investors' concerns about auditors looking objectively at decisions they have either made or recommended to management.

Accordingly, the staff believes that research, as described above, should be conducted before any final decisions are made regarding the impact of the auditor's participation in managerial functions on the auditor's independence.

IV. A COMPREHENSIVE EVALUATION OF OTHER ALTERNATIVES

One of the limitations of the White Paper is that it does not explore other more comprehensive issues that might flow from its analysis. For instance, the White Paper suggests that accounting firms increasingly should become advisors or partners with public companies. With auditors and clients working so closely together, does this suggest that auditors, rather than management, should prepare the financial statements? If the public interest focus of the profession shifts from assuring investor confidence in the markets to providing a variety of services to public company audit clients, does that suggest that the Commission should consider other approaches for achieving its statutory mission?

V. CONCLUSION

Although many of the statements and arguments in the White Paper are troublesome, the staff's review and analysis does not suggest that approaching the issues through a concise set of auditor independence principles, coupled with more precise "guidelines" and encouragement for each firm to have an auditor independence code, is inappropriate. In the staff's opinion, however, significant additional, timely research is needed before the ISB can consider whether that approach, or one of many other alternative approaches, may form the basis for independence standards that will promote investor confidence in the independent audit and in the capital markets.

Enclosure:

SEC Office of the Chief Accountant, Staff Report on Auditor Independence (March 1994)

CHAPTER NINE

Failure of Regulation

The financial tornados of recent days have knocked out the power in various sectors of our economy. The investing public has wondered about those who generate the economic power and about those who supposedly regulate its use for the public interest. They also ruminate about what might occur next, because clearly there still exists a crisis of confidence.[1]

Chapter 7 examined the failure of managers, because some of them have issued deceitful financial statements to the public. Even good managers tend to exaggerate and puff up and make everything smell like roses, only for the rest of us to discover that what we smell is just an air freshener attempting to cover up disagreeable odors. Chapter 8 investigated the failure of the accounting profession, as the Big Five—now Big Four—attempt to attenuate their responsibilities for discovering fraud and appease management. I hope, but remain unsure, that the survivors do not possess a culture similar to Andersen's. This chapter focuses on those agencies that were designed to help us and ask what happened to them.

The General Accounting Office (GAO) investigated the accounting profession and issued its report in 1996.[2] Representative John Dingell (D-MI) wrote a letter about that report on January 17, 2001, to David Walker, the comptroller general who heads up the GAO. Dingell stated that "[t]he most significant weaknesses were found in the areas of auditor independence, auditor responsibility for detecting fraud and reporting on internal controls, public participation in standard setting, the timeliness and relevancy of accounting standards, and maintaining the independence of FASB."[3]

Among other things, the representative goes on to ask the head of the GAO to determine the "status of the profession's response . . . and the likelihood that the reforms, if implemented, will be effective." As I look back on this letter, I wonder what might have ensued had Dingell been able to persuade his colleagues of these convictions or had the GAO been more critical in its analysis. More important, I doubt that many other members of Congress read the 1996 GAO report or evaluated it before the decline and fall of the Enron empire. Why do our senators and representatives guide us only after major catastrophes take place? And even then, it seems that they use the fallout only for personal political advantage.

The first section of this chapter looks at the Financial Accounting Standards Board (FASB), questioning its slowness to address special-purpose entities (SPEs) and its unwillingness or its lack of power in standing up to chief executive officers (CEOs) and chief financial officers (CFOs). The text also ponders the call for principles-based accounting and a convergence to global accounting standards. The next section examines the Securities and Exchange Commission (SEC) and compares and contrasts the Levitt period with the Pitt era. Then the text moves to Capitol Hill and the White House to assess whether the actions of Congress and our president have helped or hindered the economic system. This inspection necessarily requires a look at the campaign donations by CEOs, CFOs, and the large accounting firms. The chapter ends with a look at the court system and the importance of litigation in fighting managerial lying and cover-ups by their advisers.

FAILURE OF THE FINANCIAL ACCOUNTING STANDARDS BOARD

Section 19(a) of the Securities Act of 1933 and section 13(b) of the Securities Exchange Act of 1934 gives the SEC the authority to prescribe the form of the financial statements and the accounting methods that can be used.[4] Shortly after the SEC was formed, however, it asked the accounting profession to develop accounting standards. Apparently the commissioners thought it would be more efficient to have a private sector body create these rules since doing so would not consume SEC resources and would utilize the expertise of accounting professionals. Importantly, though the SEC in Accounting Series Releases No. 4 and 150 gave support to the private sector standard setters, it never relinquished its authority and it retained the right to overturn or amend any of these rules.

The profession responded by creating the Committee on Accounting Procedure (CAP) in 1939. In its lifetime, the CAP produced 51 Accounting Research Bulletins, most of which are now defunct. The CAP was criticized because of its patchy and inconsistent work and the part-time status of its board members. The American Institute of Certified Public Accountants (AICPA) decided to dissolve this board in 1959 and replace it with a full-time Accounting Principles Board (APB).

The APB began operations in 1959. It had a research arm, so that the APB could conduct research before the board would make decisions on accounting standards. Unfortunately, the APB soon discovered that research in accounting is unlike research in physics and chemistry inasmuch as its research efforts created conflicts rather than generating illumination. When the APB produced APB Opinions 16 and 17 on business combination accounting, it signaled the end of the board. Many people, especially many CEOs and CFOs, howled about the APB's failure to consider the views of management. At the same time, others expressed discontent that accounting firm representatives voted in ways that pleased their corporate clients. The APB issued 31 opinions during its existence, but most of them have been superseded.

The FASB replaced the APB in 1973. While the AICPA ran the CAP and the APB, the FASB is a seven-person board whose members come from management, from the securities industry, from banking, from education, and from the public accounting profession. This broader constituency supposedly makes it a more democratic organization. The FASB developed a conceptual framework that theoretically helps it to formulate standards that are more consistent than before. It has a due process procedure that meticulously allows everyone a chance to voice an opinion about a proposed rule. While the FASB has been a big improvement over the CAP and the APB, regrettably it also has problems; however, the "solutions" that some have recently proposed for overhauling the board may prove worse.

Slow and Weak

Because of its deliberative process, the FASB inherently takes a slow, almost plodding pace. At times this process can extend to ridiculous limits, as when the board took over 25 years to consider improvements in business combination accounting. Clearly, the board members realized that this topic killed the APB and that financial executives and corporate heads adamantly opposed the elimination of the fraudulent pooling-of-interests accounting.[5] In addition, the board has not reconsidered the issues covered in Chapters 3 to 5 and has left untouched the abuses discussed earlier with respect to the equity method and lease and pension accounting. Another hot topic that sat on the back burner was SPEs. The SEC staff grew concerned about accounting for SPEs around 1985 or so and asked the FASB to deal with the topic. The FASB ignored it for a while, until its Emerging Issues Task Force (EITF) issued EITF No. 90-15 in 1990, which proved a feeble effort indeed. Only after Enron and the other debacles did the FASB put the topic on its agenda and publish an opinion—which it names Interpretation No. 46.[6] It could have done something at least 15 years before Enron, but instead it did nothing.

A classic example that depicts the weakness of FASB concerns accounting for stock-based compensation. The board called on an expensing of these stock options, but CEOs yelled and screamed, running to Congress claiming that this standard would destroy capitalism.[7] As discussed later, some members of Congress accepted campaign contributions and so rallied behind the cause. At the same time, the SEC showed little backbone and refused to support the FASB. With so much pressure against it, the FASB folded and in 1995 issued Statement of Financial Accounting Standards (SFAS) No. 123, which merely requires a disclosure of the income statement effects from the use of stock options. The recent circulation of Statement No. 148 does nothing to correct the errors.[8] While I believe that the FASB could have shown more courage and required the expensing of stock options despite the howling, the example illustrates the fundamental weakness of the board.

A more up-to-date example of FASB's near impotence concerns its rule that requires business enterprises to consolidate their SPEs—sometimes. Originally the board was leaning toward requiring consolidation unless outsiders contributed at least 10 percent of the capital to the SPE and that capital is at risk. The advantage of that proposal, notwithstanding the arbitrariness of the 10 percent threshold, was that it created a "bright line" to help managers, auditors, and financial statement readers understand the accounting. Under terrific pressure from the corporate community and from bankers in the structured finance business,[9] the FASB altered its original thought so that a firm has to consolidate the SPE only when it has insufficient equity at risk. The FASB even changed the phrase "special purpose entities" to "variable interest entities" to empha-size that this new rule does not require the consolidation of all SPEs. While this inter-pretation keeps a dividing line of 10 percent, it provides several loopholes so that corporations easily are not bound by this threshold. The interpretation may move toward principles-based accounting, but it creates far greater flexibility and will allow corporate executives to do whatever they want. Auditors will be able to exercise "pro-fessional judgment" at the very time that we are uncertain whether they can. It is as if the board is saying "More Enrons, please."

To remedy the slowness and the low power of the board, I suggest greater leadership by the members of the FASB and the SEC. Further, I suggest that Congress mind its own business and quit pretending that it knows anything about accounting. When mem-bers castigate the FASB and receive corporate campaign contributions, the hypocrisy stinks and makes for bad laws. Let us now turn to some suggestions that have been made recently for improving the FASB.

Simpler Rules[10]

Walter Wriston, retired chairman of Citicorp, recently opined that the solution to accounting scandals lay in the creation of simpler rules.[11] His mistake is itself simple: There is no causal link between simplicity and ethics. I do not care how simply rule makers write the accounting regulations; there will not be automatic compliance with them. Similarly, however complex the rules become, principled individuals will still ful-fill their duties. Surely every parent has experienced the intentional disobedience of a child who clearly understands the rules but chooses to do things his or her own way. Likewise, managers who understand accounting rules completely might still have incentives to go their own way.

We should admit that Gordon Geckos who believe that greed is good do exist in the real world and that rules, whether simple or complex, will not circumscribe their actions. The central problem rests with the human heart. The avarice of some people has no bounds, and this quandary is independent of the structure of accounting rules.

Unfortunately, the theme of Wriston's commentary distracts the reader from one of its stronger points. Accounting rules are far too complex. As Wriston points out, man-agers and auditors have both pushed for more refinement in the rules to gain greater clarity about what they can and cannot do. They apparently do not realize that this process never ends, for more detailed rules always lead to further questions that require greater illumination and more complex rules.

Wriston points out that the International Accounting Standards Board (IASB) follows an approach that attempts to lay out principles rather than detailed rules. I agree that this method would be better, but it would not necessarily make accounting more ethical. The advantage of having principles instead of detailed rules is that it helps people to main-tain focus, to remain clear about the purpose of the activity. For example, I would much rather state as a principle that firms must report all commitments on the balance sheet. Then when I run into an SPE, there is no doubt that the firm's commitment should appear in the financial statements. This approach could avoid the hair-splitting, legalis-tic style corporations and auditors employ.

The question is whether such a principle would lead managers to report SPE commitments the way they ought to and whether auditors have enough chutzpah not to sign off on the audit report until the firm recognizes the liability. This leads us back full circle. Simplicity in rules might help accounting to make more sense, it could help practitioners to keep the rationale in mind, and it could assist decision makers in what to consider when thinking about what is proper. Simplicity in rules, however, does not change the character of the participants, nor does it strengthen people's backbones.[12]

Principles-based Accounting[13]

The FASB recently introduced a "proposal for a principles-based approach to U.S. standard setting."[14] I mentioned several advantages to principles-based standards in the previous section, but this approach has one major prerequisite. It requires people who have principles. Given the events of the past year or so, that presumption is at least debatable.

The FASB states that "many have expressed concerns about the quality and transparency of U.S. financial accounting and reporting. A principal concern is that accounting standards, while based on the conceptual framework, have become increasingly detailed and complex." While true, people must remember that accounting rules attempt to map the activities of the corporation into financial statements. As corporate transactions grow in complexity, we should not be surprised that accounting rules also grow in difficulty and intricacy. If we really want simple rules, perhaps instead of changing the accounting we should outlaw derivatives and structured finance.

The FASB quotes SEC chairman Harvey Pitt: "The development of rule-based accounting standards has resulted in the employment of financial engineering techniques designed solely to achieve accounting objectives rather than to achieve economic objectives." This statement is silly as well as disingenuous. Only a fool could think that managers would quit engineering financial results upon the creation of principles-based accounting.

The FASB believes that one reason for the current complexity of accounting rules is the development of exceptions to the principles. While that statement seems accurate, let us ask what would happen under a principles-based approach. Corporate managers would apply the accounting principles to their situations, bending and twisting the principles to conform to their circumstances. Exceptions to the principles would become applications of the principles themselves, as managers find ways to fit what they want to do with the accounting rules. As exceptions become the principles, accounting in practice would in fact become far more complex for investors and creditors. The investment community would have great difficulty in comprehending how corporate managers actually implemented the accounting rules. Worse, financial statements of companies might become less comparable with those in the same industry.

The FASB says that a second reason for the current complexity is that the FASB must provide interpretive and implementation guidance. In our litigious society, do we really think managers and auditors would quit asking for such advice under a principles-based system? Not for a second do I entertain that idea.

The FASB quotes the chairman of the IASB, David Tweedie: "[A principles-based approach requires] a strong commitment from auditors to resist client pressures." I agree, but wonder whether such an approach makes it easier or harder for auditors to resist those kinds of pressures. Tweedie carefully sidestepped that issue.

Finally, as I reflect on the accounting for derivatives and the accounting for SPEs, I ask whether a principles-based approach would provide better valuations, more and better disclosures, and a more candid discussion and analysis by management. Contrasting those European entities that follow IASB standards with American companies, I think not. I see no evidence that these European concerns present better valuations, more and better disclosures, or more candid discussions and analyses. Their financial statements are at least as opaque as ours.

The conclusion appears obvious. Principles-based accounting would allow us to rise above the morass of existing accounting regulations, which are incredibly difficult to decipher, while allowing greater flexibility for manipulations and deceptions. Principles-based accounting can succeed only as the power of auditors increases, as the SEC and federal prosecutors enforce the securities laws, and perhaps with some institutional changes, such as an accounting court discussed in Chapter 11.

Global Harmonization

For years some have advocated the so-called harmonization of accounting rules so that one set of accounting rules would exist for all companies everywhere in the world. Recent events have encouraged these proponents to speak up now, as if such standards would have prevented the frauds at Enron, WorldCom, Adelphia, and Tyco. Not only do I reject the notion that international rules would have stopped the frauds, I oppose the internationalization of financial reporting rules because it would decrease the quality of financial reporting. U.S. accounting rules, like those in other countries, were developed to meet the unique needs of a specific capital market within the legal and political systems of a single country. Since other nations possess different legal and economic and political institutions, financial reporting plays different roles in those countries. Harmonizing accounting rules without harmonizing these institutions seems pointless.

A framework for examining this issue is provided by Andrei Shleifer and Robert Vishny, who claim that different nations have different systems of corporate governance as a result of different modes of capital formation.[15] The U.S. society promotes widespread participation in the stock markets to reap the advantages of competition. While encouraging participation, this system also discourages untrustworthy managers from expropriating resources from the investors. For example, our system imposes fiduciary duties on management and allows stockholders to initiate derivative actions when managers breach their duties. The United States enables hostile takeovers that allow stockholders to replace ineffective managers. In comparison to other countries, the United States has achieved its policy goal of a more efficient capital market because it relies less on large investors and banks for governance of management. Since widespread investor participation is a major policy goal, the United States promotes more disclosure than other countries do.

In contrast, corporations in Europe and Japan get most of their funds from banks and permanent investors. They depend on these investors to provide more of the corporate governance than Americans do. Small investors in Europe and Japan do not receive as much protection as their American counterparts, but creditors have more power than U.S. lenders. In addition, major investors have more institutionalized power to demand information from managers and do not rely on public accounting disclosures. In this cultural context, it is not surprising that their corporations disclose less than American firms. Shleifer and Vishny also report that German bankers have actively fought against additional public disclosure because they do not want their power diminished.

Because capital markets in other parts of the world have weak protection for small investors, they have fewer participants. Large corporations are closely owned, sometimes by a family, and little relevant financial information gets disclosed publicly. Insiders obviously can obtain whatever information they want while outsiders are kept in the dark.

So, what would happen if international accounting rules replaced U.S. generally accepted accounting principles (GAAP), especially if they come from cultural contexts with weaker protections for small investors? My guess is harmonization would have little effect on corporations in the Third World because of their weak legal systems and concentrated ownership. Many will refuse to cooperate. Nevertheless, harmonized accounting rules could help those countries open up and improve the efficiency of their capital markets. Since many international accounting standards embrace existing European and Japanese practices, I doubt that harmonization will change practice very much in those countries.

With a few exceptions, international standards require less public disclosure than U.S. GAAP. Thus, accepting them here would reduce disclosures and create other negative effects. One is that many investors will avoid the additional risk from inferior disclosures by getting out of equity markets. Without their capital, competition and efficiency will decline. Another impact will be a shift to other forms of corporate governance that are retributive instead of preventive. For example, we can expect to see more derivative litigation, and entrenched managers will face more hostile takeovers because raiders will have more private information.

I expect U.S. corporate managers to embrace harmonization while they cling to the simplistic concept that higher reported earnings lead to higher security prices. They see liberal income measurement standards as dreams come true and ignore all suggestions that harmonization will increase their cost of capital and drive down security prices. Congress and the SEC must simply refuse to harmonize.

FAILURE OF THE SECURITIES AND EXCHANGE COMMISSION

Two decades ago, Pulitzer Prize winner Thomas McCraw wrote: "the rigor of SEC accounting regulation has tended to vary with the identity of the Chief Accountant and of the commissioners. But it is equally clear that . . . the SEC's strategy of using accountants to serve its own end has been successful."[16]

While McCraw seems mostly correct over the history of the SEC, recent events have challenged his two assertions. Consider the contrast between Harvey Pitt and his predecessor Arthur Levitt.

Failure by Pitt

Certified public accountants (CPAs) in recent years attempted to use the SEC to serve their professional interests, and if it were not for Enron and WorldCom, they might have succeeded. They contributed heavily to the campaigns of mostly incumbents, especially Republicans. After most of their candidates won reelection, the CPAs convinced Washington politicians to install Harvey Pitt as the SEC chairman, and he was more than willing to serve them in a kinder and gentler fashion. However, Enron and WorldCom and the other recent financial catastrophes forced Pitt to turn on his supporters, albeit grudgingly.[17]

Many commentators have pointed out that Pitt has served as legal counsel for each of the five largest accounting firms, including Arthur Andersen. While I think that fact is damaging, worse is his response to the accounting scandals. I urge readers to download Pitt's speech, "How to Prevent Future Enrons," from the SEC's website; the speech initially appeared in the *Wall Street Journal* on December 11, 2001.[18] Pitt's two major points are that the system needs "improvement and modernization" and that financial statements might be "impenetrable." The difficulty with this position is that Pitt said precious little about the lies and the thievery that took place, demonstrating to me that he does not get it—or he wants to protect his former clients. Instead of exhorting managers, directors, and auditors to tell the truth, he wants them to update their technology and provide greater efficiency in data processing. He kept on this theme of modernization until the collapse of WorldCom; then Harvey Pitt started saying and doing the right things. His slowness or unwillingness to grasp the situation proved his unfitness as an SEC commissioner.

Worst of all is Harvey Pitt's role in writing *Serving the Public Interest: A New Conceptual Framework for Auditor Independence*.[19] As discussed in Chapter 8, the accounting profession hired Pitt to write this polemic that went to the Independence Standards Board as an attempt to greatly reduce the independence rules facing CPAs. This text serves as evidence that Pitt works at the CPAs' beck and call.[20] In this book, Pitt supports loosening rules about auditor independence, and he is willing for external accountants to engage in various conflicts of interest as long as it helps the client. He even proposes that firms design their own independence rules.

Pitt avers that there is no evidence that nonaudit services impair independence in performing an audit. While evidence does exist and has been ignored, I shall simply reply that Enron serves as the classic case where Arthur Andersen employees were scared to death of enforcing the accounting rules because of the amount of money Enron brought them. As described in Chapter 8 and contained in the appendix, Michael Sutton wrote a critique so scathing that the AICPA backed down from its ludicrous position.

Pitt tried to avoid any real reforms or real enforcements when he instituted the CEO certifications,[21] according to which CEOs and CFOs had to certify "to the best of their knowledge" that the financial statements of the entity were accurate by August 14, 2002. Not only were these certifications ad hoc and possibly with no legal substance, but also they were unnecessary. We already have securities laws that prohibit fraud. Besides, if managers are willing to lie in their financial statements, I think they would have no problem lying in these certifications. While SEC officials possibly were trying to build investor morale with these symbolic actions, it is more likely that Pitt was trying to do something to deflect the criticism against him.

What we have, then, is a chairman of the organization created to protect the rights of investors working hard to minimize those rights wherever he could. Ironically, after WorldCom's disgrace, Pitt started acting like the investors' protector. I interpret these actions as merely face saving and as an attempt to retain his job. Fortunately, the media and the Democrats did not relent, and Pitt resigned on election day because of the massive criticism.

Pitt continued as a lame duck chair until the Senate confirmed President Bush's appointment of William Donaldson as the new SEC chairman on February 14, 2003. This status muddied the regulatory process because Harvey Pitt was writing and diluting rules changes for lawyers and accountants.[22] The Senate should have been quicker in its confirmation process, thereby removing Pitt from office sooner.

Levitt: Theoretical Success, Practical Failure

President Clinton appointed Arthur Levitt as chairman of the SEC as a result of Levitt's successful fund raising for the president. Once on the job, Levitt had a clear idea of what the investor needed. He chided the accountants for skirting their professional duties. He censured financial analysts for acting as selling agents for Wall Street instead of independent and objective analyzers of financial data. His speeches also called on managers to change the corporate culture and to make the changes needed. Levitt himself recalls many of these events in his book *Take on the Street*.[23]

Jim Cramer, one of the hosts on CNBC's Kudlow & Cramer, claims that Levitt's direction was more theoretical than practical.[24] Levitt did not speak up when he perceived the bubble in the market, though Alan Greenspan did complain about the stock market's "irrational exuberance." Levitt dealt with most managers and auditors by jawboning. While Levitt and his commission did enforce the laws, the staff usually pursued the medium fish—those big enough to make headlines but not big enough to possess a stable of lawyers who could make any investigation very expensive. Chapter 1 discussed the frauds at Cendant, Waste Management, and Sunbeam; Cramer reminds us that no one went to prison for these frauds. Pointing out their misdeeds in speeches or fining them insignificant amounts is not going to punish these criminals and will not prevent future Cendants, Waste Managements, or Sunbeams. Cramer wonders whether the SEC's feeble enforcements "emboldened the Ebbers and Fastows to take the awful liberties that led to such financial tragedy."

David Hilzenrath augments this analysis by pointing out that the SEC moves slowly against the Big Four accounting firms.[25] The agency has a much higher probability of going after the medium-size or small accounting firms. In addition, the penalties against medium-size or small firms exceed, sometimes greatly, those assessed against the larger firms. This fact holds under both Levitt's and Pitt's terms in office.

Cramer overstates his case a bit. After all, the accounting profession felt enough pressure from Levitt that it spent a fortune trying to buy a Congress that would be willing to appoint a more accounting-friendly SEC chairman. Additionally, Levitt did not have the resources to go after the perpetrators of fraud at Cendant, Waste Management, and

Sunbeam. Nonetheless, Cramer's major point resonates with a major thesis of this book: If you want to stop accounting fraud, enforce the laws, including the laws against those with an expensive cadre of attorneys. Sending criminals to prison for several years will do more to decrease white-collar crimes than a thousand speeches.

"Systemic Failure"

The staff to the Senate Committee on Governmental Affairs issued its report on October 8, 2002. In this report, the staff evaluates the performance of the SEC and declares systemic failure at that organization.[26] Unfortunately, the staff's review is flawed and self-serving.

The staff begins by noting that the SEC did not review any of Enron's filings in 1998, 1999, and 2000. Even today the SEC thoroughly reviews only about 10 percent of the filings received from corporations. Interestingly, however, the staff never comments on the congressional budget cuts over the previous decade that contributed to this problem since the agency did not have the funds to examine more of the filings.

Next the staff states that "better screening should have led SEC staff to select Enron's later Forms 10-K for further review." This claim remains unsubstantiated since the congressional staff never informs us what makes up this "better screening." It remains only a dream. The staff further maintains that several items by Enron were questionable and required further investigation. While true, it is hard to see the point when the SEC was not reviewing the forms in the first place.

The staff criticizes the SEC for okaying Enron's use of mark-to-market accounting. I disagree with this claim, for mark-to-market accounting is the correct and the most informative method for valuing the contracts with which Enron was engaged—as long as the managers are truthful. The problem at Enron centered on managers' lying about the values of these contracts and Arthur Andersen's not catching them in the lies. Managerial deceptions do not invalidate mark-to-market accounting. Did Andersen investigate the valuation of these contracts?; if so, did Andersen discover any discrepancies; and if so, what did Andersen do about them? These are audit failures, not SEC failures.

The staff then criticizes the SEC for granting Enron exemptions from the Public Utility Holding Company Act and from the Investment Company Act of 1940. While the staff may be correct in these assessments, it is unclear what impact these exemptions have on the accounting frauds or on the SEC's oversight responsibility with respect to reporting issues.

Overall, this staff report is disappointing. It lays out charges that we already know, charges that should be laid at the feet of managers, directors, and accountants, or charges irrelevant to the investigation. Not only that, the staff remains silent about the responsibilities of Congress.

Whither the Securities and Exchange Commission?

For the SEC to do its job, it needs great leadership, a good and dedicated staff, and resources. The president needs to appoint worthwhile people to this post, the Senate needs to be more careful in granting consent to these appointments, and the executive and legislative branches need to give the SEC the resources to carry out its responsibilities. President Bush has promised the resources, but Congress has not yet legislated a budget. Until Congress provides the SEC with an increased budget, the SEC will not have the funds necessary to enforce the securities laws as vigorously as it should.[27]

Ironically, the SEC is playing a similar power game with the FASB. The SEC needs to recognize the FASB as the accounting standards setting body so that it can collect funds from public companies, as mandated by the Sarbanes-Oxley bill. Strangely, the SEC has not yet recognized the FASB, so the FASB must continue to rely on internally generated funds. It is unclear why the SEC is dragging its feet.[28]

At times the SEC moves as slowly as the FASB. For example, it has taken years for the agency to do anything about pro forma earnings, those disclosures that Wall Street cynically calls "everything but the bad stuff." While individual investors should understand that these pro forma earnings numbers do not follow GAAP, that they come from managers who have a vested interest in what these numbers reveal, that the numbers are unaudited, and that they reduce comparability with other companies, some investors clearly do not. The SEC should have pointed out a long time ago that some managers are trying to deceive investors with their highly inflated pro forma earnings numbers. Recently the SEC initiated action on this front, but it took a very long time.[29]

In a similar vein, the SEC should have challenged those companies that itemize "nonrecurring expenses"—especially when they persist quarter after quarter.[30] Clearly, corporations display these items as nonrecurring because they do not want investors to factor them into any notion of core earnings. Some companies, such as Cisco, Procter and Gamble, and Amazon reported nonrecurring charges virtually every quarter in the past several years. If these charges are indeed nonrecurring, why are they recurring so often? This, too, is a deceptive practice, and the SEC ought to dispute its application.

At this time it is clear that many investors still feel burned and lack confidence to reenter the stock market. To the extent that investors feel better, this mood results from enforcement actions. Watching Mr. Rigas do the "perp" walk, for example, adds some credibility to the system. Convicting John Rigas and the other CEOs who had their hands in the cookie jar will add a lot of credibility. In short, the SEC has a straightforward task in restoring confidence to the economic system: Enforce the existing laws and send the criminals to prison.

FAILURE OF CONGRESS

The U.S. Constitution creates the different branches of government and lays out the basic rules by which the country operates. The Preamble says that the people of this country establish this constitution because we yearn for justice and the promotion of our general welfare, among other things. Further, Article I of the U.S. Constitution invests legislative powers in the House of Representatives and in the Senate to accomplish these goals. When I examine what Congress has done for us in promoting the general welfare of investors and creditors and justice against business frauds, I become saddened at their lack of either morality or courage in fighting corporate managers. In recent years policy matters have not driven Congress nearly as much as campaign contributions. Congress is more determined to provide a strong public crusade to give the appearance of reform rather than do anything that might actually lead to reform.

Influence of Campaign Dollars

The accounting profession has contributed about $57 million to those running for Congress over the last 12 years.[31] Despite the accounting scandals and despite the bad publicity, the Big Four provided a lot of money to politicians during the last election. Ken Rankin reports that the Big Four raised the following amounts of money for the 2002 elections[32]:

- Deloitte & Touche $2.1 million
- Ernst & Young $1.2 million
- KPMG $1.6 million
- PricewaterhouseCoopers $0.9 million

Together they raised $5.8 million to contribute to members of Congress for the 2002 elections. I doubt that it was to support further legislation such as Sarbanes-Oxley.

Of course, the accountants are not alone. Many corporations have supported and continue to support those in the House and the Senate who hold positions favorable to their cause. Consortiums such as the Business Roundtable also do this. Another good example is TechNet, a group of high-tech companies that want to use the pooling-of-interest method and do not want to expense any stock options. What have the American people received as a result of corporate campaign contributions? Have these items improved our justice or our general welfare?[33]

After receiving a ton of money from enthusiastic supporters, Congress in 1995 passed the Private Securities Litigation Reform Act, which made it more difficult for plaintiffs to file a class action suit against business enterprises, corporate managers, and public auditors and curbed the awards when plaintiffs won. Litigation attorneys naturally turned to the state courts, but this strategy was thwarted in 1998 when Congress passed the Securities Litigation Uniform Standards Act, which requires class action lawsuits brought because of accounting issues to be filed in federal court. Because it made it much harder for plaintiffs to sue and because it capped the awards, Congress encouraged managers, directors, and auditors to rape and pillage the rest of us, which in fact they proceeded to do.[34] No wonder Charles Dickens declared, "The law is an ass."

Emily Thornton, Peter Coy, and Heather Timmons analyzed the 1999 repeal of the 1933 Glass-Steagall Act, which separated commercial banking from investment banking.[35] Once the repeal took effect, conflicts of interests and illegal activities within this sector have mushroomed. Eliot Spitzer's investigation of Wall Street has pointed out repeatedly the ill effects of combining these two sets of operations. Banks lobbied Congress for a change, they got the change, and we the people got shafted.

While it did not pass, the Financial Accounting Fairness Act of 1998 provides another example of the corrupting influence of money.[36] In 1997, Representative Richard Baker (R-LA) received money from 18 different banking political action committees. Baker provided a quid pro quo when he introduced this piece of legislation in the House. The bill would have required the SEC to approve any new accounting standards issued by the FASB, a step that would take the FASB's slow process and make it much longer. The bill also would have given "aggrieved companies" the right to sue for the overthrow of any "arbitrary and capricious" standard that FASB would issue. If passed, this right would further enervate the FASB, further reduce its speed to do anything, and drain it of resources as the FASB would spend a lot of time in court. Finally, the bill would force the SEC and the FASB to consult with federal banking agencies before issuing new rules. Apparently, if the bank managers could not influence the SEC or the FASB, they hoped to influence those who regulate the banking industry.

Another great example occurred in the mid-1990s and focuses on accounting for stock options as compensation.[37] Several congressional committees held hearings. After receiving hefty campaign contributions from the proposed rule's opponents, Senator Joe Lieberman (D-CT) introduced a bill that not only would keep the SEC from enforcing the FASB rule to expense stock options, but also would require the SEC to approve every new standard issued by the FASB. Similar to Baker's strategy, the idea was to slow down, if not eviscerate, the FASB. While the bill did not pass, the FASB backed down from its expense requirement and Statement No. 123 merely required the disclosure of the stock option effects. Lieberman, TechNet, the high-tech industry, and the investment banking industry celebrated. Meanwhile, a decade later, Enron and WorldCom proved that when Congress tramples on proper accounting, we all pay the consequences.

The worst offender, because he is the most hypocritical, is Representative Mike Oxley (R-OH). After accepting a lot of money from the accounting firms, Wall Street, bankers, and others interested in unfair accounting, Oxley opposed reform wherever he turned.[38] He has opposed legislation designed to improve disclosures to investors or any measures created for their protection. He contested the appointment of John Biggs and William Webster to the new accounting oversight board, though both are highly qualified. Only when WorldCom exploded did Oxley see the writing on the wall and put his name on some legislation that allegedly would lead to reforms. While on the committees to write the Sarbanes-Oxley bill, he did his best behind the scenes to quash any real reforms, at least to the extent he could. What Gordon Gecko stands for in business, Michael Oxley represents in terms of realpolitik.

Rush to Legislate

The Enron debacle aroused the public to condemn the business world, but most politicians were loath to follow suit, thinking that perhaps Enron was merely an isolated event. WorldCom changed the minds of politicians. Clearly, the people were enraged, and Congress had to show its leadership. Unfortunately, Congress seemed more intent on presenting an appearance of reform rather than really trying to fix the system.

The Enron hearings, for example, proved a waste of time. The witnesses had little to say, for the members of Congress busily gave long-winded speeches about the rights of investors and creditors. While most witnesses cowardly but wisely invoked their Fifth Amendment right not to incriminate themselves of accounting frauds, Jeff Skilling interestingly and cleverly took the chance to speak to the committee members. The committee members never asked Skilling a single hard question, such as how anyone in his position could think that LJM2 served as a hedge for the Rhythms NetConnections $300 million gain when a low correlation existed between the Rhythms NetConnections investment and the stock of Enron. Instead of probing for answers to tough questions, members of Congress purred instead with rhetorical wizardry.

Congress passed the Sarbanes-Oxley bill in 2002, but whether it really accomplishes anything remains to be seen. It codified a number of rules and proposals already in the works by the exchanges and by various other organizations, such as requiring independent members of audit committees. It increases fines and imposes longer prison sentences, but this does nothing if the SEC or others do not or cannot enforce the laws. Having the CEO and the CFO certify to the accuracy of the financial statements is a yawner. As stated before, any CEO or CFO who is willing to lie in financial reports should have no difficulty in certifying to the accuracy of these reports, and in relying on the fragility of accounting, the underauditing by the Big Four, and lack of real enforcement by the SEC.

The bill does create the Public Company Accounting Oversight Board (PCAOB). What it will do and what it will accomplish is up in the air.[39] As the GAO analyzes it, the PCAOB "will have sweeping powers to inspect accounting firms, set rules and standards for auditing, . . . prohibit[s] auditors from providing certain nonaudit services to their audit clients and strengthening the oversight role of the board of directors."[40]

As stated, the problem with this is that we do not have a clue about what the board will actually do. We do know that the selection process of board members has been mired in ugly politics and that the accounting firms are desperately trying to restrict board activities to peer reviews just as bland and impotent as they always were.

Finally, the Sarbanes-Oxley bill purports to increase the SEC's budget so that it can better enforce the laws. Unfortunately, as this is not an appropriations bill, this section of the bill is merely symbolic. Another bill must be passed by Congress and signed by the President (or any veto overturned) before funds are disbursed to the agency. Until then, the SEC tries to perform a yeoman's task on a boy scout's budget.

No Enforcement Help

Besides errors of commission, Congress is guilty of errors of omission. It has oversight responsibility for the operations of this country, including oversight responsibility for the SEC. I do not blame the President for appointing Harvey Pitt to head the SEC, nor do I censure Congress for its confirmation; neither may have known about his support of the accounting industry. Of course, they should have been suspicious, given the monies entering their coffers. Once Enron folded, however, and Pitt began traveling around the country arguing for the modernization of accounting, both the President and Congress learned his true colors. There was no excuse for not removing him from office in late 2001.

As stated earlier, in the Sarbanes-Oxley bill Congress claimed that it would increase funds to the SEC so the agency could fight accounting frauds. While it included that paragraph in the legislation, the bill in fact gave no money to the SEC. We are still waiting for Congress to provide funds to the bureau so that it can do its job. Enforcement is key to real reform, not extending the length of prison sentences, as written in the Sarbanes-Oxley bill.

Think of it this way. Suppose one really wanted to reduce speeds on (say) the New Jersey turnpike and had two ways of doing so. One way would be to increase the number of cops on the highway and hold them responsible for enforcing the speed limit. The other way would be to increase the speeding fines to $100,000 per violation but make sure there were no funds to have police patrol the thoroughfare. Which method is more likely to reduce speeds?

Given the influence of campaign dollars and the penchant to legislate new rules instead of enforce the old rules, we have to presume that Congress prefers the perception of reform rather than the institution of real reform. Shame on Congress. As Mark Twain said, "There is no distinctively native American criminal class except Congress."

FAILURE OF THE COURTS

With respect to accounting, the judicial branch of government has served as a bulwark for finding justice and for meting out fines and sentences and judgments that acted as deterrents. As with most human institutions, the courts have not reached perfection.

Judge Barbour, for example, was hearing a complaint against WorldCom in early 2002.[41] He dismissed the lawsuit against WorldCom as one with "prejudice." A few months later, when WorldCom vomited on the financial world, Judge Barbour had detritus splattered all over his face. Judges must give credence to investor complaints, because the shortcomings of financial reports have become titanic.

Worse is the decision in *Central Bank of Denver v. First Interstate Bank of Denver.* In this 1994 case the Supreme Court ruled that professional advisers who knowingly aid and abet securities fraud are not liable to victims.[42] The Court ruled that the securities laws do not extend that far, though it invited Congress to rewrite the laws if it members saw fit. Congress did not see fit, which comes as no surprise, given the importance of campaign contributions in recent years. The consequence of this ruling is straightforward: Law firms like Vinson and Elkins and auditing firms such as Arthur Andersen can knowingly aid and abet securities fraud, but victims might not collect from the law firms or the audit firms if the courts rely on the decision in this case. What injustice! What an invitation to commit fraud!

SUMMARY AND CONCLUSION

As Cassell Bryan-Low and Ken Brown have pointed out, accounting reform is slow.[43] In reality, they overstate the case. Little has changed with respect to the FASB and the SEC and even less has changed with respect to Congress. Without improvement in these quarters, how can the public ever witness real and lasting reform?

The FASB must become responsive and increase in power so that it can withstand the onslaughts and slanders of the corporate community. Principles-based accounting has a certain appeal, but should be pursued only if an accounting court is created to deal with the nuances of practice, as described further in Chapter 11.

The SEC needs leadership, a great staff, and funds to pursue enforcement vigorously. Congress needs to discharge its oversight responsibilities, and it should open the purse strings to permit the SEC to discharge its enforcement responsibilities.

Congress should investigate further some clamps on campaign contributions, because such funds create myriad conflicts of interests to which many members succumb. Congress should also recognize that investors and creditors are members of the business world and quit biasing laws toward managers. Too many laws encourage managers to deceive the investment community. If the House and the Senate members really want reform, they should repeal the 1995 Private Securities Litigation Reform Act and the 1998 Securities Litigation Uniform Standards Act. Congress must also greatly expand the SEC's budget to allow the staff to pursue criminal investigations against the perpetrators of accounting fraud.

Finally, the courts must maintain vigilance against the evildoers in the business world. Often the courts become the institutions of last resort to provide justice to those investors and creditors cheated by corporate executives. The courts should also revisit the Continental Vending case, more fully described in Chapter 11, and require managers and auditors to deliver financial reports that fairly present the results of the entity's operations.

NOTES

1. "Loss of Trust White-Collar Damage," Editorial, *Charleston Gazette,* June 21, 2002; and J. Nocera et al., "System Failure: Corporate America Has Lost Its Way, Here's a Road Map for Restoring Confidence," *Fortune,* June 24, 2002.

2. General Accounting Office, *The Accounting Profession: Major Issues: Progress and Concerns.* Report to the Chairman, Committee on Commerce, U.S. House of Representatives (Washington, DC: GAO, September 1996).

3. J. D. Dingell, unpublished letter to David Walker, General Accounting Office, January 17, 2001.

4. For more details about this history, see: E. S. Hendriksen, *Accounting Theory,* 2nd ed. (Homewood, IL: Irwin, 1970); G. J. Previtts and B. D. Merino, *A History of Accountancy in the United States: The Cultural Significance of Accounting* (Columbus: Ohio State University Press, 1998); H. I. Wolk, M. G. Tearney, and J. L. Dodd, *Accounting Theory: A Conceptual and Institutional Approach,* 5th ed. (Cincinnati: South-Western Publishing, 2001); and S. A. Zeff, *Forging Accounting Principles in Five Countries* (Champaign, IL: Stipes Publishing Co., 1971), pp.110–268. Moonitz discusses how the Committee on Accounting Procedures and the Accounting Principles Board developed accounting standards; see: M. Moonitz, *Obtaining Agreement on Standards in the Accounting Profession,* Studies in Accounting Research No. 8 (Sarasota, FL: American Accounting Association, 1974).

5. The pooling-of-interests method to account for business combinations allowed managers to manipulate earnings and fraudulently misstate the results of operations. See J. E. Ketz and P. B. W. Miller, "Some Ethical Issues About Financial Reporting and Public Accounting and Some Proposals," *Research on Accounting Ethics* (1997), pp. 49–77 and our two 1997 essays in *Accounting Today* on "pfooling" (which is shorthand for "pooling is fooling"): "Time to

Stop Pfooling Around," September 22–October 5, and "Pfooling Around: The Psequel," November 10–23.

6. Financial Accounting Standards Board, *Consolidation of Variable Interest Entities*, Interpretation No. 46 (Norwalk CT: FASB, 2003).

7. Compare "Badly in Need of Repair—Company Reports—Companies' Accounts Are Badly in Need of Repair," *The Economist,* May 4, 2002.

8. Financial Accounting Standards Board, *Accounting for Stock-Based Compensation—Transition and Disclosure*, Statement No. 148 (Norwalk CT: FASB, 2003).

9. F. Norris, "Accounting Reform Takes Step Backward," *New York Times,* June 9, 2002; and C. S. Remond, "FASB Mulls Excluding Some SPEs from Consolidation Rules," *Dow Jones News Service,* May 8, 2002.

10. This section comes from my essay "Why Simpler Isn't Necessarily Better," September 9, 2002; see: *www.SmartPros.com.*

11. W. Wriston, "The Solution to Scandals? Simpler Rules," *Wall Street Journal,* August 5, 2002.

12. Compare B. McNamee and K. Capell, "FASB: Rewriting the Book on Bookkeeping: Will Broader, Simpler Rules Prevent Future Enrons?" *Business Week,* May 20, 2002.

13. I first wrote about this topic in "Principles-Based Standards," December 16, 2002; see *www.SmartPros.com.*

14. FASB (2002), *Proposal for a Principles-Based Approach to U.S. Standard Setting* (Norwalk CT: FASB, 2002).

15. A. Shleifer and R. Vishny, "A Survey of Corporate Governance," *Journal of Finance* (June 1997).

16. T. K. McCraw, *Prophets of Regulation* (Cambridge, MA: Harvard University Press, 1984), p. 191.

17. Many articles have described Pitt and the recent activities of the SEC. See, for example: J. H. Birnbaum, "It's Time for Him to Go," *Fortune,* October 28, 2002; K. Day, "SEC Borrows Executives as Advisers: Some Question Use of Accountants from Major Auditing Firms," *Washington Post,* January 22, 2002, p. E01; D. B. Henriques, "Chairman of S.E.C. Faces Time of Testing," *New York Times,* November 3, 2002; S. Labaton, "Audit Overseer Cited Problems in Previous Post," *New York Times,* October 31, 2002, and "Government Report Details a Chaotic S.E.C. Under Pitt," *New York Times,* December 20, 2002; M. Schroeder, "Webster's Appointment Signals Serious Partisan Divide at SEC," *Wall Street Journal,* October 28, 2002; M. Schroeder and C. Bryan-Low, "SEC's Pitt Now Faces Dissent from Within the Commission," *Wall Street Journal,* October 7, 2002. I have called for his resignation in several essays ("Harvey Pitt Has to Go," May 22, 2002, and "Harvey Pitt Has to Go: Part Deux," August 5, 2002; both at *www.SmartPros.com*) and have discussed how he undermined John Biggs as the first appointee to head the new accounting oversight board ("Big Bad John Biggs," October 31, 2002; *www.SmartPros.com*).

18. Harvey L. Pitt, "How to Prevent Future Enrons," from the SEC's website, which appeared in the *Wall Street Journal,* December 11, 2001.

19. American Institute of Certified Public Accountants, *Serving the Public Interest: A New Conceptual Framework for Auditor Independence.* Submitted to the Independence Standards Board on October 20, 1997. Written by H. L. Pitt and D. E. Birenbaum.

20. Some might argue that since the AICPA hired Harvey Pitt to write *Serving the Public Interest*, the words act as evidence against the AICPA but not Pitt. I disagree. If Pitt opposed the AICPA position but performed the work anyway, he should have served as a ghostwriter. Once he affixed his name to the document, he assumed responsibility for its content.

21. J. E. Ketz, "CEO Certifications: "D" is for Drivel" September 16, 2002; see: *www.SmartPros.com.*

22. K. Day, "SEC Staff Urges Limit to Reforms," *Washington Post,* January 22, and "SEC Allows Auditors as Tax Consultants," January 23, 2003; K. Drawbaugh, "SEC Wavers on Post-Enron Auditor, Lawyer," *Forbes,* January 21, 2003; S. Labaton and J. D. Glater, "Staff of S.E.C. Is Said to Dilute Rule Changes," *New York Times,* January 23, 2003.

23. Levitt himself recalls many of these events in his book *Take on the Street: What Wall Street and Corporate America Don't Want You to Know: What You Can Do to Fight Back* (New York: Pantheon Books, 2002).

24. J. J. Cramer, "Mr. Levitt's Legacy," *Wall Street Journal,* December 5, 2002.

25. D. S. Hilzenrath, "Big Firms Avoiding SEC Ire," *Washington Post,* January 17, 2003.

26. U.S. Senate, *Financial Oversight of Enron: The SEC and Private-Sector Watchdogs.* Report of the Staff to the Senate Committee on Governmental Affairs (Washington, DC: U.S. Senate, October 8, 2002), pp. 29–68; M. Schroeder and G. Ip, "SEC Faces Hurdles Beyond Budget in Quest to Crack Down on Fraud," *Wall Street Journal,* July 19, 2002; and J. Weil and J. Wilke, "Systemic Failure by SEC Is Seen in Enron Debacle," *Wall Street Journal,* October 7, 2002.

27. D. S. Broder, "A Budget of Dire Consequences," *Washington Post*, March 30, 2003; M. Gordon, "Bush Asks Congress to Approve Larger Budget for SEC," *Philadelphia Inquirer*, February 4, 2003; R. W. Stevenson, "Bush Proposes Big Increase in S.E.C. Budget," *New York Times,* January 12, 2003; W. M. Welch, "Congress Wary of Bush Budget," *USA Today*, February 4, 2003.

28. G. Cheney, "FASB Scrambles for Funds in Power Struggle with SEC," *Accounting Today*, March 17–April 6, 2003, p.14.

29. M. Schroeder, "SEC Orders New Disclosures in Companies' Profit Reports," *Wall Street Journal,* January 16, 2003.

30. M. Krantz, "One-Time Charges? Not Always," *USA Today,* November 21, 2001.

31. J. Toedtman, "Accounting Reform Slows to a Crawl," *Newsday,* June 6, 2002; "Push Is On for Audit Reform, Before Sting of Andersen Verdict Fades," *Financial Managers Society,* June 24, 2002; see: *www.fmsinc.org.*

32. K. Rankin, "Big 4 Poised to Wield Influence at the Ballot Box," The Electronic Accountant, September 2002; see: *www.electronicaccountant.com*; and "Despite Scandals, Profession Poised to Wield Influence in November Elections," The Electronic Accountant, October 2002; see: *www.electronicaccountant.com.*

33. In addition to the examples I present, Levitt includes an appendix that contains letters from members of Congress who tried to influence SEC rule making; see *Take on the Street,* pp. 285–307. When we connect the dots back to the donors, it is easy to see how corporate America has been attempting indirectly to influence accounting regulations.

34. L. Calabro, "I Told You So," *CFO Magazine,* September 10, 2002; W. S. Lerach, "The Chickens Have Come Home to Roost: How Wall Street, the Big Accounting Firms and Corporate Interests Chloroformed Congress and Cost America's Investors Trillions," 2002; see: *www.milberg.com/pdf/news/chickens.pdf,* p. 4; and R. B. Schmitt, M. Schroeder, and S. Murray, "Corporate-Oversight Bill Passes, Smoothing Way for New Lawsuits," *Wall Street Journal,* July 26, 2002.

35. E. Thornton, P. Coy, and H. Timmons, "The Breakdown in Banking," *Business Week,* October 7, 2002.

36. J. E. Ketz and P. B. W. Miller, "Financial Accounting Fairness Act: Fairness to Whom?" *Accounting Today*, May 25-June 7, 1998, pp. 14, 17.

37. S. Burkholder, "Former SEC Accountants, Ex-FASB Chairman Offer Advice, Caution on Post-Enron Reforms," *Pension & Benefits Reporter*, March 5, 2002; Levitt, *Take on the Street*; and J. J. Young, "Accounting as It Intertwines with the Political: The Case of Accounting for Stock Compensation," Working Paper, University of New Mexico, Presented at the Conference on Interdisciplinary Perspectives on Accounting, July 7–9, 1997.

38. G. Morgenson, "It Still Pays to See Who Did the Research," *New York Times,* December 22, 2002; Levitt, *Take on the Street.*

39. J. Freeman, "Who Will Audit the Regulators?" *Wall Street Journal,* July 8, 2002; D. L. Glass, "Can Fed Strike a Post-Enron Regulatory Balance?" *American Banker,* June 20, 2002; and S. Labaton, "New Rules on Accountants, But Also Questions," *New York Times,* July 26, 2002.

40. General Accounting Office, *Financial Statement Restatements: Trends, Market Impacts, Regulatory Responses, and Remaining Challenges.* Report to the Chairman, Committee on Banking, Housing, and Urban Affairs. U.S. Senate (Washington, DC: GAO, October 2002), appendix 23.

41. A. Weinberg, "Asleep at the Switch," *Forbes,* July 22, 2002.

42. Lerach, "The Chickens Have Come Home to Roost"; K. Eichenwald, "Enron Ruling Leaves Corporate Advisers Open to Lawsuits," *New York Times,* December 23, 2002.

43. C. Bryan-Low and K. Brown, "And Now, the Question Is: Where's the Next Enron? Accounting Textbooks Will Get Rewritten, But Few Practices in the Industry Might Change," *Wall Street Journal,* June 18, 2002.

CHAPTER TEN

Failure of Investors

Chapters 7 to 9 have spotlighted institutional failures that led to the accounting scandals of the early 21st century. While these breakdowns by managers, directors, lawyers, auditors, investment bankers, the Financial Accounting Standards Board (FASB), the Securities and Exchange Commission (SEC), and Congress have been severe, they do not absolve investors from bad decisions they made. Except for those employees in Enron and others like them who had restricted stock and could not easily sell their shares, the rest of us must recognize that we are responsible for our choices. Enron, for example, left a few clues that we could have read in its financial reports. That we chose not to heed these signals was our undoing. In addition, we accepted much higher financial risks than we thought, but that is because we did not understand how business enterprises hid these liabilities. We should remember the adage, "Buyer beware."[1]

Perhaps we noticed the young entrepreneurs who created the so-called dot-coms, and we became jealous. Our greed got the better of us, and we wanted our fair share. We saw the increases in the stock market and thought that we too could become rich quick with little effort and little risk. Charles Kindleberger reminds us that such a community mind-set puts manias into motion that later become crashes.[2] Instead of doing our homework, we got caught up in the fervor of the marketplace. We decided what to buy and what to sell with our emotions instead of our brains.

We might have thought managers were considering our needs and providing accounts and disclosures that investors and creditors wanted. Instead of acting like good stewards, managers employed the modern golden rule: The one who has the gold rules. Clearly a number of executives thought they owned the business enterprise instead of the shareholders. In the future we have to remember managers' mind-set.

Much of what I wrote in Chapters 2 to 6 was known at least a decade ago. Anyone who wanted to study financial markets could have learned this accounting lore and become knowledgeable of the tricks played by managers and approved by directors, lawyers, accountants, and investment bankers. Burned investors now have three choices:

1. They can remove themselves from Wall Street and never invest another penny. If there is no real reform in financial reporting and in how Wall Street works, this may become a rational option.

2. They can lick their wounds and complain but, next time there is an economic boom, toss their money into the hot picks without much study or care. They will be just as disappointed when the market crashes next time.

3. They can learn some finance and accounting and make better investment decisions in the future. While the major purpose of this book has been a call for real reform of corporate governance, auditing, and the legal environment in which business enterprises operate, a secondary purpose has been to instruct investors so that next time they can invest with a full knowledge of the tricks played by managers, directors, and auditors, at least with respect to off–balance sheet accounting.[3]

The first section of this chapter discusses the failure of private sector financial governance. The next section considers several aspects of accounting that were critical to making investment decisions in the late 1990s. The third section uses these accounting topics to take another look at Enron and see how the company's financial report showed that it was a mediocre investment at best. The final section provides some guidance into learning more about finance and accounting for investment purposes, including a look at the current posturing by corporations and an explanation of why investors should not be fooled into believing that substantive changes are being made.

FAILURE OF FINANCIAL GOVERNANCE

The 2002 report by the staff to the Senate Committee on Governmental Affairs criticized the labors of what they called the "private-sector watchdogs."[4] For example, the staff points out that the credit ratings agencies did not sound an alarm that Enron had problems. In part, this lack of concern resulted because the credit ratings agencies had not examined recent financial reports by Enron. Slowness to update credit ratings is typical for these agencies.[5] Investors and creditors must understand the slowness of these agencies to update the ratings and realize that ratings typically reflect old data. If investors really want updated ratings, they can fabricate their own ratings by employing models such as the Horrigan model described in Chapter 2.

The conflicts of interest caused by rewarding financial analysts on the basis of sales have been much in the news lately.[6] The job of analysts supposedly is to gather data about a particular company and provide an objective analysis of the facts, with the end result of a recommendation to buy, hold, or sell the stock. Clearly some Wall Street analysts have not been doing their job. Others who have been are conflicted by the pressure to generate revenues. Investors will either have to drop out of the market altogether, quit trusting the financial analysts and do their own analysis, or read analysts' reports but maintain a jaundiced eye about the recommendations.

Ken Brown reminds us that financial analysts brim with optimism on virtually every deal.[7] They either are psychologically bent to think like Pollyanna, or they have become the epitome of used-car salesmen. Brown reports that analysts predict that 345 firms in the Standard & Poor's 500 will have earnings growth of at least 10 percent. When economists forecast that the overall economy will grow around 3 percent, however, obviously there is an inconsistency between the two projections. I believe the latter number is the more accurate of the two. The key point is that investors cannot blindly trust financial analysts. At the least, investors need to understand what makes analysts tick, and that includes knowing their incentives. After all, if the investment is really, really hot, why do analysts bother to tell us? I would expect analysts to invest in anything that good and not share the wealth.

As Matthew Goldstein comments, perhaps the major lesson from all of these accounting scandals is that investors cannot depend on any of the other players[8]: not the managers who lied to them, the directors who did not rein in the managers, the auditors who allowed the managers to lie, the Financial Accounting Standards Board (FASB) and the Securities and Exchange Commission (SEC) that permitted shoddy accounting practices, members of Congress who nodded and winked, and not the bond rating agencies and the financial analysts. To date, little of substance has changed, so investors might anticipate more of the same from these folks. Buyer beware!

MORE ACCOUNTING

This section of the chapter touches briefly on pro forma earnings, cash flows, off-balance sheet disclosures, and the impact of the business cycle on accounting earnings. The last three of these items are important in the next section when we revisit Enron.

Pro Forma Earnings

Pro forma means "as if," so *pro forma earnings* means the earnings that would have been reported had the corporation been using some alternative method. Pro forma numbers first gained significance when the Accounting Principles Board issued Opinion No. 20 in 1971. The idea was simple but powerful: When an organization changed from one acceptable accounting method to another, it would have to recast the statements from the past couple of years into numbers applying the new method. Doing this would allow investors a contrast between the two methods, and it would give investors some data on which to build up a time series picture of the firm under the new technique. The idea was to assist the investment community in its collective evaluation of the entity's economic achievements.

I have encouraged companies to issue pro forma numbers whenever there are better and more accurate methods to report the results to the investors and creditors than those currently in generally accepted accounting principles (GAAP). Using pro forma numbers allows firms to experiment with new accounting methods so that they can assess whether the investment community likes the numbers. It also takes a positive, proactive stance to adopt with respect to capital customers.

Today, however, pro forma numbers are seldom published for the purpose of informing investors and creditors in a better manner.[9] Instead, these disclosures have become a way of undermining orthodox accounting by not recognizing a variety of items as expenses. The high-tech industry foolishly pretends that goodwill never declines in value, so it creates pro forma earnings that start as net income but exclude the amortization or impairment of goodwill, among other things. It does the same with compensation expense, depreciation, depletion, and amortization charges. These machinations also include moving expenses and losses from operating items to so-called nonrecurring items, regardless of how often they persist. As some quipster remarked, pro forma earnings are everything but the bad stuff.

The SEC recently issued new rules concerning the publication of pro forma numbers.[10] Under what the SEC terms Regulation G, companies must disclose pro forma earnings in an 8-K. More important, the SEC requires these firms to provide a reconciliation back to GAAP earnings, presumably to underscore what adjustments the corporations are actually making.

This development improves disclosures inasmuch as investors do not (or at least should not) have to guess what firms include or exclude when they compute pro forma earnings. At the same time, however, investors were foolish to believe the pro forma numbers during the past few years. When companies such as Cisco, Informix, Qualcomm, and Peregrine Systems issued pro forma numbers that attempted to undermine traditional accounting by asserting in effect that depreciation, depletion, amortization, and stock-based compensation are not expenses, why did we believe them?

Cash Flows

While this book has focused on hidden financial risk, I also have discussed some shenanigans with respect to the income statement. One good way of assessing the earnings of a firm is to contrast the income with the firm's operating cash flows. I particularly recommend estimating the firm's free cash flows.[11] Not only does cash represent an asset more valuable than receivables or adjustments to market values, but it pays the bills and promotes corporate liquidity.[12]

Cash flows from operating activities roughly equal the corporate earnings plus (or minus) items that enter the income statement without corresponding cash flow minus the increase in the firm's net working capital. Items that enter the income statement but are not cash flows encompass equity earnings (see Chapter 3), changes in the fair value of investments (see Chapter 3), depreciation, depletion, and amortization. Changes in the net working capital include increases and decreases in accounts receivable, inventory, and accounts payable. Once these modifications are made, the cash generated by the firm's operating activities during the period can be determined.

There are several ways to compute free cash flow. Under one method, free cash flow equals earnings before interest and taxes (EBIT) minus taxes plus depreciation, depletion, and amortization minus capital expenditures and minus the change in net working capital. While this method relates free cash flow to operating earnings, it ignores things that do influence value and is subject to some degree of manipulation by management (e.g., in its placement of certain types of revenues and expenses). A second technique is to calculate free cash flow as cash from operating activities less the capital expenditures of the business entity. This technique includes all activities of the business enterprise. Its only disadvantage is that it too is subject to managerial discretion of where to display the results of certain types of operations. The third way to compute free cash flow, and the one I prefer, is as cash from operating activities less the cash from investing activities. The major advantage is that it avoids all problems of where management places items such as adjustments for investment activities or property and plant acquisitions and dispositions.

Valuation models employ these free cash flows to estimate the corporation's value. Even if a person does not attempt to value the firm or the stock, computing free cash flow imparts information inasmuch as it indicates in a crude manner whether the firm has generated enough cash to produce economic value for the shareholders. Negative cash flows often indicate that a firm has performed poorly or might hint that corporate managers are engaging in corporate fraud. While it is nearly impossible for an outsider to distinguish between the two, usually it does not matter. Both situations constitute bad news.

One word of warning. Corporate executives have learned that the investment community esteems cash flow analysis, and they have devised ways to distort the signals in their favor. Watch out for accounting mischief in this area.[13]

Off-Balance Sheet Disclosures

As companies, especially those in the high-tech industry, have endeavored to remove expenses from the income statement with their pro forma disclosures, many corporations have eradicated their liabilities from the balance sheet. I have talked about these off-balance sheet items throughout this book, especially in Chapters 1 to 6. People now realize that Enron's undoing centered on its special-purpose entities and their removing debts from the balance sheets. Investors must understand that off-balance debts pervade corporate America.[14]

Analytical adjustments for certain types of off-balance accounting can be made, as was discussed in Chapters 3 to 5. Doing so, of course, assumes the footnotes are adequate and complete. Other types of off-balance sheet accounting, particularly the various forms of special-purpose entities (SPEs), do not provide enough data to make an adjustment. Even the new FASB pronouncement Interpretation No. 46, issued in 2003, might be of only limited help, given the wiggle room that it contains. In addition, some SPEs involve guarantees by the business enterprise, and it is doubtful that financial reports adequately disclose these contingent liabilities.

Corporations must disclose any related party transactions, which include many transactions with their SPEs and contingent liabilities.[15] During the past few years, financial executives often met these requirements superficially by writing impenetrable footnotes. Warren Buffett has remarked that people should never invest in a business they cannot understand. My corollary to this is that people should never invest in a firm whose financial report they cannot understand. When managers write opaque financial reports, they are usually hiding something.

Economic Cycle

The Young model presented in Chapters 7 and 8 captured the essence of managerial fraud and certified public accountant (CPA) underauditing (Exhibits 7.1 and 8.3). As a manager feels pressure to perform, he or she seizes the opportunity to cook the books, and the auditor grants permission. The pressure continues or intensifies and requires more exploitation. This process continues until either something great happens that allows managers to hide their deceptions or the fraud becomes public knowledge.

Sadly, when Arthur Andersen discovered the fraud at Waste Management, it concocted a scheme to sweep everything under the rug. The partner in charge proposed that the fraud—which was in the neighborhood of $3 billion after taxes—get reversed by amortizing it into the income statement over a 10-year period. In other words, Andersen proposed adding $300 million (after taxes) to the expenses of Waste Management each year for 10 years, thereby eliminating the initial fraud. While the reversal scheme itself is fraudulent and the auditors would act as accessories after the fact, they were hoping that enough good things would happen in the future decade so that Waste Management could absorb these hits. It was Andersen's way of keeping everything quiet, but it did not work.

This illustration helps to point out a critical insight when investing over the business cycle. While managers sometimes can hide frauds by undoing them during periods of economic boom, periods of economic bust force them into a seemingly infinite loop because good things are not happening by which they can cover up past frauds.[16] Managers must continue their frauds because of the continual pressure to make the numbers, so they stay on the merry-go-round until it crashes.

Mark Bradshaw, Scott Richardson, and Richard Sloan put it this way[17]: Firms with high accruals (earnings associated with relatively low cash flows from operations) tend to reverse course in future years and report low accruals (i.e., lower earnings relative to the cash flows). The good earnings reports followed by bad earnings reports tend to catch the interest of the SEC enforcement arm and lead to enforcement actions. Bradshaw, Richardson, and Sloan chide analysts for not foreseeing these reductions in earnings; they also reprimand auditors for not qualifying the audit opinions. The authors further believe that investors are not using all of the information contained in the cash flows statements; otherwise they would not be surprised by these shifts in fortune.

Buyer beware!

ENRON—A REPRISE

I previously remarked that I think it hard, if not impossible, to know when a firm is committing accounting fraud. This comment, however, does not imply that investors cannot know that problems exist. Consistent with the ideas in the previous section, at least three clues lingered at Enron, and investors should have smelled the bad cologne.

Cash Flows

Exhibit 10.1 presents three different estimates of Enron's free cash flow for the years 1998 to 2000. Panel A shows free cash flow as earnings before interest and taxes less taxes plus depreciation (and depletion and amortization) minus capital expenditures and minus the change in net working capital. Panel B depicts free cash flow as cash from operating activities less capital expenditures, and panel C portrays free cash flow as cash from operations less cash from investing activities.

Exhibit 10.1   Free Cash Flow Analysis of Enron (in Millions of Dollars)

Panel A: FCF as EBIT after Taxes—Capital Expenditures

	2000	1999	1998
EBIT	$1,953	$ 802	$1,378
Effective Income Tax Rate	30.7%	9.2%	20.0%
EBIT × (1 – T)	1,353	728	1,102
Depreciation	855	870	827
Capital Expenditures	3,158	2,674	2,009
Change in Net Working Capital	1,769	(1,000)	(233)
Free Cash Flow	($4,429)	($1,816)	$1,501

Panel B: FCF as CFO—Capital Expenditures

	2000	1999	1998
Cash from Operating Activities	$4,779	$1,228	$1,640
Capital Expenditures	3,158	2,674	2,009
Free Cash Flow	$1,621	($1,446)	($ 369)

Panel C: FCF as CFO—CFI

	2000	1999	1998
Cash from Operating Activities	$4,779	$1,228	$1,640
Cash from Investing Activities	4,264	3,507	3,965
Free Cash Flow	$ 515	($2,279)	($2,325)

Note: Parentheses denote negative numbers.

Over the three-year period from 1998 to 2000, the first method yields a free cash outflow of $(881) million, the second method reveals a free cash outflow of $(194) million, and the third method shows free cash flow of $(4) billion. While the numbers are somewhat different, all three methods depict a significant cash drain for Enron. As stated earlier, I prefer the last method because it includes the flows from all operating activities and because it minimizes the impact of managerial manipulations.[18] In this case, it does not matter much, for all three methods provide a negative picture of Enron. But given the stock prices in early 2001, it appears that few investors paid attention to cash flow. The numbers—the reported fraudulent numbers!—reveal an ill firm.[19] Certainly these free cash flow numbers do not support the lofty prices attained by Enron's common stock.

Off-Balance Sheet Disclosures

Exhibit 10.2 contains the infamous footnote 16 from Enron's 2000 annual report. When reading it, I am amazed at how little it says.

Take any paragraph you want, and read it slowly and carefully. Do you really know what Enron is doing? In particular, do you know what risks the firm is accepting on the investors' behalf? Unfortunately, the footnote is a paragon of goobledly-gook. Enron's

---

Exhibit 10.2   Enron's Related Party Transactions Footnote

In 2000 and 1999, Enron entered into transactions with limited partnerships (the Related Party) whose general partner's managing member is a senior officer of Enron. The limited partners of the Related Party are unrelated to Enron. Management believes that the terms of the transactions with the Related Party were reasonable compared to those which could have been negotiated with unrelated third parties.

In 2000, Enron entered into transactions with the Related Party to hedge certain merchant investments and other assets. As part of the transactions, Enron (i) contributed to newly formed entities (the Entities) assets valued at approximately $1.2 billion, including $150 million in Enron notes payable, 3.7 million restricted shares of outstanding Enron common stock and the right to receive up to 18.0 million shares of outstanding Enron common stock in March 2003 (subject to certain conditions) and (ii) transferred to the Entities assets valued at approximately $309 million, including a $50 million notes payable and an investment in an entity that indirectly holds warrants convertible into common stock of an Enron equity method investee. In return, Enron received economic interests in the Entities, $309 million in notes receivable, of which $259 million is recorded at Enron's carryover basis of zero, and a special distribution from the Entities in the form of $1.2 billion in notes receivable, subject to changes in the principal for amounts payable by Enron in connection with the execution of additional derivative instruments. Cash in these Entities of $172.6 million is invested in Enron demand notes. In addition, Enron paid $123 million to purchase share-settled options from the Entities on 21.7 million shares of Enron common stock. The Entities paid Enron $10.7 million to terminate the share-settled options on 14.6 million shares of Enron common stock outstanding. In late 2000, Enron entered into share-settled collar arrangements with the Entities on 15.4 million shares of Enron common stock. Such arrangements will be accounted for as equity transactions when settled.

In 2000, Enron entered into derivative transactions with the Entities with a combined notional amount of approximately $2.1 billion to hedge certain merchant investments and other assets. Enron's notes receivable balance was reduced by $36 million as a result of premiums owed on derivative transactions. Enron recognized revenues of approximately $500 million related to the subsequent change in the market value of these derivatives, which offset market value changes of certain merchant investments and price risk management activities. In addition, Enron recognized $44.5 million and $14.1 million of interest income and interest expense, respectively, on the notes receivable from and payable to the Entities.

Exhibit 10.2 *(Continued)*

In 1999, Enron entered into a series of transactions involving a third party and the Related Party. The effect of the transactions was (i) Enron and the third party amended certain forward contracts to purchase shares of Enron common stock, resulting in Enron having forward contracts to purchase Enron common shares at the market price on that day, (ii) the Related Party received 6.8 million shares of Enron common stock subject to certain restrictions and (iii) Enron received a note receivable, which was repaid in December 1999, and certain financial instruments hedging an investment held by Enron. Enron recorded the assets received and equity issued at estimated fair value. In connection with the transactions, the Related Party agreed that the senior officer of Enron would have no pecuniary interest in such Enron common shares and would be restricted from voting on matters related to such shares. In 2000, Enron and the Related Party entered into an agreement to terminate certain financial instruments that had been entered into during 1999. In connection with this agreement, Enron received approximately 3.1 million shares of Enron common stock held by the Related Party. A put option, which was originally entered into in the first quarter of 2000 and gave the Related Party the right to sell shares of Enron common stock to Enron at a strike price of $71.31 per share, was terminated under this agreement. In return, Enron paid approximately $26.8 million to the Related Party.

In 2000, Enron sold a portion of its dark fiber inventory to the Related Party in exchange for $30 million cash and a $70 million note receivable that was subsequently repaid. Enron recognized gross margin of $67 million on the sale.

In 2000, the Related Party acquired, through securitizations, approximately $35 million of merchant investments from Enron. In addition, Enron and the Related Party formed partnerships in which Enron contributed cash and securities and the Related Party contributed $17.5 million in cash. Subsequently, Enron sold a portion of its interest in the partnership through securitizations. See Note 3 [not included here]. Also, Enron contributed a put option to a trust in which the Related Party and Whitewing hold equity and debt interests. At December 31, 2000, the fair value of the put option was a $36 million loss to Enron.

In 1999, the Related Party acquired approximately $371 million of merchant assets and investments and other assets from Enron. Enron recognized pre-tax gains of approximately $16 million related to these transactions. The Related Party also entered into an agreement to acquire Enron's interests in an unconsolidated equity affiliate for approximately $34 million.

---

officials do not identify the related parties, they do not reveal the purpose of the limited partnerships, they typically do not say what type of derivative transactions are undertaken, they declare nothing about collateral, they say nothing about guarantees (and neither does the previous footnote, supposedly about guarantees), and they do not give even a remote idea of how much risk the firm has procured. Enron's footnote 16 serves as a perfect illustration of my advice not to invest in any firm whose financial report you cannot understand.[20]

Economic Cycle

As the U.S. economy moved into recession in 2000, the huge accruals amassed by Enron had to reverse. A number of commentators have focused on the income from Enron's use of mark-to-market accounting.[21] The usual complaint is that Enron added $1.9 billion to income from these activities, and Jeff Skilling and Ken Lay fudged these numbers. While true, investors and creditors should have realized two things. First, this $1.9 billion gain came with no cash flows, so it should be subtracted out when determining the firm's free cash flow. Second, large embellishments to earnings because of noncash accruals are generally followed by sizable decrements to income, again because of noncash accruals. Call it the financial what-goes-up-must-come-down principle.

When the economy goes into a recession, managers do not have room in which to maneuver with their voodoo accounting. The downturn forces financial executives to take negative accruals, earnings fall sharply, and the firm's problems become apparent to all. Blemishes appear everywhere. Enron was no exception, as the recession left it and Andersen no room in which to lie any more.

Even though outsiders could not work out the deceptions, they still could have recognized several Enron conundrums. Enron did not have the cash flow of a hot stock, it published garbage for important disclosures, and recessions tend to be days of reckoning. Investors and creditors failed to glean the information from Enron's financial report and from macroeconomic data and interpret it correctly. While managers, directors, general counsel, auditors, investment bankers, the FASB, the SEC, and Congress failed the investment community, the investment community also failed. The evidence was there; the analysis was not.

Buyer beware!

RULES FOR INVESTING

In his speech "How to Prevent Future Enrons," SEC chairman Harvey Pitt testified that financial statements often are "arcane and impenetrable."[22] Further, he asserted that "[i]nvestors and employees concerned with preserving and increasing their retirement funds deserve comprehensive financial reports they can easily interpret and understand." This is a foolish approach for the market system, first because the only way to really simplify financial reports is to outlaw complex transactions and second because investors must diligently learn business, finance, and accounting if they expect to understand what they read in financial reports.

Suppose you or a loved one needs heart surgery. You meet the surgeons who will perform the surgery, and they speak with an "arcane and impenetrable" lexicon. Do you really want to prohibit their using professional language just because you do not understand what is discussed? I think it a more profitable experience to free the doctors to do their job, using whatever professional techniques they deem best, while studying and learning these methods to the extent that we can. By so doing we would be in a better position to dialog with the doctors without impeding their efforts.

Rather than dumbing down the financial statements, the SEC or other regulators should educate investors to protect themselves. There are two key ways to do this: diversify one's portfolio and gain knowledge of accounting and finance.

Risk and Diversification

According to some pundit, the three most important factors in real estate are location, location, and location. I modify that for finance by claiming that the three most important things to do when investing is diversify, diversify, and diversify.

I mentioned the capital asset pricing model in Chapter 2. For convenience, I duplicate the capital market line and the security market line in Exhibit 10.3. (It appeared earlier as Exhibit 2.5.) I mentioned the capital asset pricing model earlier to formalize the notion of risk as the standard deviation of market returns in the capital market line and as beta in the security market line. Later I mentioned that this risk is a function of the financial structure of a business enterprise, so that as the firm adds debt to its financial structure, the beta (also known as the systematic risk) goes up.

One of the assumptions of the capital asset pricing model is that the investor holds a diversified portfolio. The idea is that the risk of the portfolio contains some aspects that can be diversified away. Exhibit 10.4 displays this notion. When an investor holds only one stock, the total risk includes a portion that the market does not compensate. By purchasing other securities, investors can reduce the total risk of the portfolio. Different

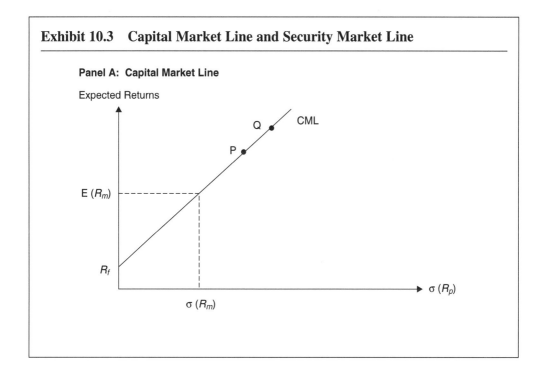

Exhibit 10.3   Capital Market Line and Security Market Line

Panel A: Capital Market Line

Expected Returns

Q

P

CML

$E(R_m)$

R_f

$\sigma(R_m)$

$\sigma(R_p)$

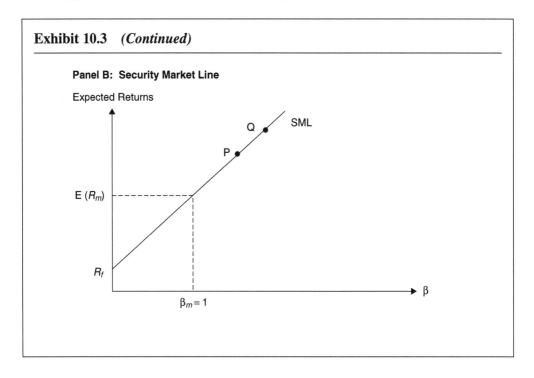

Exhibit 10.3 *(Continued)*

Panel B: Security Market Line

studies suggest that as few as eight well-diversified securities can essentially wring out all of the undiversified risk from the portfolio, while some suggest a number closer to 25. The point is that when investors hold few securities in their portfolios, they are accepting much higher risk than is necessary to obtain some return.

An employee of Enron, for example, who held only Enron stock possessed very high risk. When the returns are going up, that may be okay, but when the returns turn south, the investors can feel the pinch in a hurry as the losses mount up.

Develop Expertise

Investors now have a choice: They can learn a lot about finance and accounting so that they can make informed choices. Alternatively, they can choose to let others make those choices. Investors effect the latter approach by investing in mutual funds.

To make your own choices, you should have the knowledge and skills to understand thoroughly finance and accounting. I provide some suggestions for furthering one's skills in Exhibit 10.5. The first section lists some elementary texts that build solid foundations in finance and in accounting. The material there constitutes the minimum expertise that I think a person needs before making investment decisions. The second section is for those who want to get serious about accounting. It lists intermediate and advanced texts that cover the complex material in the world of accounting. If you really want to understand what is contained in an annual report, you have to gain proficiency in these topics. The last list does the same thing for financial investments. Those who read and study these texts will gain the knowledge to make good decisions, as long as they keep their eye on the ball.

Exhibit 10.4   Effect of Diversification on Risk

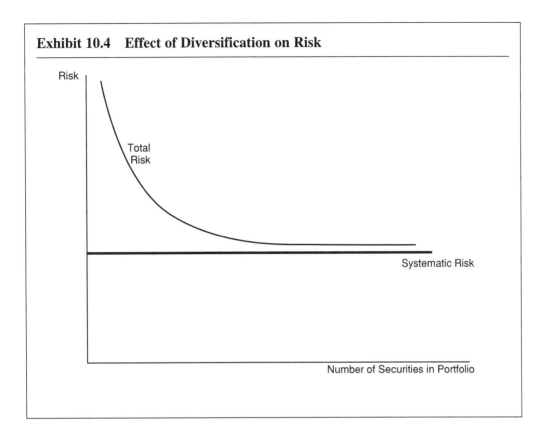

Reducing the information content of company reports to a level that anyone who graduated high school can read them is the wrong approach. It's like asking Tolstoy to reduce all of the tough sections of *War and Peace* so that someone with a comic book reading level can understand it. The edits can be made, but so much is lost in the process. The better approach is to advise investors of their obligations to learn the complexities of accounting and finance.

Exhibit 10.5   Suggestions for Further Reading

Elementary Accounting and Finance Texts

Brigham, E. F. and J. F. Houston. (1998). *Fundamentals of Financial Management*, 8th ed. New York: Dryden.
    Good coverage of the basics of investments.

Higgins, R. C. (2000). *Analysis for Financial Management*. New York: Irwin.
    Excellent treatment of key topics in investments.

Exhibit 10.5 *(Continued)*

Stickney, C. P., and R. L. Weil. (2002). *Financial Accounting: An Introduction to Concepts, Methods, and Uses*, 10th ed. Mason, OH: South-Western.

Good coverage of the basics of financial accounting.

Accounting for the Serious Investor

Beams, F. A., J. H. Anthony, R. P. Clement, and S. H. Lowensohn. (2003). *Advanced Accounting*, 8th ed. Upper Saddle River, NJ: Prentice- Hall.

The first half of the book gives detailed coverage of business combination accounting, including foreign currency transactions and translations.

Revsine, L., D. W. Collins, and W. B. Johnson. (2002). *Financial Reporting and Analysis*, 2nd ed. Upper Saddle River, NJ: Prentice-Hall.

Provides an intermediate coverage of most topics in financial accounting.

Trombley, M. A. (2003). *Accounting for Derivatives and Hedging*. New York: McGraw-Hill Irwin.

Accounting for derivatives per SFAS No. 133.

White, G. I., A. C. Sondhi, and D. Fried. (2003). *The Analysis and Use of Financial Statements*, 3rd ed. New York: John Wiley & Sons.

Discusses how an investor can interpret accounting reports.

Finance for the Serious Investor

Damodaran, A. (1996). *Investment Valuation: Tools and Techniques for Determining the Value of Any Asset*. New York: John Wiley & Sons.

Discusses the valuation of hard-to-measure assets.

Fabozzi, F. J. (2000). *Fixed Income Analysis for the Chartered Financial Analyst Program*. New York: Fabozzi Associates.

Supplies a comprehensive treatment of fixed income securities.

Kolb, R. W. (1999). *Futures, Options, and Swaps,* 3rd ed. London: Blackwell.

A good treatment of derivatives.

Reilly, F. K., and K. C. Brown. (2000). *Investment Analysis and Portfolio Management*, 6th ed. New York: Dryden.

Provides an intermediate coverage of most topics in investments.

White, G. I., A. C. Sondhi, and D. Fried. (2003). *The Analysis and Use of Financial Statements*, 3rd ed. New York: John Wiley & Sons.

Besides accounting, this text also furnishes excellent coverage of topics in investments.

SUMMARY AND CONCLUSION

At this time many corporations have put on a good public relations campaign to tell investors that their firms present honest and accurate accounting numbers.[23] Should investors believe them? Is there an Enron out there just waiting for cash? How do investors know?

Investors did not heed the advice of Alan Greenspan when he talked about "irrational exuberance"; instead, we guffawed at those comments. The investing public made a major mistake by not realizing that a big bubble existed in the stock market. Likewise, we became hypnotized by high earnings, even if they were of poor quality because of low cash flows attached to them. And we did not worry about omitted liabilities, even though Enron at least indicated that it had plenty of omissions. Off-balance sheet items abound, but we were too lazy to adjust for them and learn the truth about the amount of financial risk in the system. Admittedly, managers lied and others played games of one sort or another, but we have to confess that some of the blame rests with us.

Ken Brown[24] and Jonathan Weil[25] remind us that several key issues radiate in this financial season. Brown in particular points out that four areas of accounting abuse continue to pop up on the scene:

1. Some sales really are not sales, such as securitizations with recourse (see Chapter 6).
2. Valuing assets on a mark-to-market basis (consider the cash flows of these markups).
3. Off-the-book accounts (while everywhere, investors need to hunt them down and understand their implications).
4. The funny business of merger accounting (remember the shenanigans of Tyco).

Accounting is fragile. Investors must gain an understanding of the strengths and weaknesses of this domain. Recent accounting abuses in 2003 at Ahold, AOL, HealthSouth, Medco, and Sprint remind us of the need for constant vigilance.

NOTES

1. Compare D. Q. Mills, *Buy, Lie, and Sell High: How Investors Lost Out on Enron and the Internet Bubble* (Upper Saddle River, NJ: Prentice-Hall, 2002).
2. C. P. Kindleberger, *Manias, Panics, and Crashes: A History of Financial Crises,* 4th ed. (New York: John Wiley & Sons, 2000).
3. In case it matters to anyone, my portfolio primarily consists of my retirement funds in TIAA-CREF. At the beginning of 2001, my retirement funds were totally invested in stocks. By July 2001, however, I had transferred all of my TIAA-CREF retirement funds into fixed income securities, money market funds, and real estate.
4. U.S. Senate, *Financial Oversight of Enron: The SEC and Private-Sector Watchdogs.* Report of the Staff to the Senate Committee on Governmental Affairs (Washington, DC: U.S. Senate, October 8, 2002).

5. B. Mattson-Teig, "A Closer Look," *National Real Estate Investor,* November 1, 2002.

6. For example, see C. Mollenkamp and P. Beckett, "Bank of America, Citigroup Will Post Massive Charges," *Wall Street Journal,* December 24, 2002; and G. Morgenson, "It Still Pays to See Who Did the Research," *New York Times,* December 22, 2002.

7. K. Brown, "Heard on the Street: Analysts: Still Coming Up Rosy When Looking to Future Profits," *Wall Street Journal,* January 27, 2003.

8 M. Goldstein, "Avoiding the Next Enron," parts 1 and 2, *Dow Jones News Service,* February 14–15, 2002.

9 Compare C. Bryan-Low and K. Brown, "And Now, the Question Is: Where's the Next Enron? Accounting Textbooks Will Get Rewritten, but Few Practices in the Industry Might Change," *Wall Street Journal,* June 18, 2002, p. C1.

10. M. Schroeder, "SEC Orders New Disclosures in Companies' Profit Reports," *Wall Street Journal,* January 16, 2003; and Securities and Exchange Commission, "SEC Adopts Rules on Provisions of Sarbanes-Oxley Act: Actions Cover Non-GAAP Financials, From 8-K Amendments, Trading During Blackout Periods, Audit Committee Financial Expert Requirements," January 13, 2003; see: *www.sec.gov/news/extra/finfrds.html.*

11. The relationship between accounting earnings and cash flows from operating activities is discussed in: M. J. Gombola and J. E. Ketz, "A Note on Cash Flow and Classification Patterns of Financial Ratios," *Accounting Review* (January 1983), pp. 105–114, and "Financial Ratio Patterns in Retail and Manufacturing Organizations," *Financial Management* (Summer 1983), pp. 45–56; D. F. Hawkins and W. J. Campbell, *Equity Valuation: Models, Analysis and Implications* (Charlottesville, VA: Financial Executives Research Foundation, 1978); J. E. Ketz and J. A. Largay III, "Reporting Income and Cash Flows from Operations," *Accounting Horizons* (June 1987), pp. 9–17; and J. A. Largay and C. P. Stickney, "Cash Flows, Ratio Analysis and the W. T. Grant Company Bankruptcy," *Financial Analysts Journal* (July-August 1980), pp. 51–54. Recommended readings on free cash flow include: R. C. Higgins, *Analysis for Financial Management* (New York: Irwin, 2000); F. K. Reilly and K. C. Brown, *Investment Analysis and Portfolio Management,* 6th ed. (New York: Dryden, 2000); and G. I. White, A. C. Sondhi, and D. Fried, *The Analysis and Use of Financial Statements,* 2nd ed. (New York: John Wiley & Sons, 1998).

12. J. Aldersley, "Mocking Myths Pays Dividends," *Sun Herald,* June 23, 2002; M. Davis, "Tyco Topples Cash Flow Target," January 22, 2003; see: *www.thestreet.com*; A. Rappaport, "Show Me the Cash Flow!" *Fortune,* September 16, 2002, pp. 193–194; and G. Zuckerman and M. Benson, "S&P Draws Up List of Firms That May Face Cash Shortfall," *Wall Street Journal,* May 16, 2002, p. C1.

13. A. Berenson, "Changing the Definition of Cash Flow Helped Tyco," *New York Times,* December 31, 2003; and M. Maremont and L. P. Cohen, "Tyco's Internal Report Finds Extensive Accounting Tricks," *Wall Street Journal,* December 31, 2002.

14. Bryan-Low and Brown, "And Now, the Question Is: Where's the Next Enron?"; S. Lubove and E. MacDonald, "Debt? Who, Me? Enron Is Hardly Alone When It Comes to Creative Off-Balance Sheet Accounting," *Forbes,* February 18, 2002; K. Pender, "There May Be More Enrons," *San Francisco Chronicle,* January 24, 2002, p. B1; and R. Thomas, "Avoiding the Next Enron," *Dow Jones News Service,* February 26, 2002.

15. Financial Accounting Standards Board, *Accounting for Contingencies,* SFAS No. 5 (Stamford, CT: FASB Statements, 1975), and *Related Party Disclosures,* SFAS No. 57 (Stamford, CT: FASB, 1982).

16. Compare W. S. Lerach, "The Chickens Have Come Home to Roost: How Wall Street, the Big Accounting Firms and Corporate Interests Chloroformed Congress and Cost America's Investors Trillions," 2002; see: *www.milberg.com/pdf/news/chickens.pdf.*

17. M. T. Bradshaw, S. A. Richardson, and R. G. Sloan, "Do Analysts and Auditors Use Information in Accruals?" *Journal of Accounting Research* (June 2001), pp. 45–74.

18. Compare White, Sondhi, and Fried, *The Analysis and Use of Financial Statements,* 2nd ed., pp. 104–117).

19. Compare C. Higson, "Did Enron's Investors Fool Themselves?" *Business Strategy Review,* no. 4 (2001), pp. 1–6.

20. Goldstein, "Avoiding the Next Enron," February 14, 2002; M. Ingram, "Financial Disclosure Is Good—But It Doesn't Always Help," *The Globe and Mail,* February 5, 2002, p. B16; and S. Pearlstein and P. Behr, "At Enron, the Fall Came Quickly," *Washington Post,* December 2, 2001, p. A01.

21. For example, D. Feldstein, "What Was Bottom Line at Enron? Disturbing Signs Not Easy to Spot in Annual Report," *Houston Chronicle,* March 18, 2002.

22. Harvey Pitt, "How to Prevent Future Enrons," *Wall Street Journal,* December 11, 2001.

23. See: A. Clendenning, "Preventing 'Enronitis': Companies Coming Clean About Anything that Could Smell Fishy," *Pittsburgh Post-Gazette,* February 16, 2002, p. A7; E. MacDonald, "False Front," *Forbes* (October 14, 2002); J. McFarland, "Companies Putting on a Squeaky Clean Face," *The Globe and Mail,* February 14, 2002, p. B1; T. S. Mulligan, "The Fall of Enron; Companies Simplifying Accounting; Complex Methods Lose Favor as Firms Scurry to Prove Worth," *Los Angeles Times,* February 19, 2002; M. Rivituso, "Avoiding the Next Enron," *Fortune,* February 22, 2002; A. Schmelkin, "Preferred Issues: Disclosures Up in 10Ks, But What's It All Mean?" *American Banker,* March 18, 2002.

24. K. Brown, "Creative Accounting: How to Buff a Company," *Wall Street Journal,* February 21, 2002.

25. J. Weil, "Accounting-Standards Panel Takes on Hot-Button Issues," *Wall Street Journal,* January 13, 2003.

Part IV

Making Financial Reports Credible

CHAPTER ELEVEN

Andersen Has the Solution—Really!

The purpose of financial accounting and reporting is to provide information about the firm to outsiders, particularly to investors and creditors. Companies convey information about their economic status and their economic accomplishments during the past year or quarter by publishing financial reports that contain the balance sheet, the income statement, the statement of changes in stockholders' equity, and the cash flow statement, supplemented by footnotes and schedules.

Unfortunately, as documented in Chapter 1, in recent days this purpose was trampled and crumpled and cursed by managers, general counsel, accountants, corporate directors, and investment bankers. During this period the Financial Accounting Standards Board (FASB) acted like Caspar Milquetoast, while the Securities and Exchange Commission (SEC) leadership blamed everything on the need for accountants to modernize their ways. Congress professed a need for reform, while creating roadblocks for actual advancement and accepting campaign contributions from those they supposedly are reforming. Better enforcement is needed—not new rules. Even if stock market prices sputter upward, there is no guarantee they will maintain an upward trend, especially as financial statements continue to lack credibility. Oh, they may be improved for a while as managers and their professional advisers watch the "perp walks" by managers charged with various corporate frauds and want to be excluded from that club, but at best this is merely a short-term phenomenon. The system still has major problems, and unless these issues are addressed, the events of Enron, Adelphia, WorldCom, and Tyco will be repeated.

Chapter 2 sets the stage by discussing the importance of financial structure to investors and creditors. Financial leverage forms an important variable when assessing the riskiness of stocks and bonds, whether in terms such as modern portfolio theory or particular items of interest, such as the prediction of corporate failure and the prediction of bond ratings. Debt matters to investors and creditors, so managers ought to disclose the truth about corporate debt to them.

Lack of truthfulness and transparency when reporting on the entity's liabilities leads to three basic types of problems for the investment community. As I described hiding debt with the equity method, with lease accounting, and with pension accounting in Chapters 3 to 5, some understatements of debt can be remedied with analytical adjustments, by which the investor or the financial analyst modifies the reported financial numbers to make them more meaningful and more useful. Such analytical adjustments require corporations to disclose enough data to facilitate this process. If managers at least disclose these data honestly, the investors and financial analysts can analyze the firm properly. The essence of the problem of understating debts is that it imposes costs on the investment community to learn enough accounting to recognize the shortcomings and to take the time and effort to make these amendments.

The second type of problem was encountered with take-or-pay contracts and special-purpose entities (SPEs) in Chapter 6. The main problem with asset securitizations, SPE borrowings, and synthetic leases is that managers of business enterprises who employ these business tactics rarely divulge what is transpiring. They do not account for these transactions fully, if at all, in their financial statements, nor do they provide full and meaningful disclosures in the footnotes. Because so much data are missing, investors and financial analysts cannot reconstruct and analytically adjust the transactions. They are forced to be aware of the issues and protect themselves by increasing the financial reporting risk premium that is added to the firm's cost of capital.

Outright fraud constitutes the third and most serious problem. While many managers and directors rejoice over exaggerations, half truths, and nondisclosures, some executives lust for more. Corporate executives at Enron, Global Crossing, and WorldCom, among others, lied to investors and creditors for their own personal gain. In addition to anguish over what corporate America has done to the rest of us, what distresses me is the recent publication of various books and articles claiming that investors and creditors can discover fraud in the financial reports. This assertion is patently untrue. One's suspicions might be aroused by a cash flow analysis, but it is virtually impossible to distinguish between corporate fraud and financial difficulties. As discussed in Chapter 10, investors must protect themselves by diversifying their portfolios and understanding the risks of investments.

What amazes the public about the events of 2001 and 2002 is not the extent of management deceit and greed—the public already suspected that to be the case. More astonishing is how broken the system of checks and balances is. Corporate governance does not work; the directors are too busy playing golf. Auditors do not capture misdeeds; they covet consulting engagements. The FASB is a political Ping Pong ball, going wherever it is paddled. The SEC is hampered with insufficient funds because Congress makes promises but takes no actions. It also has been led during this period by a man who spent the early months after Enron trying to modernize accounting. Only after the implosion of WorldCom did he realize that the American economy was under attack from within. Members of Congress also contributed to the problems by pontificating about how to reform the system, but hamstringing the institutions so that little reform can actually occur. Meanwhile, they have their hands in the pockets of campaign donors, which of course include many managers, directors, general counsel, auditors, financial analysts, and investment bankers.

Chapters 7 through 10 drive home the point that all of these actors within the financial community failed to uphold the public interest. While the incredible stock market declines of recent years have forced a reassessment by participants in the system, we must understand that we face a choice. One possibility is to look partially, almost superficially, at the issues, modify the system in some small measure, and hope everything will be okay. If that path is taken, things will improve for a short time, but only for a while. New financial explosions and revelations will occur, and we shall again ask ourselves why.

A better approach is to make deeper changes and especially to modify the culture. Managers must consider themselves stewards of the investment community instead of lords and ladies in some corporate fiefdoms. The other participants need to accept the responsibility to do their parts, rather than to request bribes from the corporate lords and ladies. We can improve the credibility of financial accounting.

The most ironic aspect of this economic meltdown is that former leaders of Arthur Andersen proposed long-range solutions some 30 to 40 years ago. If we had followed their advice, we might not have found ourselves in this sinkhole. We still have a chance to listen to their voices, and if we follow their advice now, we shall restore confidence in the financial system and improve capital formation in this country. How that once-glorious accounting firm suffered such setbacks is beyond my comprehension, but fortunately we need not follow its path. The leaders of Arthur Andersen proposed three topics that are of special interest: the principle of accounting, the importance of socialization within the firm, and an Accounting Court.

Before exploring a solution to the culture that creates accounting scandals, this chapter examines how some business managers marginalize the investment community. Then the text focuses on the framework of accounting, especially at what has been called the postulates, the principles, or the objectives of accounting. I discuss the famous Continental Vending case, which gets to the heart of the matter and related issues in the profession's Rule 203. The solution to accounting scandals rests on some commonsensical notions. While difficult to implement, the solution serves as a starting point from which to build a culture that encourages truth telling in accounting reports.

ARTHUR ANDERSEN FORGETS ITS ROOTS

Unfortunately, recently some managers have forgotten the purpose of accounting and have viewed corporate assets as their own. Certified public accountants (CPAs) ought to know better, for the profession preaches and teaches better ethics than this. As an illustration, consider the case of telecom accounting, which was briefly discussed in Chapter 1. Sadly but tellingly, Arthur Andersen played a key role in inventing a new twist to creative accounting.[1]

Global Crossing, Qwest, and other companies in the telecom industry recently engaged in swaps of bandwidth. A typical contract had one company leasing some of its bandwidth in return for obtaining access to some of the bandwidth of another corporation. How should the telecoms account for these transactions? Accounting Principles Board (APB) Opinion No. 29 applies, and it classifies barter transactions into two types, depending on whether the assets are similar or dissimilar. Trading a car for another auto is an example of a similar asset swap, while trading a car for a computer illustrates the bartering of dissimilar assets. Of course, some items may be hard to distinguish, and in those cases accountants will need to exercise professional judgment.[2]

APB Opinion No. 29 states that gains and losses are recognized in the case of exchanging dissimilar assets but not in the case of trading similar assets. In essence, the telecoms asserted that the trades were dissimilar, but that seems ridiculous. Both items were bandwidths; it was like trading a Ford for a Dodge. Since both assets are cars, it seems clear that these trades were of similar assets. Calling different bandwidths dissimilar assets does not stretch one's incredulity—it defies it.

The more interesting feature of this story is that Arthur Andersen was the architect of this accounting diversion. Andersen prepared a document instructing companies in the telecom industry how to create the illusion of accounting gains and have enormous latitude in fabricating how much profit they wanted to display. The accounting firm, presumably for a fee, then peddled this position to its clients in the telecom industry, who in turn thought that deceiving the investment community was all right.

That attitude, apparently encrusted many corporate cultures, creating an environment in which managers commit unethical if not illegal acts. We need to change this corporate culture. The best place to begin is to recall the objectives of financial accounting and reporting and keep in mind what accountants are about.

The downfall of Andersen should serve as an important object lesson for the remaining accounting firms. Firms need to remember their roots, so they can grow into strong trees, with boughs to shade others. Without changes, the blight that destroyed Andersen might annihilate the rest of the nation's accounting firms.

PURPOSE OF FINANCIAL REPORTING

The remainder of this chapter concerns how to fix the problem and manufacture credible financial reports. I begin with Arthur Andersen's insights into what it called the "postulate of accounting," supplementing this insight with comments from accounting rule makers, from Judge Friendly in the Continental Vending case, and a look at Rule 203.

Andersen's Postulate of Accounting[3]

I love reading accounting texts, especially the older ones that helped shape the profession. One book that made a deep impression on me was *The Postulate of Accounting: What It Is; How It Is Determined; How It Should Be Used*, written by Arthur Andersen and published in 1960.[4] Even today I find the book insightful and foundational.

When the book was written, the Committee on Accounting Procedure (CAP) had come under virulent attack because it allowed many accounting alternatives and produced accounting bulletins that were inconsistent with one another. The American Institute of Certified Public Accountants (AICPA) responded to this criticism by replacing the CAP with the Accounting Principles Board (APB) in 1959, and it created the Accounting Research Division in that same year. The AICPA's objectives were to reduce the number of accounting alternatives and to make the rules as nearly consistent as possible. The strategy to implement this plan was to undertake research that would produce the postulates and the principles of accounting. Once this groundwork was completed, then the APB could establish the accounting rules.

Leonard Spacek, senior partner at Arthur Andersen, clearly had a hand in writing *The Postulate of Accounting*. In this book, Arthur Andersen held that there was only one postulate of accounting, and that postulate is *fairness*:

> Each party to the accounting is entitled to a fair statement of his economic rights and interests. Any misstatement of the rights of one group will necessarily misstate those of another group.
>
> Financial reporting is concerned with ascertaining the rights of all parties and impartially applying the accounting principles thereto.
>
> To ascertain those conditions that are prerequisite, we must look to the purpose of the financial statements. It would seem that this purpose, as universally recognized by the standard short-form accountant's certificate, is to give a fair presentation of financial position and results of operations. Accordingly, essential prerequisite conditions are those which result in fairness—which "present fairly."
>
> Thus, financial statements cannot be so prepared as to favor the interests of any one segment without doing injustice to others; and such statements could not meet the test of fairness which the public demands always be present in public financial reporting.[5]

The obvious possible deficiency of this postulate rests with the potential for ambiguity. Realizing that the postulate of fairness might be interpreted in many ways, Andersen then provides an illustration. The firm claims that "Liabilities and obligations of a business entity should be recognized and recorded in the period incurred and should be eliminated in the period in which they cease to exist."[6] The firm goes on to explain how this principle is fair to management, labor, stockholders, creditors, customers, and the public. As discussed in Chapter 2 of this book, stockholders need to understand the nature and extent of corporate liabilities so they can better assess the value of their equity. Creditors need similar information.

Wanting still more specificity, Andersen demonstrates how accounting regulators could extend this principle to leases. (Recall that this book was written in 1960, long before the issuance of SFAS No. 13.) Andersen concludes that leases and liabilities are sufficiently similar to treat them in the same manner[7]; accordingly, business enterprises should capitalize lease obligations at an appropriate discount rate and place this amount on the corporation's balance sheet.

Unfortunately, today's partners in Arthur Andersen did not remember this procedure. If we substitute "special-purpose entity debt" for "lease obligation," the logic is the same. Only by consolidating SPE debt can labor, stockholders, creditors, customers, and the public achieve fairness. Anything else is patently unfair. In addition, some SPEs create contingent liabilities. The same argument that Andersen uses in its 1960 book can be applied to contingent liabilities; business enterprises should report fully, clearly, and accurately the nature and the extent of these liabilities.

Today's external auditors—indeed, all who are genuinely interested in accounting and financial reporting—can learn a lot from the principles and standards of yesterday's accounting leaders. I urge external auditors and others to read *The Postulate of Accounting* and recapture the vision of Leonard Spacek.[8]

Concepts from Standards Setters

The Accounting Principles Board partially followed the lead of Arthur Andersen when it wrote Statement No. 4 in 1970. This statement is not an APB Opinion, so the AICPA never said it was binding on practicing CPAs, but the text reveals some movement by the profession toward a better understanding of the goals of accounting. In the statement, the APB said that "[a]ccounting is a service activity. Its function is to provide quantitative information, primarily financial in nature, about economic entities that is intended to be useful in making economic decisions." Though the statement is mostly a hodge-podge that justifies practice, this declaration and a few others like it set a pattern on which the FASB can build.

The FASB discussed and debated the foundations of financial accounting in its conceptual framework project beginning in the mid-1970s. After describing the users of financial statements and the environment in which financial reporting operates in its 1978 Statement of Financial Concepts No. 1, the FASB listed these objectives of financial accounting: "Financial reporting should provide information that is useful to present and potential investors and creditors and other users in making rational investment, credit, and similar decisions. The information should be comprehensible to those who have a reasonable understanding of business and economic activities and are willing to study the information with reasonable diligence."

It added some details about that information later: "Financial reporting should provide information to help present and potential investors and creditors and other users in assessing the amounts, timing, and uncertainty of prospective cash receipts from dividends or interest and the proceeds from the sale, redemption, or maturity of securities or loans."

To convey this information to the investment community, the business world relies on balance sheets, income statements, statements of changes in stockholders' equity, and statements of cash flows. The FASB avers: "Financial reporting should provide information about the economic resources of an enterprise, the claims to those resources (obligations of the enterprise to transfer resources to other entities and owners' equity), and the effects of transactions, events, and circumstances that change resources and claims to those resources."

While the FASB did not mention "fairness" as it approached the fundamental aspects of financial accounting, it seems to me that it ends up in essentially the same place by virtue of the great emphasis it placed on financial statement users. In other words, the FASB operationalized the term *fairness* by calling on corporate managers to measure assets and liabilities and stockholders' equity, revenues, and expenses as accurately as possible and then to communicate these results without distortion to the firm's investors and potential investors.

Continental Vending Case

The single most important legal case that involves accountants is *U.S. v. Simon* (1969), popularly known as the Continental Vending case.[9] The case requires external auditors to ensure that financial reports are constructed and conveyed in such a manner that they communicate the results fairly to the investment community.

Briefly, the facts are as follows. Harold Roth was president of Continental Vending Machine Corporation and owned about 25 percent of it and its affiliate, Valley Commercial Corporation. From time to time Continental would raise cash by giving Valley negotiable notes, and Valley would discount them at the bank and hand over the proceeds to Continental. On its books, Continental had a "Valley payable." In addition, Roth would borrow money from the parent corporation in an indirect manner. Continental would loan money to Valley, giving rise to a "Valley receivable," and Valley in turn would lend the cash to Roth. Roth used the funds primarily to play in the stock market. Exhibit 11.1 captures the essence of these relationships.

Near the end of fiscal 1962, Valley could not pay off its debts. Roth pledged his securities, most of which were Continental stocks and bonds, as collateral. When the financial statements were prepared, the firm netted a portion of the Valley receivable against the Valley payable, did not disclose the fact that Roth had borrowed money from the firm, and did not disclose the nature of the loan's collateral. Shortly thereafter, Continental had a cash flow problem. The securities held as collateral lost value, and the firm declared bankruptcy.

Federal prosecutors charged three persons in Lybrand, Ross Brothers, and Montgomery (this accounting firm later merged to become Coopers & Lybrand, which in turn later merged to become PricewaterhouseCoopers) with criminal fraud. While agreeing with the facts presented by the federal prosecutors, the defendants relied on a number of expert witnesses, all of whom stated that the deficiencies just mentioned were not part of generally accepted accounting principles (GAAP). The trial judge

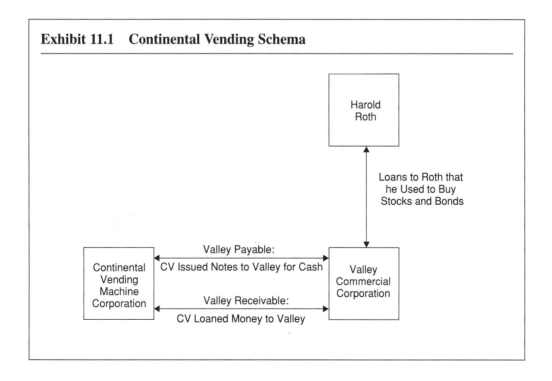

Exhibit 11.1   Continental Vending Schema

issued directions to the jury that negated this perspective by maintaining that "the 'critical test' was whether the financial statements as a whole 'fairly presented the financial position of Continental as of September 30, 1962, and whether it accurately reported the operations for fiscal 1962." The jury found the defendants guilty; they appealed; the circuit court did not reverse the decision; and the Supreme Court denied certiorari.[10]

The major result of this case is that the courts do not rely exclusively on whether the external auditors attest to an entity's application of GAAP. Instead, the standard is fairness. This is the proper outcome, for managers cannot be allowed to loot corporations and cover it up with transactions that abide by GAAP.

A. A. Sommer, former commissioner at the SEC, put this case into perspective:

> Judge [Henry J.] Friendly . . . said in effect that the first law for accountants was not compliance with generally accepted accounting principles, but rather full and fair disclosure, fair presentation, and if the principles did not produce this brand of disclosure, accountants could not hide behind the principles but had to go beyond them and make whatever additional disclosures were necessary for full disclosure. In a word, "present fairly" was a concept separate from "generally accepted accounting principles," and the latter did not necessarily result in the former.[11]

While the FASB shied away from the concept of "fairness," the courts have embraced it warmly. Interestingly, the courts ended up in a place quite similar to that in Statement of Financial Concepts No.1. The courts said that corporate managers should report assets and liabilities and stockholders' equity, revenues, and expenses as fairly as possible and then communicate these results fairly to the firm's investors and potential investors.

Rule 203

The accounting profession has listened to the words of Judge Friendly only halfheartedly. The concession is made in Rule 203 of the AICPA's Code of Professional Conduct, which states that when a member of the AICPA performs an audit, he or she will follow GAAP unless some unusual circumstance exists that makes the financial statements misleading. In that case the CPA may depart from GAAP.

The profession's orientation is backward. It assumes that GAAP produce fair and accurate results unless the accountant can prove otherwise. By putting the burden of proof on the accountant, it reveals its bias for GAAP. The trial judge and the circuit judge in the Continental Vending case, however, stated unequivocally that fairness was the first principle.

As FASB considers moving to a principles-based system, accountants need to get their priorities straight.[12] This refocus will succeed only if CPAs and managers and others in the system utilize the shift to create more and better information for the investment community.

Audit Report

I can sum up this section by reviewing what an auditor says in an audit report. For a reminder, Exhibit 11.2 reproduces KPMG's audit report of General Electric. What does

KPMG mean when it states that "the aforementioned financial statements . . . present fairly, in all material respects, the financial position of General Electric Company and consolidated affiliates at December 31, 2001 and 2000, and the results of their operations and their cash flows for each of the years in the three-year period ended December 31, 2001" if not that it abides by the concept of fairness? Does the next phrase, "in conformity with accounting principles generally accepted in the United States of America," explain what this means, or does it circumscribe what is intended by fairness? Given the Continental Vending rule, I think it ought to mean that fairness is what the profession is seeking, and that accounting rules generally are helpful to attain fairness; when they are not, accounting professionals promise to do what is necessary so that the reports are fair to financial statement readers.

Exhibit 11.2   Independent Auditor's Report

TO SHARE OWNERS AND BOARD OF DIRECTORS OF
GENERAL ELECTRIC COMPANY

We have audited the accompanying statement of financial position of General Electric Company and consolidated affiliates as of December 31, 2001 and 2000, and the related statements of earnings, changes in share owners' equity and cash flows for each of the years in the three-year period ended December 31, 2001. These consolidated financial statements are the responsibility of the Company's management. Our responsibility is to express an opinion on these consolidated financial statements based on our audits.

We conducted our audits in accordance with auditing standards generally accepted in the United States of America. Those standards require that we plan and perform the audit to obtain reasonable assurance about whether the financial statements are free of material misstatement. An audit includes examining, on a test basis, evidence supporting the amounts and disclosures in the financial statements. An audit also includes assessing the accounting principles used and significant estimates made by management, as well as evaluating the overall financial statement presentation. We believe that our audits provide a reasonable basis for our opinion.

In our opinion, the aforementioned financial statements appearing on pages F-2 to F-7, F-11 and F-27 to F-52 present fairly, in all material respects, the financial position of General Electric Company and consolidated affiliates at December 31, 2001 and 2000, and the results of their operations and their cash flows for each of the years in the three-year period ended December 31, 2001, in conformity with accounting principles generally accepted in the United States of America.

As discussed in note 1 to the consolidated financial statements, the Company in 2001 changed its method of accounting for derivative instruments and hedging activities and impairment of certain beneficial interests in securitized assets.

/s/ KPMG LLP

SOCIALIZATION[13]

Herb Miller, a retired partner from Arthur Andersen and a former accounting professor, wrote an important essay entitled "Collectivization of Judgment," which first appeared in the *Arthur Andersen Chronicle* in January 1974.[14] He begins by asserting that professional judgment lies at the heart of the accounting profession, in part because few measurements, recognitions, and aggregations of accounting data can be undertaken in an objective fashion. Accounting is essentially subjective; thus, accountants must hone their individual professional judgment to carry out the tasks they take on. Society holds accountants responsible for their decisions, whether in their roles as corporate financial officers or as external auditors; hence they need to exercise good professional judgment to meet their responsibilities.

After noting these fundamental considerations, Miller focuses on the collectivization of judgment. He states that "[j]udgment develops from the interaction of education and experience." However, "the quality of the judgment developed by the interaction of education and experience is not automatically assured." Accounting firms and professional associations such as the AICPA engage in various activities that help increase the quality of a person's judgment.

Miller then contrasts judgment developed by a profession vis-à-vis judgment cultivated by a professional firm, and he argues that the profession's activities cannot enhance the quality of personal judgment nearly as much as partners and managers in the accounting firm. Essentially, the accounting profession has attempted to improve judgment by increasing the uniformity of accounting standards. Miller argues that creating rules under the guise of self-regulation does not enhance professional judgment by individual accountants because it replaces judgment with a sense of uniformity, whether uniformity is justified or not. Worse, if an audit problem develops, the accountant is held responsible for his or her mistakes, but the profession is not. Since the civil and criminal courts do not hold the profession responsible for the construction of bad rules, there is a disconnect between standard setting and consequences. The profession has a penchant for creating accounting and auditing rules, but these rules in fact reduce professional judgment.

Collectivization of judgment by the firm is quite a different matter to Miller. Because the firm suffers when the individual is hauled before civil or criminal court, the firm has incentives to develop the judgment of its personnel. In addition, senior partners can develop the professional judgment of junior partners by having the latter observe the problem-solving abilities of the former in real and specific instances. Likewise, junior partners can train managers and so on. The result is a firm that has a high quality of professional judgment.

While Miller's original essay concentrated on what he saw as encroachment on professional judgment by the AICPA (today he would say the FASB) as it legislates proper accounting and auditing, I am struck by its relevance today. As we view the ashes of Arthur Andersen, I wonder what happened to Miller's vision. Did the firm forget the wisdom of one of its own partners, or were other forces at play that led to the firm's demise?

Miller correctly anticipated the transition from a judgment-based to a rules-based profession. When he wrote this paper, the Accounting Principles Board had passed perhaps 27 of its 31 opinions. Today there are 148 Statements of Financial Accounting Standards, 7 Statements of Financial Accounting Concepts, and scores of interpretations and other related documents. The proliferation of accounting rules has truly been staggering. We cannot determine whether Miller is correct in his contention that this increase in rules has diminished professional judgment. If he is correct, such attenuation should be observed in all accounting firms.

On the other hand, Miller seems incorrect in his assertion that accounting firms can and does cultivate professional judgment in their own staff. The audit failures of Enron, Global Crossing, Waste Management, and Sunbeam—as well as others—serve as evidence to the contrary. For example, why did Arthur Andersen ever allow a partner in charge of an audit, such as David Duncan, to overrule a technical partner, such as Carl Bass? I find it amazing that a firm with the collective wisdom of Arthur Andersen could have such a breakdown in its own internal control system.

If Enron were the firm's only audit failure, we could talk about some renegade partner or two. But the number of audit failures by Arthur Andersen suggests instead disintegration in its own culture. Either Miller is wrong in his assertion about how firms develop professional judgment, or his own firm ignored him.

I believe that Herb Miller is generally correct and that what he says applies to issues of ethics and fairness as well as to evaluations of whether accounting methods are proper or improper. If the FASB does move toward principles-based accounting, principled individuals must carry out the tasks. Education can help, but accounting firms will carry most of the burden. If they can socialize their employees to do the right things and to value fairness to investors and creditors, we shall be well on our way to repairing the damage done to the U.S. economic system in recent years.

ANDERSEN'S ACCOUNTING COURT[15]

A number of accounting leaders and members of Congress have proposed some structure to investigate accounting issues. Most of these suggestions focus on accounting and auditing failures. Enron, of course, supplies the motivation for these initiatives. For example, James Copeland, CEO of Deloitte Touche Tohmatsu, has proposed a body similar to the National Transportation Safety Board. Just as that association examines air, rail, and auto catastrophes, the accounting body would probe for reasons behind financial failures.

Harvey Pitt, former chairman of the SEC, has suggested an organization that acts as an adjunct to the SEC. It would deal with ethical violations, while the SEC would handle criminal activities.

As I think about these proposals, my mind harkens back to the original proposal for such an organization. Leonard Spacek, then chief executive officer of Arthur Andersen, first proposed an Accounting Court in 1957.[16] While his idea differs from today's thoughts, it is worth exploring because it helps us to understand how the profession has evolved over the past 50 years and how we can make progress today.

Spacek concentrates on the myriad alternatives that exist for various accounting issues, all of which fall under the umbrella of GAAP. He begins with the fundamental observation that managers own the financial statements and that these executives have incentives to present the financial report "in the most favorable light." Spacek claims that public accountants have a responsibility for deciding which treatment is the best accounting method for the occasion. And there's the rub. Managers can counter that another alternative is equally a part of GAAP, and an auditor cannot force the company to apply the better method.

Spacek's solution is an Accounting Court. Corporate managers, external auditors, investors, creditors, and other stakeholders could take a particular case to the Accounting Court, which would scrutinize the facts of the situation. By applying accounting theory and accounting case law, the Accounting Court would judge what is the best accounting method for the case.

Spacek thought that the Committee on Accounting Procedure and the Accounting Principles Board were incapable of resolving accounting issues. If he were alive today, I assume he would say the same about the FASB and perhaps even the International Accounting Standards Board (IASB). He argued that "we need the case method of arriving at decisions on accounting principles." He thought that the legislative approach of the CAP, the APB, the FASB, and even the so-called principles-based approach of the IASB had too many generalities and could not, by their very nature, deal with the facts of a particular situation. Spacek also contended that legislative schemes could not challenge existing GAAP because they tend to freeze GAAP with certain multiple solutions. The legislative process not only immobilizes efforts to improve accounting, but also helps bad accounting methods to drive out good accounting ones. Spacek thought an Accounting Court would have to justify its choices, so the judges would tend to choose the better accounting principles and would tend to establish a case law that other firms and auditors would have to follow unless they could prove that a better accounting treatment existed. They would have to demonstrate this proof publicly before the court.[17]

In 1969, in *Unaccountable Accounting*, Abraham Briloff expanded the function of an accounting court to what he called a Trade Court.[18] Like Spacek's Accounting Court, the Trade Court would decide accounting principles on a case-by-case basis. Unlike Spacek's idea, Briloff's Trade Court would adjudicate lawsuits and criminal actions against corporate executives and directors and their auditors.

Copeland's idea is similar to Spacek's except that he waits until the patient dies before asking what medicine the doctor should have administered. At least Spacek understood the need to dispense medicine while the patient was still alive. Briloff apparently found Spacek's idea appealing but thought it needed additional teeth to make it work. Pitt's idea looks similar to Briloff's though all the teeth have been pulled.

As I look at the history of this concept of an Accounting Court, I find two aspects interesting. First, Leonard Spacek envisioned the need for improved accounting, and he proposed a significant, concrete way of striving for this ideal. If the profession had captured his vision, it likely would have improved financial reporting in this country and have staved off a lot of the problems that the profession finds itself in. The second aspect is the respect I feel for Leonard Spacek and my amazement at how Arthur Andersen has changed over the years. I doubt that the firm would have dropped out of auditing if Spacek had been at the helm.

SUMMARY AND CONCLUSION

As I have said several times, principles-based accounting standards require principled people. To have principled people, society needs to set in motion forces that will encourage behaviors that add to the common good and work for the public interest. At the same time it needs to have and use a series of disincentives for those who break the public trust. With respect to accounting, I agree with Levitt's oft-quoted declaration that we need a culture change.

The process is simple to state: Managers and their professional advisers have to renounce the philosophy of "earnings management" and replace it with an attitude that understands that investors and creditors are members of the business community. Managers must learn that investors and creditors are not outside the process—they are not the enemy and they are not to be despised. They are the capital customers of the business, and because of this, managers need to treat them with as much respect as they treat their product customers.[19]

A simple example explains the difference in viewpoint. Consider when a firm applies straight-line depreciation to a piece of equipment. Everyone in the business community understands that this is not an engineering marvel, for no one knows the life or the salvage value of the property, and thus the computation of depreciation is somewhat arbitrary and inaccurate. What happens next, however, depends very much on the mind-sets of managers and their professional advisers. One way of viewing this situation is to think of it as an opportunity to massage corporate earnings. If earnings otherwise are small this year, managers might lengthen the life of the equipment and increase the estimate of the salvage value. In this manner, depreciation expense is lowered and net income is increased. Alternatively, if earnings are healthy during this fiscal period, managers could decrease the life of the asset and reduce the salvage value. Depreciation is enlarged, but this protects the firm against the proverbial rainy day. Unfortunately, as we learned from the Waste Management case, this process eventually spirals out of control (the infinite loop of the Young model in Chapters 7 and 8).

The better approach is for managers to approach this depreciation computation with an eye to investors and creditors. Managers can attempt to determine as best it can what the life and the salvage value will be. Next, and very importantly, they would provide disclosures in the financial statements that provide details about how the business enterprise computes depreciation. Even better, the firm might create an Investors Committee of investors and creditors, with absolutely no one employed by the corporation on the committee. Managers could then ask this committee how to depreciate the property and what disclosures it would like to see so that business operations can best be understood.

We need a dream similar to Spacek's. He envisioned a business world in which managers would treat all financial statement readers with fairness. He argued that financial accounting should disclose what was necessary to allow a knowledgeable reader to possess all the material facts so that he or she could make an informed investment or credit or other business decision. If the business culture can capture this old vision, then investors and creditors would make capital more available and they would reduce the cost of capital. Managers add value to firms and to society when they treat investors, creditors, and other financial statement users fairly.

In practice, this improved culture must be tended with great care and patience. The best institution to develop and maintain this proper attitude between managers and the investment community is the firm. As Miller pointed out, others will not work as well because accounting firms have the authority and the responsibility to see that employees carry out these goals. Senior partners can teach and mentor young accountants in how to discharge their tasks professionally and ethically. Senior partners can reward and advance those who are objective and independent and maintain high integrity, and they can fire those less able. A well-functioning firm creates value not only for its professionals, but for the business and economic world as well.

While Miller focused his "collectivization of judgment" on the accounting firm, corporate managers certainly could employ the idea as well. Instead of promoting the notion of "earnings management," it would be so much more refreshing to hear a senior manager telling a young hire how to treat investors and creditors with fairness and integrity.

Principles-based accounting is a worthwhile idea to the extent that standard setters indicate the financial reporting goal for a new idea or new application, and they present some strategies as well. In practice, however, principles-based accounting is a pipedream because managers, lawyers, accountants, and investment bankers can easily bend and twist GAAP to manage the firm's earnings. Principles, such as those espoused by the International Accounting Standards Committee and now the International Accounting Standards Board, are so general and so subjective that firms can meet the letter of the law but do so in ways most unfair to investors and creditors. Spacek foresaw this when he advocated an Accounting Court. It is a useful idea for augmenting general accounting principles.

Last is the need for real enforcement. When managers or others do things that harm the investment community, they should be prosecuted to the utmost. To minimize criminal or tortuous behavior, society must punish the offenders. It is ludicrous that when managers and accountants at Enron, WorldCom, Adelphia, and Tyco broke the law, Congress passed the Sarbanes-Oxley bill. We do not need new rules when the old rules are broken. We need a justice system that punishes the wrongdoers. If federal prosecutors had dealt with the criminals at Boston Chicken, Waste Management, Sunbeam, and Cendant, then the current round of scandals likely would not have happened. In the same way, if we do not adequately deal with the felons this time, we can be sure that they or their clones will haunt us in the near future. Prison time or lawsuits would supply major disincentives to illicit behavior.

While I do not wish to end on a melodramatic note, I do view this time as a turning point. I am optimistic that much good is possible, given a new culture, a new ethic of fairness, firms that properly and thoroughly socialize their employees in strong professional commitments, an Accounting Court that can help sort out the details, and a justice system that makes it distasteful to cheat financial statement users. Without these changes, though, we should expect higher costs of capital throughout all sectors of the economy, thereby depressing asset prices. If the culture surrounding accounting becomes sufficiently bad, such as experienced during the early part of the 21st century, we can expect more dishonesty and more stock market crashes. We might even experience huge numbers of people withdrawing their funds from the stock market and perhaps even from the banking system. If we do not effect significant, meaningful changes, the consequences will prove calamitous.

The choice is ours. As for me, I choose the Arthur Andersen path of yesteryear.

NOTES

1. This text is adapted in part from my column "Telecom Swaps," which appeared on October 7, 2002, at: *www.SmartPros.com.* See A. Berenson, *The Numbers: How the Drive for Quarterly Earnings Corrupted Wall Street and Corporate America* (New York: Random House, 2003); B. L. Toffler, *Final Accounting: Ambition, Greed, and the Fall of Arthur Andersen* (New York: Broadway Books, 2003).

2. I simplify the example in the text. The opinion makes the situation more complex when cash is received or given. For details, see Accounting Principles Board Opinion No. 29, *Accounting for Nonmonetary Transactions* (New York: AICPA, 1973). For explanation, see D. E. Kieso, J. J. Weygandt, and T. D. Warfield, *Intermediate Accounting*, 10th ed. (New York: John Wiley & Sons, 2001), pp. 512–516.

3. See my article "Andersen's Accounting Postulate," *Accounting Today,* June 17–July 7, pp. 6–7.

4. Arthur Andersen, *The Postulate of Accounting: What It Is; How It Is Determined; How It Should Be Used* (Chicago: Arthur Andersen, 1960).

5. Ibid., pp. 3, 5, 25, and 29.

6. Ibid., p. 37.

7. Ibid., pp. pp. 40–42. I made the same point in Chapter 4. See Exhibit 4.2, especially panels B and C.

8. While Harvey Kapnick, Andersen's CEO after Spacek, wrote that we should consider dropping "fairly present" from the audit report, this stance should not be interpreted as a renunciation of Spacek's push for the principle for fairness. Kapnick explains that today's rules "are saddled with financial reporting concepts that place great reliance on historical cost, realization, and matching." See H. Kapnick, "Let's Abandon 'Generally Accepted,'" in R. R. Sterling, ed., *Institutional Issues in Public Accounting* (Lawrence, KS: Scholars Book Co., 1974), p. 384. In other words, Kapnick directed his criticism to the standard setters who enact rules that are unfair.

9. *U.S. v. Simon* [425 F.2d 796 (2d Cir. 1969)].

10. The three defendants, however, did not pay any penalty, for then-President Nixon pardoned them.

11. Quoted in A. J. Briloff, *The Truth about Corporate Accounting* (New York: Harper & Row, 1981), p. 5.

12. Magill and Previtts correctly point out that auditors have not realized the significance of the Continental Vending case and still think that generally accepted accounting principles would save them in court. See H. T. Magill and G. J. Previtts, *CPA Professional Responsibilities: An Introduction* (Cincinnati: South-Western Publishing, 1991). This thinking is quite dangerous as we recall that some of the underhanded tricks foisted on us by Enron's management actually met the letter of the law. Arthur Andersen failed in part because it relied on generally accepted accounting principles instead of fairness—as its predecessor warned it not to do.

13. I first wrote about this in "The Disintegration of Professional Judgment: Miller's 'Collectivization of Judgment,'" April 29, 2002; see: *www.SmartPros.com.* Also see Toffler, *Final Accounting*; and M. Swartz and S. Watkins, *Power Failure: The Inside Story of the Collapse of Enron* (New York: Doubleday, 2003).

14. H. E. Miller, "Collectivization of Judgment," *Arthur Andersen Chronicle* (January 1974), pp. 32–39.

15. This section is taken from my article "Andersen's Accounting Court," *Accounting Today,* July 22–August 4, 2002, pp. 6–7.

16. Leonard Spacek, "The Need for an Accounting Court," *The Accounting Review* (July 1958), pp. 368–379.

17. An interesting variation would have the FASB adopt a principles-based approach to develop a suitable framework and create an Accounting Court that would deal with the details of applying these principles to specific instances.

18. A. J. Briloff, *Unaccountable Accounting* (New York: Harper & Row, 1969).

19. P. Miller and P. R. Bahnson, *Quality Financial Reporting* (New York: McGraw-Hill, 2002).

Bibliography

Accounting Principles Board. (1970). *Conceptual Framework for Financial Accounting and Reporting: Elements of Financial Statements and Their Measurement*, APB Statement No. 4. New York: AICPA.

Accounting Principles Board. (1971). *The Equity Method of Accounting for Investments in Common Stock*, APB Opinion No. 18. New York: AICPA.

Accounting Principles Board. (1971). *Accounting Changes*, APB Opinion No. 20. New York: AICPA.

Accounting Principles Board. (1973). *Accounting for Nonmonetary Transactions*, APB Opinion No. 29. New York: AICPA.

Ackman, D. (2002). "Andrew Fastow, Fall Guy." *Forbes*. October 3.

Airline Financial News. (2002). "US Airways Awash in Problems Despite Guarantee." *Airline Financial News*. July 15.

Akst, D. (2002). "Why Business Needs a More Powerful S.E.C." *New York Times*. November 3.

Aldersley, J. (2002). "Mocking Myths Pays Dividends." *Sun Herald*. June 23.

Altman, E. I. (1968). "Financial Ratios, Discriminant Analysis and the Prediction of Corporate Bankruptcy." *Journal of Finance*. September, pp. 589–609.

Altman, E. I. (1971). *Corporate Bankruptcy in America*. New York: Heath.

Altman, E. I. (1993). *Corporate Financial Distress and Bankruptcy: A Complete Guide to Predicting and Avoiding Distress and Profiting from Bankruptcy*. New York: John Wiley & Sons.

American Accounting Association. (1977). *Statement on Accounting Theory and Theory Acceptance*. Report of Committee on Concepts and Standards for External Financial Reports. Sarasota FL: AAA.

American Bar Association. (2002). *Preliminary Report of the American Bar Association Task Force on Corporate Responsibility*. www.abanet.org/buslaw/corporateresponsibility/preliminary_report.pdf. July 16.

American Institute of Certified Public Accountants. (1992). *Code of Professional Conduct as amended January 14, 1992*. New York: AICPA.

American Institute of Certified Public Accountants. (1997). *Considerations of Fraud in a Financial Statement Audit*, Statement on Auditing Standards No. 82. New York: AICPA.

American Institute of Certified Public Accountants. (1997). *Serving the Public Interest: A New Conceptual Framework for Auditor Independence.* Submitted to the Independence Standards Board on October 20, 1997. Written by H. L. Pitt and D. E. Birenbaum.

Armstrong, M. B. (1987). "Moral Development and Accounting Education." *Journal of Accounting Education.* Spring, pp. 27–43.

Armstrong, M. B. (1993). *Ethics and Professionalism for CPAs.* Cincinnati, OH: South-Western Publishing.

Armstrong, M. B., J. E. Ketz, and D. Owsen. (2003). "Ethics Education in Accounting: Moving Towards Ethical Motivation and Ethical Behavior." *Journal of Accounting Education*, pp. 1–16.

Arthur Andersen. (1960). *The Postulate of Accounting: What It Is; How It Is Determined; How It Should Be Used.* Chicago: Arthur Andersen.

Associated Press. (2002). "US Airways Files Bankruptcy Plan." *New York Times.* December 22.

Association for Investment Management and Research. (1993). *Financial Reporting in the 1990s and Beyond.* Charlottesville VA: AIMR.

Ayres, F. L., and D. E. Logue. (2002). "Risk Management in the Shadow of Enron." *Journal of Business Strategy.* July–August.

"Badly in Need of Repair—Company Reports—Companies' Accounts Are Badly in Need of Repair." (2002). *The Economist.* May 4.

Balsi, J., D. Kruse, and A. Bernstein. *In the Company of Owners: The Truth about Stock Options (And Why Every Employee Should Have Them).* New York: Basic Books.

Bank and Lender Liability Litigation Reporter. (2002). "How Scrutiny of SPEs Will Affect Financing in the Middle Market." *Bank and Lender Liability Litigation Reporter.* August 29.

Barboza, D. (2002). "El Paso's Off-Balance Sheet Partnerships Baffle Analysts." *Milwaukee Journal Sentinel.* July 23.

Barboza, D. (2002). "Dynegy to Pay $3 Million in Settlement with S.E.C." *New York Times.* September 25, p. C6.

Barrionuevo, A., J. Weil, and J. R. Wilke. (2002). "Enron's Fastow Charged with Fraud-Complaint by U.S. Signals Peril for Other Ex-Officials; Merrill Lynch Role Is Cited." *Wall Street Journal.* October 3, p. A3.

Bazerman, M. H., G. Loewenstein, and D. A. Moore. (2002). "Why Good Accountants Do Bad Audits." *Harvard Business Review.* November, pp. 97–102.

Beams, F. A., J. H. Anthony, R. P. Clement, and S. H. Lowensohn. (2003). *Advanced Accounting*, 8th ed. Upper Saddle River, NJ: Prentice-Hall.

Beauprez, J. (2002). "Reforming Corporate Boards on Agenda: Directors too Close to Execs, Critics Say." *Denver Post.* June 9.

Bebeau, M. J. (1994). "Influencing the Moral Dimension of Dental Practice." In Rest and Varvaez, ed., *Moral Development in the Professions.* Hillsdale, NJ: Lawrence Erlbaum Associates.

Beckett, P., and J. Sapsford. (2002). "Energy Deals Made $200 Million in Fees for Citigroup, J. P. Morgan." *Wall Street Journal.* July 24.

Bedipo-Memba, A. (1998). "Boston Chicken Files for Protection, Lays Off 500, Shuts 178 Restaurants." *Wall Street Journal*. October 6.

Behr, P., and A. Witt. (2002). "Visionary's Dream Led to Risky Business." *Washington Post*. July 28, p. A01.

Behr, P., and A. Witt. (2002). "Dream Job Turns into a Nightmare." *Washington Post*. July 29, p. A01.

Behr, P., and A. Witt. (2002). "Concerns Grow Amid Conflicts." *Washington Post*. July 30, p. A01.

Behr, P., and A. Witt. (2002). "Losses, Conflicts Threaten Survival." *Washington Post*. July 31, p. A01.

Behr, P., and A. Witt. (2002). "Hidden Debts, Deals Scuttle Last Chance." *Washington Post*. August 1, p. A01.

Berenson, A. (2002). "Changing the Definition of Cash Flow Helped Tyco." *New York Times*. December 31.

Berenson, A. (2003). *The Number: How the Drive for Quarterly Earnings Corrupted Wall Street and Corporate America*. New York: Random House.

Bergsman, S. (2002). "Serious Questions about Synthetic Leases." *National Real Estate Investor*. May 1.

Bergsman, S. (2002). "Scrutinizing Synthetic Leases." *Shopping Center World*. July 1.

Berkowitz, A. L. (2002). *Enron: A Professional's Guide to the Events, Ethical Issues, and Proposed Reforms*. Chicago: Commerce Clearing House.

Bilodeau, O. (2002). "Lawyers Fingered in Enron Report." *Fulton County Daily Report*. October 11.

Birnbaum, J. H. (2002). "It's Time for Him to Go." *Fortune*. October 28, pp. 99, 100, 102.

Bloom, A. (1987). *The Closing of the American Mind: How Higher Education Has Failed Democracy and Impoverished the Souls of Today's Students*. New York: Simon and Schuster.

Borrus, A., and P. Dwyer. (2002). "To Expense or Not to Expense." *Business Week*. July 29.

Boynton, W. C., and W. G. Kell. (1996). *Modern Auditing*, 6th ed. New York: John Wiley & Sons.

Bradshaw, M. T., S. A. Richardson, and R. G. Sloan. (2001). "Do Analysts and Auditors Use Information in Accruals?" *Journal of Accounting Research*. June, pp. 45–74.

Brannigan, M., and N. Harris. (2002). "Delta Air Changes Pension Plan to Slash Costs over Five Years." *Wall Street Journal*. November 19.

Brealey, R. A., and S. C. Myers. (2002). *Principles of Corporate Finance*, 7th ed. New York: McGraw Hill-Irwin.

Brewster, M. (2003). *Unaccountable: How the Accounting Profession Forfeited a Public Trust*. Hoboken, NJ: John Wiley & Sons.

Brigham, E. F., and J. F. Houston. (1998). *Fundamentals of Financial Management*, 8th ed. New York: Dryden.

Briloff, A. J. (1972). *Unaccountable Accounting*. New York: Harper & Row.

Briloff, A. J. (1976). *More Debits than Credits*. New York: Harper & Row.

Briloff, A. J. (1981). *The Truth about Corporate Accounting*. New York: Harper & Row.

Broder, D. S. (2003). "A Budget of Dire Consequences." *Washington Post*. March 30.

Brooks, L. (2000). *Professional Ethics for Accountants*, 2nd ed. Minneapolis, MN: West.

Brown, K. (2002). "Creative Accounting: How to Buff a Company." *Wall Street Journal*. February 21.

Brown, K. (2002). "Heard on the Street: Andersen Staff Works to Tie Up Loose Ends-Andersen Might Face More Legal Problems Beyond Guilty Verdict." *Wall Street Journal*. June 17.

Brown, K. (2002). "Heard on the Street: Auditors' Methods Make It Hard to Uncover Fraud by Executives." *Wall Street Journal*. July 8.

Brown, K. (2003). "Heard on the Street: Analysts: Still Coming Up Rosy When Looking to Future Profits." *Wall Street Journal*. January 27.

Bryan-Low, C. (2002). "Heard on the Street: Pension Funds Take Spotlight—Numbers Released by S&P Bring Attention to Issue of Accounting for Costs." *Wall Street Journal*. October 25.

Bryan-Low, C. (2002). "Weak Pension Funds Become the Market's Latest Worry." *Wall Street Journal*. November 17.

Bryan-Low, C. (2002). "SEC May Take Tougher Tone on Accountants in Bad Audits." *Wall Street Journal*. December 13.

Bryan-Low, C., and K. Brown. (2002). "And Now, the Question Is: Where's the Next Enron? Accounting Textbooks Will Get Rewritten, but Few Practices in the Industry Might Change." *Wall Street Journal*. June 18, p. C1.

Bryan-Low, C., and K. Brown. (2002). "Questioning the Books: After Enron, Accounting Reform Is Slow to Come—Lack of Progress Risks Loss of Investor Confidence." *Asian Wall Street Journal*. June 19, p. A5.

Bryan-Low, C., and C. Mollenkamp. (2003). "'Off the Books' Cleanup Turns Out to Be Tough." *Wall Street Journal*. January 13.

Bryce, R. (2002). *Pipe Dreams: Greed, Ego, and the Death of Enron*. Cambridge, MA: Perseus Book Group.

Buffett, W. (2001 and earlier). Chairman's Letter to BerkshireHathaway Shareholders. www.berkshirehathaway.com/letters.

Buffett, W. (2002). "Stock Options, the Megabucks Battle." *Mercury News*. April 15.

Burkholder, S. (2002). "Former SEC Accountants, Ex-FASB Chairman Offer Advice, Caution on Post-Enron Reforms." *Pension & Benefits Reporter*. March 5.

Bush, G. W. (2002). "Speech in New York City, July 9." *Wall Street Journal*. July 9.

"Bush Seeks Tougher Penalties in Assault on Corporate Fraud." (2002). *Wall Street Journal*. July 9.

"Bush Selects Donaldson for Top Post at the SEC." (2002). *Wall Street Journal*. December 10.

Business Wire. (2002). "Fitch Rates Constellation Energy's $500MM Senior Notes 'A–'." *Business Wire*. August 27.

Business Wire. (2002). "NRG Energy, Inc. Updates Financial Situation." *Business Wire*. September 16.

Business Wire. (2002). "Willis Lease Finance Closes New, Increased Warehouse Credit Facility and Announces Partners for Planned Securitization." *Business Wire*. September 17.

Butler, J. R. Jr., and J. E. Steiner. (2001). "New Rules of Engagement for Workouts: REMICs and Distressed Real Estate Loans." *Real Estate Issues*. January 1.

Byron, C. (2002). "Krispy Kreme Bites." *New York Post*. February 11.

Calabro, L. (2002). "I Told You So." *CFO Magazine*. September 10.

Carcello, J. V., D. R. Hermanson, and T. L. Neal. (2002). "Disclosures in Audit Committee Charters and Reports." *Accounting Horizons*. December, pp. 291–304.

Carmichael, D. R., D. Guy, and L. A. Lach. (2003). *Ethics for CPAs: Meeting Expectations in Challenging Times*. New York: John Wiley & Sons.

CBS News. (2000). "IBM Workers: Pension Change Hurts." *CBS News*. April 25.

Ceron, G. F. (2002). "Schwab Annual Report Spells Out Synthetic Lease Details." *Dow Jones Newswires*. May 2.

"CFOs to the Rescue: After Enron and AHERF, Financial Oversight Is Playing a Far More Pivotal Role." (2002). *Modern Healthcare*. June 17.

Chang, J. (2002). "Wall Street Sharpens Focus on Off-Balance Sheet Items: Impact on Chemical Industry Has Been Negligible as Companies Have Provided Reasonable Disclosures." *Chemical Market Reporter*. April 8.

Chen, K. (2002). "Unfunded Pension Liabilities Soared in 2001 to $111 Billion." *Wall Street Journal*. July 26.

Cheney, G. (2003). "FASB Scrambles for Funds in Power Struggle with SEC." *Accounting Today*. March 17–April 6, p. 14.

Clendenning, A. (2002). "Preventing 'Enronitis:' Companies Coming Clean About Anything that Could Smell Fishy." *Pittsburgh Post-Gazette*. February 16, p. A7.

Coallier, D. L. (2002). "Buyer Beware of Off-the-Books Funding: An Enron-Inspired Accounting Change Would Force Acquirers to Determine Whether They Have Bought a Live Time Bomb." *Mergers and Acquisitions Journal*. October 1.

"Communicating Trustworthiness." (2002). *International Accounting Bulletin*. June 14.

Cramer, J. J. (2002). "Mr. Levitt's Legacy." *Wall Street Journal*. December 5.

Crenshaw, A. B., and B. D. Fromson. (2002). "A Conflict for CPAs?" *Washington Post*. March 29, 1998, p. H1.

Crouhy, M. (2000). *Risk Management*. New York: McGraw-Hill.

Cruver, B. (2002). *Anatomy of Greed: The Unshredded Truth from an Enron Insider*. New York: Carroll and Graf Publishers.

Cummins, C., and A. Barrionuevo. (2002). "El Paso Investors Question Booking of Power Contracts." *Wall Street Journal*. July 23.

Damodaran, A. (1996). *Investment Valuation: Tools and Techniques for Determining the Value of Any Asset*. New York: John Wiley & Sons.

Davenport, T. (2002). "In Focus: SEC Proposal Could Cloud Off-Balance Sheet Picture." *American Banker*. November 4.

Davidson, S., ed. (1979). *The Accounting Establishment in Perspective*. Chicago: Arthur Young & Company.

Davis, M. (2002). "Questions Raised about El Paso's Corp.'s Bond Deal, Trading Liabilities." *Houston Chronicle*. July 11.

Davis, M. (2003). "Tyco Topples Cash Flow Target." www.thestreet.com. January 22.

Day, K. (2002). "SEC Borrows Executives as Advisers: Some Question Use of Accountants from Major Auditing Firms." *Washington Post*. June 8.

Day, K. (2003). "SEC Staff Urges Limit to Reforms." *Washington Post*. January 22, p. E01.

Day, K. (2003). "SEC Allows Auditors as Tax Consultants: Agency Abandons Proposed Ban." *Washington Post*. January 23, p. A01.

Deener, B. (2002). "Corporate Directors Return to School for Training Seminars." *Dallas Morning News*. June 10.

Delaney, P. R., B. J. Epstein, J. A. Adler, and M. F. Foran. (2000). *GAAP 2000: Interpretation and Application of Generally Accepted Accounting Principles 2000*. New York: John Wiley & Sons.

DeMarco, D. (1996). *The Heart of Virtue: Lessons from Life and Literature Illustrating the Beauty and Value of Moral Character*. San Francisco, CA: Ignatius Press.

de Teran, N. (2002). "CDOs Mushroom Despite a Slide in Their Ratings." *eFinancial News*. June 12.

Dingell, J. D. (2001). Unpublished Letter to David Walker, General Accounting Office. January 17.

Dingwall, R., and P. Lewis, eds. (1983). *The Sociology of the Professions: Lawyers, Doctors and Others*. London: Macmillan.

Dini, J. (2002). "Can One Good Man Save Accounting?" *Institutional Investor*. July 1.

DiStefano, J. N. (2002). "SEC Makes Allegations about PNC Financial's Accounting Reports." *Philadelphia Inquirer*. July 19.

Dirsmith M., and J. E. Ketz. (1987). "A Fifty-Cent Test: An Approach to Teaching Integrity." *Advances in Accounting*, pp. 129–141.

Dobson, J., and M. B. Armstrong. (1995). "Applications of Virtue Ethics Theory: A Lesson from Architecture." *Research on Accounting Ethics*, pp. 187–202.

Doherty, J. (2002). "Pay Me Later? An Increase in Underfunded Pension Plans Could Pose Trouble for Companies and Shareholders." *Barron's*. October 21.

Dow Jones Business News. (2002). "GE Sees 1st-Quarter Charge of About $1 Billion from Goodwill Elimination." *Dow Jones*. March 8.

Dow Jones Business News. (2002). "Andersen Partner Was Barred after Criticizing Enron Deals." *Wall Street Journal*. May 10.

Dow Jones Business News. (2002). "Elan to Take $542 Million in Charges for 3rd Quarter." *Dow Jones Business News*. September 30.

Dow Jones Corporate Filings Alert. (2002). "General Motors Details Use of Special Purpose Entities." *Dow Jones*. February 25.

Dow Jones Corporate Filings Alert. (2002). "Goodyear Tire Had $339.2M Invested in SPE at June 30." *Dow Jones*. August 7.

Dow Jones Newswires. (2002). "Northwest Will Take a Charge of $700 Million for Pensions." *Wall Street Journal*. November 6.

Drawbaugh, K. (2002). "US SEC Proposes Pro Forma, Off-Balance Sheet Rules." *Reuters English News Service*. October 31.

Drawbaugh, K. (2003). "SEC Wavers on Post-Enron Auditor, Lawyer." *Forbes*. January 21.

Dugan, I. J. (2002). "A Decade of Greed Undid a Once-Proud Profession." *College Journal from the Wall Street Journal*. www.collegejournal.com.

Duhigg, C. (2002). "Ethicists at the Gate: Can Harvard Business School Make Its Graduates Behave?" *Boston Globe*. December 8.

Eavis, P. (2002). "Many Numbers Still Don't Add Up at Tyco." www.TheStreet.com. December 31.

Eichenwald, K. (2002). "Enron Ruling Leaves Corporate Advisers Open to Lawsuits." *New York Times*. December 23.

EIU Viewswire. (2002). "USA Finance-Commercial Paper Chase." *CFO Magazine*. June 27.

Elstein, A. (2002). "GE Sheds Light on Its Finances—in Its Annual Report, Conglomerate Provides More Detailed Profit Figures—Company Tries to Reassure Investors in the Wake of Enron's Collapse." *Asian Wall Street Journal*. March 11.

Emerging Issues Task Force. (1990). *Impact of Nonsubstantive Lessors, Residual Value Guarantees, and Other Provisions in Leasing Transactions*, EITF 90–15. Stamford CT: EITF.

Emshwiller, J. R. (2002). "Enron's 'SPE' Transactions Raise Questions on Roles of Executives." *Wall Street Journal*. September 30.

Epstein, M. J. and A. D. Spalding, Jr. (1993). *The Accountant's Guide to Legal Liability and Ethics*. Homewood, IL: Irwin.

Etzioni, A. (2002). "When It Comes to Ethics, B-Schools Get an F." *Washington Post*. August 4, p. B4.

"Faith in Corporate Ethics Not Yet Restored." (2002). www.SmartPros.com. December 9.

Fabozzi, F. J. (2000). *Fixed Income Analysis for the Chartered Financial Analyst Program*. New York: Fabozzi Associates.

Feldstein, D. (2002). "What Was Bottom Line at Enron? Disturbing Signs Not Easy to Spot in Annual Report." *Houston Chronicle*. March 18.

Financial Accounting Standards Board. (1975). *Accounting for Contingencies*, SFAS No. 5. Stamford, CT: FASB.

Financial Accounting Standards Board. (1976). *Accounting for Leases*, SFAS No. 13. Stamford, CT: FASB.

Financial Accounting Foundation (1977). *Statement of Position on Study Entitled, "The Accounting Establishment."* Stamford, CT: FASB.

Financial Accounting Standards Board. (1978). *Objectives of Financial Reporting by Business Enterprises*, SFAC No. 1. Stamford, CT: FASB.

Financial Accounting Standards Board. (1980). *Accounting and Reporting by Defined Benefit Pension Plans*, SFAS No. 35. Stamford, CT: FASB.

Financial Accounting Standards Board. (1981). *Disclosure of Long-Term Obligations*, SFAS No. 47. Stamford, CT: FASB.

Financial Accounting Standards Board. (1982). *Related Party Disclosures*, SFAS No. 57. Stamford, CT: FASB.

Financial Accounting Standards Board. (1985). *Employers' Accounting for Pensions*, SFAS No. 87. Stamford, CT: FASB.

Financial Accounting Standards Board. (1985). *Employers' Accounting for Settlements and Curtailments of Defined Benefit Pension Plans and for Termination Benefits*, SFAS No. 88. Stamford, CT: FASB.

Financial Accounting Standards Board. (1985). *Elements of Financial Statements*, SFAC No. 6. Stamford, CT: FASB.

Financial Accounting Standards Board. (1990). *Employers' Accounting for Postretirement Benefits Other than Pensions*, SFAS No. 106. Norwalk, CT: FASB.

Financial Accounting Standards Board. (1993). *Accounting for Certain Investments in Debt and Equity Securities*, SFAS No. 115. Norwalk, CT: FASB.

Financial Accounting Standards Board. (1995). *Accounting for Stock-Based Compensation*, SFAS No. 123. Norwalk, CT: FASB.

Financial Accounting Standards Board. (1998). *Employers' Disclosures about Pensions and Other Postretirement Benefits: An Amendment of FASB Statements No. 87, 88, and 106*, SFAS No. 132. Norwalk, CT: FASB.

Financial Accounting Standards Board. (2000). *Accounting for Transfers and Servicing of Financial Assets and Extinguishments of Liabilities*, SFAS No. 140. Norwalk, CT: FASB.

Financial Accounting Standards Board. (2001). *Business Combinations*, SFAS No. 141. Norwalk, CT: FASB.

Financial Accounting Standards Board. (2001). *Goodwill and Other Intangible Assets*, SFAS No. 142. Norwalk, CT: FASB.

Financial Accounting Standards Board. (2002). *Proposal for a Principles-Based Approach to U.S. Standard Setting*. Norwalk, CT: FASB.

Financial Accounting Standards Board. (2002). *Consolidation of Certain Special-Purpose Entities*. Proposed Interpretation. June 28. Norwalk, CT: FASB.

Financial Accounting Standards Board. (2002). *Guarantor's Accounting and Disclosure Requirements for Guarantees, Including Indirect Guarantees of Indebtedness of Others*, Interpretation No. 45. Norwalk, CT: FASB.

Financial Accounting Standards Board. (2003). *Consolidation of Variable Interest Entities*, Interpretation No. 46. Norwalk, CT: FASB.

Financial Accounting Standards Board. (2003). *Accounting for Stock-Based Compensation-Transition and Disclosure*, Statement No. 148. Norwalk, CT: FASB.

Financial Executives International. (2002). "Special Purpose Entities: Understanding the Guidelines." *FEI Issues Alert*. January.

Fink, R. (2002). "The Fear of all Sums: To Restore Investor Trust, Many Companies Are Disclosing More Information, According to a CFO Survey. But It May Not Be Enough." *CFO Magazine*. August 1.

Flesher, D. L., and T. K. Flesher. (1986). "Ivar Kreuger's Contribution to U.S. Financial Reporting." *The Accounting Review*. July, pp. 421–434.

Fox, L. (2003). *Enron: The Rise and Fall*. Hoboken, NJ: John Wiley & Sons.

France, M., and D. Carney. "Why Corporate Crooks Are Tough to Nail." *Business Week*. July 1.

Freeman, J. (2002). "Who Will Audit the Regulators?" *Wall Street Journal*. July 8.

Friedson, E. (1986). *Professional Powers: A Study of the Institutionalization of Formal Knowledge*. Chicago, IL: University of Chicago Press.

Galbraith, S. (2003). "With Guidance Like This . . . ." *Wall Street Journal*. January 7.

Garver, R. (2002). "FASB Proposes Special-Entity Asset Pullback." *American Banker*. July 2.

Gately, E. (2002). "U-Haul Parent Alters Accounting Practices amid Greater Scrutiny." *East Valley Tribune*. August 27.

General Accounting Office (GAO). (1996). *The Accounting Profession: Major Issues: Progress and Concerns*. Report to the Chairman, Committee on Commerce, U.S. House of Representatives. Washington, DC: GAO. September.

General Accounting Office (GAO). (2002). *Financial Statement Restatements: Trends, Market Impacts, Regulatory Responses, and Remaining Challenges*. Report to the Chairman, Committee on Banking, Housing, and Urban Affairs, U.S. Senate. Washington, DC: GAO. October.

Georgiades, G. (2001). *Miller GAAP Financial Statement Disclosures Manual*. New York: Aspen.

Glass, D. L. (2002). "Can Fed Strike a Post-Enron Regulatory Balance?" *American Banker*. June 20.

Glater, J. D. (2003). "Pricewaterhouse Taking a Stand, and a Big Risk." *New York Times*. January 1.

Glazer, A. S., and H. R. Jaenicke. (2002). "A Pathology of the Independence Standards Board's Conceptual Framework Project." *Accounting Horizons*. December, pp. 329–352.

Goldstein, M. (2002). "Avoiding the Next Enron." *Dow Jones News Service*. February 14.

Goldstein, M. (2002). "Avoiding the Next Enron [Part 2]." *Dow Jones News Service*. February 15.

Gombola, M. J., and J. E. Ketz. (1983). "A Note on Cash Flow and Classification Patterns of Financial Ratios." *Accounting Review*. January, pp. 105–114.

Gombola, M. J., and J. E. Ketz. (1983). "Financial Ratio Patterns in Retail and Manufacturing Organizations." *Financial Management*. Summer, pp. 45–56.

Gordon, M. (2003). "Bush Asks Congress to Approve Larger Budget for SEC." *Philadelphia Inquirer*. February 4.

Gough, R. W. (1998). *Character Is Destiny: The Value of Personal Ethics in Everyday Life*. Rocklin, CA: Prima Publishing.

Greenman, F. E. (1999). "Business School Ethics—An Overlooked Topic." *Business and Society Review*. Summer, pp. 171–176.

Hartgraves A. L., and G. J. Benston. (2002). "The Evolving Accounting Standards for Special Purpose Entities and Consolidations." *Accounting Horizons*. September, pp. 245–258.

Hawkins, D. F., and W. J. Campbell. (1978). *Equity Valuation: Models, Analysis and Implications*. Charlottesville, VA: Financial Executives Research Foundation.

Hendriksen, E. S. (1970). *Accounting Theory*, 2nd ed. Homewood, IL: Irwin.

Henriques, D. B. (2002). "Chairman of S.E.C. Faces Time of Testing." *New York Times*. November 3.

Higgins, R. C. (2000). *Analysis for Financial Management*. New York: Irwin.

Higson, C. (2001). "Did Enron's Investors Fool Themselves?" *Business Strategy Review*. Issue 4, pp. 1–6.

Hill, A., and A. Hill. (1997). *Just Business: Christian Ethics for the Marketplace*. Downers Grove, IL: Intervarsity Press.

Hill, A., and A. Michaels. (2002). "Hostile Terrain." *Financial Times*. August 13.

Hilzenrath, D. S. (2002). "Big Four Firms Face Post-Enron Scrutiny." *Washington Post*. June 7.

Hilzrenrath, D. S. (2003). "Big Firms Avoiding SEC Ire." *Washington Post*. January 17, p. E01.

Homer, E. (2002). "Sale/Leaseback Flow to Swell as FASB Prepares to Drain Synthetic Leases." *Private Placement Letter*. June 17.

Homer, E. (2002). "Synthetic Leases: Extinct, or Just Evolving?" *Asset Securitization Report*. July 8.

Homer, E. (2002). "Synthetic Intelligence: How Will FASB Decisions Truly Affect Synthetic Issues?" *Private Placement Letter*. July 8.

Homer, E. (2002). "Synthetic Leases—One Hundred, Fifty-four Million Dollars." *Asset Securitization Report*. September 9.

Homer, E. (2002). "Lease Pros Come Out Swinging at Synthetic Lease/CTL Conference." *Private Placement Letter*. November 4.

Horrigan, J. O. (1966). "The Determination of Long-Term Credit Standing with Financial Ratios." *Journal of Accounting Research*. Supplement, pp. 44–62.

Howell, R. (2002). "How Accounting Executives Looked the Wrong Way." *Financial Times*. August 13.

Huffington, A. (2003). *Pigs at the Trough: How Corporate Greed and Political Corruption Are Undermining America*. New York: Crown Publishers.

Hughes, J. (2002). "Ethics in a Culture of Greed." *Christian Science Monitor*. July 3.

Hussein, M. E., and J. E. Ketz. (1980). "Ruling Elites of the FASB: A Study of the Big Eight." *Journal of Accounting Auditing and Finance*. Summer, pp. 354–367.

Hussein, M. E., and J. E. Ketz. (1991). "Accounting Standards-Setting in the U.S.: An Analysis of Power and Social Exchange." *Journal of Accounting and Public Policy*. Spring, pp. 59–81.

Ijiri, Y. (1980). *Recognition of Contractual Rights and Obligations*. Research Report. Stamford, CT: FASB.

Ingram, M. (2002). "Financial Disclosure Is Good—But It Doesn't Always Help." *The Globe and Mail*. February 5, p. B16.

Ivanovich, D. (2002). "Economist Raised Doubts about Partnerships/ Enron Researcher Raised Issue in '99." *Houston Chronicle*. March 19.

Ivanovich, D., and S. Brewer. (2002). "The Andersen Verdict: Verdict May Aid Government's Case Against Enron." *Houston Chronicle*. June 16.

Jarnagin, B. D. (2000). *2001 U.S. Master GAAP Guide*. Chicago, IL: Commerce Clearing House.

Johnson, T. J. (1972). *Professions and Power*. London: Macmillan.

Julavits, R. (2002). "Labor Department Probing PNC's Accounting Snafu." *American Banker*. August 15.

Julavits, R. (2002). "PNC Leadership Changes May Be Far from Over." *American Banker*. August 19.

Kansas, D. (2002). "Plain Talk: Pension Liabilities a Big Concern." *Dow Jones News Service*. October 1.

Kapnick, H. (1974). "Let's Abandon 'Generally Accepted.'" In R. R. Sterling, ed. *Institutional Issues in Public Accounting*. Lawrence, KS: Scholars Book Co.

Keegan, J., and B. Tunick. (2002). "Shell Shocked." *Investment Dealers Digest*. July 8.

Keeton, A. (2002). "Boeing CEO Assures Investors on Special Purpose Entity." *Dow Jones News Service*. March 19.

Ketz, J. E. (1998). "Is There an Epidemic of Underauditing?" *Journal of Corporate Accounting and Finance*. Fall, pp. 25–35.

Ketz, J. E. (2002). "The Pitfalls of Accounting." *Accounting Today*. February 25–March 17, pp. 7, 10.

Ketz, J. E. (2002). "FASB: Carpe Diem Before You Start Smelling Like Carp!" *Accounting Today*. April 8–21, pp. 9, 26.

Ketz, J. E. (2002). "The Disintegration of Professional Judgment: Miller's 'Collectivization of Judgment.'" www.SmartPros.com. April 29.

Ketz, J. E. (2002). "Financial Analysts Should Analyze the Financials." www.SmartPros.com. May 6.

Ketz, J. E. (2002). "More Rhetoric Will Not Prevent Future Enrons." *Accounting Today*. May 6–19, pp. 7, 33.

Ketz, J. E. (2002). "Adelphia Is Latest Example of Awful Accounting." *Accounting Today*. May 20–June 2, p. 7.

Ketz, J. E. (2002). "Harvey Pitt Has to Go." www.SmartPros.com. May 22.

Ketz, J. E. (2002). "Can We Prevent Future Enrons?" *Journal of Corporate Accounting and Finance*. May–June 2002, pp. 3–11.

Ketz, J. E. (2002). "Andersen's Accounting Postulate." *Accounting Today*. June 17–July 7, pp. 6–7.

Ketz, J. E. (2002). "The Andersen Verdict: Questions Worth Asking." www.SmartPros.com. July 15.

Ketz, J. E. (2002). "Andersen's Accounting Court." *Accounting Today*. July 22–August 4, pp. 6–7.

Ketz, J. E. (2002). "Harvey Pitt Has to Go: Part Deux." www.SmartPros.com. August 5.

Ketz, J. E. (2002). "The Market Cannot Police Itself." *Accounting Today*. August 5–18, pp. 6, 9.

Ketz, J. E. (2002). "Yawn—Another Bush Speech: Does the President Get It?" www.SmartPros.com. August 19.

Ketz, J. E. (2002). "Why Simpler Isn't Necessarily Better." www.SmartPros.com. September 9.

Ketz, J. E. (2002). "CEO Certifications: 'D' is for Drivel." www.SmartPros.com. September 16.

Ketz, J. E. (2002). "FASB, O FASB, Where Is Thy Sting?" www.SmartPros.com. September 23.

Ketz, J. E. (2002). "Merrill's Stab at Quality of Earnings." *Accounting Today*. September 23–October 6, pp. 8, 25.

Ketz, J. E. (2002). "Telecom Swaps: The SEC Finally Arrives at the Scene of the Crime." www.SmartPros.com. October 7.

Ketz, J. E. (2002). "Big Bad John Biggs." www.SmartPros.com. October 31.

Ketz, J. E. (2002). "Principles-Based Standards." www.SmartPros.com. December 16.

Ketz, J. E. (2002). "Why Didn't the Private-Sector Watchdogs Bark?" *Accounting Today.* November 25–December 15, pp. 8–9.

Ketz, J. E. (2003). "What Happens When Government Is of the CEO, by the CEO, and for the CEO?" *Accounting Today.* Forthcoming.

Ketz, J. E. (2003). "Corporate Governance: As Oxymoronic as Business Ethics." *Accounting Today.* January 27–February 9, pp. 6, 34.

Ketz, J. E., R. Doogar, and D. E. Jensen. (1990). *Cross-Industry Analysis of Financial Ratios: Comparabilities and Corporate Performance.* New York: Quorum Books.

Ketz, J. E., and J. A. Largay III. (1987). "Reporting Income and Cash Flows from Operations." *Accounting Horizons.* June, pp. 9–17.

Ketz, J. E., and P. B. W. Miller. (1997). "Some Ethical Issues About Financial Reporting and Public Accounting and Some Proposals." *Research on Accounting Ethics.* Pp. 49–77.

Ketz, J. E., and P. B. W. Miller. (1997). "Bury 'Dumb Analysts' Argument." *Accounting Today.* June 2–15, pp. 14, 16.

Ketz, J. E., and P. B. W. Miller. (1997). "Time to Stop Pfooling Around." *Accounting Today.* September 22–October 5, pp. 28, 31.

Ketz, J. E., and P. B. W. Miller. (1997). "Pfooling Around: the Psequel." *Accounting Today.* November 10–23, pp. 14, 17.

Ketz, J. E., and P. B. W. Miller. (1998). "Looking at a White Paper Through Rose-Colored Glasses." *Accounting Today.* February 9–22, pp. 12, 16.

Ketz, J. E., and P. B. W. Miller. (1998). "Financial Accounting Fairness Act: Fairness to Whom?" *Accounting Today.* May 25–June 7, pp. 14, 17.

Ketz, J. E., and P. B. W. Miller. (1999). "Elan Managers Play the Market for a Sucker." *Accounting Today.* November 22–December 12, pp. 14, 16, 17.

Kidder, R. M. (1996). *How Good People Make Tough Choices: Resolving the Dilemmas of Ethical Living.* New York: Fireside.

Kieso, D. E., J. J. Weygandt, and T. D. Warfield. (2001). *Intermediate Accounting*, 10th ed. New York: John Wiley & Sons.

Kindleberger, C. P. (2000). *Manias, Panics, and Crashes: A History of Financial Crises*, 4th ed. New York: John Wiley & Sons.

KPMG v. Securities and Exchange Commission. "United States Court of Appeals for the District of Columbia Circuit." Argued February 15, 2002. Decided May 14, 2002. No. 01-1131.

Kohlberg, L. (1984). *The Psychology of Moral Development*, 2nd ed. San Francisco, CA: Harper & Row.

Kolb, R. W. (1999). *Futures, Options, and Swaps*, 3rd ed. Malden, MA: Blackwell.

Krantz, M. (2001). "One-Time Charges? Not Always." *USA Today.* November 21.

Labaton, S. (2002). "New Rules on Accountants, but Also Questions." *New York Times.* July 26.

Labaton, S. (2002). "Audit Overseer Cited Problems in Previous Post." *New York Times.* October 31.

Labaton, S. (2002). "Government Report Details a Chaotic S.E.C. Under Pitt." *New York Times*. December 20.

Labaton, S., and J. D. Glater. (2003). "Staff of S.E.C. Is Said to Dilute Rule Changes." *New York Times*. January 22.

Lambert, W., A. Galloni, and P. Dvorak. (2002). "A Global Journal Report: Enron Uproar Focuses a More Critical Eye on Accounting Abroad—Off-Balance Sheet Financing Clouds Economic Health of Certain Nations—Japan Is Among Those Using 'Tricks.'" *Asian Wall Street Journal*. July 15, p. A1.

Largay, J. A., and C. P. Stickney. (1980). "Cash Flows, Ratio Analysis and the W. T. Grant Company Bankruptcy." *Financial Analysts Journal*. July–August, pp. 51–54.

Larson, M. S. (1977). *The Rise of Professionalism: A Sociological Analysis*. Los Angeles: University of California Press.

Lemieux, P. (2002). "Our Government: The Ultimate Enron." *National Post*. June 25.

Lenzner, R., and M. Swibel. (2002). "Warning: Credit Crunch; Regulators Want $1 Trillion or More of Hidden Corporate Debt Moved into Plain View. The Reform Could Stifle the Credit-Driven Economy." *Forbes*. August 12.

Lerach, W. S. (2002). "The Chickens Have Come Home to Roost: How Wall Street, the Big Accounting Firms and Corporate Interests Chloroformed Congress and Cost America's Investors Trillions." www.milberg.com/pdf/news/chickens.pdf.

Lev, B. (1988). "Toward a Theory of Equitable and Efficient Accounting Policy." *The Accounting Review*. January, pp. 1–22.

Lev, B. (2003). "Accounting's Paper Maze: Sorting Out Reform Priorities." *Wall Street Journal*. January 28.

Levine, G. (2002). "Ex-Tyco Exec Walsh: I Did It, I'll Pay; Ebbers Cronies Quit WorldCom." *Forbes*. December.

Levitt, A. (1998). "The Numbers Game." Remarks by Chairman Arthur Levitt, presented at the NYU Center for Law and Business, New York. www.sec.gov/news/speech/speecharchive.shtml. September 28.

Levitt, A. (2000). "Renewing the Covenant with Investors." Remarks by Chairman Arthur Levitt, presented at the NYU Center for Law and Business, New York. www.sec.gov/news/speech/speecharchive.shtml. May 10.

Levitt, A. (2002). *Take on the Street: What Wall Street and Corporate America Don't Want You to Know: What You Can Do to Fight Back*. New York: Pantheon Books.

Lewis, C. S. (1952). *Mere Christianity*, 2nd ed. New York: Macmillan.

Liesman, S., J. Weil, and M. Schroeder. (2002). "Accounting Profession Faces a Credibility Crisis." *College Journal from the Wall Street Journal*. www.collegejournal.com.

Loftus, P. (2002). "Cisco Details Synthetic Leases Worth at Least $1.6B." *Dow Jones News Service*. March 11.

Loomis, C. J. (2002). "Whatever It Takes." *Fortune*. November 25, p. 74.

"Loss of Trust White-Collar Damage." (2002). Editorial, *Charleston Gazette*. June 21.

Lubove, S., and E. MacDonald. (2002). "Debt? Who, Me? Enron Is Hardly Alone When It Comes to Creative Off-Balance Sheet Accounting." *Forbes*. February 18.

MacDonald, E. (2002). "The Cable Fable." *Forbes*. August 18.

MacDonald, E. (2002). "False Front." *Forbes*. October 14.

Madison, R. L. (2002). "Is Failure to Teach Ethics the Causal Factor?" www.SmartPros.com. December 18.

Magill, H. T. and G. J. Previtts. (1991). *CPA Professional Responsibilities: An Introduction.* Cincinnati, OH: South-Western Publishing.

Maremont, M. (2002). "Inquiry at Tyco Is Unlikely to Settle Accounting Issues." *Wall Street Journal.* December 13.

Maremont, M., and L. P. Cohen. (2002). "Probe of Tyco Is Expanded to Include Its Auditor PwC." *Wall Street Journal.* September 30.

Maremont, M., and L. P. Cohen. (2002). "Tyco's Internal Report Finds Extensive Accounting Tricks." *Wall Street Journal.* December 31.

Mason, E. (1998). "White Paper or Whitewash?" *Accounting Today.* January 5–25.

Mason, E. (1998). *Random Thoughts: The Writings of Eli Mason.* New York: Eli Mason.

Mason, E. (2003). "SAS 99: A View from a Skeptic." *Accounting Today.* December 16–January 5, pp. 6–7.

Mattson-Teig, B. (2002). "A Closer Look." *National Real Estate Investor.* November 1.

Maynard, M. (2002). "US Airways to Cut Costs $1.8 Billion a Year." *New York Times.* December 22.

McCartney, S. (2002). "American Air Asks Workers to Forgo Pay Raises in 2003." *Wall Street Journal.* December 9.

McCraw, T. K. (1984). *Prophets of Regulation.* Cambridge, MA: Harvard University Press.

McFarland, J. (2002). "Companies Putting on a Squeaky Clean Face." *The Globe and Mail.* February 14, p. B1.

McKay, B. (2002). "Coca-Cola: Real Thing Can Be Hard to Measure." *Wall Street Journal.* January 23, p. C16.

McKay, B., and K. Brown. (2002). "Coke to Abandon Forecasts to Focus on Long-Term Goals." *Wall Street Journal.* December 16.

McNamee, M., and K. Capell. (2002). "FASB: Rewriting the Book on Bookkeeping: Will Broader, Simpler Rules Prevent Future Enrons?" *Business Week.* May 20.

Melancon, B. C. (1998). "The Changing Strategy for the Profession, the CPA, and the AICPA: What This Means for the Education Community." *Accounting Horizons.* December, pp. 397–406.

Merx, K. (2002). "Off the Books, Not off the Wall: Off-Balance-Sheet Financing Makes Some Squirm, but It's Legit and Common." *Crain's Detroit Business.* May 13.

Miles, R. P., and T. Osborne. (2001). *The Warren Buffett CEO: Secrets of the Berkshire Hathaway Managers.* New York: John Wiley & Sons.

Miller, H. E. 1974. "Collectivization of Judgment." *The Arthur Andersen Chronicle.* January, pp. 32–39.

Miller, P. B. W., and P. R. Bahnson. (2002). *Quality Financial Reporting.* New York: McGraw-Hill.

Mills, D. Q. (2002). *Buy, Lie, and Sell High: How Investors Lost Out on Enron and the Internet Bubble.* Upper Saddle River, NJ: Prentice-Hall.

Mintz, S. M. (1995). "Virtue Ethics and Accounting Education." *Issues in Accounting Education.* Fall, pp. 247–267.

Mollenkamp, C., and P. Beckett. (2002). "Bank of America, Citigroup Will Post Massive Charges." *Wall Street Journal.* December 24.

Montagna, P. D. (1974). *Certified Public Accounting: A Sociological View of a Profession in Change.* Houston, TX: Scholars Book Co.

Morgenson, G. (2002). "A Friend of Main St. or Wall St.?" *New York Times.* November 3.

Morgenson, G. (2002). "It Still Pays to See Who Did the Research." *New York Times.* December 22.

Moonitz, M. (1974). *Obtaining Agreement on Standards in the Accounting Profession,* Studies in Accounting Research No. 8. Sarasota, FL: American Accounting Association.

Mulford, C. W. and E. E. Comiskey. (2002). *The Financial Numbers Game: Detecting Creative Accounting Practices.* New York: John Wiley & Sons.

Mulligan, T. S. (2002). "The Fall of Enron; Companies Simplifying Accounting; Complex Methods Lose Favor as Firms Scurry to Prove Worth." *Los Angeles Times.* February 19.

Murray, S. D. (2002). "Letter from Delaware: Fleet Week." *The Daily Deal.* July 11.

Muto, S. (2002). "Firms Use Synthetic Leases Despite Criticism—Some Charge Leases Hide Potential Liabilities from the Balance Sheet." *Wall Street Journal.* February 20.

Muto, S. (2002). "'Synthetic Lease' Arrangement Thrive in U.S. Despite Scrutiny—Critics Say Financing Method Hides Potential Liabilities from Balance Sheet—Accounting Maneuver Can Be Used to Boost Earnings per Share." *Asian Wall Street Journal.* February 22.

National Commission on Fraudulent Financial Reporting. (1987). *Report of the National Commission on Fraudulent Financial Reporting.* Washington DC: NCFFR.

Nelson, B. (2003). "FASB Puts Banks in a Bind." *Forbes.* January 1.

Nelson, S. B. (2002). "FleetBoston May Have to Hike Its Reserves by Up to $600 Million." *Boston Globe.* August 27.

Nelson, S. B. (2002). "FleetBoston Financial Changes Accounting of 'Special Purpose Entities.'" *Boston Globe.* August 28.

Nessen, R. L. (2002). "The Appropriate Solution—Synthetic Leases vs. Bond Net Lease." www.crico.com/articles.

Nocera, J., J. Kahn, D. Rynecki, C. Leaf, J. Fox, K. Brooker, and S. Tully. (2002). "System Failure: Corporate America Has Lost Its Way. Here's a Road Map for Restoring Confidence." *Fortune.* June 24.

Norris, F. (2002). "Accounting Reform Takes Step Backward." *New York Times.* June 9.

Norris, F. (2002). "Using a Weak Pension Plan as a Cash Cow." *New York Times.* December 20.

Norris, F. (2002). "Will Auditing Reform Die Before It Begins?" *New York Times.* December 27.

Norris, F. (2003). "Should Tyco's Auditors Have Told More?" *New York Times.* January 3.

Norris, F. (2003). "Accounting Rules Changed to Bar Tactics Used by Enron." *New York Times.* January 16.

O'Connor, C. M. (2002). "How Dreamworks Works: Anatomy of Movie-Backed Deals." *Asset Securitization Report.* November 4.

Oliver, M. Patricia. (2002). "Off-Balance Sheet Representations/Warranties." *Hoosier Banker.* August 1.

O'Reilly, V. M., P. J. McDonnell, B. N. Winograd, J. S. Gerson, and H. R. Jaenicke. (1998). *Montgomery's Auditing*, 12th ed. New York: John Wiley & Sons.

Pearlstein, S., and P. Behr. (2001). "At Enron, the Fall Came Quickly." *Washington Post*. December 2, p. A01.

Pender, K. (2002). "There May Be More Enrons." *San Francisco Chronicle*. January 24, p. B1.

Pincoffs, E. (1986). *Quandaries and Virtues*. Lawrence, KS: University Press of Kansas.

Pitt, Harvey L. (2001). "How to Prevent Future Enrons." *Wall Street Journal*. December 11.

Pizzo, S. P. (2002) "Making Accounting Add Up." *Forbes*. February 26.

Plitch, P. (2002). "Independent Directors May Not Be Cure-all." *Associated Press Newswires*. August 30.

Ponemon, L. A., and A. Glazer. (1990). "Accounting Education and Ethical Development: The Influence of Liberal Learning on Students and Alumni in Accounting Practice." *Issues in Accounting Education*. Fall, pp. 195–208.

Powers, W., R. S. Troubh, and H. S. Winokur, Jr. (2002). *Report of Investigation by the Special Investigative Committee of the Board of Directors of Enron Corp*. February 1.

Pratt, S. P. (2002). *Cost of Capital: Estimation and Applications*, 2nd ed. Hoboken, NJ: John Wiley & Sons.

Prentice, R. (2002). "An Ethics Lesson for Business Schools." *New York Times*. August 20.

Previtts, G. J., and B. D. Merino. 1998. *A History of Accountancy in the United States: The Cultural Significance of Accounting*. Columbus, OH: Ohio State University Press.

PRNewswire. (2002). "S&P: Timber Securitizations Unique Among ABS Transactions." *PRNewswire*. June 6.

Pulliam S., and J. Sandberg. (2002). "New WorldCom Report to SEC Will Acknowledge More Flaws." *Wall Street Journal*. September 19.

"Push Is on for Audit Reform, Before Sting of Andersen Verdict Fades." (2002). *Financial Managers Society*. www.fmsinc.org. June 24.

Raghunathan, A. (2002). "Interim CEO Must Simplify Enron to Save It." *Dallas Morning News*. August 18.

Rankin, K. (2002). "Big 4 Poised to Wield Influence at the Ballot Box." *The Electronic Accountant*. www.electronicaccountant.com. September.

Rankin, K. (2002). "Despite Scandals, Profession Poised to Wield Influence in November Elections." *The Electronic Accountant*. www.electronicaccountant.com. October.

Rappaport, A. (2002). "Show Me the Cash Flow!" *Fortune*. September 16, pp. 193–194.

Reese, C. (2002). "Avoiding the Next Enron." *Fortune*. April 15, p. 358.

Reilly, F. K., and K. C. Brown. (2000). *Investment Analysis and Portfolio Management*, 6th ed. New York: Dryden.

Remond, C. S. (2002). "FASB Mulls Excluding Some SPEs from Consolidation Rules." *Dow Jones News Service*. May 8.

Rest, J. (1986). *Moral Development: Advances in Research and Theory*. New York: Praeger.

Rest, J., D. Varvaez, M. J. Bebeau, and S. T. Thoma. (1999). *Postconventional Moral Thinking: A Neo-Kohlbergian Approach*. Hillsdale, NJ: Lawrence Erlbaum Associates.

Revell, J. (2002). "Beware the Pension Monster." *Fortune*. December 9, pp. 99, 100, 102, 104, 106.

Revsine, L., D. W. Collins, and W. B. Johnson. (2002). *Financial Reporting and Analysis*, 2nd ed. Upper Saddle River, NJ: Prentice-Hall.

Reynolds, R. R. (2002). "Enron Held Too Much Influence over Andersen, Partner Says." *Dow Jones Business News*. May 31.

Reynolds, R. R. (2002). "WRAP: Jury Finds Andersen Guilty on Obstruction Charge." *Dow Jones Energy Service*. June 15.

Rittenhouse, L. J. (2002). *Do Business with People You Can Trust: Balancing Profits and Principles*. New York: AndBEYOND Communications.

Rivituso, M. (2002). "Avoiding the Next Enron." *Fortune*. February 22.

Ryan, Stephen G. (2002). *Financial Instruments and Institutions: Accounting and Disclosure Rules*. Hoboken, NJ: John Wiley & Sons.

Sapsford, J., and P. Beckett. (2002). "Citigroup Deals Helped Enron to Disguise Its Debts as Trades." *Wall Street Journal*. July 22.

Schilit, H. (2002). *Financial Shenanigans: How to Detect Accounting Gimmicks and Fraud in Financial Reports*. New York: McGraw-Hill.

Schmelkin, A. (2002). "Preferred Issues: Disclosures Up in 10Ks, But What's It All Mean?" *American Banker*. March 18.

Schmitt, R. B. (2002). "Companies Add Ethics Training: Will It Work?" *Wall Street Journal*. November 4, p. B1.

Schmitt, R. B., M. Schroeder, and S. Murray. (2002). "Corporate-Oversight Bill Passes, Smoothing Way for New Lawsuits." *Wall Street Journal*. July 26.

Schroeder, M. (2002). "Webster's Appointment Signals Serious Partisan Divide at SEC." *Wall Street Journal*. October 28.

Schroeder, M. (2003). "SEC Orders New Disclosures in Companies' Profit Reports." *Wall Street Journal*. January 16.

Schroeder, M., and C. Bryan-Low. (2002). "SEC's Pitt Now Faces Dissent from Within the Commission." *Wall Street Journal*. October 7.

Schroeder, M., and G. Ip. (2002). "SEC Faces Hurdles Beyond Budget in Quest to Crack Down on Fraud." *Wall Street Journal*. July 19.

Schroeder, M., and E. MacDonald. (1999). "SEC Enforcement Actions Target Accounting Fraud." *Wall Street Journal*. September 29.

Securities and Exchange Commission. (1994). Staff Report on Auditor Independence. Prepared by the Office of the Chief Accountant. March.

Securities and Exchange Commission. (1996). *SEC v. Michael Monus, Patrick Finn, John Anderson and Jeffrey Walley*. Case No. 4:95 CV 975 (N.D. OH, filed May 2, 1995). Litigation release No. 14819. Accounting and Auditing Enforcement Release No. 761. Washington DC: Securities and Exchange Commission.

Securities and Exchange Commission. (1997). Staff Analysis of AICPA White Paper: A New Conceptual Framework for Auditor Independence. December 11.

Securities and Exchange Commission. (1998). SEC Statement of Policy on the Establishment and Improvement of Standards Related to Auditor Independence. Financial Reporting Release No. 50.

Securities and Exchange Commission. (1998). In the matter of Sensormatic Electronics Corp. Accounting and Auditing Enforcement Release No. 1020. Washington, DC: Securities and Exchange Commission.

Securities and Exchange Commission. (1998). Report of the internal investigation of independence issues at PricewaterhouseCoopers LLP. US SEC AP file No. 3-9809. Washington, DC: Securities and Exchange Commission.

Securities and Exchange Commission. (1999). SEC Charges 68 Individuals, Entities with Fraud and/or Abuses of the Financial Reporting Process. Press Release. September 28. www.sec.gov/news/finfraud.html.

Securities and Exchange Commission. (1999). Details of the 30 Enforcement Actions. September 28. www.sec.gov/news/extra/finfrds.html.

Securities and Exchange Commission. (2003). SEC Adopts Rules on Provisions of Sarbanes-Oxley Act: Actions Cover Non-GAAP Financials, From 8-K Amendments, Trading During Blackout Periods, Audit Committee Financial Expert Requirements. January 13. www.sec.gov/news/press/2003-6.htm.

Setaishi, S. (2002). "Accountability: Boeing Cap May See $1.2B Change to Books." *Dow Jones News Service*. March 14.

Shaub, M. (1994). "Limits to the Effectiveness of Accounting Ethics Education." *Business and Professional Ethics Journal*, pp. 129–145.

Shleifer, A., and R. Vishny. (1997). "A Survey of Corporate Governance." *Journal of Finance*. June.

Sickinger. T. (2002). "In Search of the Bottom Line." *The Oregonian*. March 31, p. F01.

Sieroty, C. H. (2002). "US Airways Files for Chapter 11." *Washington Times*. August 11.

Silverman, G. (2002). "Second Bank Falls Foul of Regulators." *Financial Times*. July 19.

Sisaye, S. (1997). "An Overview of the Institutional Approach to Accounting Ethics Education." *Research on Accounting Ethics*, pp. 233–244.

Skipworth, D. (2001). *Statement 140—A Study of Securitization Disclosures.* Research Report. (Norwalk CT: FASB).

Smith, R. and J. R. Emshwiller. (2002). "Skilling's Role in 'Braveheart' Project Under Investigation." *Wall Street Journal*. December 16.

Sorid, D. (2002). "Audit Committee Disclaimer Comes Under Fire." *Forbes*. December 24.

Sorkin, A. R. (2003). "Tyco, After the Glitter and the Agile Math." *New York Times*. January 1.

Sorkin, A. R., and A. Berenson. (2002). "Tyco Admits Using Accounting Tricks to Inflate Earnings." *New York Times*. December 31.

Spacek, L. (1958). "The Need for an Accounting Court." *The Accounting Review*. July, pp. 368–379.

Sterling, R. R. (1973). "Accounting Power." *Journal of Accountancy*. January, pp. 61–67.

Sterling, R. R. (1973). "Accounting Research, Education and Practice." *Journal of Accountancy*. September, pp. 44–52.

Sterling, R. R., ed. (1974). *Institutional Issues in Public Accounting*. Lawrence, KS: Scholars Book Co.

Sterling, R. R. (1979). *Toward a Science of Accounting*. Houston, TX: Scholars Book Co.

Sterling, R. R. (1990). "Positive Accounting: An Assessment." *Abacus,* pp. 97–135.

Stevens, M. (1981). *The Big Eight*. New York: Macmillan.

Stevens, M. (1991). *The Big Six: The Selling Out of America's Top Accounting Firms*. New York: Simon & Schuster.

Stevenson, R. W. (2003). "Bush Proposes Big Increase in S.E.C. Budget." *New York Times*. January 12.

Stewart, I. (1997). "Teaching Accounting Ethics: The Power of Narrative." *Accounting Education: A Journal of Theory, Practice, and Research*, pp. 173–184.

Stickney, C. P., and R. L. Weil. (2002). *Financial Accounting: An Introduction to Concepts, Methods, and Uses*, 10th ed. Mason, OH: South-Western Publishing.

Stone, C. A., and A. Zissue. (2002). "Synthetic Collaterized Loan Obligations: Olan Enterprises, PLC." *Journal of Derivatives*. March 22.

Storey, R. K. (1964). *The Search for Accounting Principles—Today's Problems in Perspective*. New York: AICPA.

Sunder, S. (2002). "Knowing What Others Know: Common Knowledge, Accounting, and Capital Markets." *Accounting Horizons*. December, pp. 305–318.

Sutton, M. H. (1997). Unpublished letter to W. T. Allen, Chairman of the Independence Standards Board. December 11.

Sutton, M. H. (2002). "Financial Reporting at a Crossroads." *Accounting Horizons*. December, pp. 319–328.

Swartz, M. and S. Watkins. (2003). *Power Failure: The Inside Story of the Collapse of Enron*. New York: Doubleday.

TechNet. (2002). "Stock Option Accounting." www.technet.org/issues/stock.html.

Thangavelu, P. (2002). "SPE Controversy Having Impact on Commercial MBS Market." *American Banker*. August 19.

Thomas, R. (2002). "Avoiding the Next Enron." *Dow Jones News Service*. February 26.

Thorne, L. (1998). "The Role of Virtue in Auditors' Ethical Decision Making: An Integration of Cognitive-Developmental and Virtue-Ethics Perspectives." *Research on Accounting Ethics*, pp. 291–308.

Thornton, E., P. Coy, and H. Timmons. (2002). "The Breakdown in Banking." *Business Week*. October 7.

Toedtman, J. (2002). "Accounting Reform Slows to a Crawl." *Newsday*. June 6.

Toffler, B. (2003). *Final Accounting: Ambition, Greed, and the Fall of Arthur Andersen*. New York: Broadway Books.

Townsend, P. (2002). "Asset-Backed Securities Market Feels the Pinch." *eFinancial News*. June 12.

Townsend, P. (2002). "Whole-Business Deals Come Under Scrutiny." *eFinancial News*. June 12.

Trevino, L. K., and K. A. Nelson. (1999). *Managing Business Ethics: Straight Talk About How to Do It Right*, 2nd ed. New York: John Wiley & Sons.

Trombley, M. A. (2003). *Accounting for Derivatives and Hedging*. New York: McGraw-Hill Irwin.

Tunick, B. (2002). "The Looming Pension Liability: Analysts Focus on Problem that FASB Rules Ignore." *Investment Dealers Digest*. October 14.

Turner, L. (2002). Financial Institutions and Collapse of Enron. Congressional Testimony before the Committee on Senate Governmental Affairs. July 23.

Tyco International Ltd. (2002). Form 8-K. December 30.

"UAL Files for Creditor Shield But Vows to Keep Flying." (2002). *Wall Street Journal.* December 9.

Ultramares Corporation v. Touche [255 N.Y. 170, 174 N.E. 441].

United States v. Simon [425 F 2d 796 (2d Cir. 1969)].

U.S. Senate. (1976). *The Accounting Establishment*, Report of the Staff to the Senate Subcommittee on Reports, Accounting, and Management, Committee on Government Operations. Washington DC: U.S. Senate. December.

U.S. Senate. (2002). *Financial Oversight of Enron: The SEC and Private-Sector Watchdogs*, Report of the Staff to the Senate Committee on Governmental Affairs. Washington DC: U.S. Senate. October 8.

Useem, J. (2002). "In Corporate America It's Cleanup Time: Under Pressure, A Slew of Companies Are Now Changing the Way They Do Business. Will It Last?" *Fortune.* September 16.

"Volcker Calls for Non-Exec Board Structure in Large Corporations." (2002). www.SmartPros.com. November 5.

Von Brachel, J. (1997). "Professional Issues: New AICPA Chairman: Creating a Future." *Journal of Accountancy.* November.

Walsh, M. W. (2003). "Companies Fight Shortfalls in Pension Funds." *New York Times.* January 13.

Weil, J. (2002). "Heard on the Street: Board Members Draw Scrutiny for Roles at Other Companies." *Wall Street Journal.* December 9.

Weil, J. (2003). "Accounting-Standards Panel Takes on Hot-Button Issues." *Wall Street Journal.* January 13.

Weil, J., and J. Wilke. (2002). "Systemic Failure by SEC Is Seen in Enron Debacle." *Wall Street Journal.* October 7.

Weinberg, A. (2002). "Asleep at the Switch." *Forbes.* July 22.

Weinberg, A. (2002). "Tyco Counts Sheep, But Can Investors Sleep?" *Forbes.* December 31.

Welch, W. M. (2003). "Congress Wary of Bush Budget." *USA Today.* February 4.

Wheat, A. (2002). "Keeping an Eye on Corporate America." *Fortune.* November 25, pp. 44–46.

Whelan, S. T. (2002). "Operating Assets: The Latest Securitization Niche." *Equipment Leasing Today.* August 1.

White, G. I., A. C. Sondhi, and D. Fried. (1998). *The Analysis and Use of Financial Statements*, 2nd ed. New York: John Wiley & Sons.

White, G. I., A. C. Sondhi, and D. Fried. (2003). *The Analysis and Use of Financial Statements*, 3rd ed. New York: John Wiley & Sons.

Williams, P. (2002). "Accounting Involves Ethics, not Just Technical Issues." *Strategic Finance.* September.

Windal, F. W. and R. N. Corley. (1980). *The Accounting Professional: Ethics, Responsibility, and Liability.* Englewood Cliffs, NJ: Prentice-Hall.

Windal, F. W. (1991). *Ethics and the Accountant: Text and Cases*. Englewood Cliffs, NJ: Prentice-Hall.

Wolk, H. I., J. R. Francis, and M. G. Tearney. (1992). *Accounting Theory: A Conceptual and Institutional Approach*, 3rd ed. Cincinnati, OH: South-Western Publishing.

Wolk, H. I., M. G. Tearney, and J. L. Dodd. (2001). *Accounting Theory: A Conceptual and Institutional Approach*, 5th ed. Cincinnati, OH: South-Western Publishing.

Wriston, W. (2002). "The Solution to Scandals? Simpler Rules." *Wall Street Journal*. August 5.

Young, J. J. (1997). Accounting as It Intertwines with the Political: The Case of Accounting for Stock Compensation. Working Paper, University of New Mexico. Presented at the Interdisciplinary Perspectives on Accounting Conference. July 7–9.

Young, M. R., ed. (2000). *Accounting Irregularities and Financial Fraud*. San Diego, CA: Harcourt Professional Publishing.

Young, M. R., ed. (2002). *Accounting Irregularities and Financial Fraud,* 2nd ed. San Diego, CA: Harcourt Professional Publishing.

Zeff, S. A. (1971). *Forging Accounting Principles in Five Countries*. Champaign, IL: Stipes Publishing Company.

Zuckerman, G., and M. Benson. (2002). "S&P Draws Up List of Firms That May Face Cash Shortfall." *Wall Street Journal*. May 16, p. C1.

Index